Z[illegible]S
6TH SINGLE

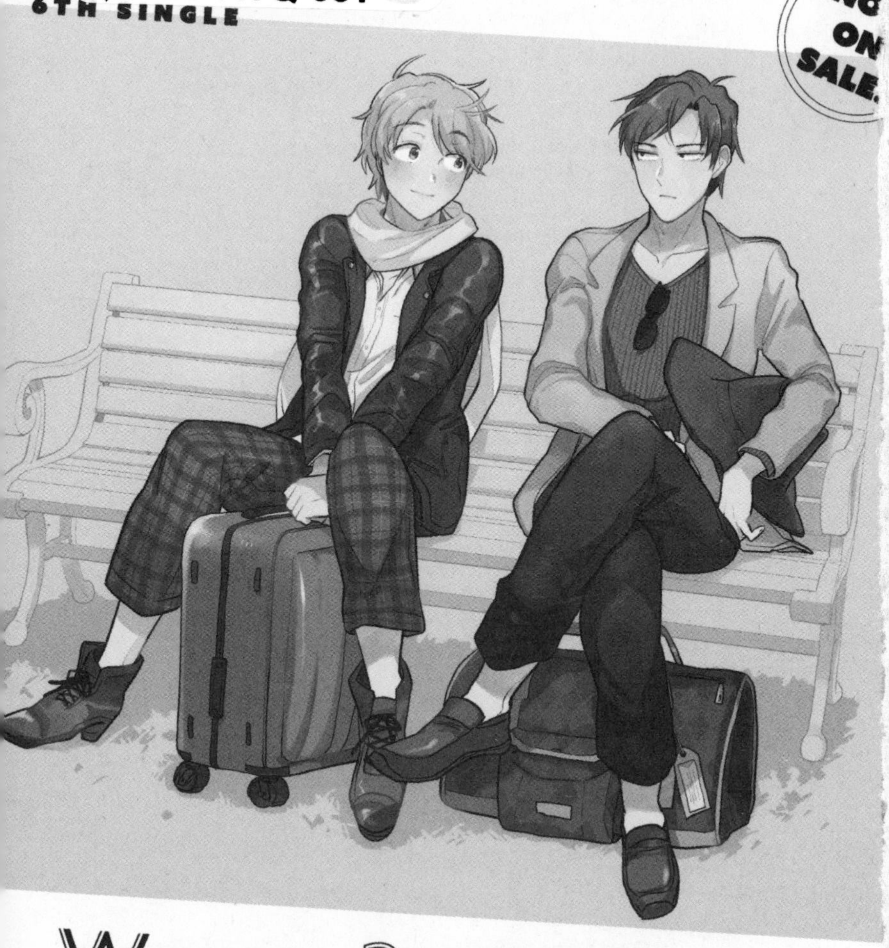
NO
ON
SALE.

# Wanna Be With You

## Commemorative launch events

1. In-store mini concert and polaroid session!
June 18, 1:00 p.m.: Blue Records Shibuya, 8F Event Space
June 18, 9:00 p.m.: Blue Records Ikebukuro, 1F Patio Plaza

2. "Wanna Be With You" commemorative concert!
July 2/Kamikitazawa EAST/OPEN 5:30 p.m./START 6:00 p.m. ¥2500
For details, see venue website or flyer included with CD.

. Personally signed love letter from Yuya Niyodo and Kazuki Yoshino! ♡
10 lucky winners will receive hand-signed love letters written by the members of ZINGS for someone they care about!
Entry form included with single! For details, see flyer included with CD.
Note: Winners will receive letters in lieu of public announcement. Letters will be printed.

What are you doing?

the flow

wing Followers
71

**PHANTOM OF THE IDOL ☆ CONTENTS BOT**
<<<-----SET 15---P.003----->>>

**Aya the Eternally Reborn**
Uh, excuse me, what happened with the ZINGS calendar?
My timeline is NOT breathing (in a good way lmao) #ZINGS
7 12

**PHANTOM OF THE IDOL ☆ CONTENTS BOT**
<<<-----SET 16---P.032----->>>

**Haruka@Not online much**
They couldn't announce this earlier?!?!?!? I have a job heah!
If anyone can go to Yokomase Fest, please report! srsly!
2 1

**PHANTOM OF THE IDOL ☆ CONTENTS BOT**
<<<-----SET 17---P.059----->>>

**PHANTOM OF THE IDOL ☆ CONTENTS BOT**
<<<-----SET 18---P.083----->>>

**yumi**
Today this total hottie came into work, but I'm like 99% sure he was practicing for parties, which...no seriously, who practices tambourine??
2

**PHANTOM OF THE IDOL ☆ CONTENTS BOT**
<<<-----SET 19---P.099----->>>

**Kazemaru ver2.0**
Chikage Yura at the Shinano Talent Agency? I saw the president once and she was a beautiful woman in glasses so you bet I still stan
12 9

**PHANTOM OF THE IDOL ☆ CONTENTS BOT**
<<<-----SET 20---P.124----->>>

**Tsugiko**
Could this be the Up Next effect?!
Hurry up and give us a chance to spend! I'll do anythiiing! $$$$
3

**PHANTOM OF THE IDOL ☆ CONTENTS BOT**
<<<-----SET 21---P.145----->>>

**Mai-yan ☆ Please check my pinned trading post**
Replying to: Kazuki Yoshino
I see Niyodo-kun's photo was from Lasole too
So you were hanging out together~! ❤❤❤❤
1

**PHANTOM OF THE IDOL ☆ CONTENTS BOT**
<<<-----SET 22---P.165----->>>

# Set 15

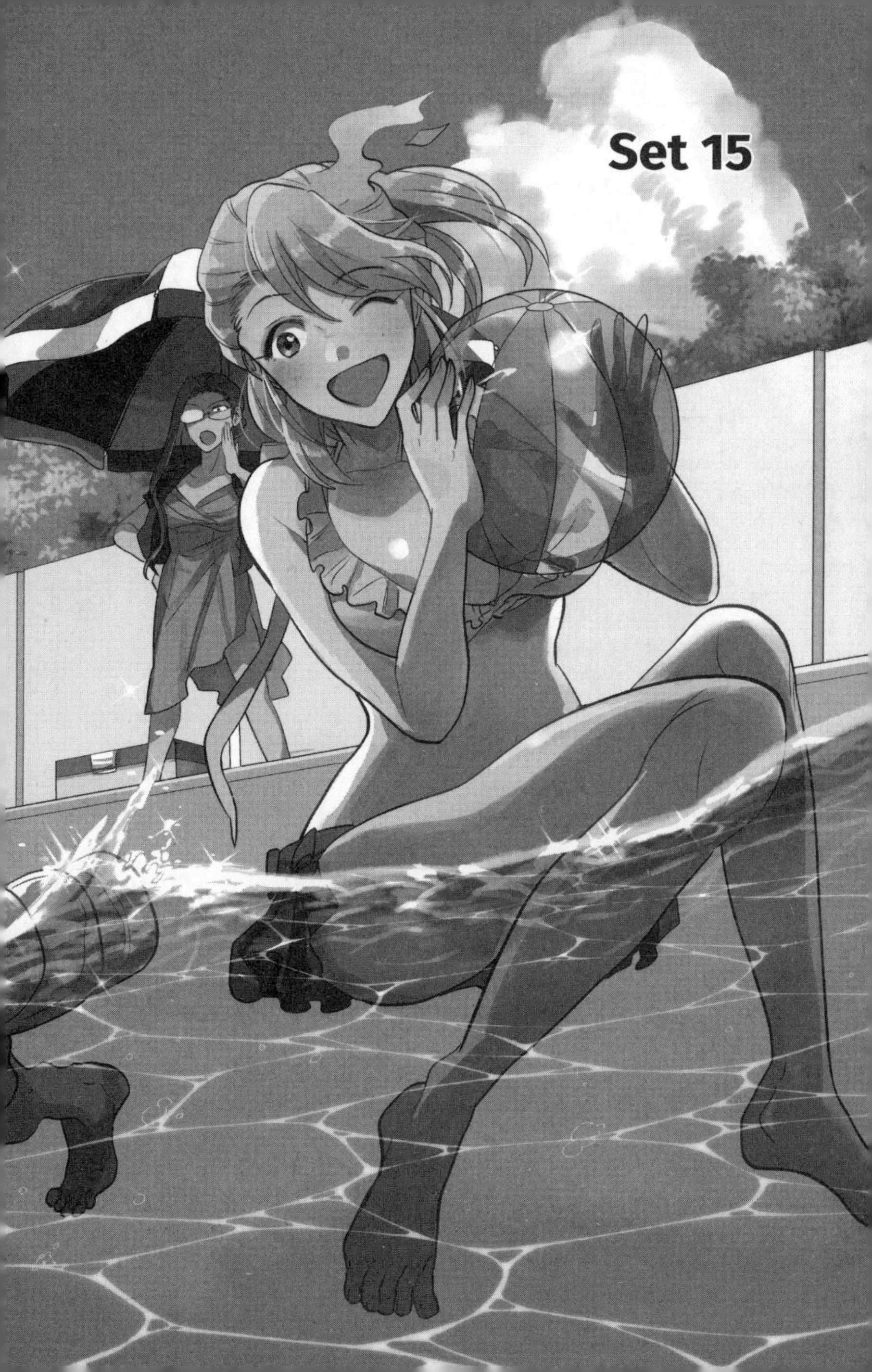

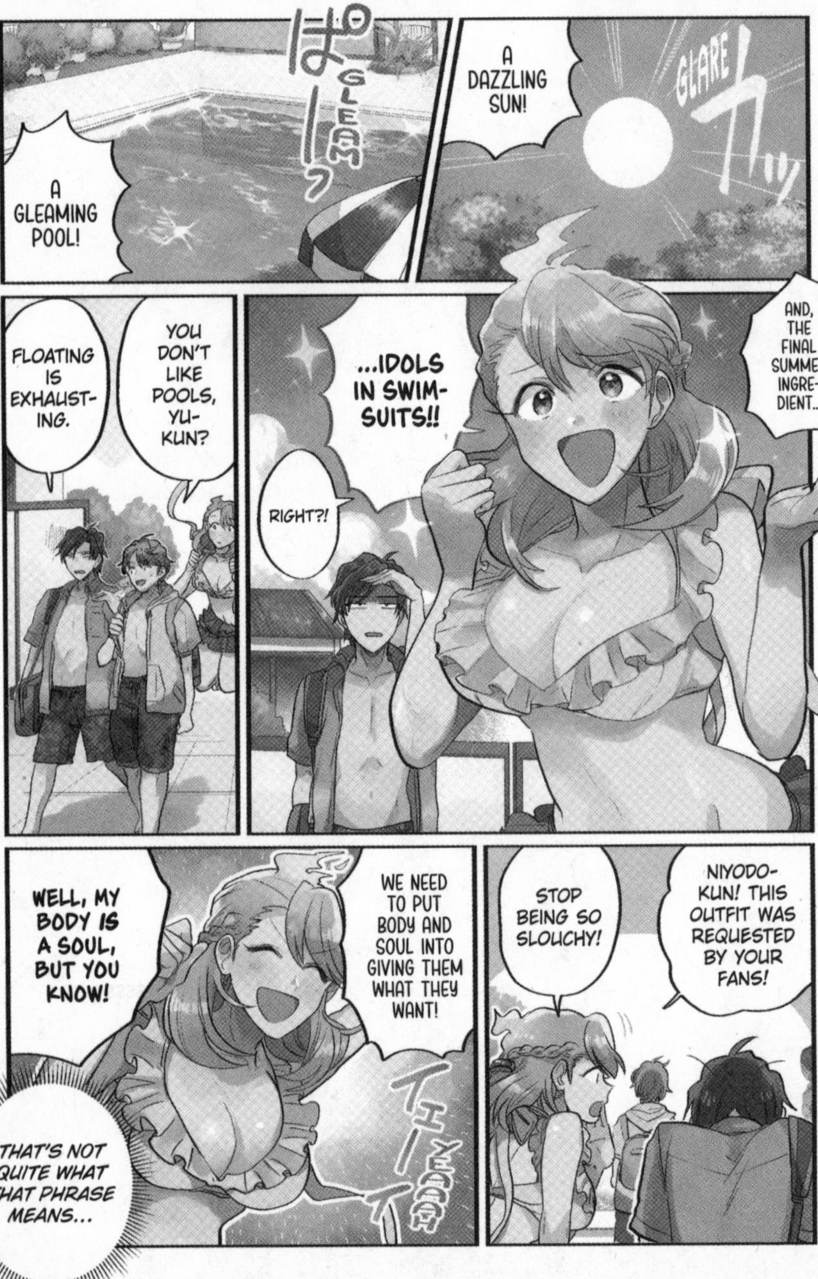
A DAZZLING SUN!
GLARE
GLEAM
A GLEAMING POOL!
AND, THE FINAL SUMMER INGREDIENT...
...IDOLS IN SWIMSUITS!!
RIGHT?!
YOU DON'T LIKE POOLS, YU-KUN?
FLOATING IS EXHAUSTING.
NIYODO-KUN! THIS OUTFIT WAS REQUESTED BY YOUR FANS!
STOP BEING SO SLOUCHY!
WE NEED TO PUT BODY AND SOUL INTO GIVING THEM WHAT THEY WANT!
WELL, MY BODY IS A SOUL, BUT YOU KNOW!
イェーイ
YEAAAH
THAT'S NOT QUITE WHAT THAT PHRASE MEANS...

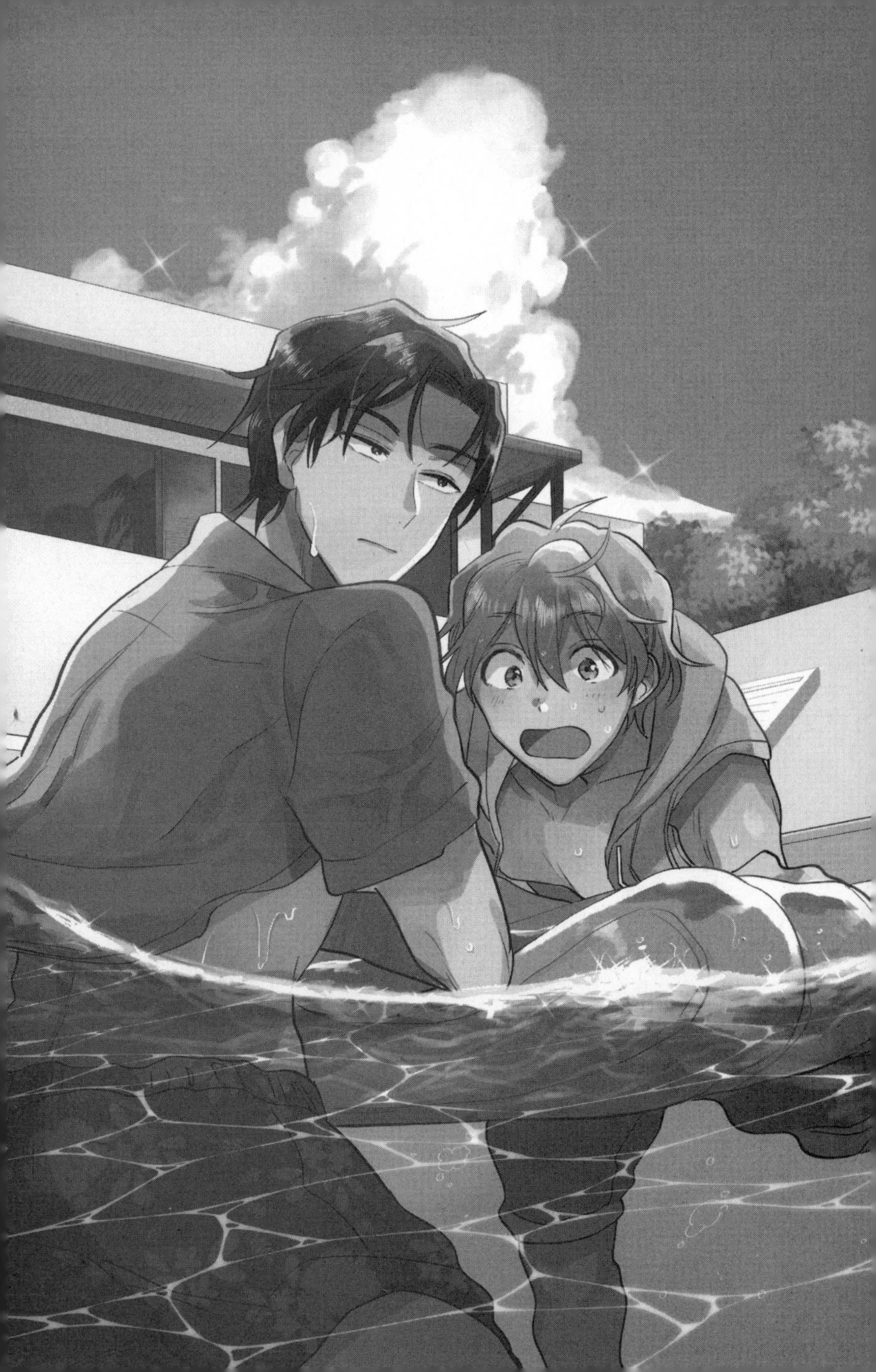

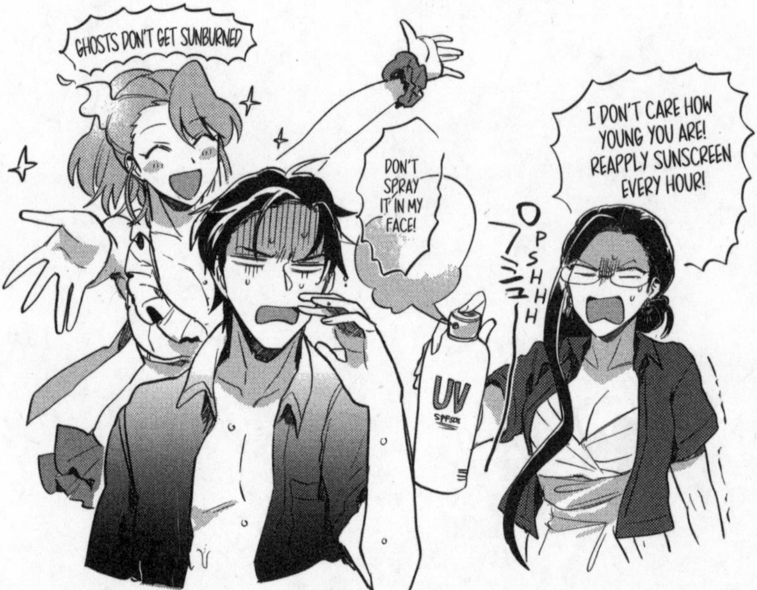
I DON'T CARE HOW YOUNG YOU ARE! REAPPLY SUNSCREEN EVERY HOUR!
PSHHH
DON'T SPRAY IT IN MY FACE!
GHOSTS DON'T GET SUNBURNED
UV

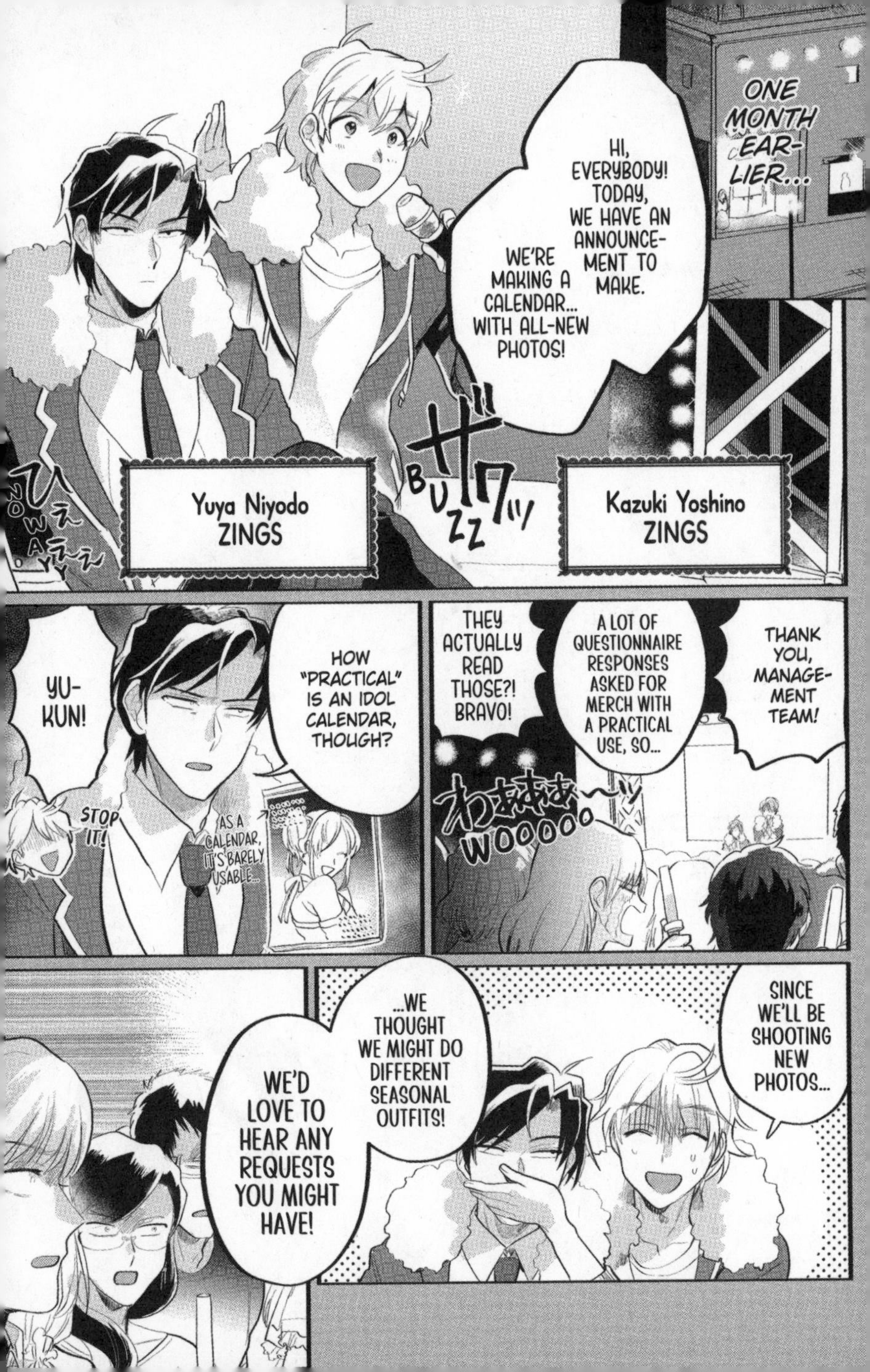
ONE MONTH EAR-LIER...
HI, EVERYBODY! TODAY, WE HAVE AN ANNOUNCE-MENT TO MAKE.
WE'RE MAKING A CALENDAR... WITH ALL-NEW PHOTOS!
BUZZ
Kazuki Yoshino ZINGS
Yuya Niyodo ZINGS
NO WAY
THANK YOU, MANAGE-MENT TEAM!
A LOT OF QUESTIONNAIRE RESPONSES ASKED FOR MERCH WITH A PRACTICAL USE, SO...
THEY ACTUALLY READ THOSE?! BRAVO!
WOOOOO
HOW "PRACTICAL" IS AN IDOL CALENDAR, THOUGH?
YU-KUN!
AS A CALENDAR, IT'S BARELY USABLE...
STOP IT!
SINCE WE'LL BE SHOOTING NEW PHOTOS...
...WE THOUGHT WE MIGHT DO DIFFERENT SEASONAL OUTFITS!
WE'D LOVE TO HEAR ANY REQUESTS YOU MIGHT HAVE!

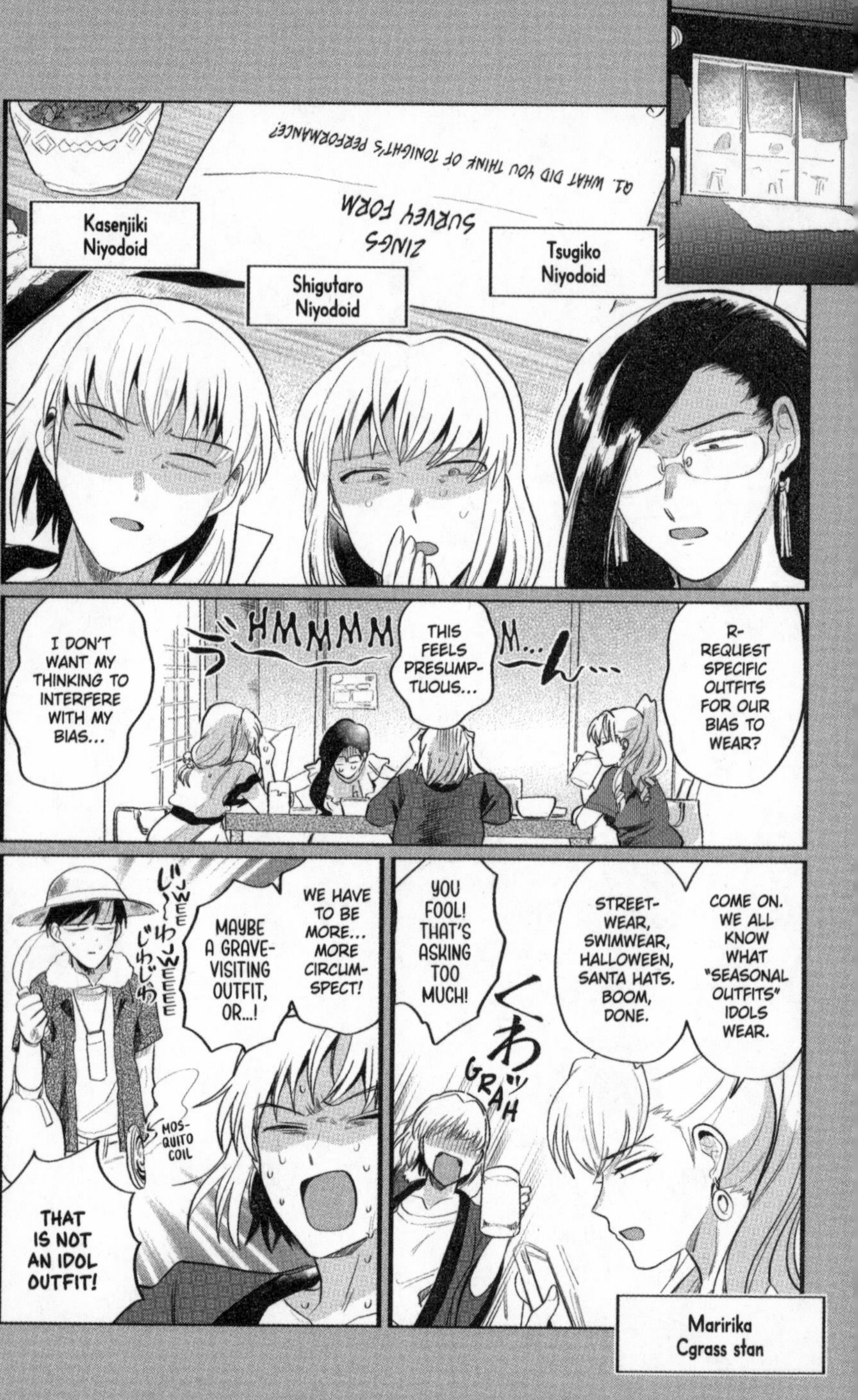
ZINGS
SURVEY FORM
Q1. WHAT DID YOU THINK OF TONIGHT'S PERFORMANCE?
Tsugiko Niyodoid
Shigutaro Niyodoid
Kasenjiki Niyodoid
R-REQUEST SPECIFIC OUTFITS FOR OUR BIAS TO WEAR?
HMMMMM...M...
THIS FEELS PRESUMPTUOUS...
I DON'T WANT MY THINKING TO INTERFERE WITH MY BIAS...
COME ON. WE ALL KNOW WHAT "SEASONAL OUTFITS" IDOLS WEAR.
STREETWEAR, SWIMWEAR, HALLOWEEN, SANTA HATS. BOOM, DONE.
GRAH
YOU FOOL! THAT'S ASKING TOO MUCH!
Maririka Cgrass stan
WE HAVE TO BE MORE... MORE CIRCUMSPECT!
MAYBE A GRAVE-VISITING OUTFIT, OR...!
JWEE
JWEEEE
MOSQUITO COIL
THAT IS NOT AN IDOL OUTFIT!

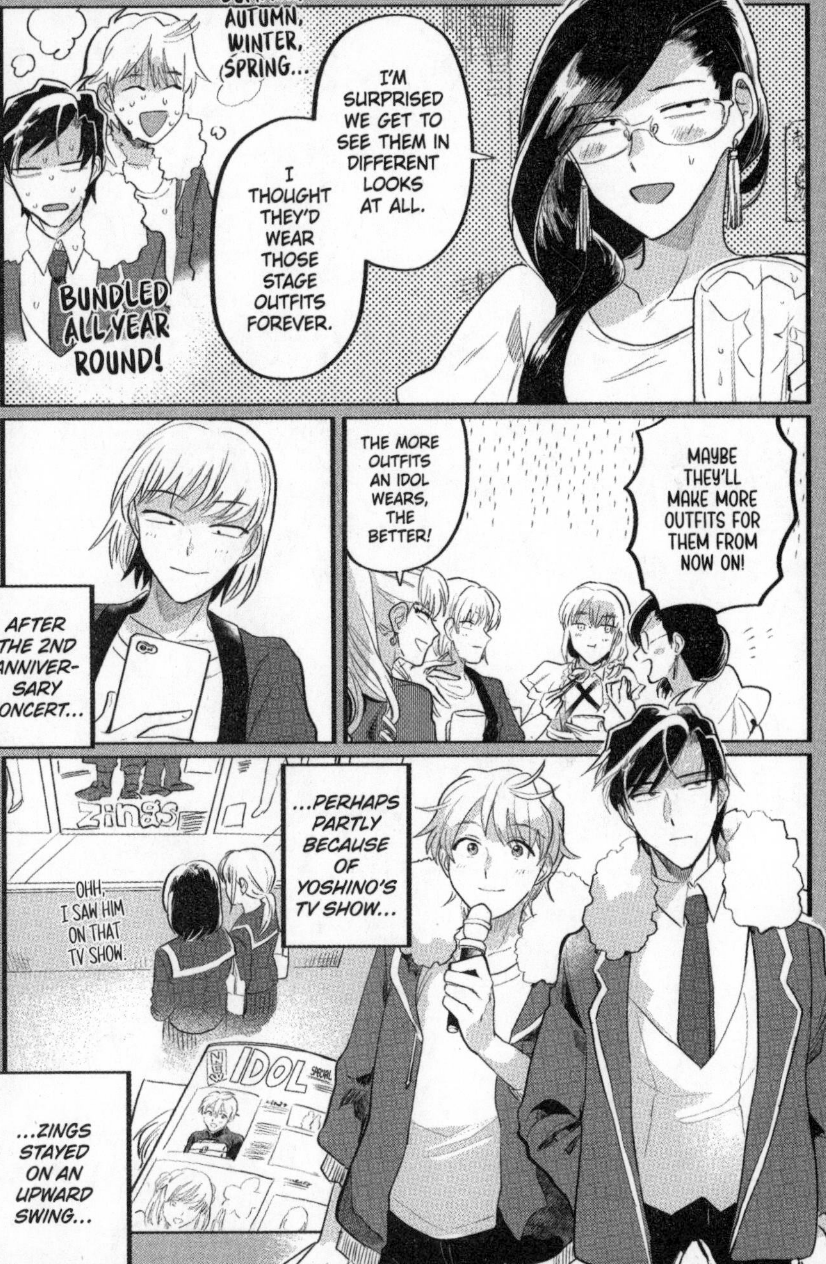
I'M SURPRISED WE GET TO SEE THEM IN DIFFERENT LOOKS AT ALL.
I THOUGHT THEY'D WEAR THOSE STAGE OUTFITS FOREVER.
SUMMER, AUTUMN, WINTER, SPRING...
BUNDLED ALL YEAR ROUND!
MAYBE THEY'LL MAKE MORE OUTFITS FOR THEM FROM NOW ON!
THE MORE OUTFITS AN IDOL WEARS, THE BETTER!
AFTER THE 2ND ANNIVERSARY CONCERT...
...PERHAPS PARTLY BECAUSE OF YOSHINO'S TV SHOW...
Zings
OHH, I SAW HIM ON THAT TV SHOW.
IDOL
SPECIAL
...ZINGS STAYED ON AN UPWARD SWING...

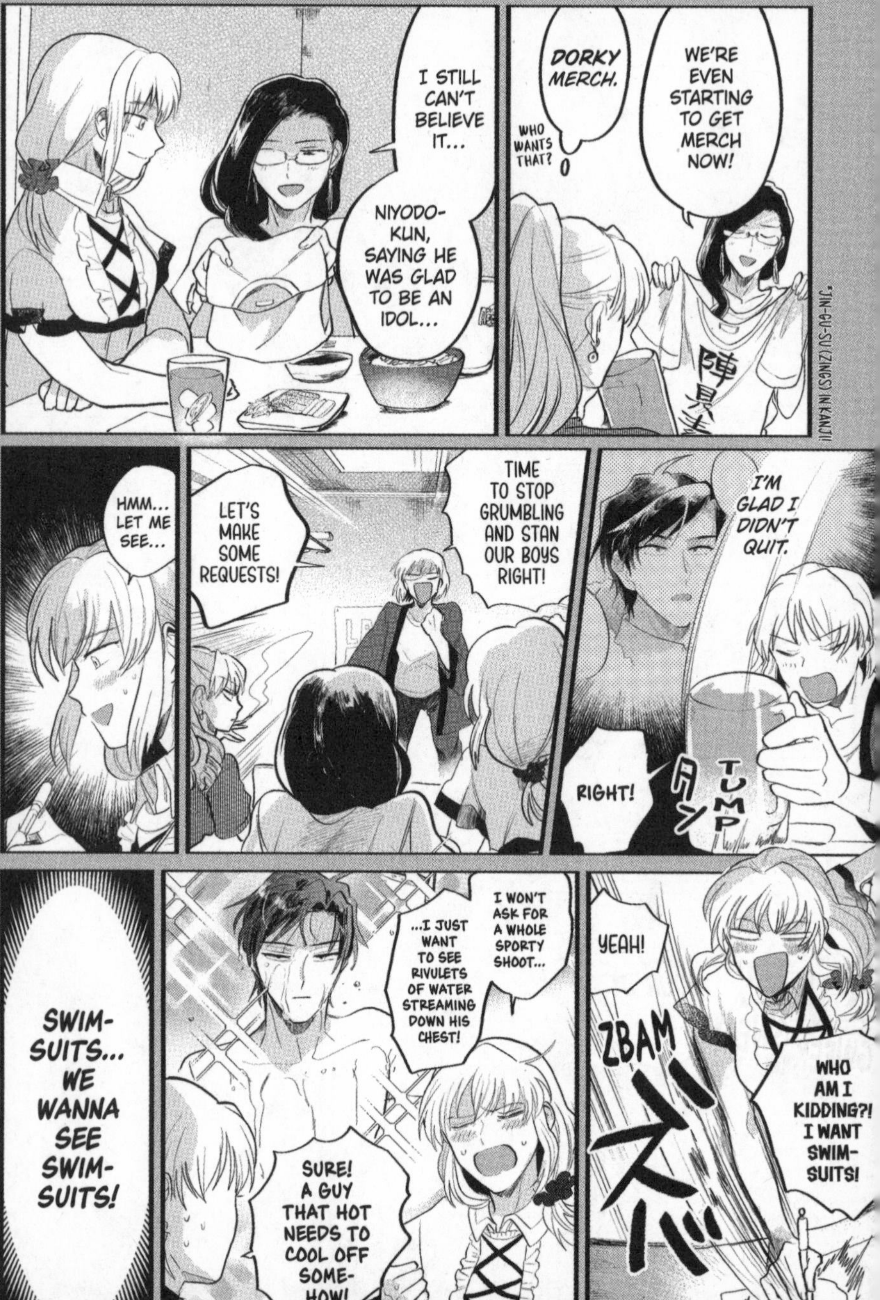
WE'RE EVEN STARTING TO GET MERCH NOW!
DORKY MERCH.
WHO WANTS THAT?
*JIN-GU-SU (ZINGS) IN KANJI!
I STILL CAN'T BELIEVE IT...
NIYODO-KUN, SAYING HE WAS GLAD TO BE AN IDOL...
I'M GLAD I DIDN'T QUIT.
TUMP
RIGHT!
TIME TO STOP GRUMBLING AND STAN OUR BOYS RIGHT!
LET'S MAKE SOME REQUESTS!
HMM... LET ME SEE...
YEAH!
ZBAM
WHO AM I KIDDING?! I WANT SWIM-SUITS!
I WON'T ASK FOR A WHOLE SPORTY SHOOT...
...I JUST WANT TO SEE RIVULETS OF WATER STREAMING DOWN HIS CHEST!
SURE! A GUY THAT HOT NEEDS TO COOL OFF SOME-HOW!
SWIM-SUITS... WE WANNA SEE SWIM-SUITS!

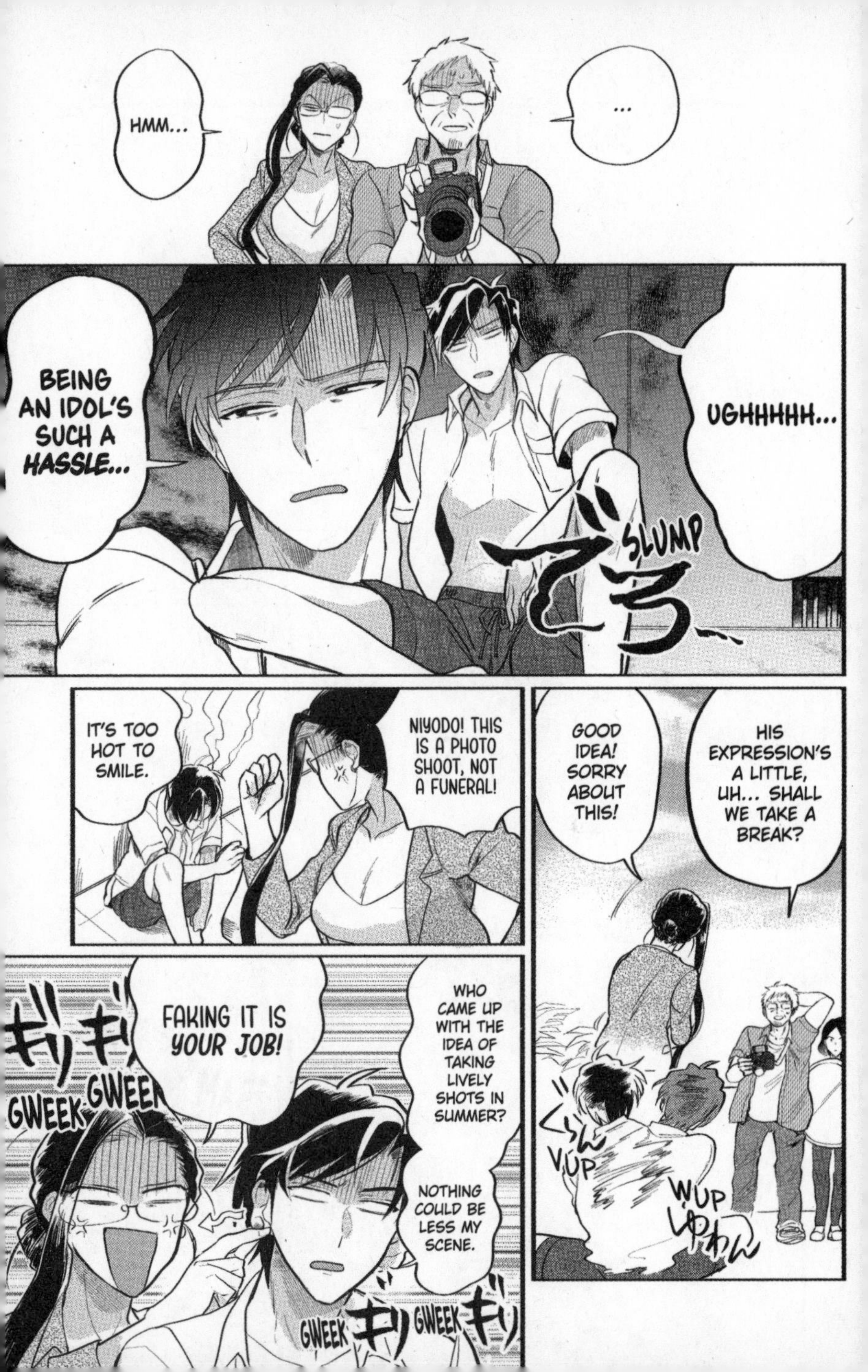
...
HMM...
UGHHHHH...
SLUMP
BEING AN IDOL'S SUCH A HASSLE...
HIS EXPRESSION'S A LITTLE, UH... SHALL WE TAKE A BREAK?
GOOD IDEA! SORRY ABOUT THIS!
VUP
WUP
NIYODO! THIS IS A PHOTO SHOOT, NOT A FUNERAL!
IT'S TOO HOT TO SMILE.
WHO CAME UP WITH THE IDEA OF TAKING LIVELY SHOTS IN SUMMER?
NOTHING COULD BE LESS MY SCENE.
FAKING IT IS *YOUR JOB*!
GWEEK GWEEK
GWEEK GWEEK

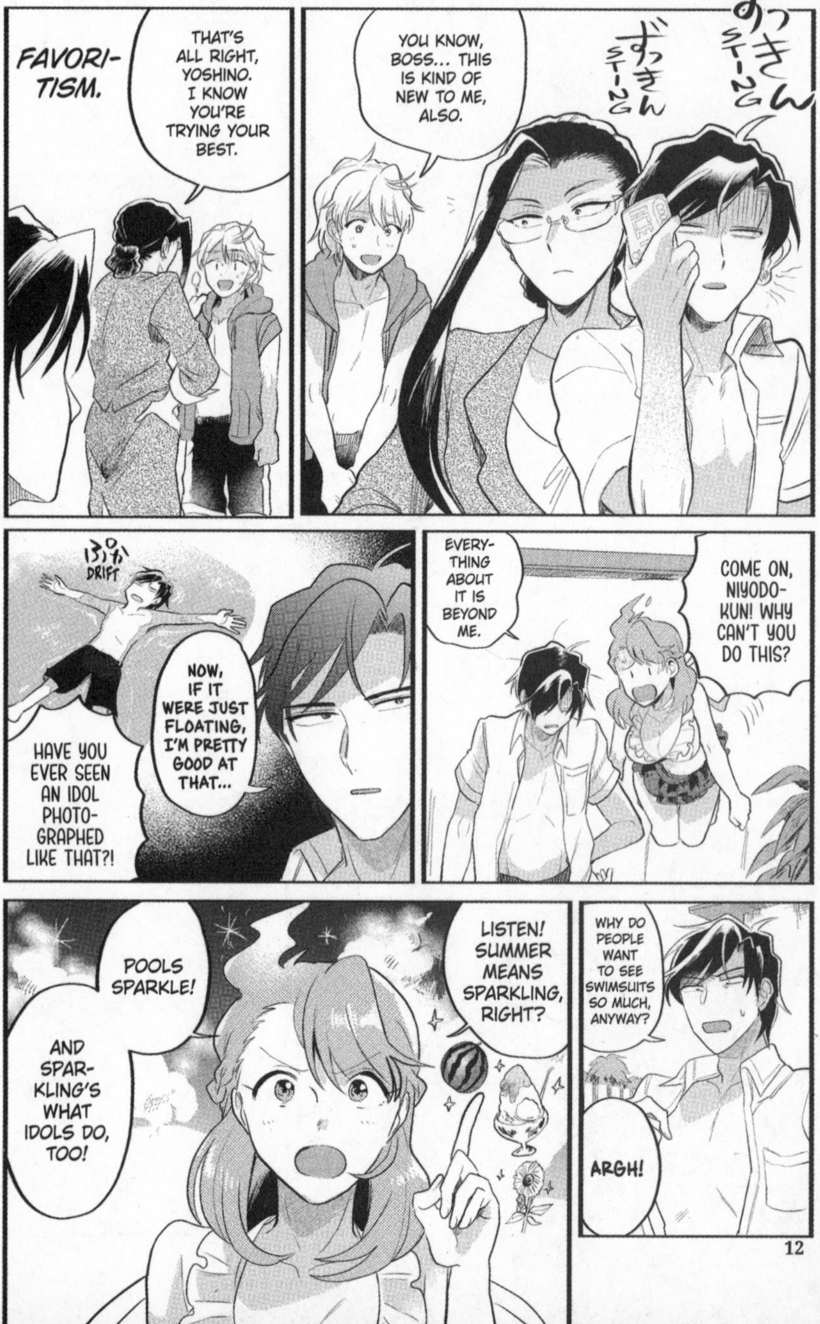
ずっきん STING
ずっきん STING
YOU KNOW, BOSS... THIS IS KIND OF NEW TO ME, ALSO.
THAT'S ALL RIGHT, YOSHINO. I KNOW YOU'RE TRYING YOUR BEST.
FAVORI-TISM.
COME ON, NIYODO-KUN! WHY CAN'T YOU DO THIS?
EVERY-THING ABOUT IT IS BEYOND ME.
ぷか DRIFT
HAVE YOU EVER SEEN AN IDOL PHOTO-GRAPHED LIKE THAT?!
NOW, IF IT WERE JUST FLOATING, I'M PRETTY GOOD AT THAT...
WHY DO PEOPLE WANT TO SEE SWIMSUITS SO MUCH, ANYWAY?
ARGH!
LISTEN! SUMMER MEANS SPARKLING, RIGHT?
POOLS SPARKLE!
AND SPAR-KLING'S WHAT IDOLS DO, TOO!

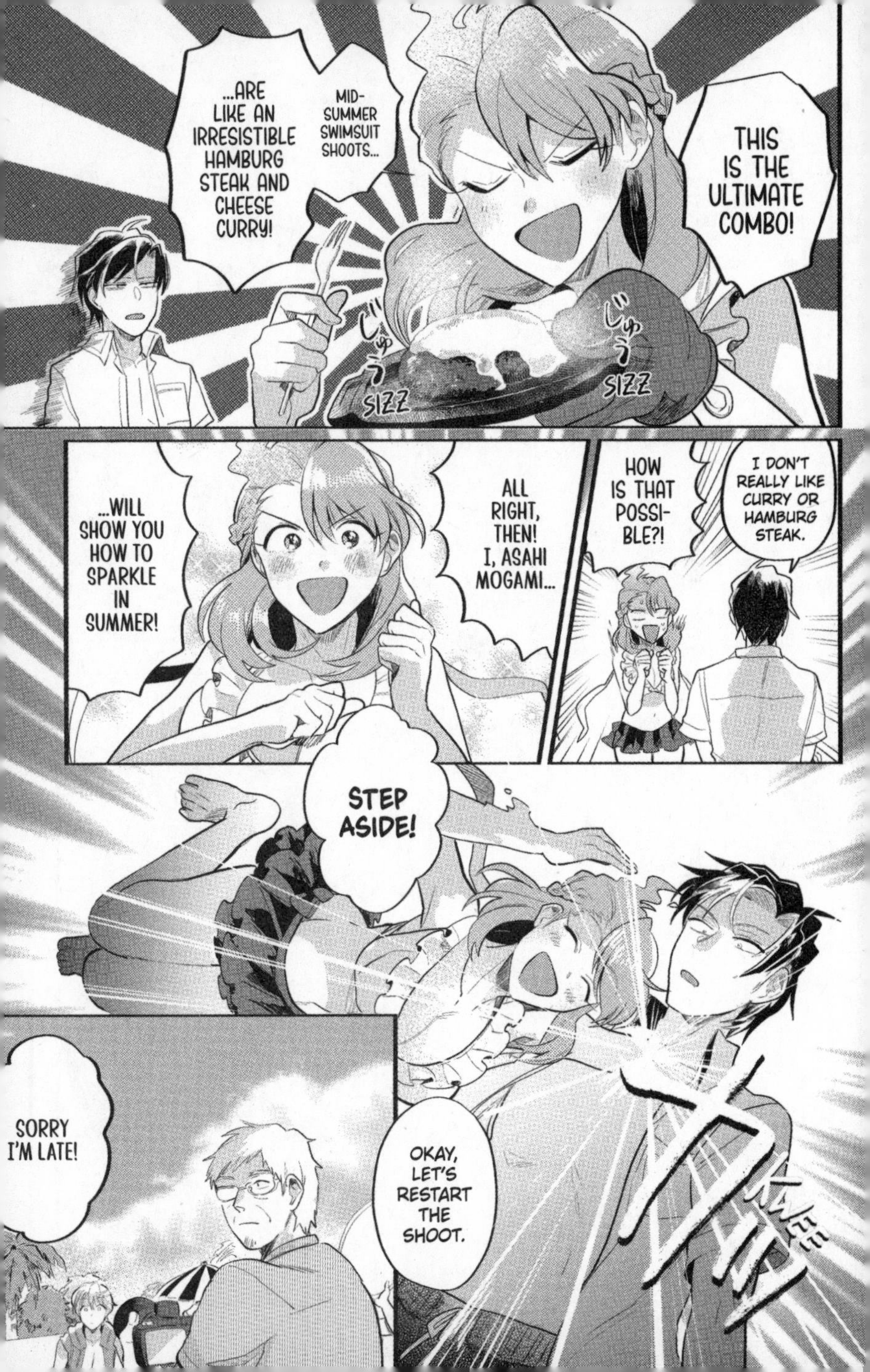
THIS IS THE ULTIMATE COMBO!
MID-SUMMER SWIMSUIT SHOOTS...
...ARE LIKE AN IRRESISTIBLE HAMBURG STEAK AND CHEESE CURRY!
じゅう SIZZ
じゅう SIZZ
I DON'T REALLY LIKE CURRY OR HAMBURG STEAK.
HOW IS THAT POSSIBLE?!
ALL RIGHT, THEN! I, ASAHI MOGAMI...
...WILL SHOW YOU HOW TO SPARKLE IN SUMMER!
STEP ASIDE!
SWEE
OKAY, LET'S RESTART THE SHOOT.
SORRY I'M LATE!

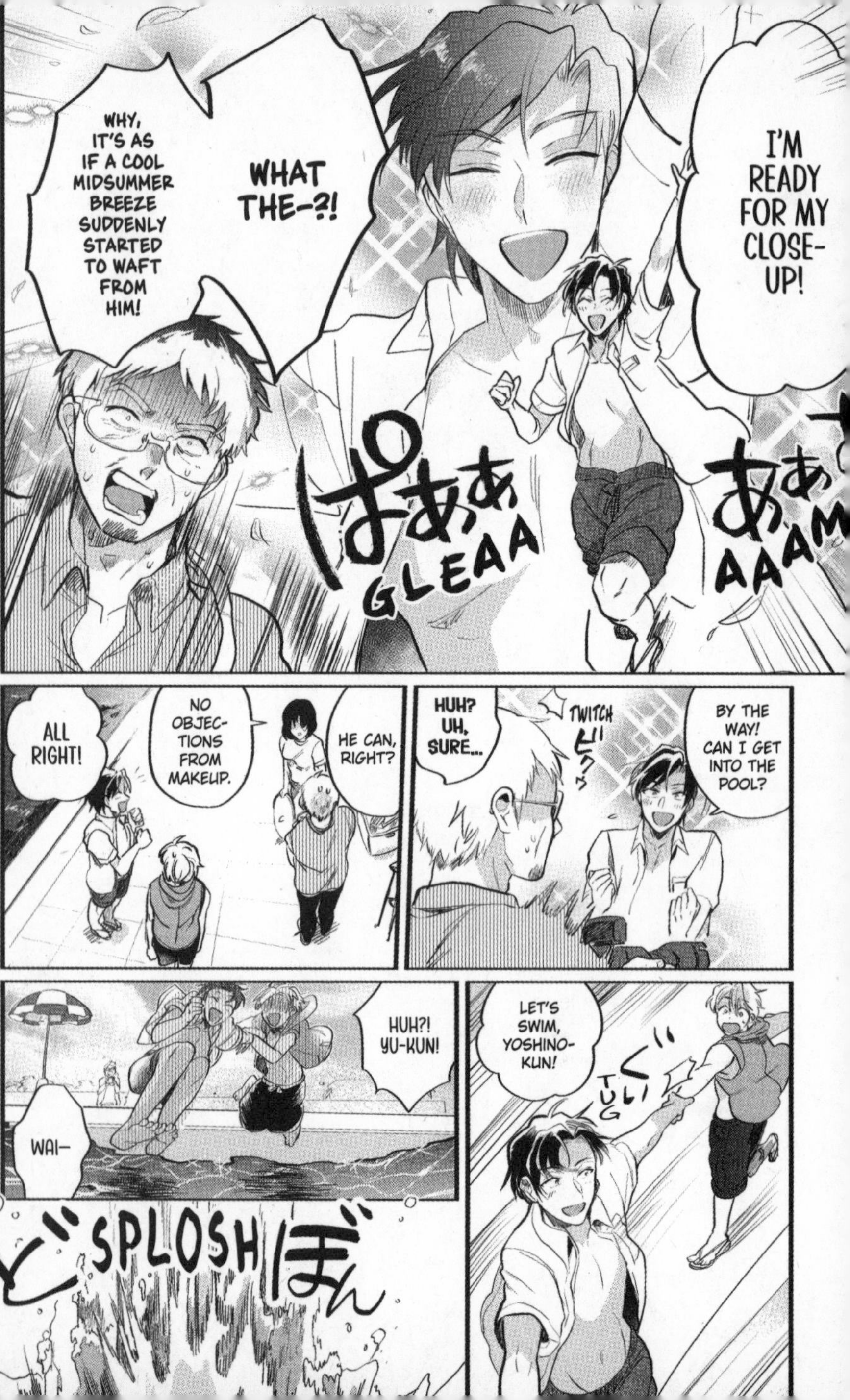
I'M READY FOR MY CLOSE-UP!
あぁ AAAM
ぱぁぁ GLEAA
WHAT THE-?!
WHY, IT'S AS IF A COOL MIDSUMMER BREEZE SUDDENLY STARTED TO WAFT FROM HIM!
BY THE WAY! CAN I GET INTO THE POOL?
ビクッ TWITCH
HUH? UH, SURE...
HE CAN, RIGHT?
NO OBJECTIONS FROM MAKEUP.
ALL RIGHT!
LET'S SWIM, YOSHINO-KUN!
ぐい TUG
HUH?! YU-KUN!
WAI-
どぼん SPLOSH

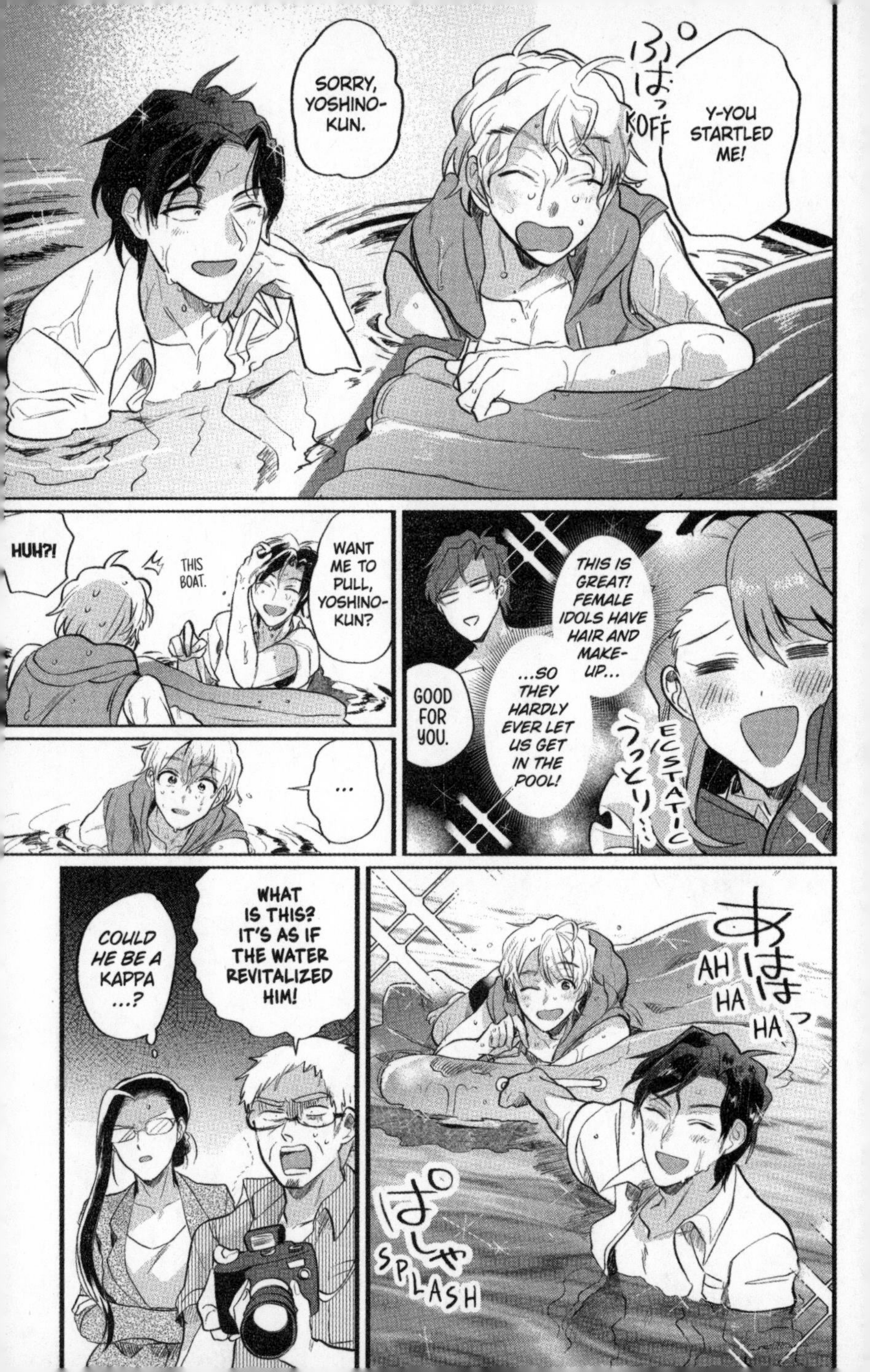
ぷはっ KOFF
Y-YOU STARTLED ME!
SORRY, YOSHINO-KUN.
THIS IS GREAT! FEMALE IDOLS HAVE HAIR AND MAKE-UP...
...SO THEY HARDLY EVER LET US GET IN THE POOL!
うっとり… ECSTATIC
GOOD FOR YOU.
WANT ME TO PULL, YOSHINO-KUN?
THIS BOAT.
HUH?!
...
あははっ AH HA HA
ぱしゃ SPLASH
WHAT IS THIS? IT'S AS IF THE WATER REVITALIZED HIM!
COULD HE BE A KAPPA ...?

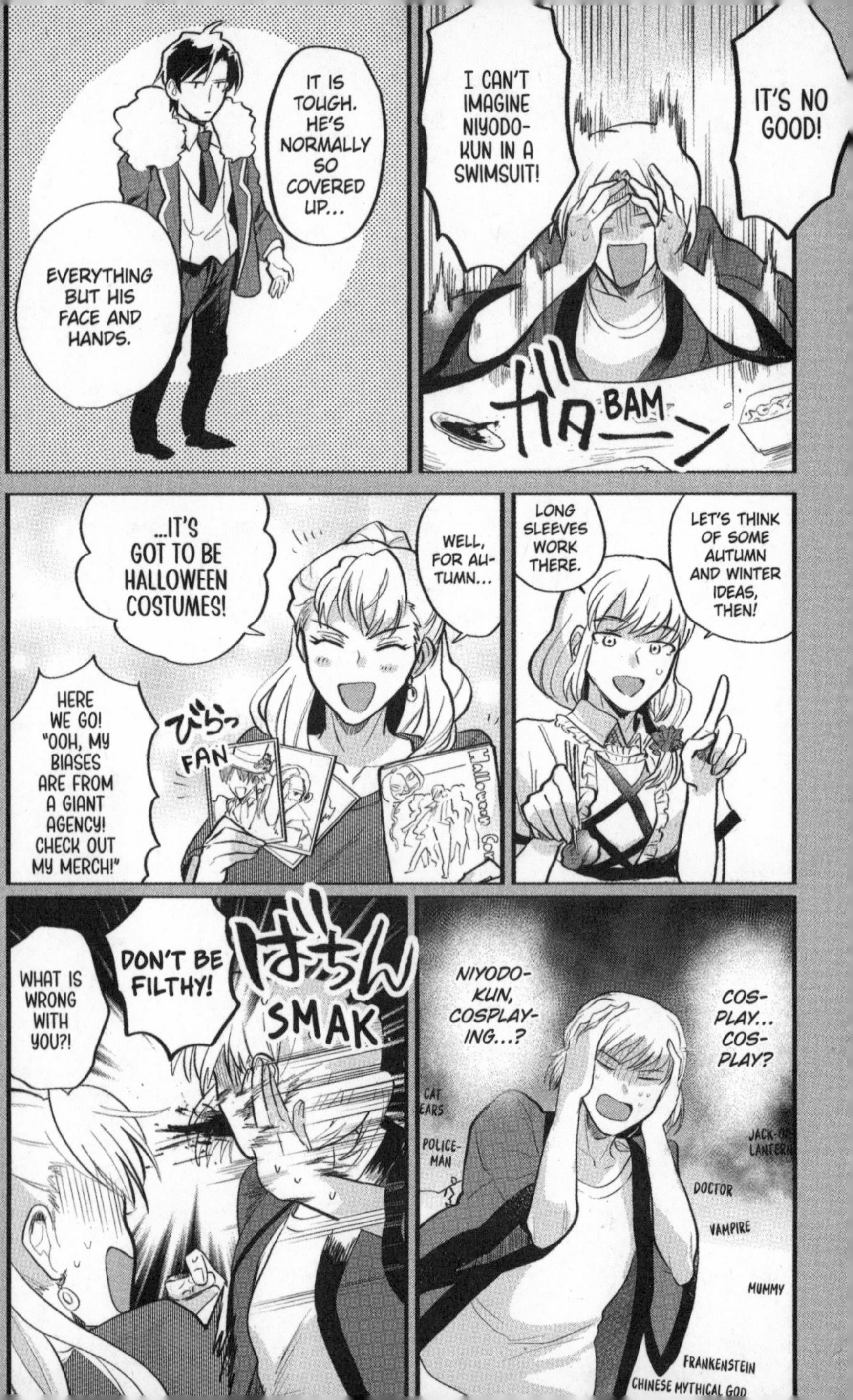
IT'S NO GOOD!
I CAN'T IMAGINE NIYODO-KUN IN A SWIMSUIT!
ガバーン BAM
IT IS TOUGH. HE'S NORMALLY SO COVERED UP...
EVERYTHING BUT HIS FACE AND HANDS.
LET'S THINK OF SOME AUTUMN AND WINTER IDEAS, THEN!
LONG SLEEVES WORK THERE.
WELL, FOR AUTUMN...
...IT'S GOT TO BE HALLOWEEN COSTUMES!
HERE WE GO! "OOH, MY BIASES ARE FROM A GIANT AGENCY! CHECK OUT MY MERCH!"
びらっ FAN
COSPLAY... COSPLAY?
NIYODO-KUN, COSPLAYING...?
CAT EARS
POLICEMAN
JACK-O'- LANTERN
DOCTOR
VAMPIRE
MUMMY
FRANKENSTEIN
CHINESE MYTHICAL GOD
ばちん SMAK
DON'T BE FILTHY!
WHAT IS WRONG WITH YOU?!

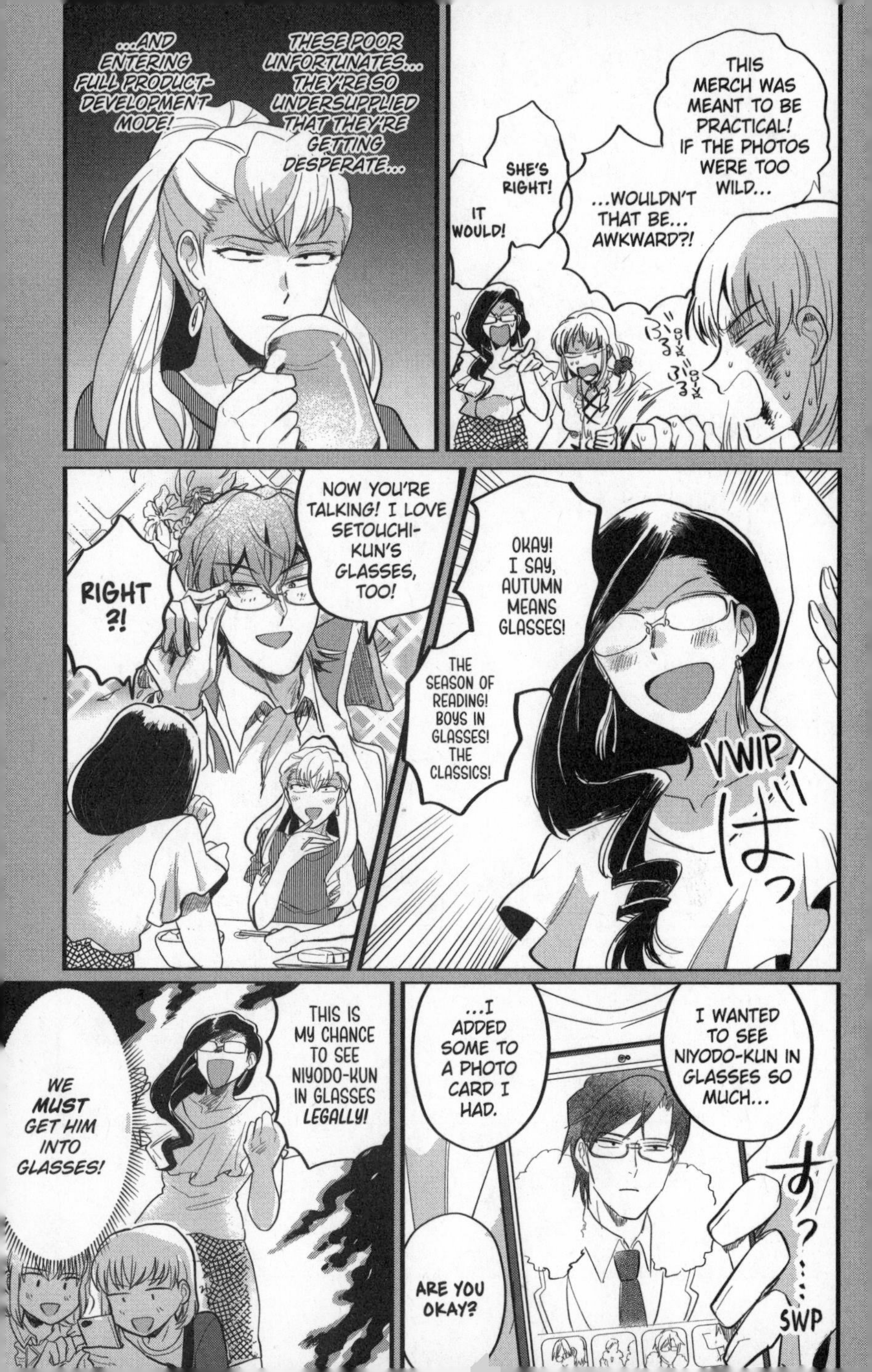
THIS MERCH WAS MEANT TO BE PRACTICAL! IF THE PHOTOS WERE TOO WILD...
...WOULDN'T THAT BE... AWKWARD?!
SHE'S RIGHT!
IT WOULD!
THESE POOR UNFORTUNATES... THEY'RE SO UNDERSUPPLIED THAT THEY'RE GETTING DESPERATE...
...AND ENTERING FULL PRODUCT-DEVELOPMENT MODE!
OKAY! I SAY, AUTUMN MEANS GLASSES!
THE SEASON OF READING! BOYS IN GLASSES! THE CLASSICS!
VWIP
ばっ
NOW YOU'RE TALKING! I LOVE SETOUCHI-KUN'S GLASSES, TOO!
RIGHT?!
I WANTED TO SEE NIYODO-KUN IN GLASSES SO MUCH...
...I ADDED SOME TO A PHOTO CARD I HAD.
ARE YOU OKAY?
すっ
SWP
THIS IS MY CHANCE TO SEE NIYODO-KUN IN GLASSES LEGALLY!
WE MUST GET HIM INTO GLASSES!

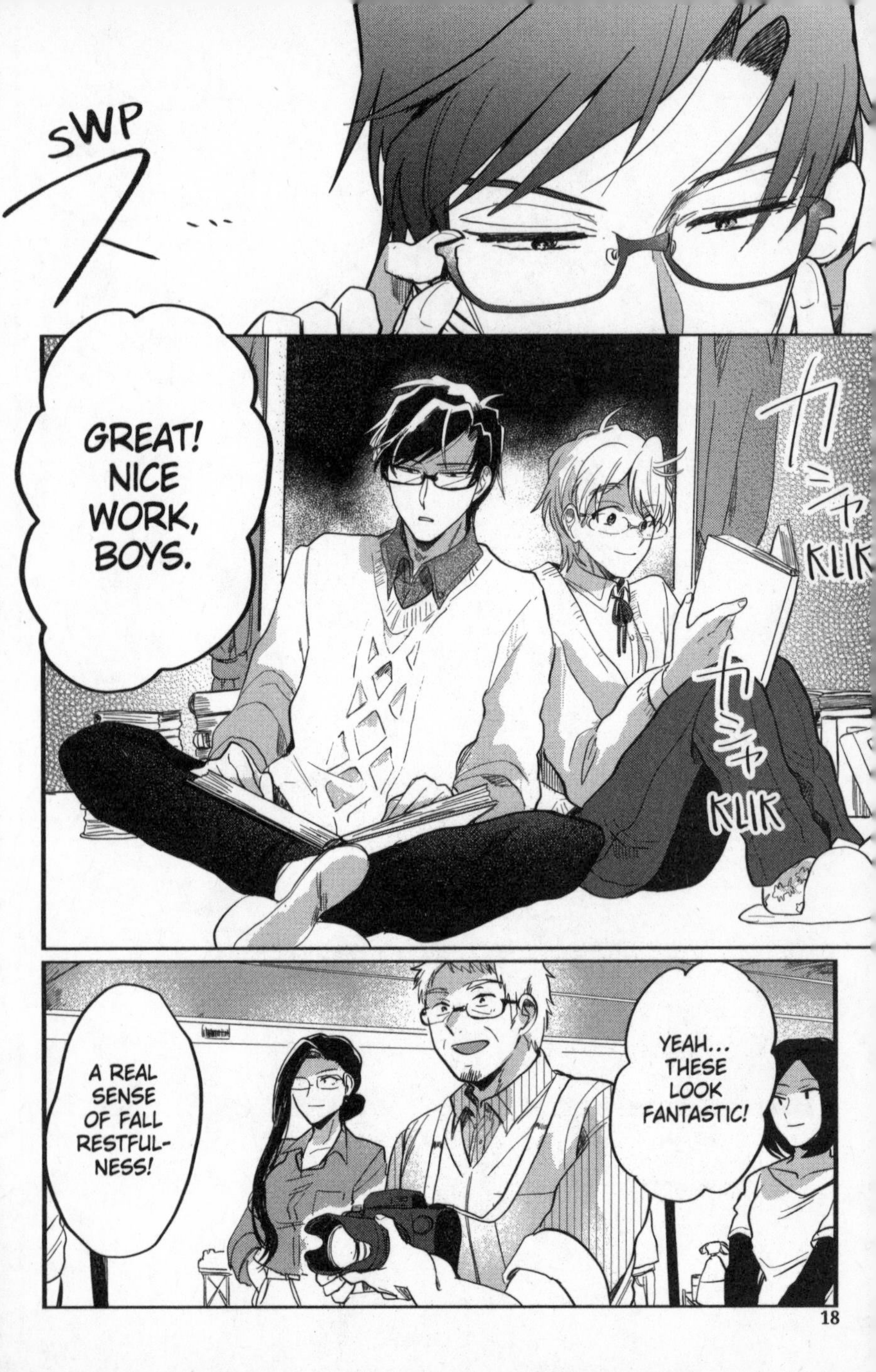
SWP
ス...
カシャ
KLIK
カシャ
KLIK
GREAT! NICE WORK, BOYS.
YEAH... THESE LOOK FANTASTIC!
A REAL SENSE OF FALL RESTFUL-NESS!

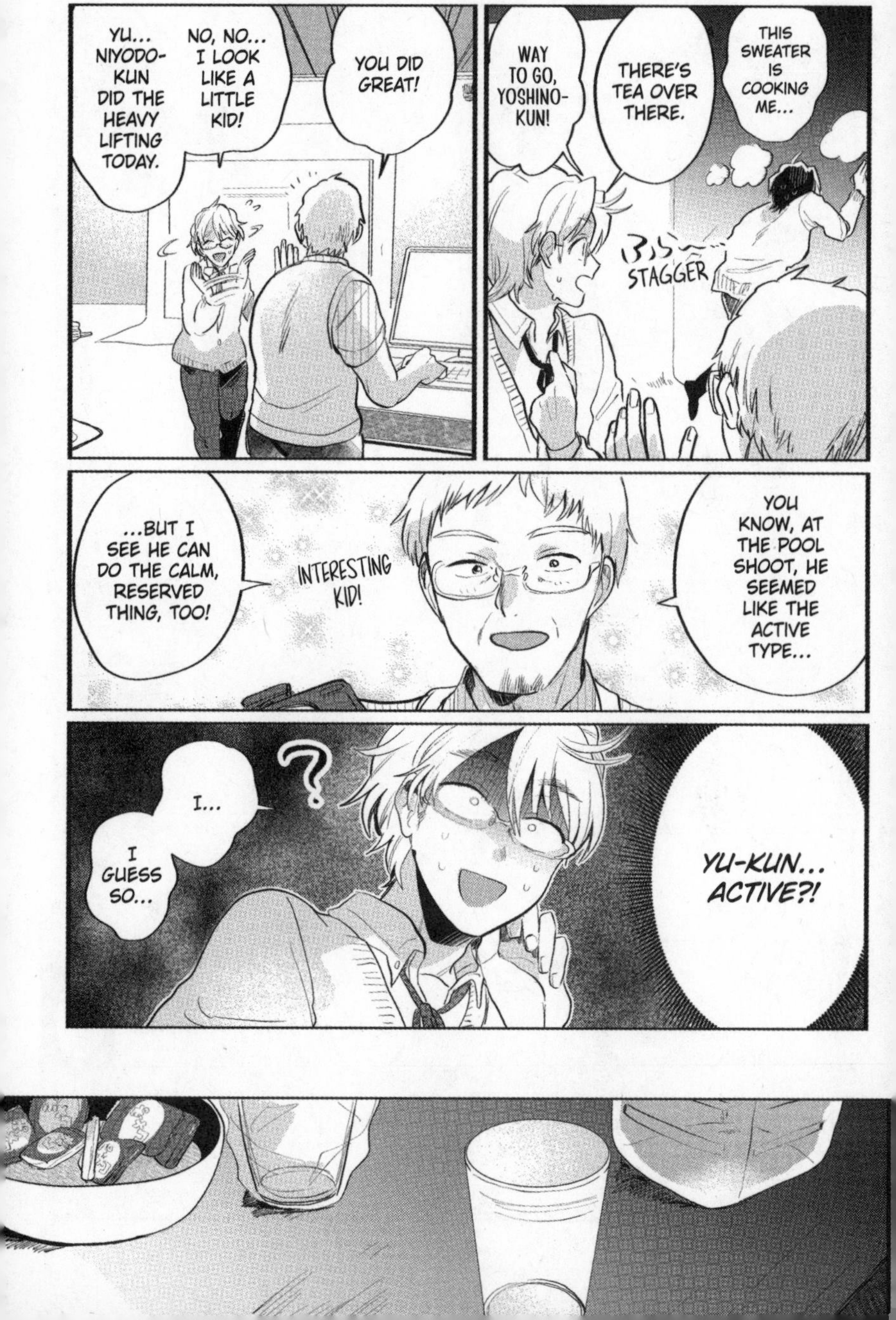
THIS SWEATER IS COOKING ME...
THERE'S TEA OVER THERE.
WAY TO GO, YOSHINO-KUN!
STAGGER
YOU DID GREAT!
NO, NO... I LOOK LIKE A LITTLE KID!
YU... NIYODO-KUN DID THE HEAVY LIFTING TODAY.
YOU KNOW, AT THE POOL SHOOT, HE SEEMED LIKE THE ACTIVE TYPE...
INTERESTING KID!
...BUT I SEE HE CAN DO THE CALM, RESERVED THING, TOO!
YU-KUN... ACTIVE?!
I...
I GUESS SO...

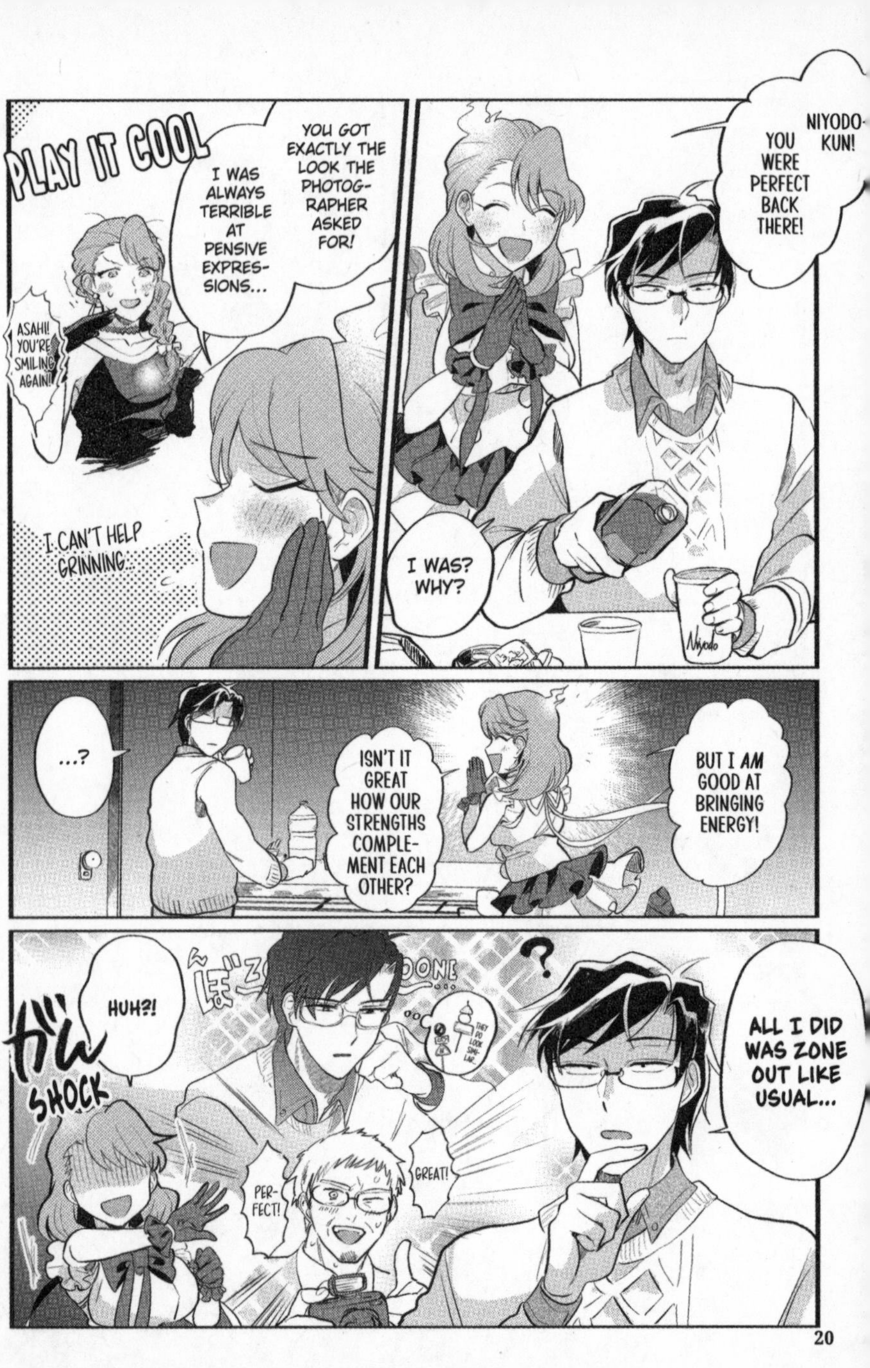
NIYODO-KUN! YOU WERE PERFECT BACK THERE!
I WAS? WHY?
YOU GOT EXACTLY THE LOOK THE PHOTOG-RAPHER ASKED FOR!
I WAS ALWAYS TERRIBLE AT PENSIVE EXPRES-SIONS...
PLAY IT COOL
ASAHI! YOU'RE SMILING AGAIN!
I CAN'T HELP GRINNING...
BUT I *AM* GOOD AT BRINGING ENERGY!
ISN'T IT GREAT HOW OUR STRENGTHS COMPLE-MENT EACH OTHER?
...?
ALL I DID WAS ZONE OUT LIKE USUAL...
?
THEY DO LOOK SIMI-LAR...
HUH?!
がん
SHOCK
GREAT!
PER-FECT!

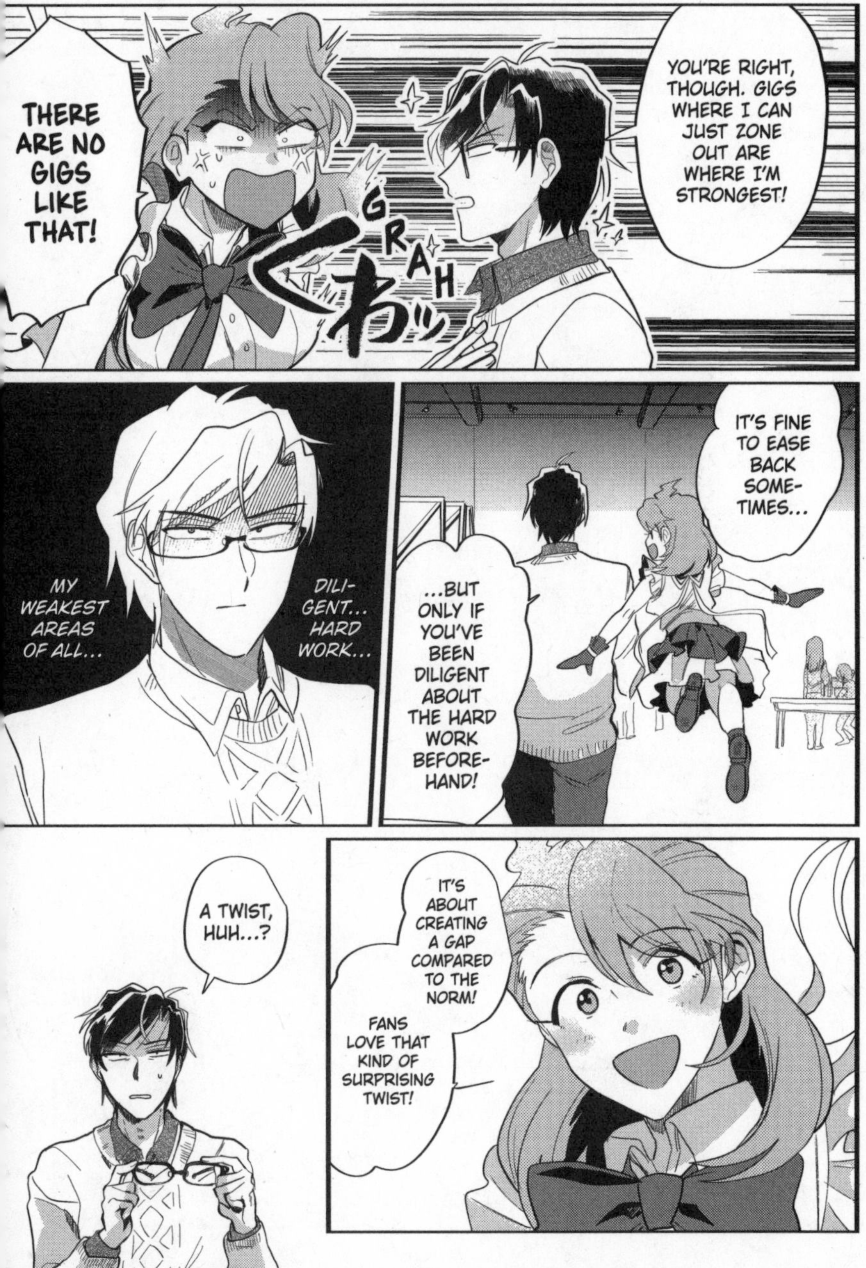
YOU'RE RIGHT, THOUGH. GIGS WHERE I CAN JUST ZONE OUT ARE WHERE I'M STRONGEST!
GRAH
THERE ARE NO GIGS LIKE THAT!
IT'S FINE TO EASE BACK SOME-TIMES...
...BUT ONLY IF YOU'VE BEEN DILIGENT ABOUT THE HARD WORK BEFORE-HAND!
DILI-GENT... HARD WORK...
MY WEAKEST AREAS OF ALL...
IT'S ABOUT CREATING A GAP COMPARED TO THE NORM!
FANS LOVE THAT KIND OF SURPRISING TWIST!
A TWIST, HUH...?

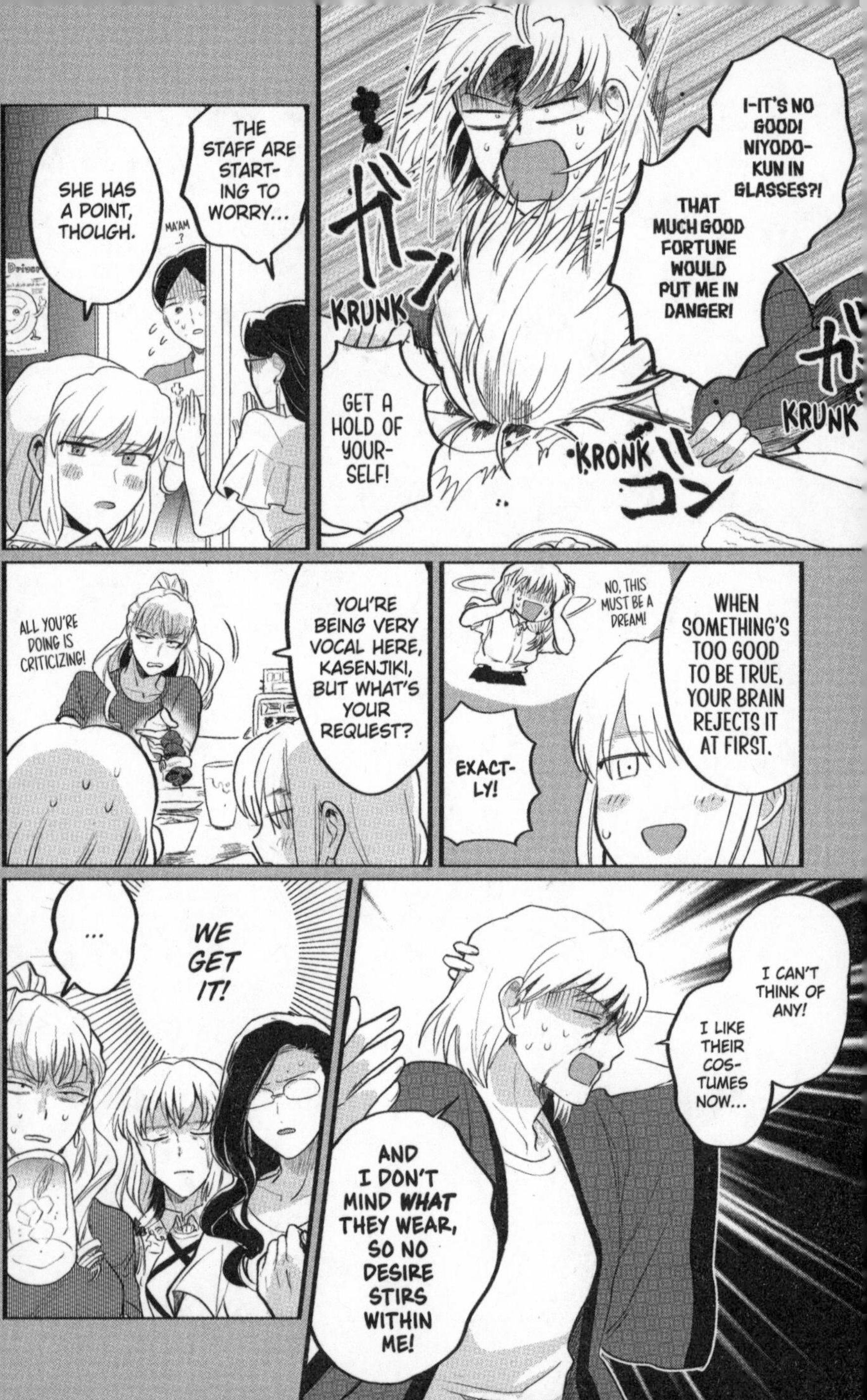
I-IT'S NO GOOD! NIYODO-KUN IN GLASSES?!
THAT MUCH GOOD FORTUNE WOULD PUT ME IN DANGER!
ガン
KRUNK
ガ
KRUNK
KRONK
コン
GET A HOLD OF YOURSELF!
THE STAFF ARE STARTING TO WORRY...
MA'AM ...?
SHE HAS A POINT, THOUGH.
WHEN SOMETHING'S TOO GOOD TO BE TRUE, YOUR BRAIN REJECTS IT AT FIRST.
NO, THIS MUST BE A DREAM!
EXACTLY!
YOU'RE BEING VERY VOCAL HERE, KASENJIKI, BUT WHAT'S YOUR REQUEST?
ALL YOU'RE DOING IS CRITICIZING!
I CAN'T THINK OF ANY!
I LIKE THEIR COSTUMES NOW...
AND I DON'T MIND WHAT THEY WEAR, SO NO DESIRE STIRS WITHIN ME!
...
WE GET IT!

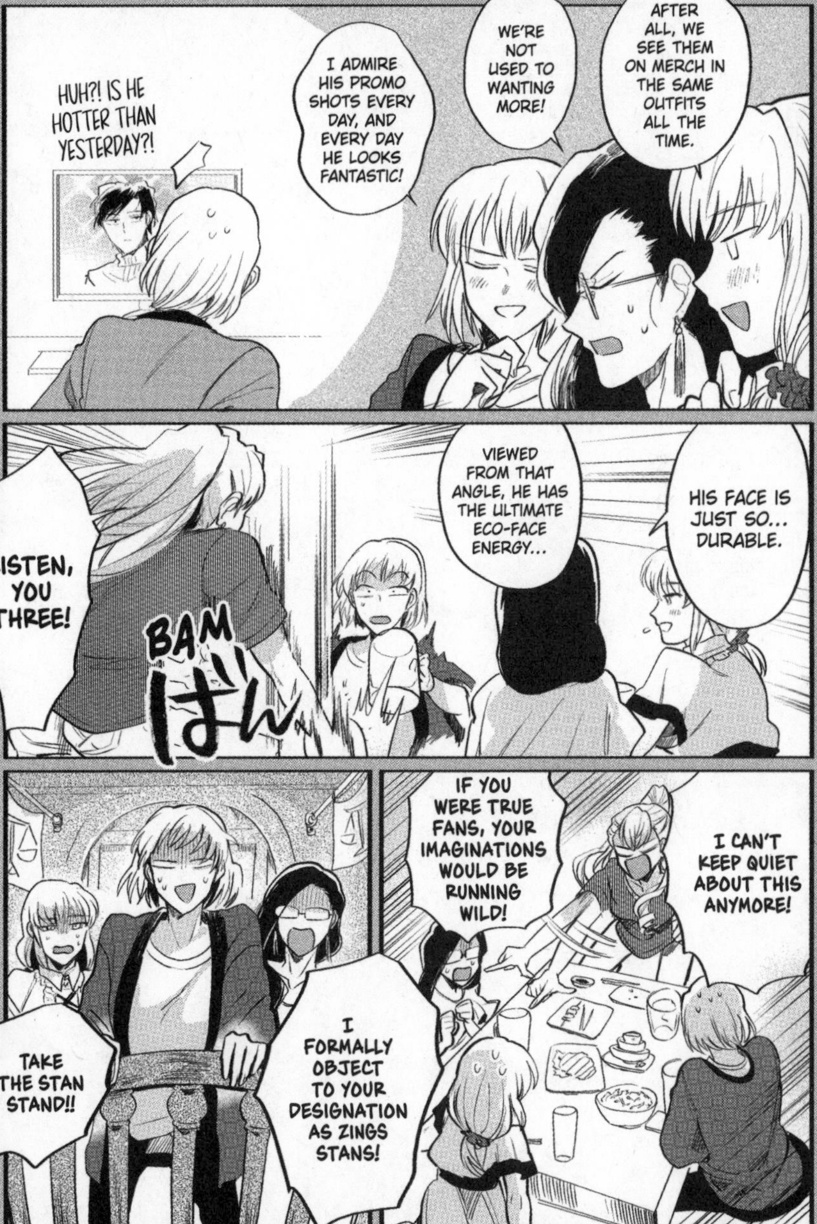
AFTER ALL, WE SEE THEM ON MERCH IN THE SAME OUTFITS ALL THE TIME.
WE'RE NOT USED TO WANTING MORE!
I ADMIRE HIS PROMO SHOTS EVERY DAY, AND EVERY DAY HE LOOKS FANTASTIC!
HUH?! IS HE HOTTER THAN YESTERDAY?!
HIS FACE IS JUST SO... DURABLE.
VIEWED FROM THAT ANGLE, HE HAS THE ULTIMATE ECO-FACE ENERGY...
LISTEN, YOU THREE!
BAM
ばん
I CAN'T KEEP QUIET ABOUT THIS ANYMORE!
IF YOU WERE TRUE FANS, YOUR IMAGINATIONS WOULD BE RUNNING WILD!
I FORMALLY OBJECT TO YOUR DESIGNATION AS ZINGS STANS!
TAKE THE STAN STAND!!

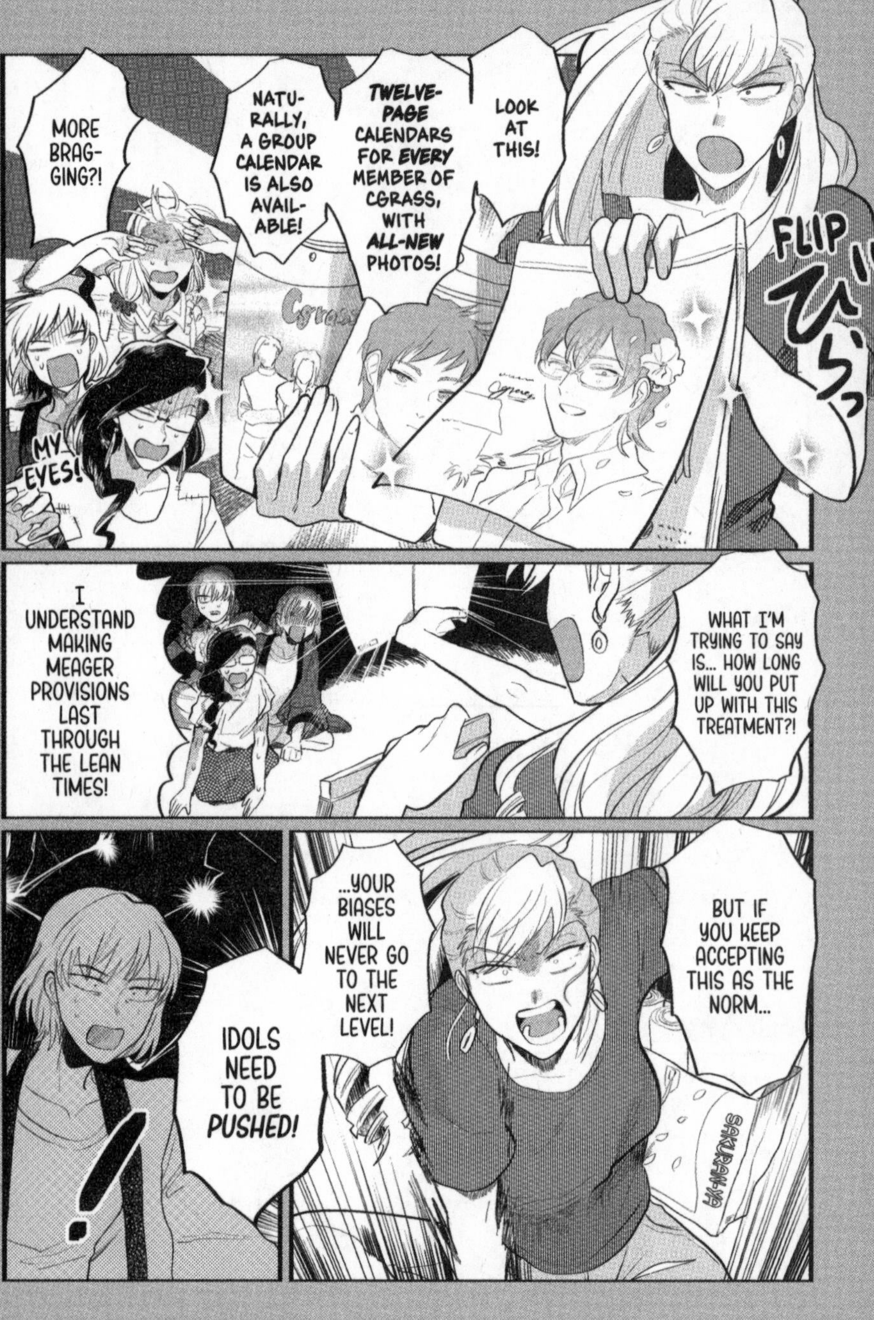
FLIP
ひらっ
LOOK AT THIS!
**TWELVE-PAGE** CALENDARS FOR **EVERY** MEMBER OF CGRASS, WITH **ALL-NEW** PHOTOS!
NATU-RALLY, A GROUP CALENDAR IS ALSO AVAIL-ABLE!
Cgrass
MORE BRAG-GING?!
MY EYES!
WHAT I'M TRYING TO SAY IS... HOW LONG WILL YOU PUT UP WITH THIS TREATMENT?!
I UNDERSTAND MAKING MEAGER PROVISIONS LAST THROUGH THE LEAN TIMES!
BUT IF YOU KEEP ACCEPTING THIS AS THE NORM...
...YOUR BIASES WILL NEVER GO TO THE NEXT LEVEL!
SAKURAI-YA
IDOLS NEED TO BE **PUSHED!**
!

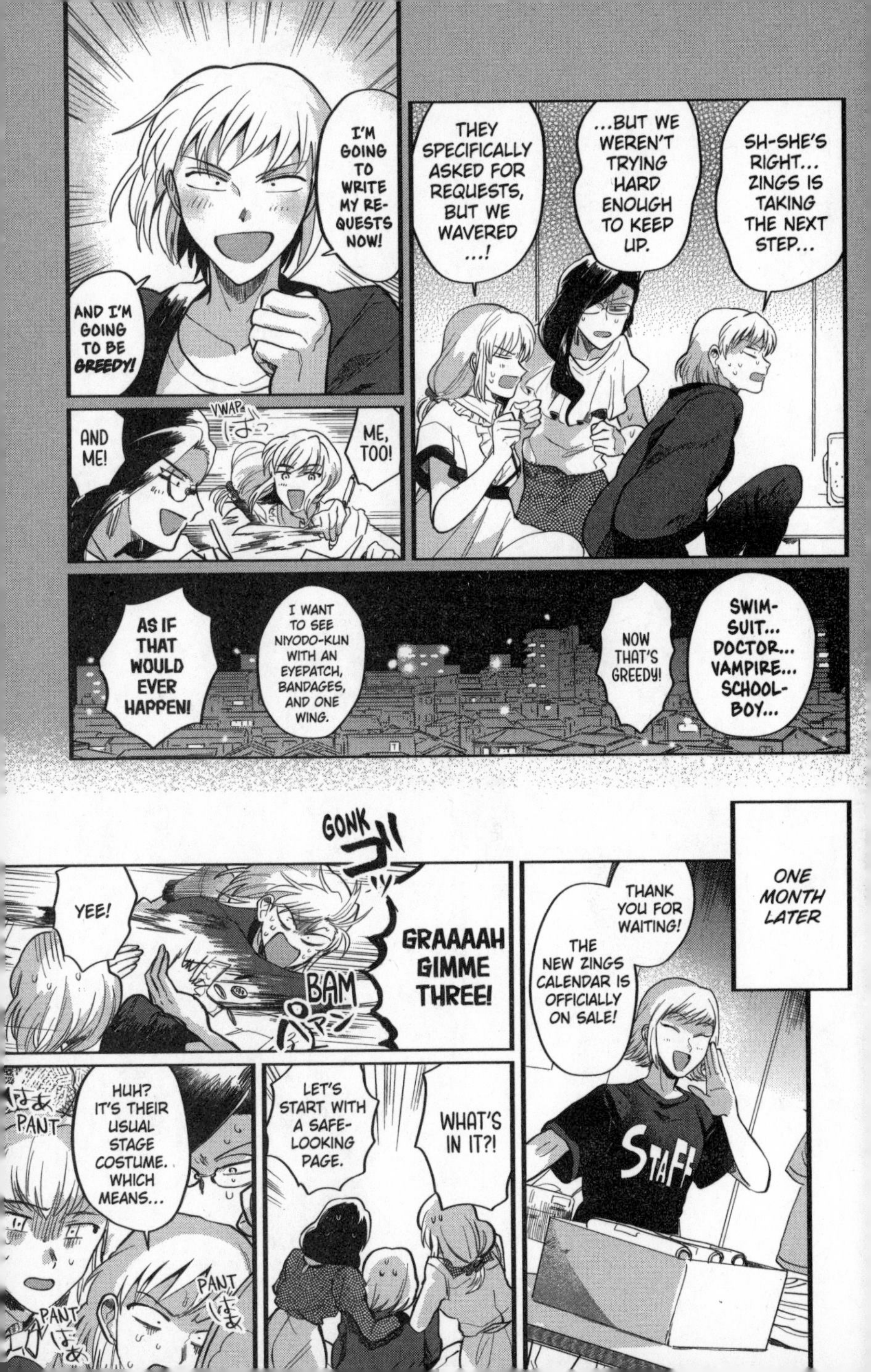
SH-SHE'S RIGHT... ZINGS IS TAKING THE NEXT STEP...
...BUT WE WEREN'T TRYING HARD ENOUGH TO KEEP UP.
THEY SPECIFICALLY ASKED FOR REQUESTS, BUT WE WAVERED ...!
I'M GOING TO WRITE MY RE-QUESTS NOW!
AND I'M GOING TO BE GREEDY!
ME, TOO!
VWAP
AND ME!
SWIM-SUIT... DOCTOR... VAMPIRE... SCHOOL-BOY...
NOW THAT'S GREEDY!
I WANT TO SEE NIYODO-KUN WITH AN EYEPATCH, BANDAGES, AND ONE WING.
AS IF THAT WOULD EVER HAPPEN!
ONE MONTH LATER
THANK YOU FOR WAITING!
THE NEW ZINGS CALENDAR IS OFFICIALLY ON SALE!
STAFF
GONK
GRAAAAH GIMME THREE!
BAM
YEE!
WHAT'S IN IT?!
LET'S START WITH A SAFE-LOOKING PAGE.
HUH? IT'S THEIR USUAL STAGE COSTUME. WHICH MEANS...
PANT
PANT
PANT

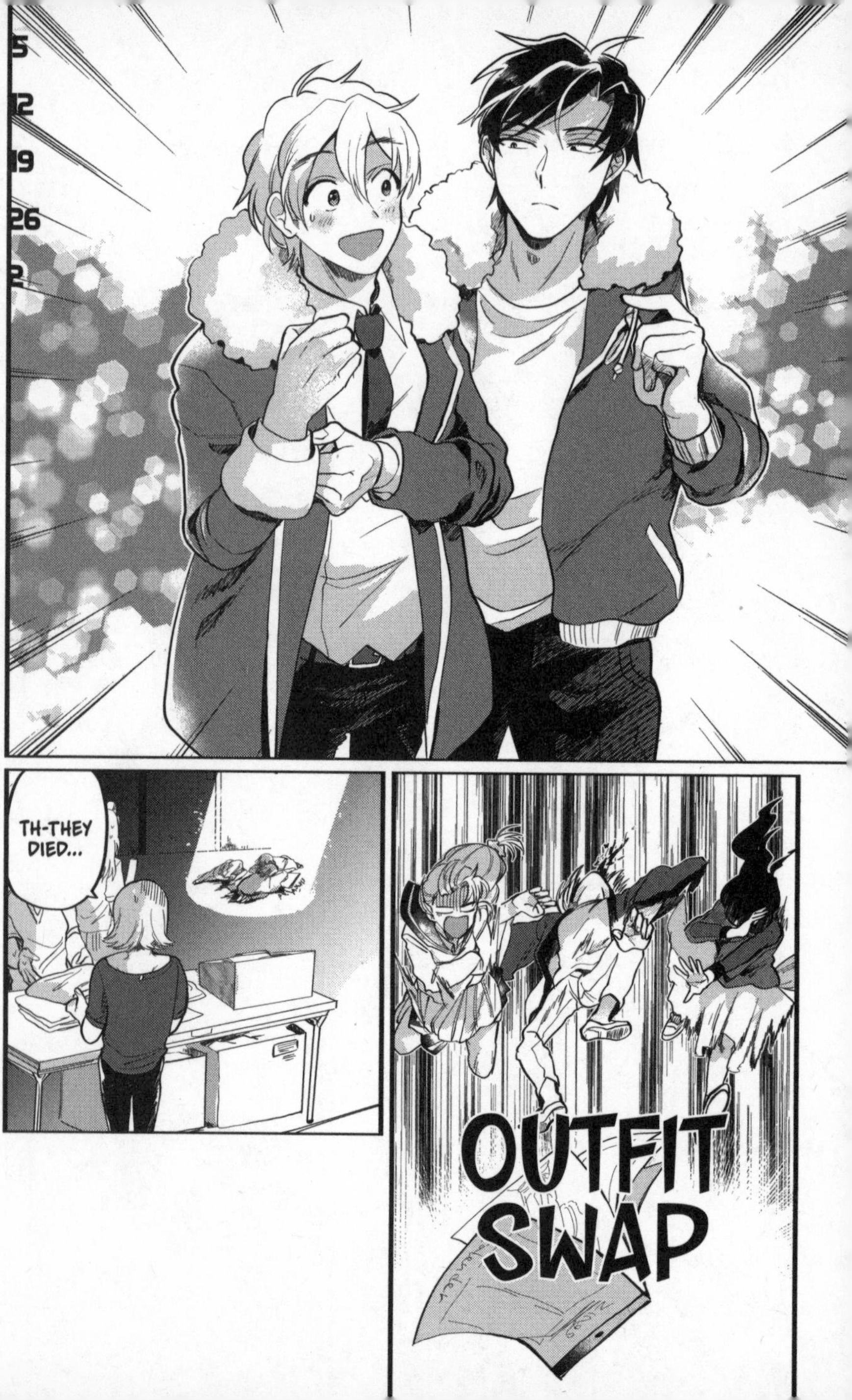
OUTFIT SWAP
TH-THEY DIED...

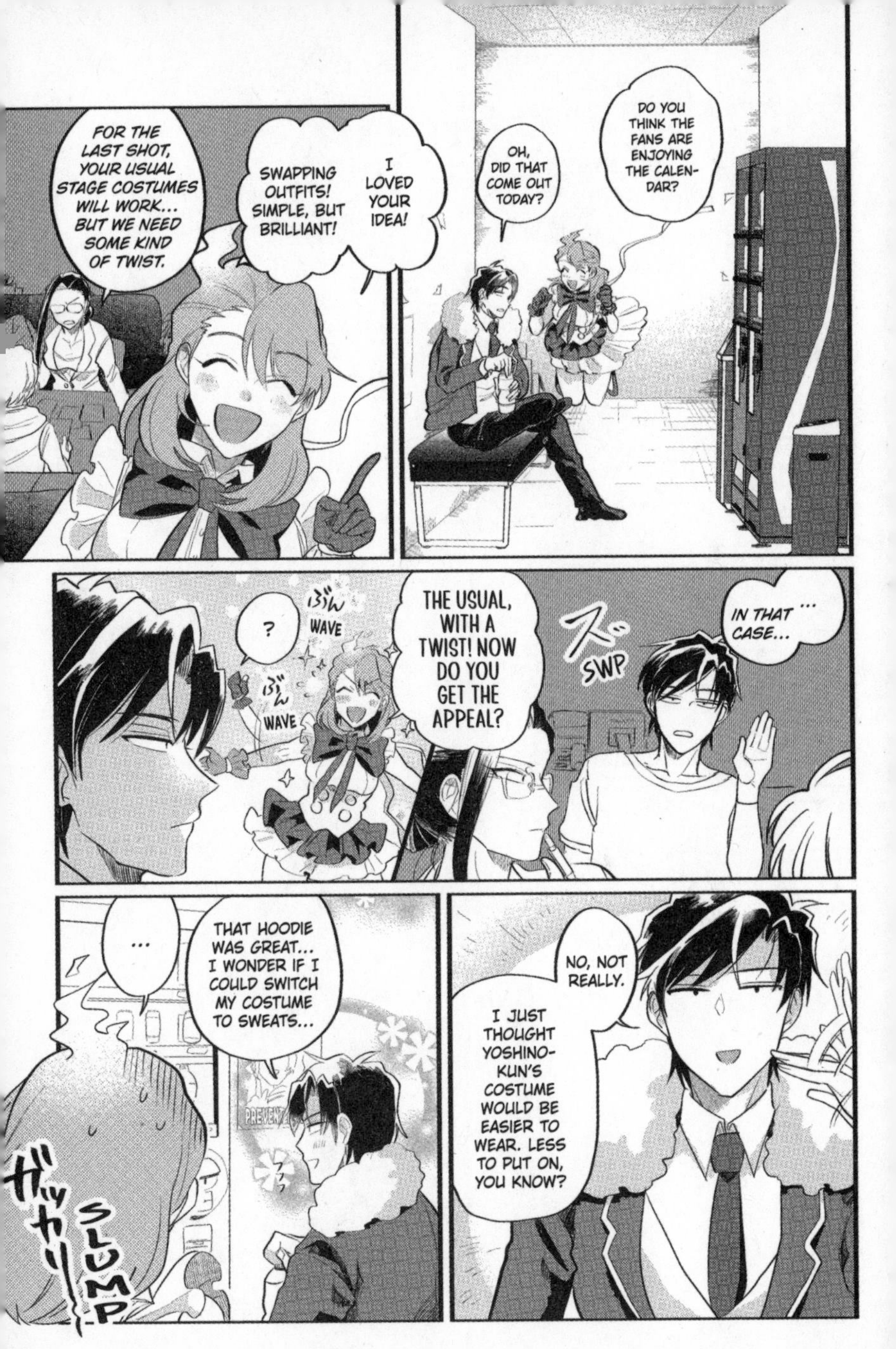
DO YOU THINK THE FANS ARE ENJOYING THE CALEN-DAR?
OH, DID THAT COME OUT TODAY?
I LOVED YOUR IDEA!
SWAPPING OUTFITS! SIMPLE, BUT BRILLIANT!
FOR THE LAST SHOT, YOUR USUAL STAGE COSTUMES WILL WORK... BUT WE NEED SOME KIND OF TWIST.
IN THAT CASE...
SWP
THE USUAL, WITH A TWIST! NOW DO YOU GET THE APPEAL?
ぶん WAVE
?
ぶん WAVE
NO, NOT REALLY.
I JUST THOUGHT YOSHINO-KUN'S COSTUME WOULD BE EASIER TO WEAR. LESS TO PUT ON, YOU KNOW?
THAT HOODIE WAS GREAT... I WONDER IF I COULD SWITCH MY COSTUME TO SWEATS...
...
ガッカリ SLUMP

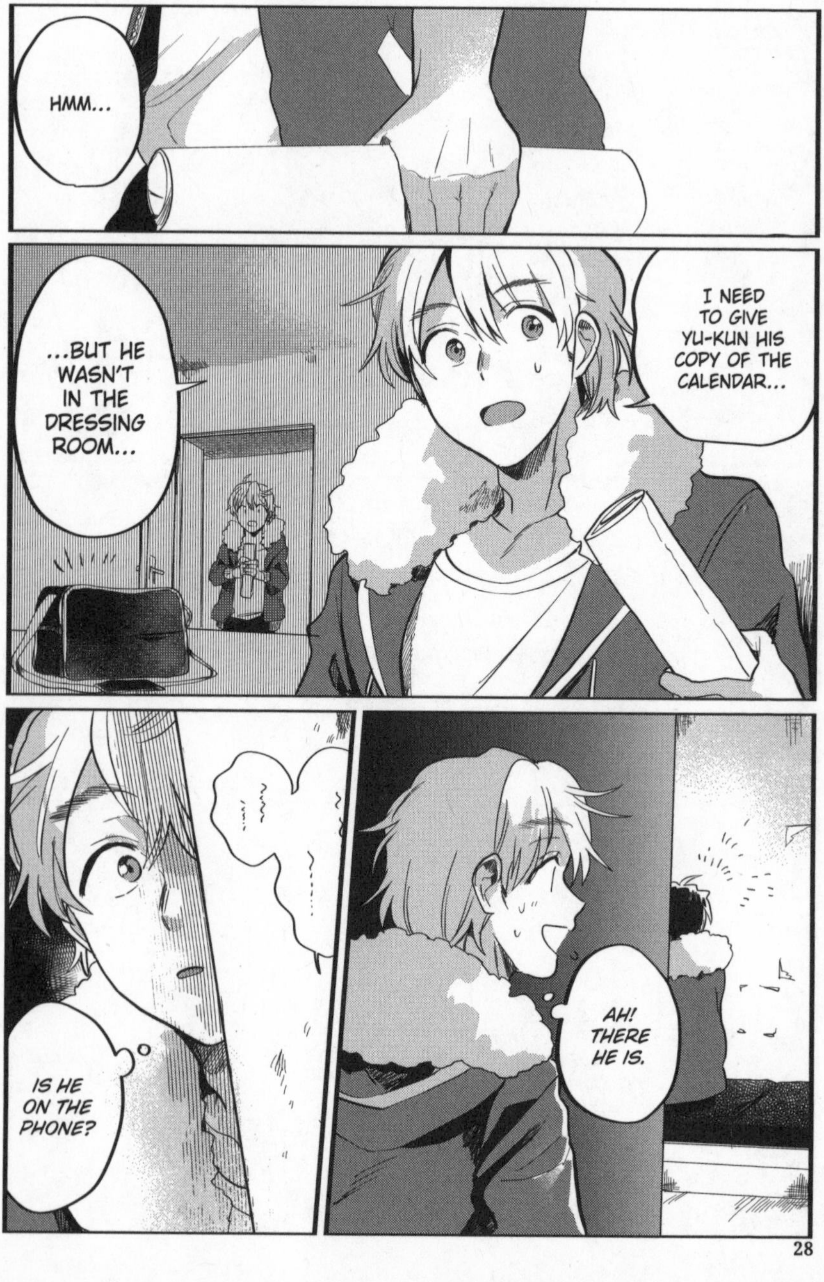
HMM...
I NEED TO GIVE YU-KUN HIS COPY OF THE CALENDAR...
...BUT HE WASN'T IN THE DRESSING ROOM...
AH! THERE HE IS.
IS HE ON THE PHONE?

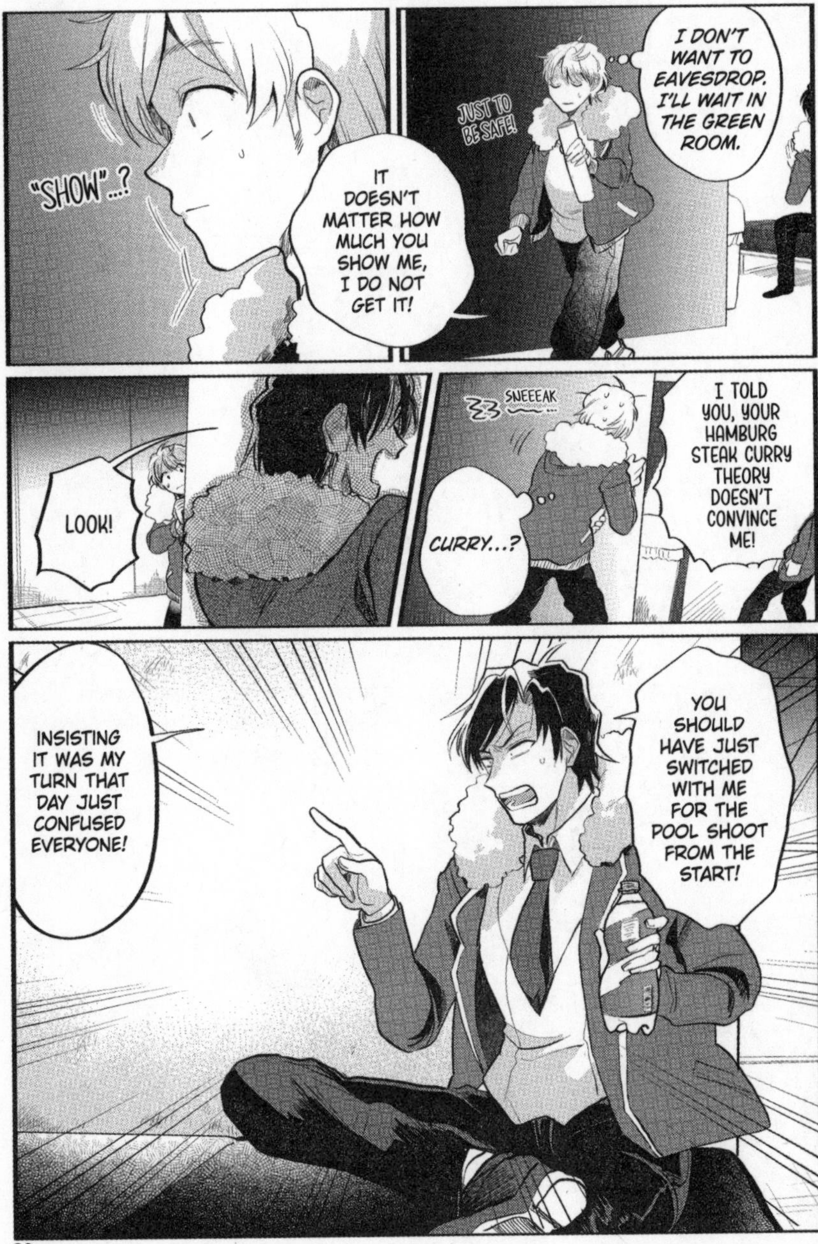
I DON'T WANT TO EAVESDROP. I'LL WAIT IN THE GREEN ROOM.
JUST TO BE SAFE!
IT DOESN'T MATTER HOW MUCH YOU SHOW ME, I DO NOT GET IT!
"SHOW"...?
I TOLD YOU, YOUR HAMBURG STEAK CURRY THEORY DOESN'T CONVINCE ME!
SNEEEAK...
CURRY...?
LOOK!
YOU SHOULD HAVE JUST SWITCHED WITH ME FOR THE POOL SHOOT FROM THE START!
INSISTING IT WAS MY TURN THAT DAY JUST CONFUSED EVERYONE!

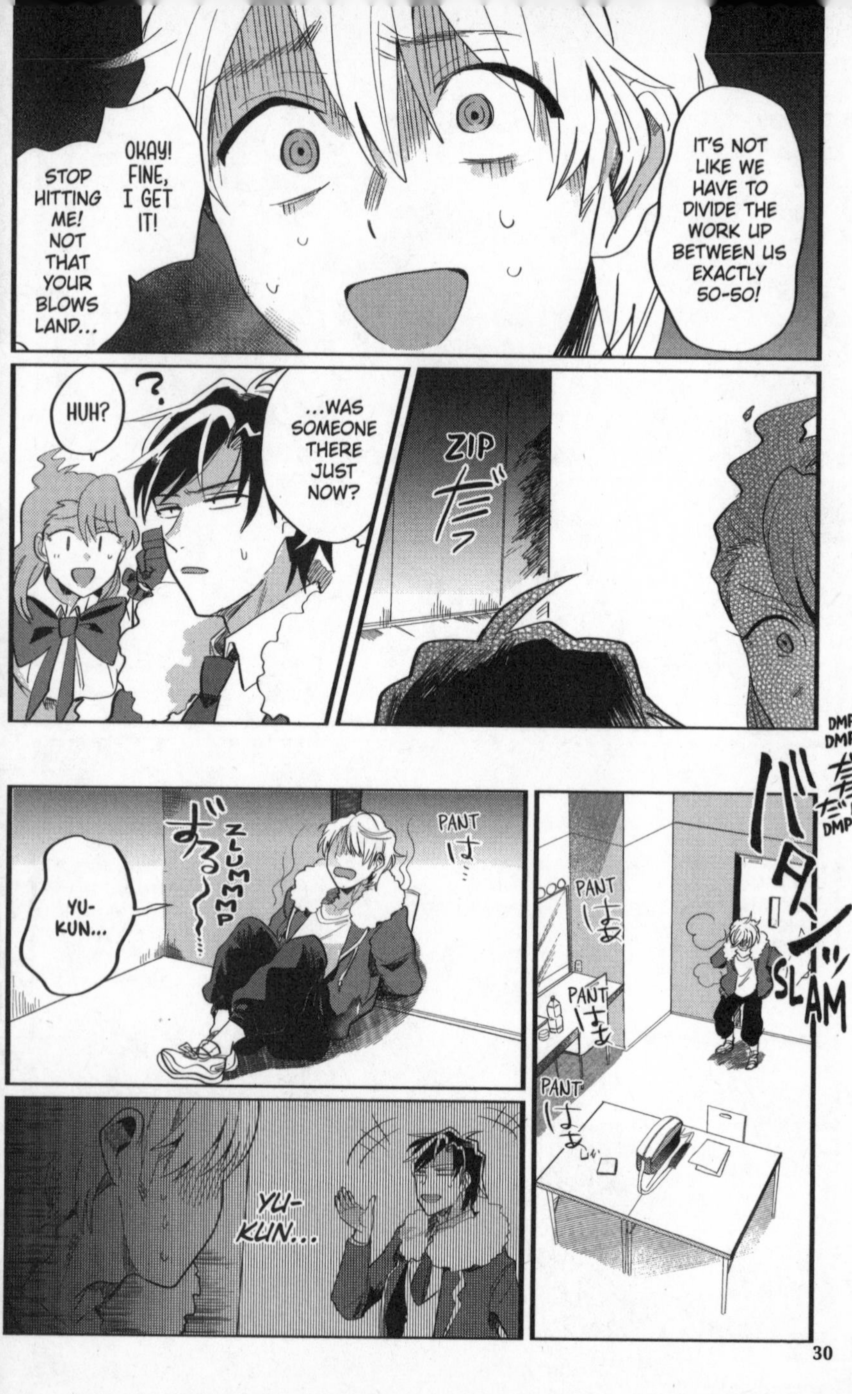
IT'S NOT LIKE WE HAVE TO DIVIDE THE WORK UP BETWEEN US EXACTLY 50-50!
OKAY! FINE, I GET IT!
STOP HITTING ME! NOT THAT YOUR BLOWS LAND...
ZIP だっ
...WAS SOMEONE THERE JUST NOW?
?
HUH?
DMP DMP だだ
DMP DMP だだ
バタン
SLAM
PANT はぁ
PANT はぁ
PANT はぁ
PANT は...
ずる～ ZLUMMMP
YU-KUN...
YU-KUN...

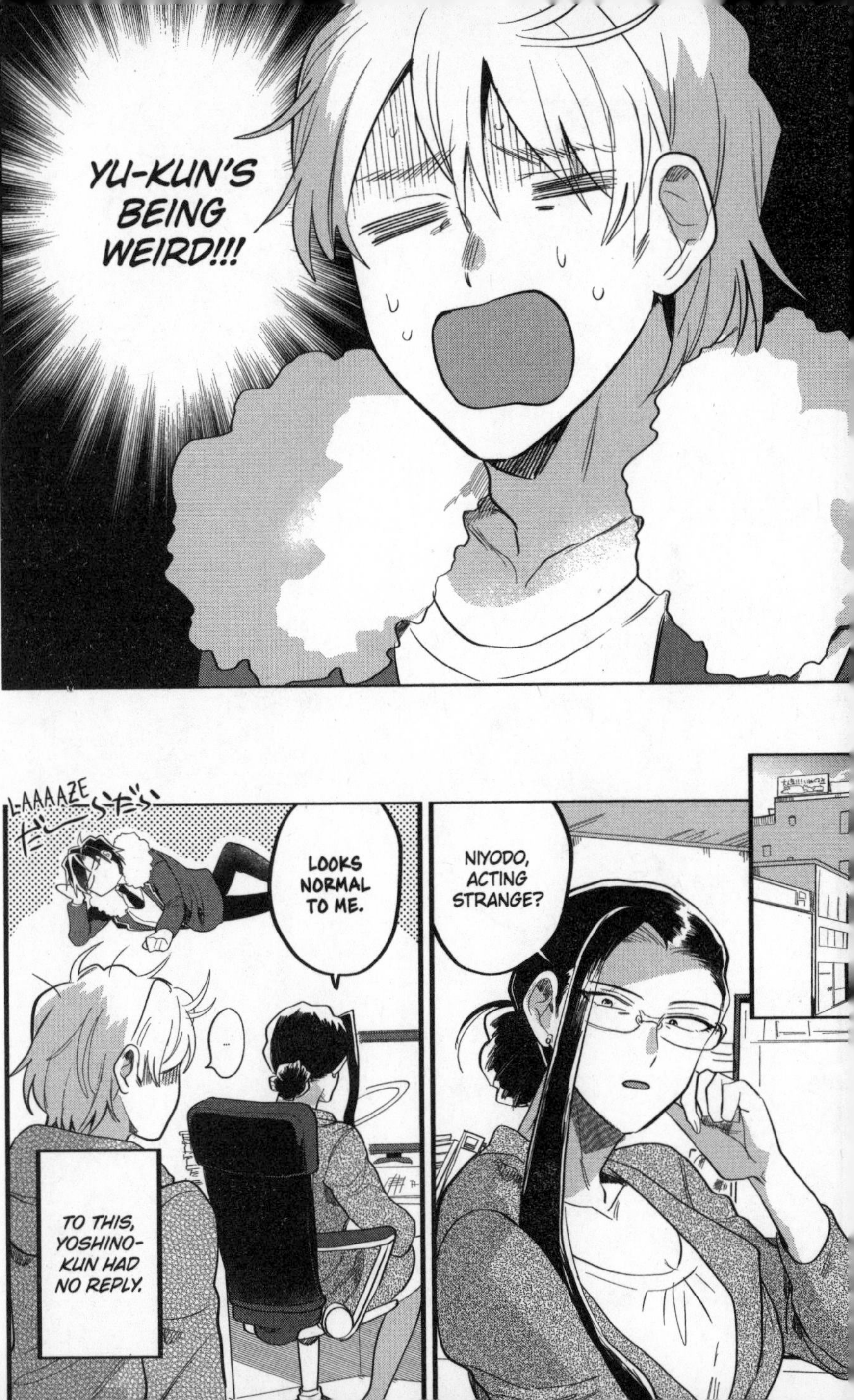
YU-KUN'S BEING WEIRD!!!
NIYODO, ACTING STRANGE?
LOOKS NORMAL TO ME.
L-AAAAZE
...
TO THIS, YOSHINO-KUN HAD NO REPLY.

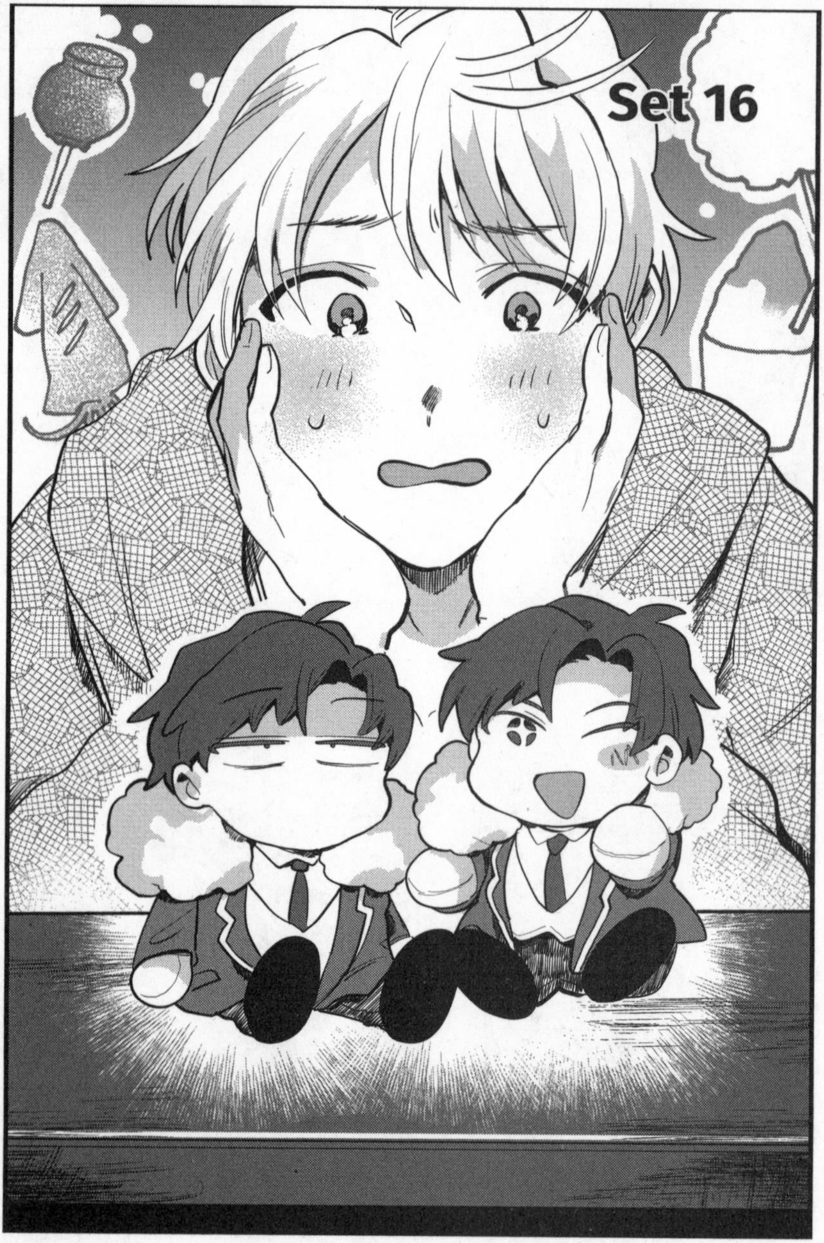
Set 16

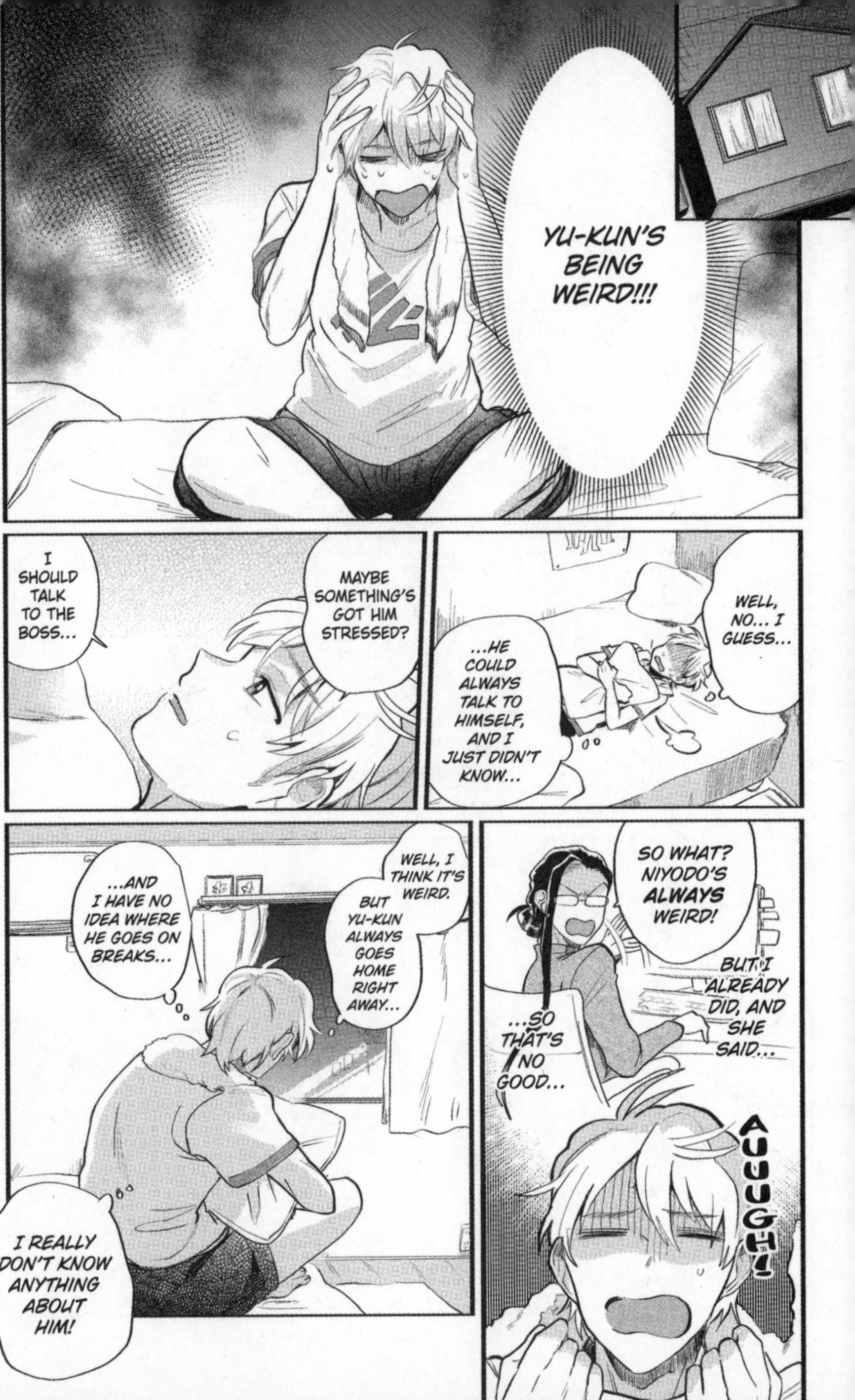
YU-KUN'S BEING WEIRD!!!
WELL, NO... I GUESS...
...HE COULD ALWAYS TALK TO HIMSELF, AND I JUST DIDN'T KNOW...
MAYBE SOMETHING'S GOT HIM STRESSED?
I SHOULD TALK TO THE BOSS...
BUT I ALREADY DID, AND SHE SAID...
SO WHAT? NIYODO'S ALWAYS WEIRD!
...SO THAT'S NO GOOD...
AUUUGH!
WELL, I THINK IT'S WEIRD.
BUT YU-KUN ALWAYS GOES HOME RIGHT AWAY...
...AND I HAVE NO IDEA WHERE HE GOES ON BREAKS...
I REALLY DON'T KNOW ANYTHING ABOUT HIM!

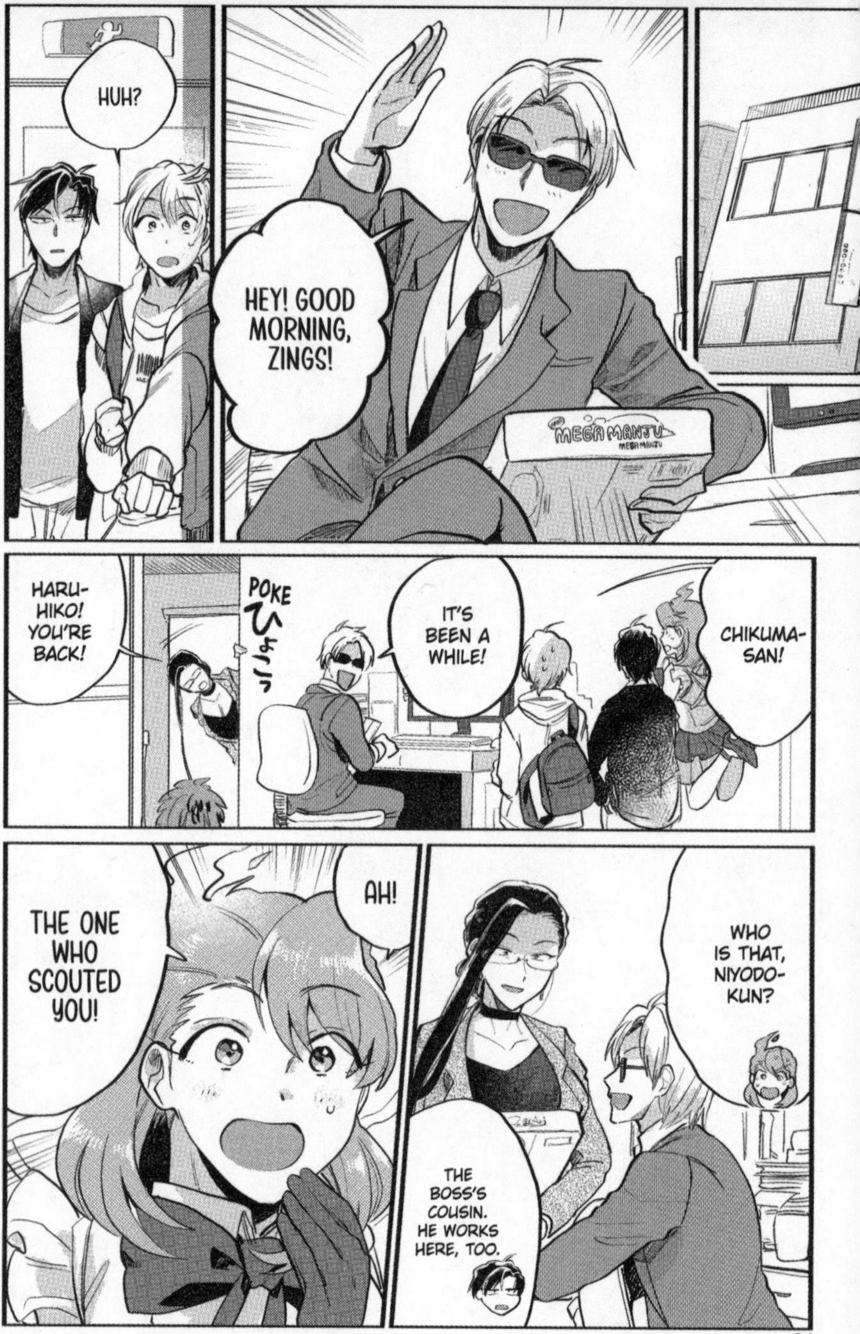
HEY! GOOD MORNING, ZINGS!
MEGA MANJU
HUH?
CHIKUMA-SAN!
IT'S BEEN A WHILE!
POKE
HARU-HIKO! YOU'RE BACK!
WHO IS THAT, NIYODO-KUN?
THE BOSS'S COUSIN. HE WORKS HERE, TOO.
AH!
THE ONE WHO SCOUTED YOU!

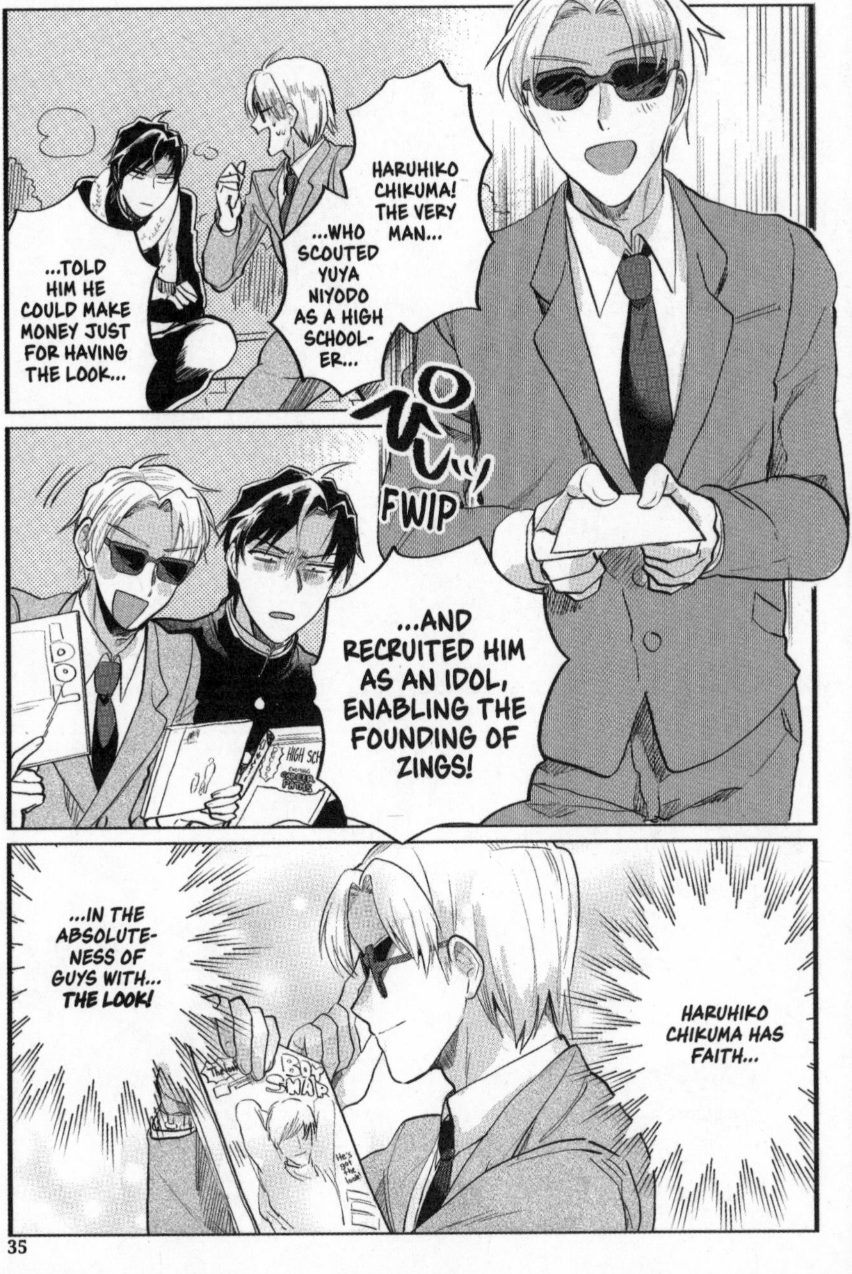
HARUHIKO CHIKUMA! THE VERY MAN...
...WHO SCOUTED YUYA NIYODO AS A HIGH SCHOOL-ER...
...TOLD HIM HE COULD MAKE MONEY JUST FOR HAVING THE LOOK...
FWIP
...AND RECRUITED HIM AS AN IDOL, ENABLING THE FOUNDING OF ZINGS!
IDOL
HIGH SCH
CAREER PATHS
HARUHIKO CHIKUMA HAS FAITH...
...IN THE ABSOLUTE-NESS OF GUYS WITH... THE LOOK!
BOY SNAP
He's got the look!

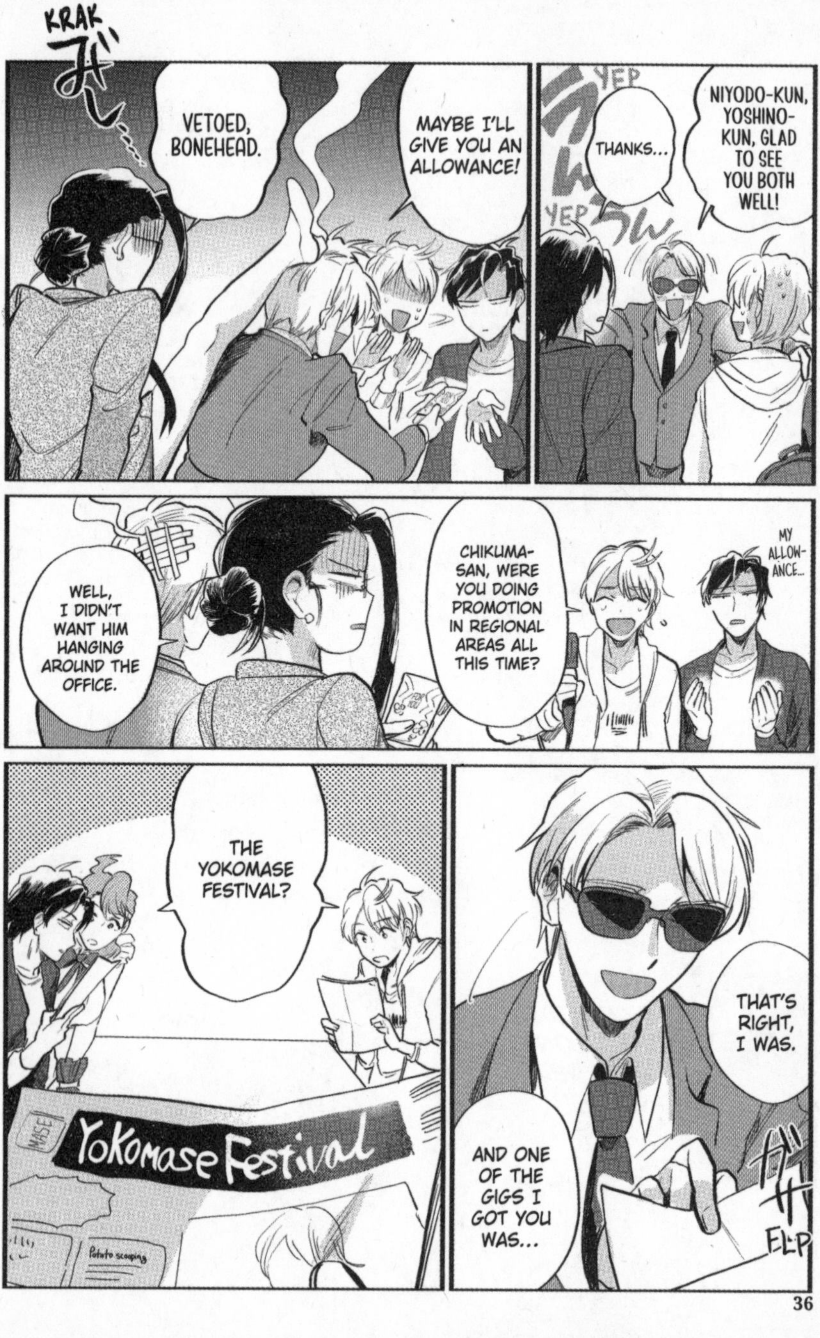
YEP
NIYODO-KUN, YOSHINO-KUN, GLAD TO SEE YOU BOTH WELL!
THANKS...
YEP
MAYBE I'LL GIVE YOU AN ALLOWANCE!
KRAK
VETOED, BONEHEAD.
MY ALLOWANCE...
CHIKUMA-SAN, WERE YOU DOING PROMOTION IN REGIONAL AREAS ALL THIS TIME?
WELL, I DIDN'T WANT HIM HANGING AROUND THE OFFICE.
THAT'S RIGHT, I WAS.
AND ONE OF THE GIGS I GOT YOU WAS...
FLIP
THE YOKOMASE FESTIVAL?
MASE
Yokomase Festival
Potato scooping

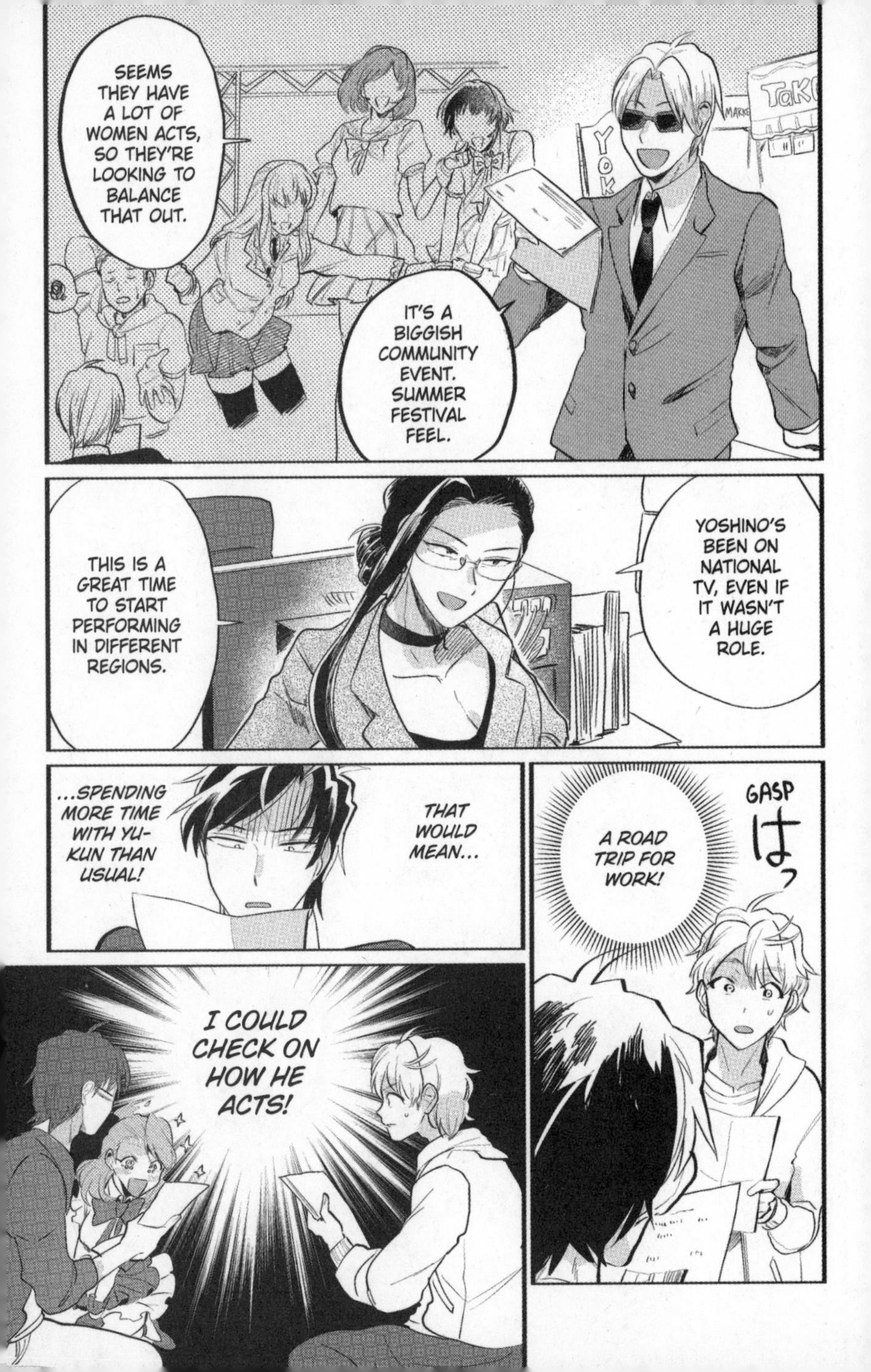
IT'S A BIGGISH COMMUNITY EVENT. SUMMER FESTIVAL FEEL.
SEEMS THEY HAVE A LOT OF WOMEN ACTS, SO THEY'RE LOOKING TO BALANCE THAT OUT.
YOSHINO'S BEEN ON NATIONAL TV, EVEN IF IT WASN'T A HUGE ROLE.
THIS IS A GREAT TIME TO START PERFORMING IN DIFFERENT REGIONS.
GASP
はっ
A ROAD TRIP FOR WORK!
THAT WOULD MEAN...
...SPENDING MORE TIME WITH YU-KUN THAN USUAL!
I COULD CHECK ON HOW HE ACTS!

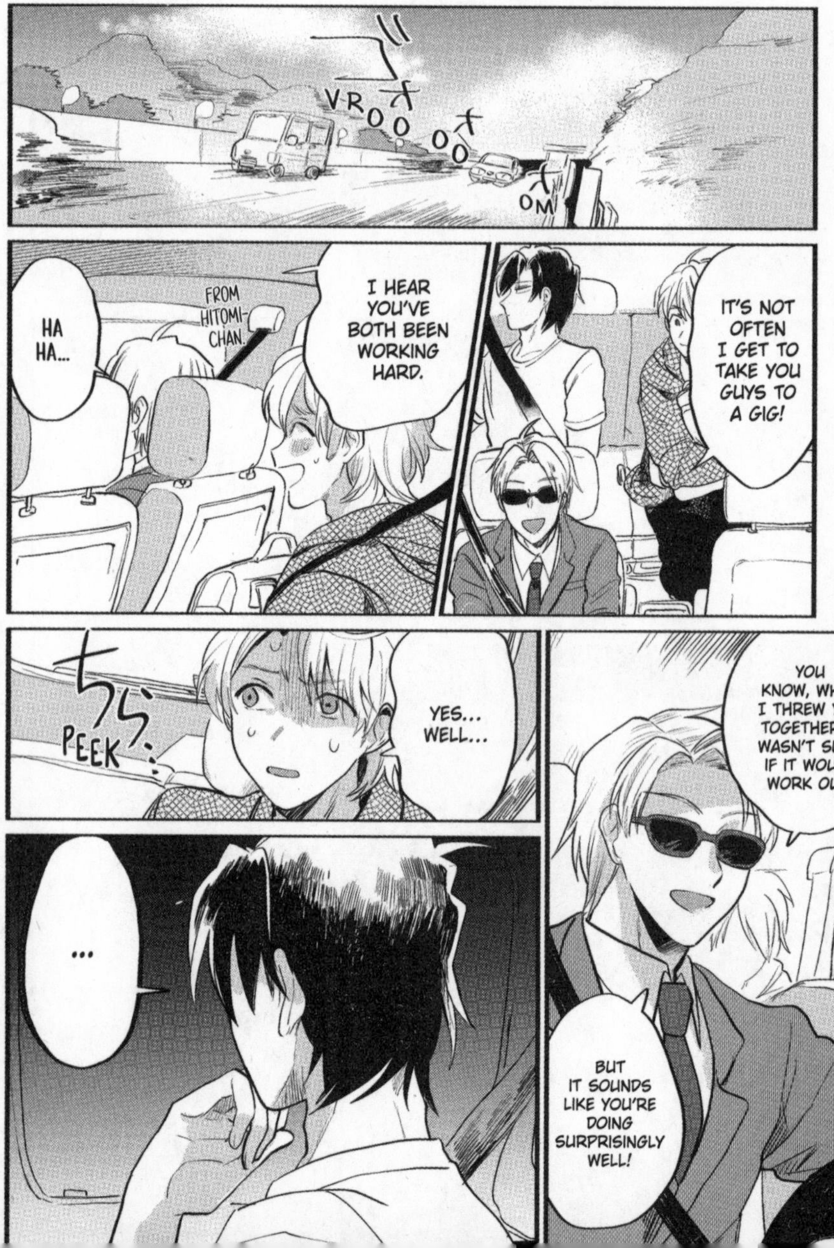
VROOOOOOM
IT'S NOT OFTEN I GET TO TAKE YOU GUYS TO A GIG!
I HEAR YOU'VE BOTH BEEN WORKING HARD.
FROM HITOMI-CHAN.
HA HA...
YOU KNOW, WHEN I THREW YOU TOGETHER, I WASN'T SURE IF IT WOULD WORK OUT.
BUT IT SOUNDS LIKE YOU'RE DOING SURPRISINGLY WELL!
YES... WELL...
PEEK
...

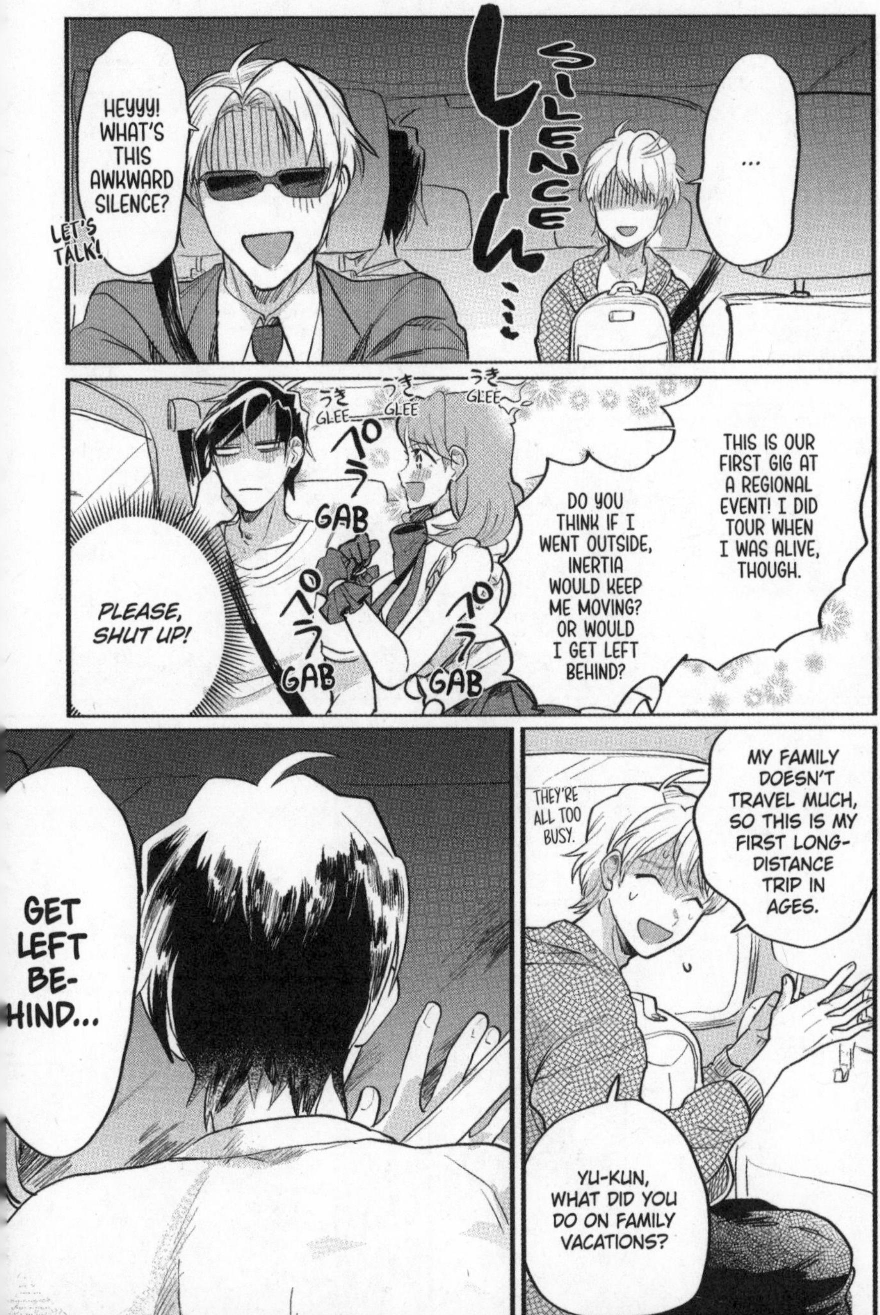

しーん…
SILENCE
...
HEYYY! WHAT'S THIS AWKWARD SILENCE?
LET'S TALK!
うき GLEE
うき GLEE
うき GLEE
THIS IS OUR FIRST GIG AT A REGIONAL EVENT! I DID TOUR WHEN I WAS ALIVE, THOUGH.
DO YOU THINK IF I WENT OUTSIDE, INERTIA WOULD KEEP ME MOVING? OR WOULD I GET LEFT BEHIND?
ペラ GAB
ペラ GAB
ペラ GAB
PLEASE, SHUT UP!
MY FAMILY DOESN'T TRAVEL MUCH, SO THIS IS MY FIRST LONG-DISTANCE TRIP IN AGES.
THEY'RE ALL TOO BUSY.
YU-KUN, WHAT DID YOU DO ON FAMILY VACATIONS?
GET LEFT BE-HIND...

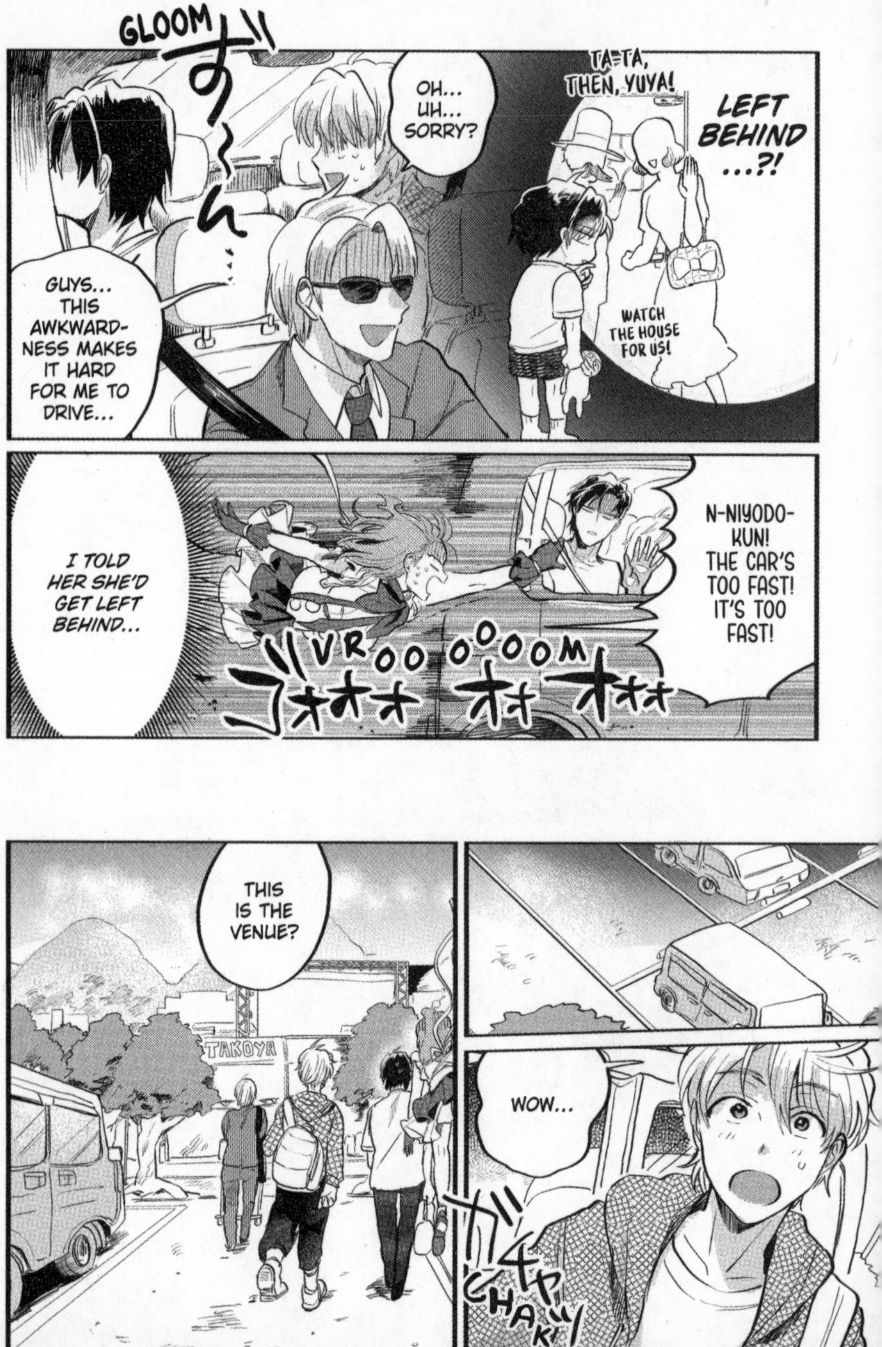
TA-TA, THEN, YUYA!
LEFT BEHIND ...?!
WATCH THE HOUSE FOR US!
OH... UH... SORRY?
GLOOM
GUYS... THIS AWKWARD-NESS MAKES IT HARD FOR ME TO DRIVE...
N-NIYODO-KUN! THE CAR'S TOO FAST! IT'S TOO FAST!
VROOOOOOM
I TOLD HER SHE'D GET LEFT BEHIND...
WOW...
CHAK
THIS IS THE VENUE?
TAKOYA

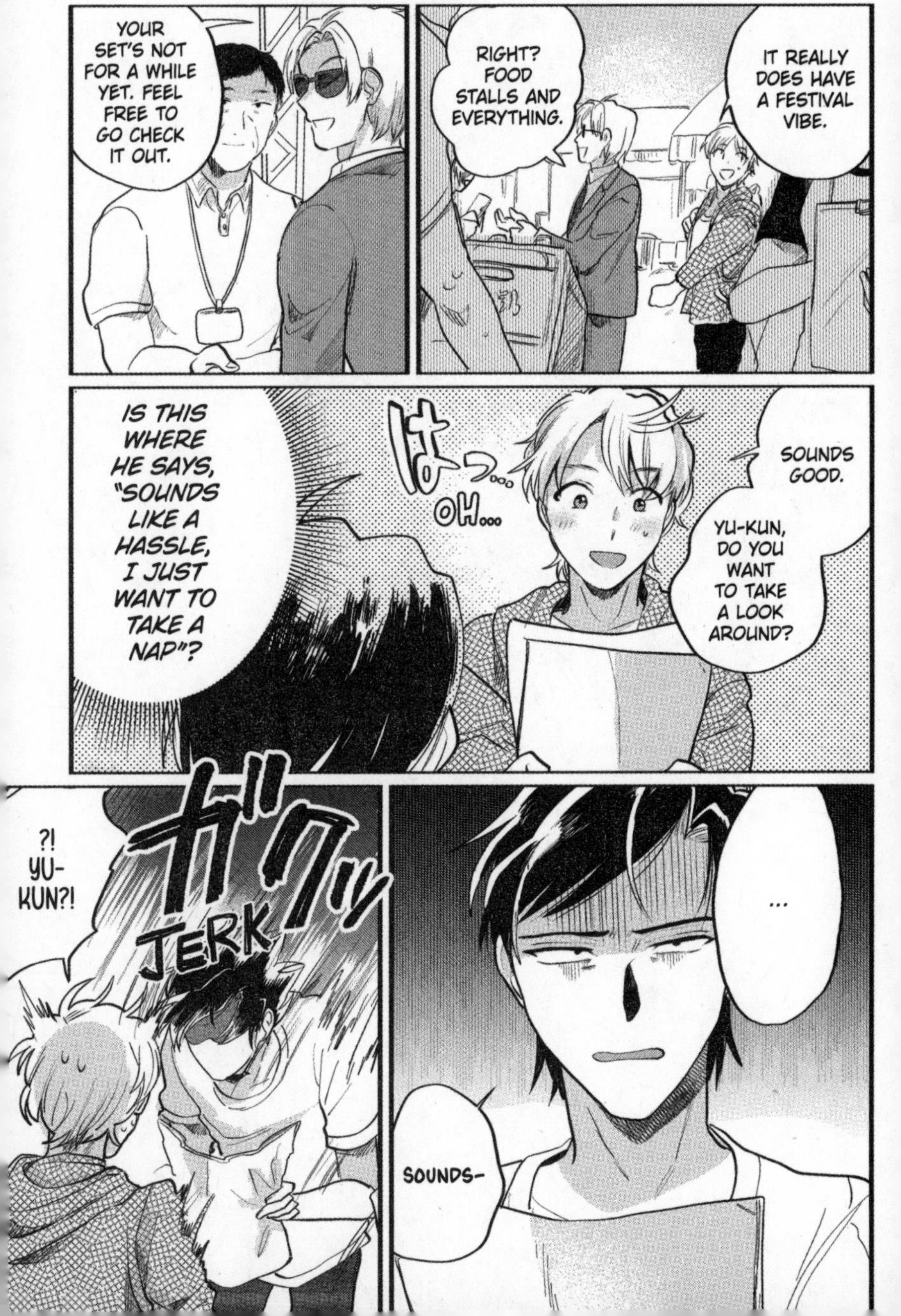
IT REALLY DOES HAVE A FESTIVAL VIBE.
RIGHT? FOOD STALLS AND EVERYTHING.
YOUR SET'S NOT FOR A WHILE YET. FEEL FREE TO GO CHECK IT OUT.
SOUNDS GOOD.
YU-KUN, DO YOU WANT TO TAKE A LOOK AROUND?
はっ...
OH...
IS THIS WHERE HE SAYS, "SOUNDS LIKE A HASSLE, I JUST WANT TO TAKE A NAP"?
...
SOUNDS-
ガクッ
JERK
?! YU-KUN?!

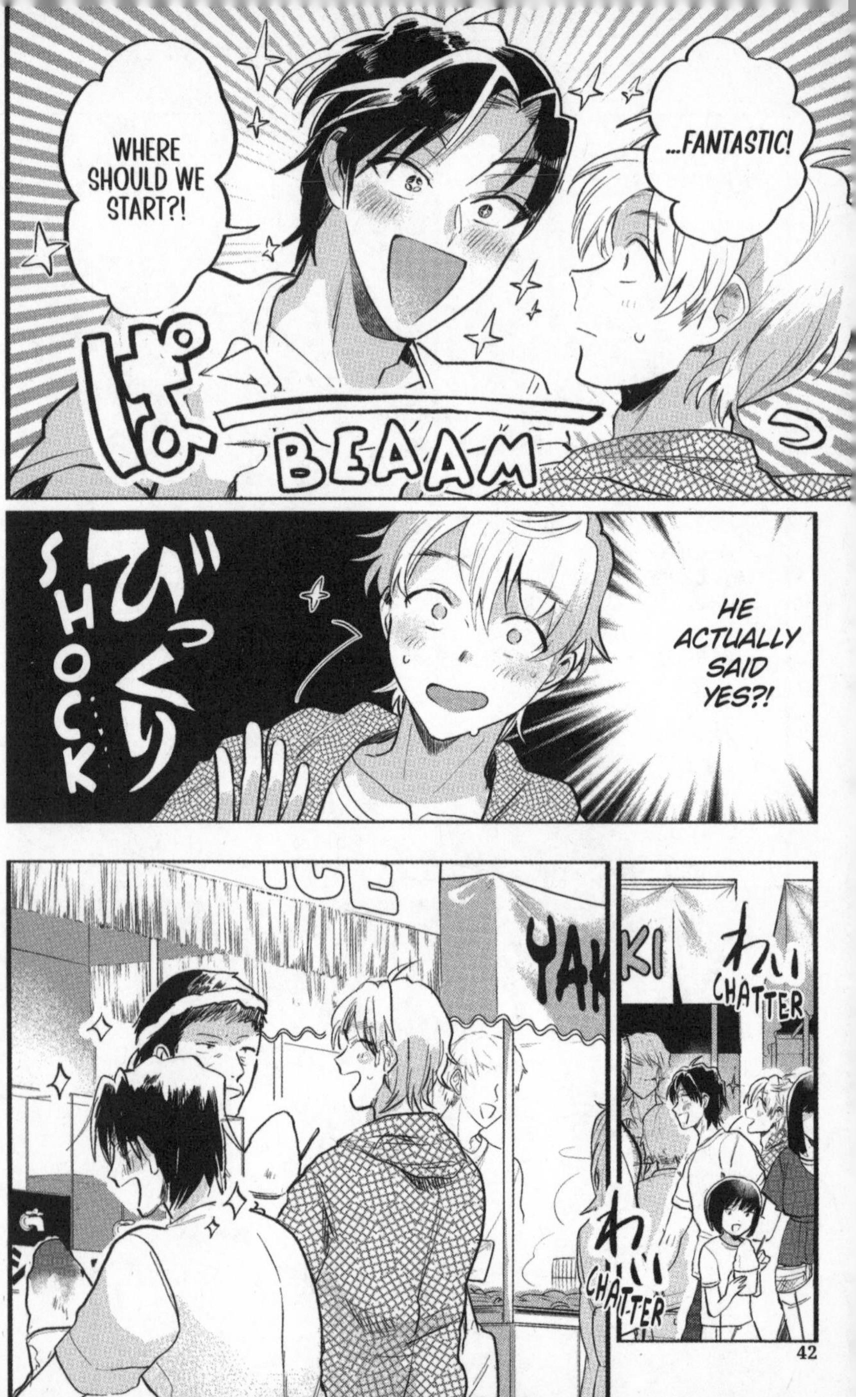
...FANTASTIC!
WHERE SHOULD WE START?!
ぱ
BEAAM
HE ACTUALLY SAID YES?!
びっくり
SHOCK
わい
CHATTER
わい
CHATTER
ICE

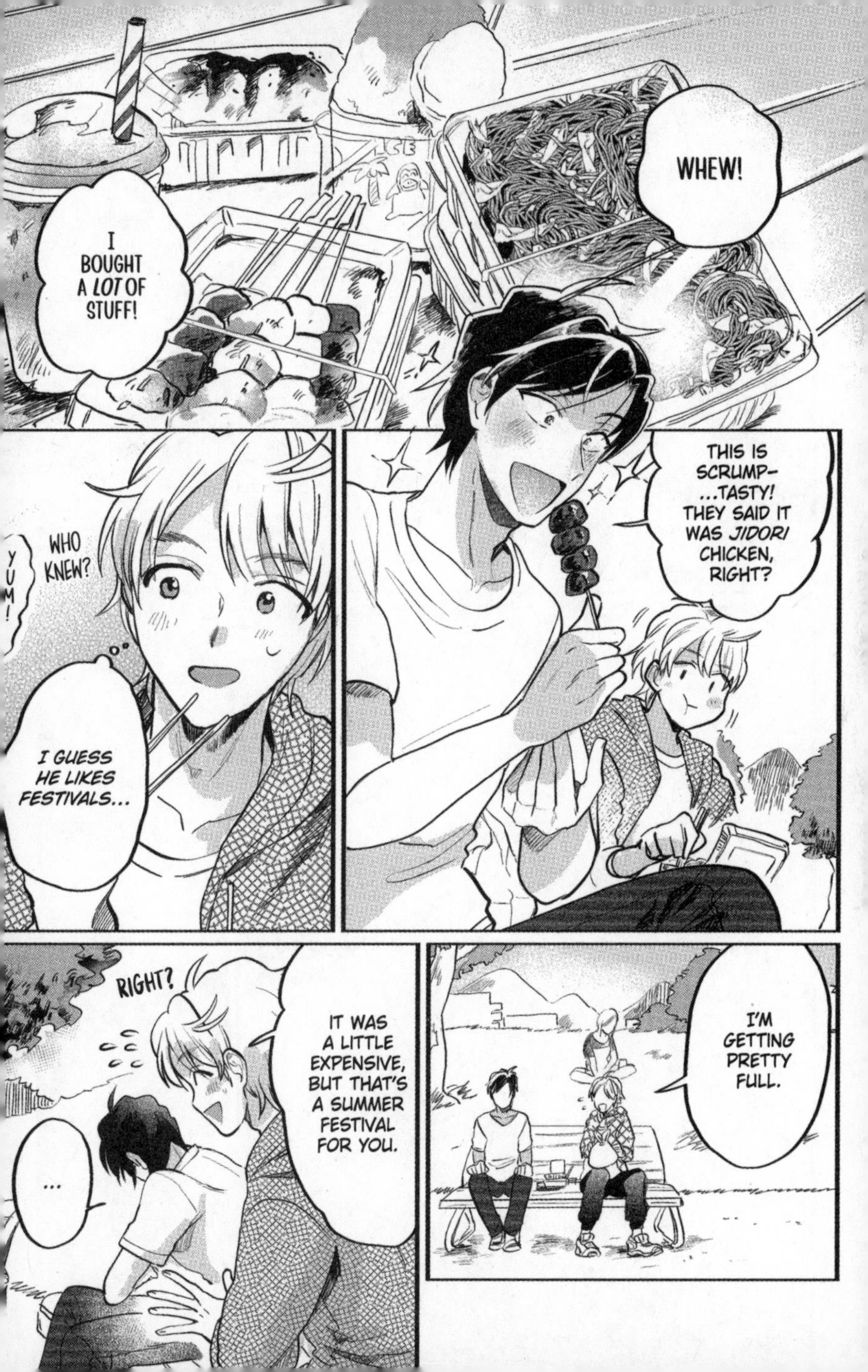
WHEW!
I BOUGHT A *LOT* OF STUFF!
THIS IS SCRUMP- ...TASTY! THEY SAID IT WAS *JIDORI* CHICKEN, RIGHT?
WHO KNEW?
YUM!
*I GUESS HE LIKES FESTIVALS...*
I'M GETTING PRETTY FULL.
IT WAS A LITTLE EXPENSIVE, BUT THAT'S A SUMMER FESTIVAL FOR YOU.
RIGHT?
...

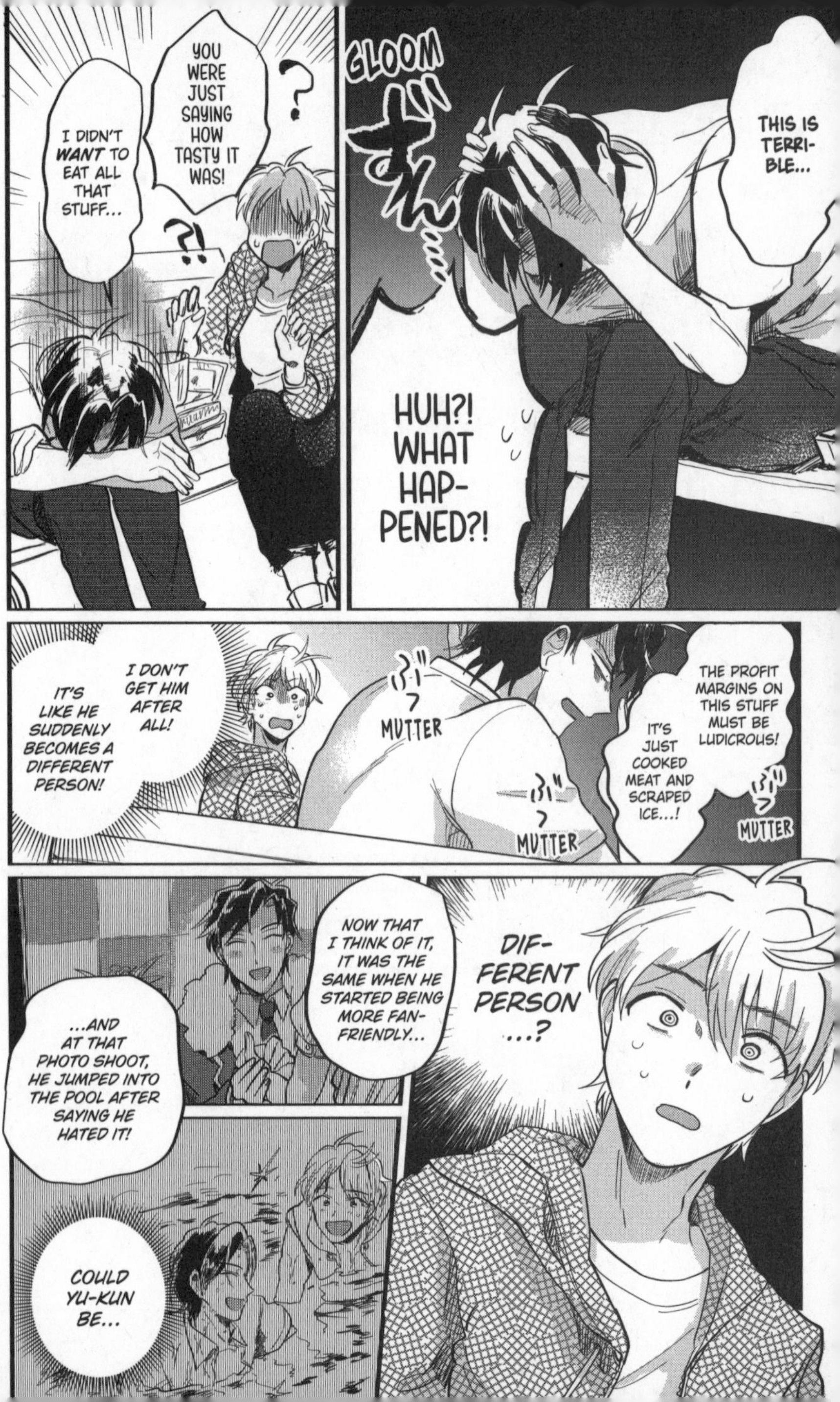
GLOOM
THIS IS TERRIBLE...
HUH?! WHAT HAPPENED?!
YOU WERE JUST SAYING HOW TASTY IT WAS!
?
I DIDN'T *WANT* TO EAT ALL THAT STUFF...
?!
THE PROFIT MARGINS ON THIS STUFF MUST BE LUDICROUS!
MUTTER
IT'S JUST COOKED MEAT AND SCRAPED ICE...!
MUTTER
MUTTER
I DON'T GET HIM AFTER ALL!
IT'S LIKE HE SUDDENLY BECOMES A DIFFERENT PERSON!
DIFFERENT PERSON...?
NOW THAT I THINK OF IT, IT WAS THE SAME WHEN HE STARTED BEING MORE FAN-FRIENDLY...
...AND AT THAT PHOTO SHOOT, HE JUMPED INTO THE POOL AFTER SAYING HE HATED IT!
COULD YU-KUN BE...

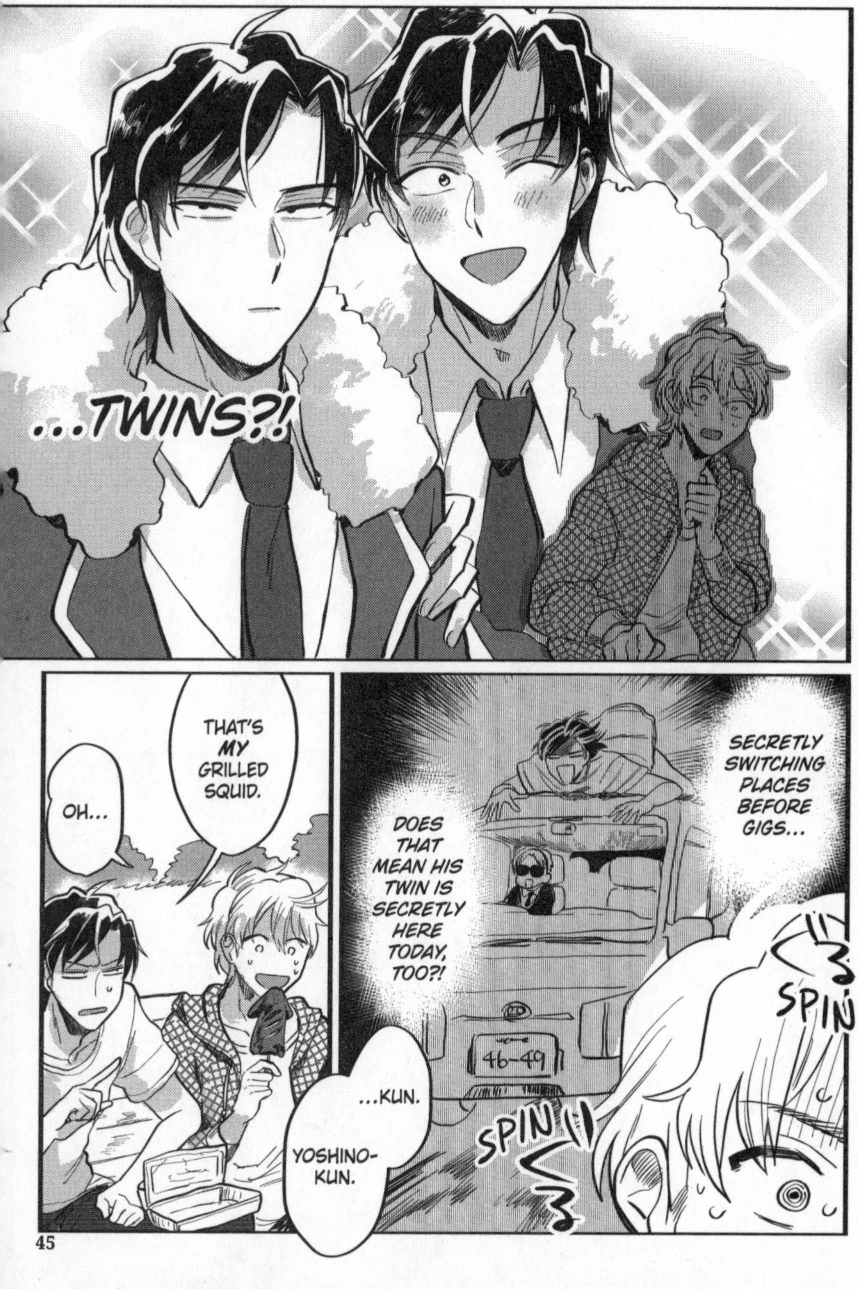
...TWINS?!
SECRETLY SWITCHING PLACES BEFORE GIGS...
DOES THAT MEAN HIS TWIN IS SECRETLY HERE TODAY, TOO?!
46-49
SPIN
SPIN
THAT'S MY GRILLED SQUID.
OH...
...KUN.
YOSHINO-KUN.

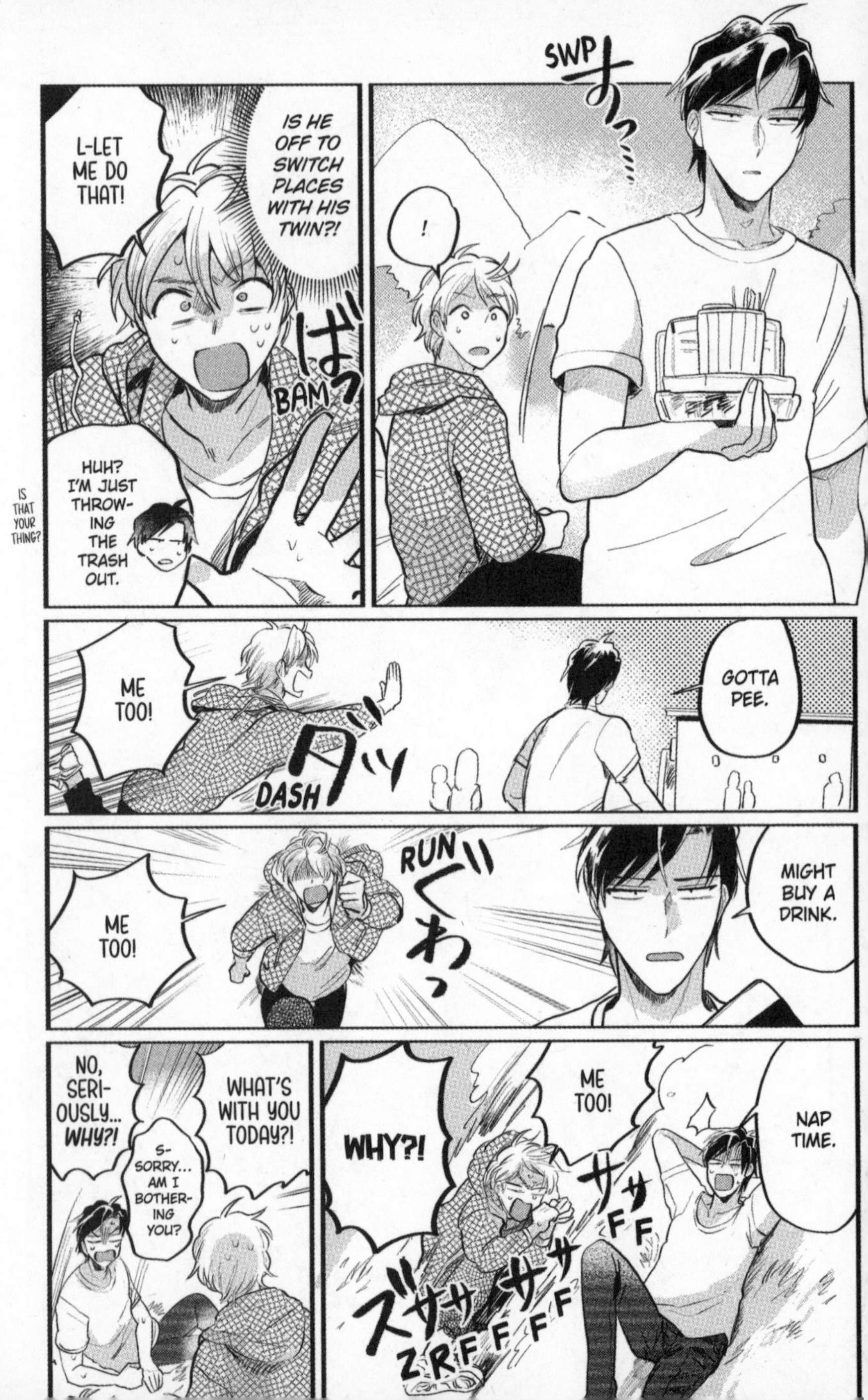
SWP
!
IS HE OFF TO SWITCH PLACES WITH HIS TWIN?!
L-LET ME DO THAT!
BAM
HUH? I'M JUST THROWING THE TRASH OUT.
IS THAT YOUR THING?
GOTTA PEE.
DASH
ME TOO!
MIGHT BUY A DRINK.
RUN
ME TOO!
NAP TIME.
ME TOO!
SFF
WHY?!
ZRFFFF
WHAT'S WITH YOU TODAY?!
NO, SERIOUSLY... WHY?!
S-SORRY... AM I BOTHERING YOU?

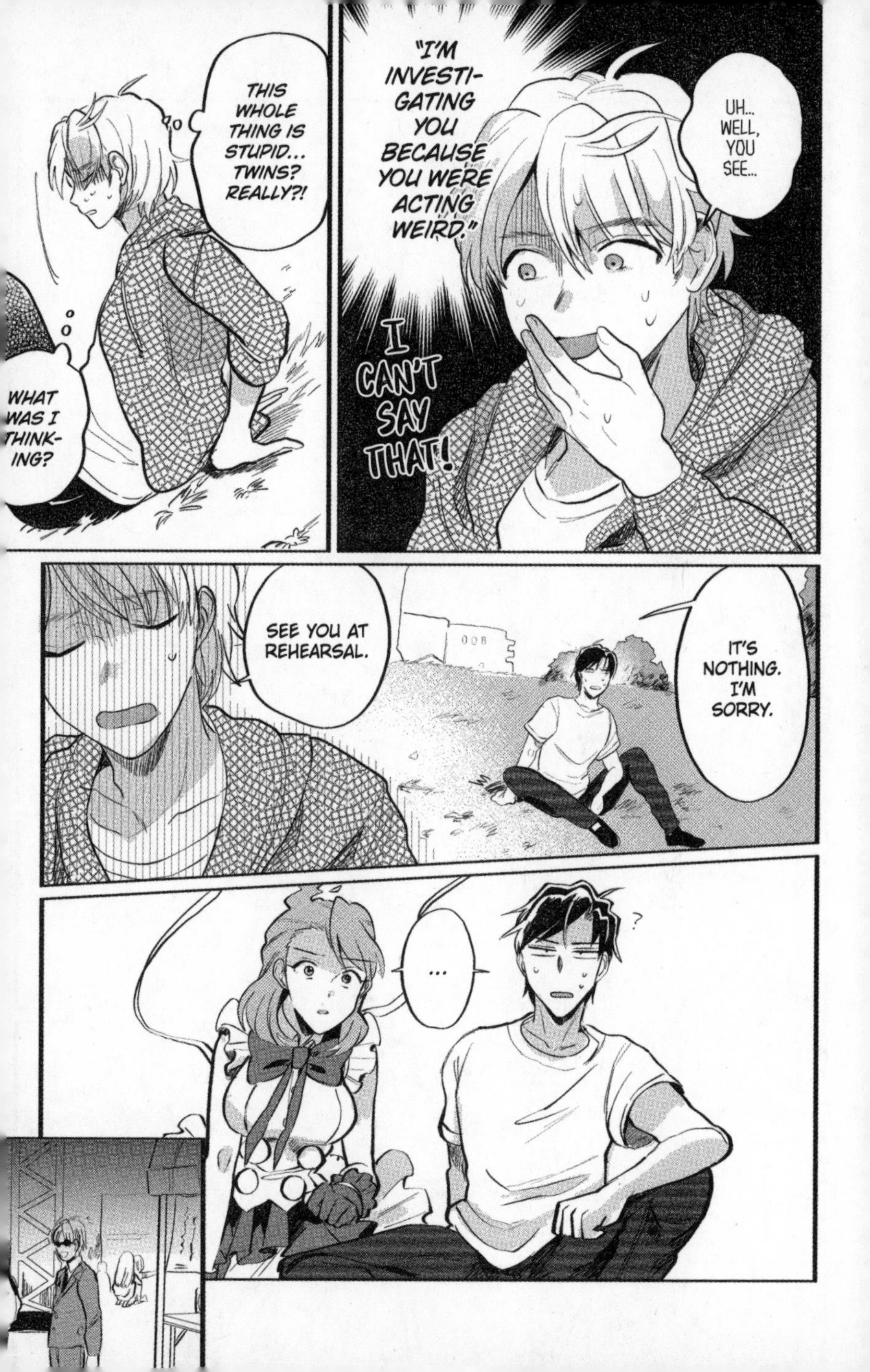
UH... WELL, YOU SEE...
"I'M INVESTIGATING YOU BECAUSE YOU WERE ACTING WEIRD."
I CAN'T SAY THAT!
THIS WHOLE THING IS STUPID... TWINS? REALLY?!
WHAT WAS I THINKING?
IT'S NOTHING. I'M SORRY.
SEE YOU AT REHEARSAL.
?
...

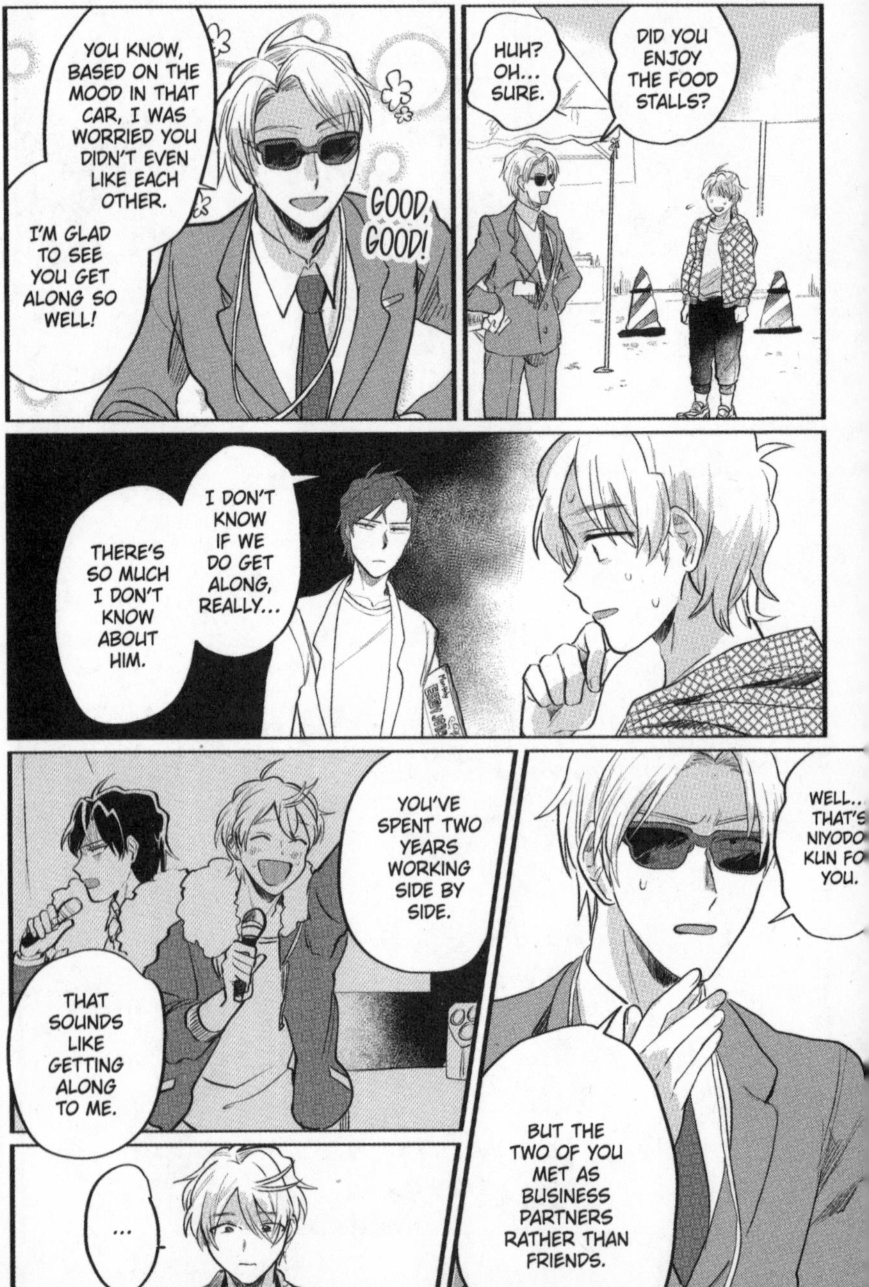
DID YOU ENJOY THE FOOD STALLS?
HUH? OH... SURE.
YOU KNOW, BASED ON THE MOOD IN THAT CAR, I WAS WORRIED YOU DIDN'T EVEN LIKE EACH OTHER.
GOOD, GOOD!
I'M GLAD TO SEE YOU GET ALONG SO WELL!
I DON'T KNOW IF WE DO GET ALONG, REALLY...
THERE'S SO MUCH I DON'T KNOW ABOUT HIM.
WELL.. THAT'S NIYODO KUN FO YOU.
BUT THE TWO OF YOU MET AS BUSINESS PARTNERS RATHER THAN FRIENDS.
YOU'VE SPENT TWO YEARS WORKING SIDE BY SIDE.
THAT SOUNDS LIKE GETTING ALONG TO ME.
...

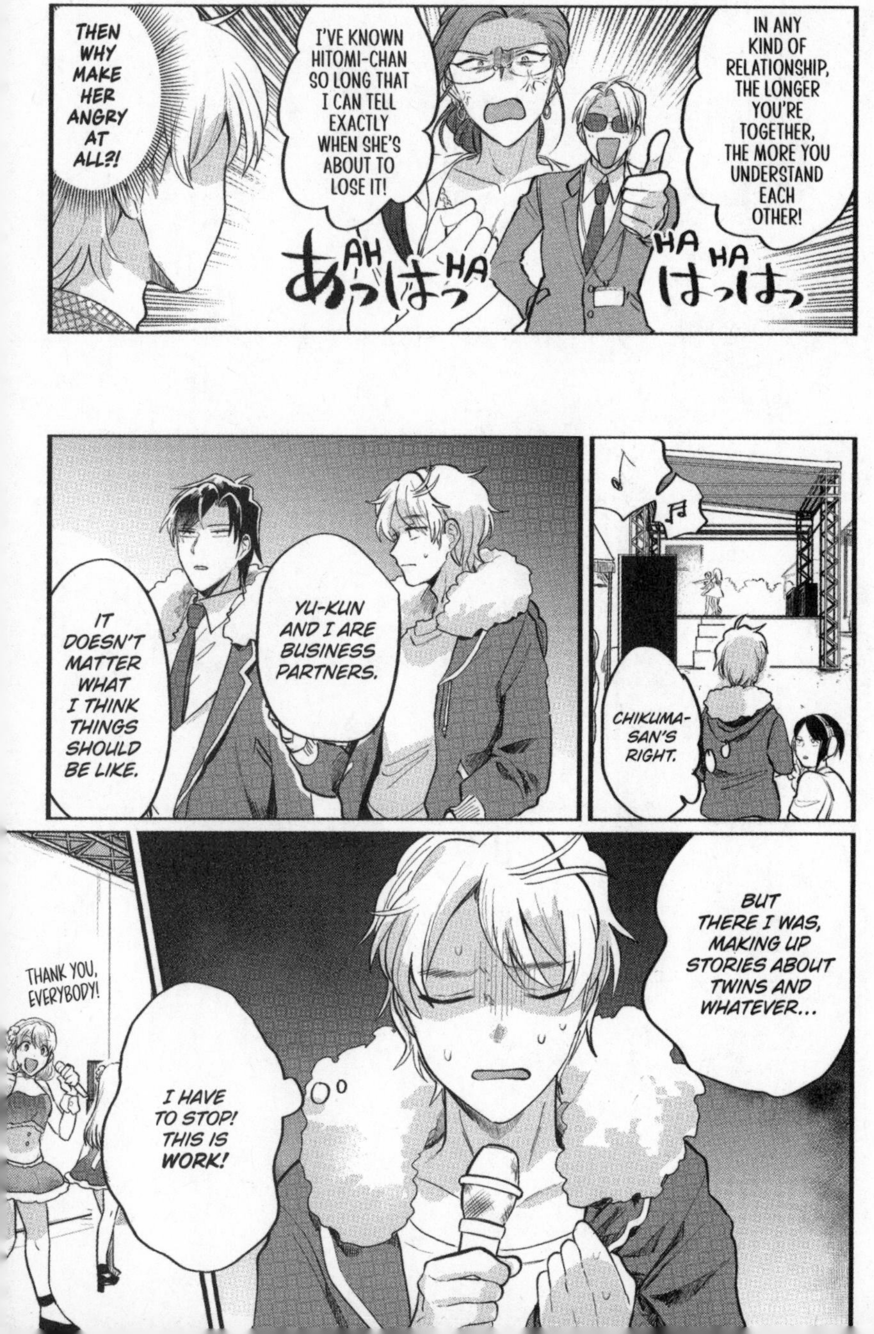
IN ANY KIND OF RELATIONSHIP, THE LONGER YOU'RE TOGETHER, THE MORE YOU UNDERSTAND EACH OTHER!
HA HA はっはっ
I'VE KNOWN HITOMI-CHAN SO LONG THAT I CAN TELL EXACTLY WHEN SHE'S ABOUT TO LOSE IT!
AH HA あっはっ
THEN WHY MAKE HER ANGRY AT ALL?!
CHIKUMA-SAN'S RIGHT.
YU-KUN AND I ARE BUSINESS PARTNERS.
IT DOESN'T MATTER WHAT I THINK THINGS SHOULD BE LIKE.
BUT THERE I WAS, MAKING UP STORIES ABOUT TWINS AND WHATEVER…
I HAVE TO STOP! THIS IS WORK!
THANK YOU, EVERYBODY!

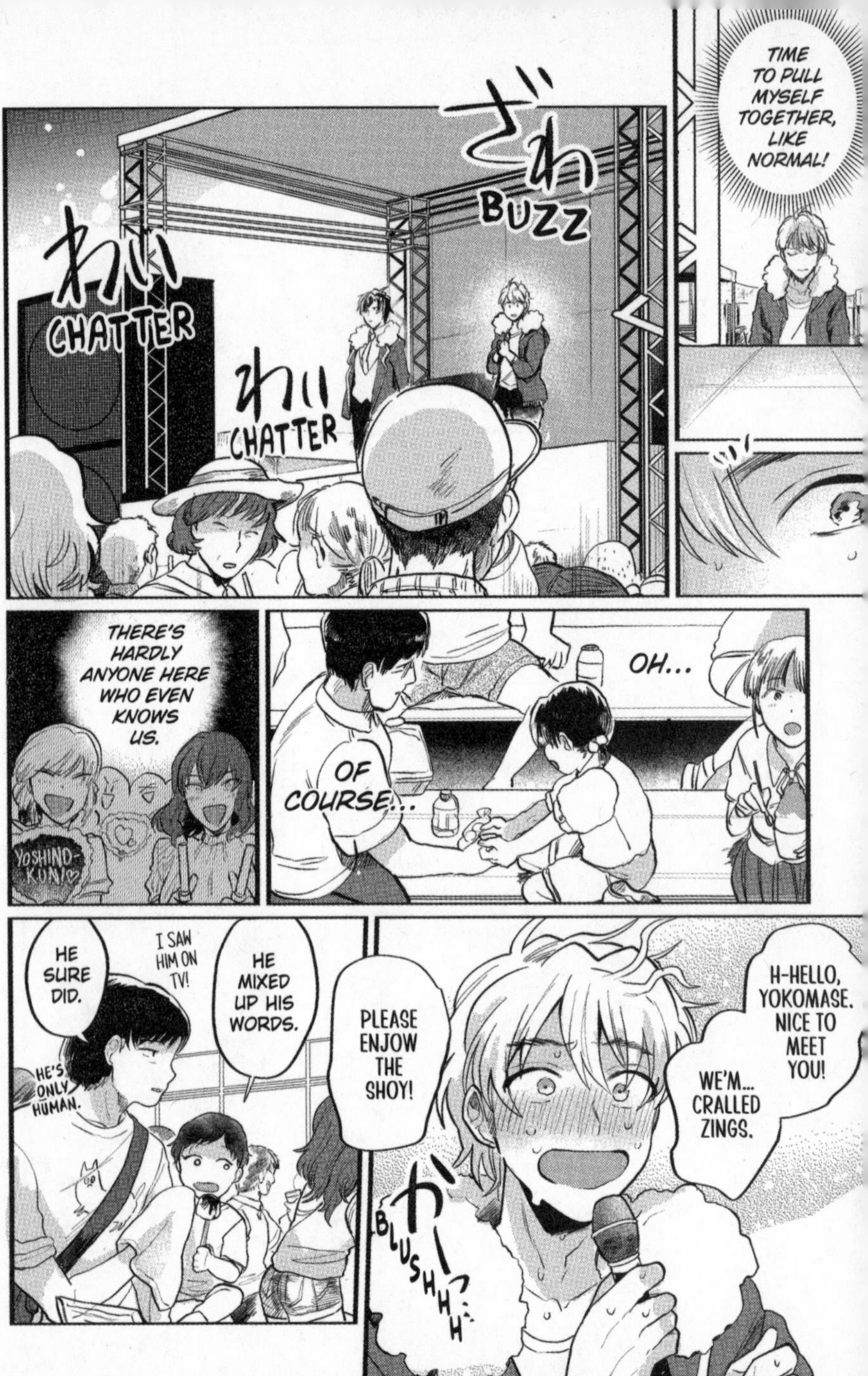
TIME TO PULL MYSELF TOGETHER, LIKE NORMAL!
ざわ
BUZZ
わい
CHATTER
わい
CHATTER
OH...
OF COURSE...
THERE'S HARDLY ANYONE HERE WHO EVEN KNOWS US.
YOSHINO-KUN♡
H-HELLO, YOKOMASE. NICE TO MEET YOU!
WE'M... CRALLED ZINGS.
PLEASE ENJOW THE SHOY!
か
BLUSHHHH...
HE MIXED UP HIS WORDS.
I SAW HIM ON TV!
HE SURE DID.
HE'S ONLY HUMAN.

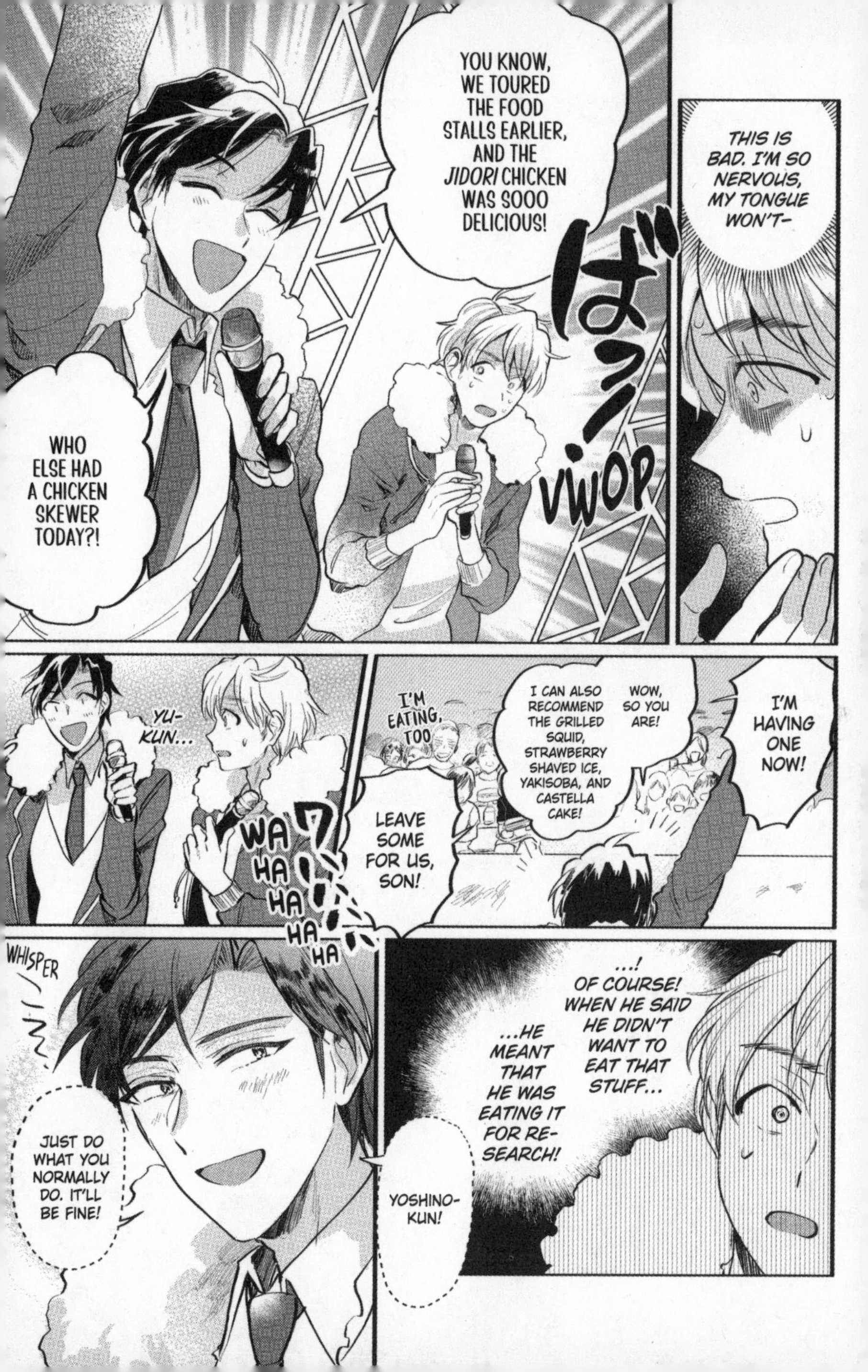
THIS IS BAD. I'M SO NERVOUS, MY TONGUE WON'T-
YOU KNOW, WE TOURED THE FOOD STALLS EARLIER, AND THE *JIDORI* CHICKEN WAS SOOO DELICIOUS!
ばっ
VWOP
WHO ELSE HAD A CHICKEN SKEWER TODAY?!
I'M HAVING ONE NOW!
WOW, SO YOU ARE!
I CAN ALSO RECOMMEND THE GRILLED SQUID, STRAWBERRY SHAVED ICE, YAKISOBA, AND CASTELLA CAKE!
I'M EATING, TOO
LEAVE SOME FOR US, SON!
YU-KUN...
WA HA HA HA HA
...! OF COURSE! WHEN HE SAID HE DIDN'T WANT TO EAT THAT STUFF...
...HE MEANT THAT HE WAS EATING IT FOR RE-SEARCH!
YOSHINO-KUN!
WHISPER
JUST DO WHAT YOU NORMALLY DO. IT'LL BE FINE!

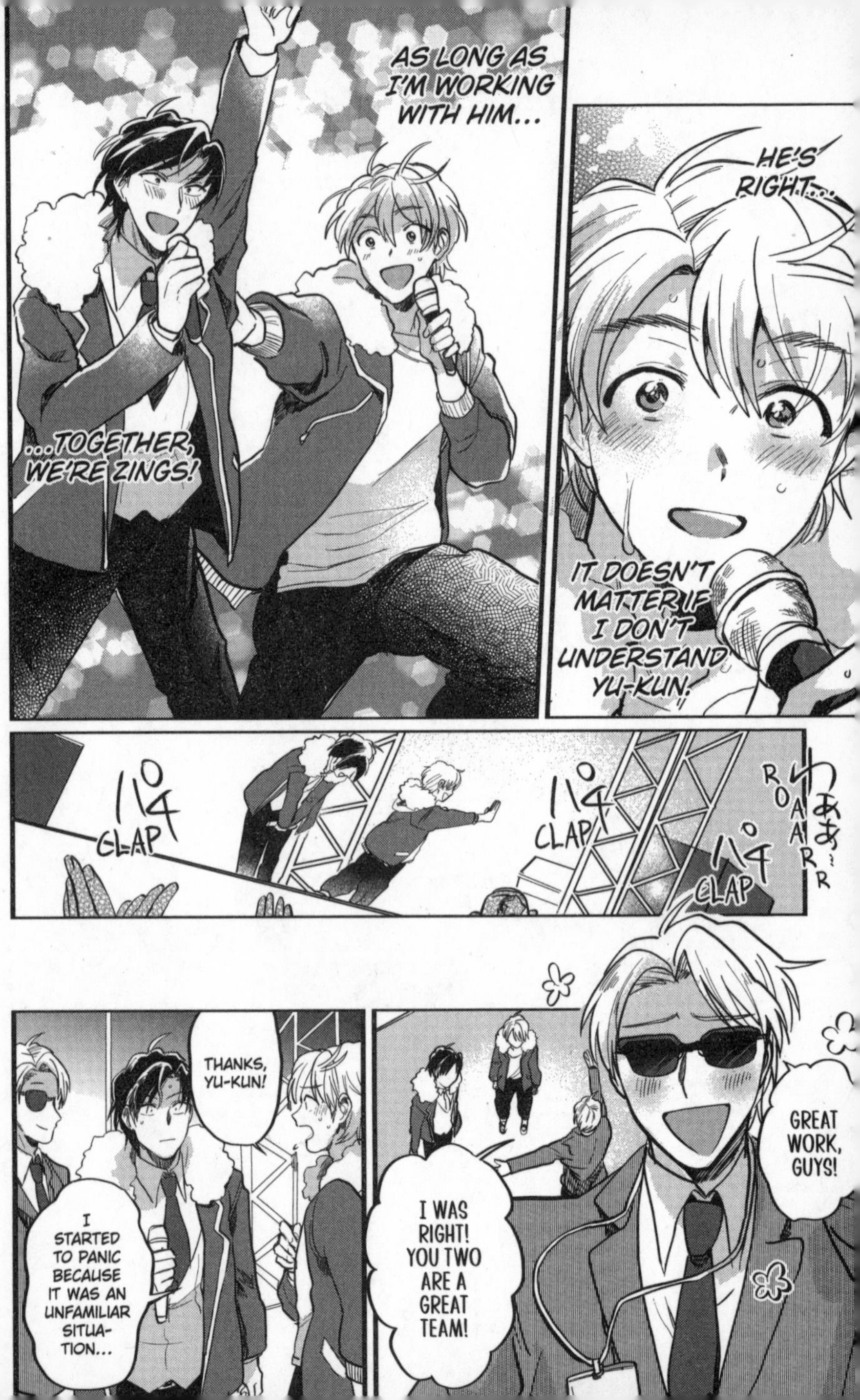
HE'S RIGHT...
IT DOESN'T MATTER IF I DON'T UNDERSTAND YU-KUN.
AS LONG AS I'M WORKING WITH HIM...
...TOGETHER, WE'RE ZINGS!
わああ ROAAARR
パチ CLAP
パチ CLAP
パチ CLAP
GREAT WORK, GUYS!
I WAS RIGHT! YOU TWO ARE A GREAT TEAM!
THANKS, YU-KUN!
I STARTED TO PANIC BECAUSE IT WAS AN UNFAMILIAR SITUA-TION...

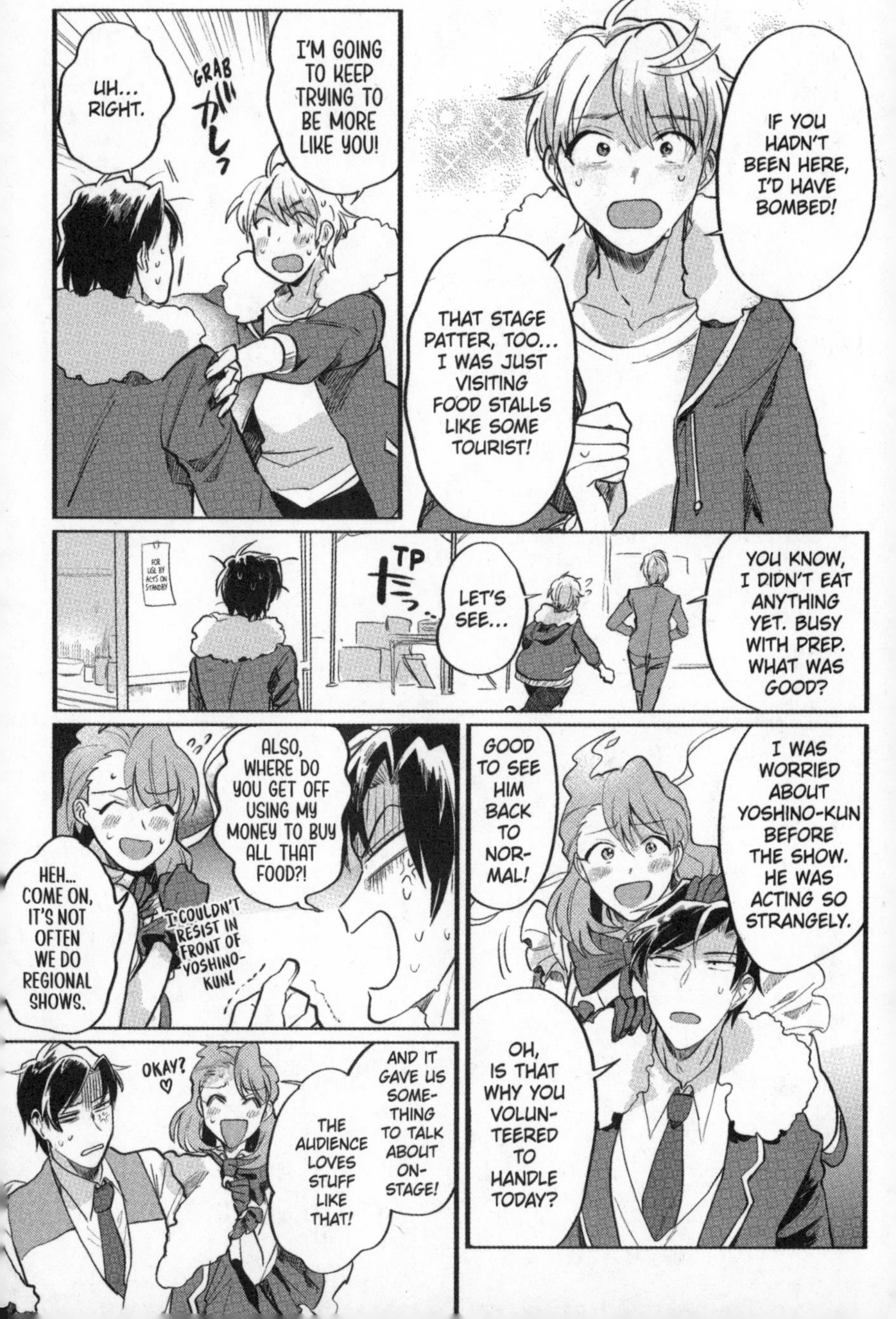
IF YOU HADN'T BEEN HERE, I'D HAVE BOMBED!
THAT STAGE PATTER, TOO... I WAS JUST VISITING FOOD STALLS LIKE SOME TOURIST!
I'M GOING TO KEEP TRYING TO BE MORE LIKE YOU!
GRAB
がしっ
UH... RIGHT.
YOU KNOW, I DIDN'T EAT ANYTHING YET. BUSY WITH PREP. WHAT WAS GOOD?
LET'S SEE...
TP
FOR USE BY ACTS ON STANDBY
I WAS WORRIED ABOUT YOSHINO-KUN BEFORE THE SHOW. HE WAS ACTING SO STRANGELY.
GOOD TO SEE HIM BACK TO NOR-MAL!
OH, IS THAT WHY YOU VOLUN-TEERED TO HANDLE TODAY?
ALSO, WHERE DO YOU GET OFF USING MY MONEY TO BUY ALL THAT FOOD?!
HEH... COME ON, IT'S NOT OFTEN WE DO REGIONAL SHOWS.
I COULDN'T RESIST IN FRONT OF YOSHINO-KUN!
AND IT GAVE US SOME-THING TO TALK ABOUT ON-STAGE!
THE AUDIENCE LOVES STUFF LIKE THAT!
OKAY? ♡

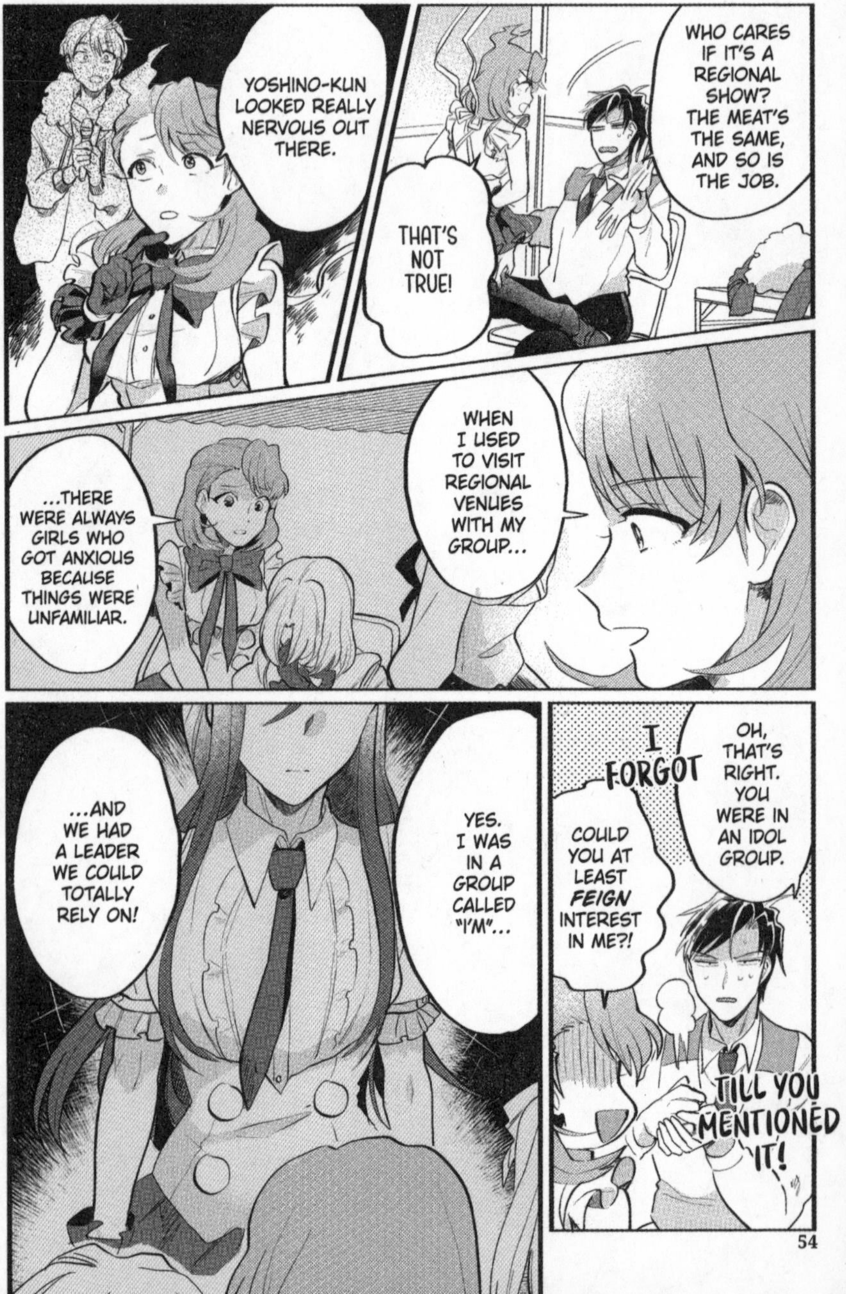
WHO CARES IF IT'S A REGIONAL SHOW? THE MEAT'S THE SAME, AND SO IS THE JOB.
THAT'S NOT TRUE!
YOSHINO-KUN LOOKED REALLY NERVOUS OUT THERE.
WHEN I USED TO VISIT REGIONAL VENUES WITH MY GROUP...
...THERE WERE ALWAYS GIRLS WHO GOT ANXIOUS BECAUSE THINGS WERE UNFAMILIAR.
OH, THAT'S RIGHT. YOU WERE IN AN IDOL GROUP.
I FORGOT
COULD YOU AT LEAST *FEIGN* INTEREST IN ME?!
TILL YOU MENTIONED IT!
YES. I WAS IN A GROUP CALLED "I'M"...
...AND WE HAD A LEADER WE COULD TOTALLY RELY ON!

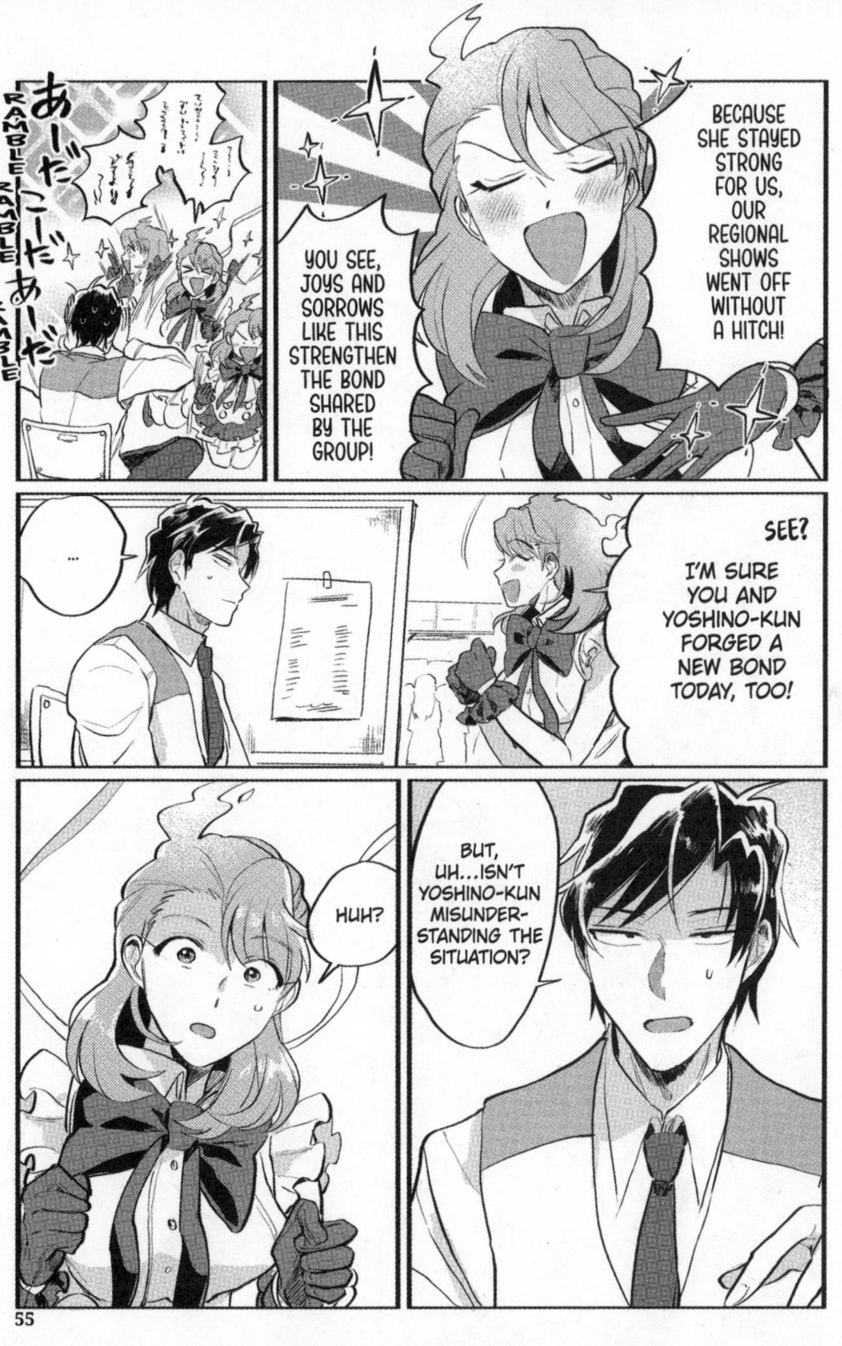
BECAUSE SHE STAYED STRONG FOR US, OUR REGIONAL SHOWS WENT OFF WITHOUT A HITCH!
YOU SEE, JOYS AND SORROWS LIKE THIS STRENGTHEN THE BOND SHARED BY THE GROUP!
あーだこーだあーだ
RAMBLE RAMBLE RAMBLE
SEE?
I'M SURE YOU AND YOSHINO-KUN FORGED A NEW BOND TODAY, TOO!
...
BUT, UH...ISN'T YOSHINO-KUN MISUNDER-STANDING THE SITUATION?
HUH?

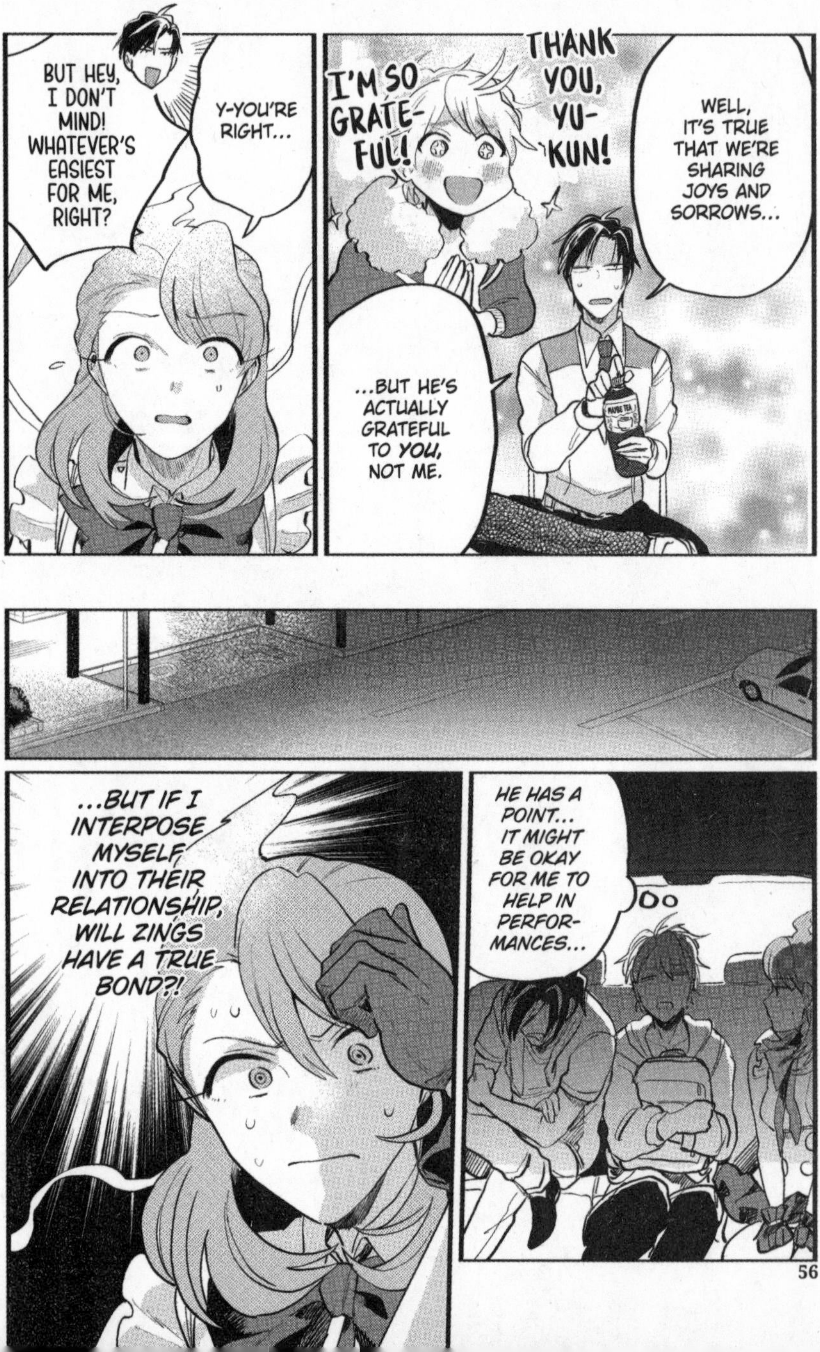
WELL, IT'S TRUE THAT WE'RE SHARING JOYS AND SORROWS...
THANK YOU, YU-KUN!
I'M SO GRATE-FUL!
...BUT HE'S ACTUALLY GRATEFUL TO *YOU*, NOT ME.
Y-YOU'RE RIGHT...
BUT HEY, I DON'T MIND! WHATEVER'S EASIEST FOR ME, RIGHT?
HE HAS A POINT... IT MIGHT BE OKAY FOR ME TO HELP IN PERFOR-MANCES...
...BUT IF I INTERPOSE MYSELF INTO THEIR RELATIONSHIP, WILL ZINGS HAVE A TRUE BOND?!

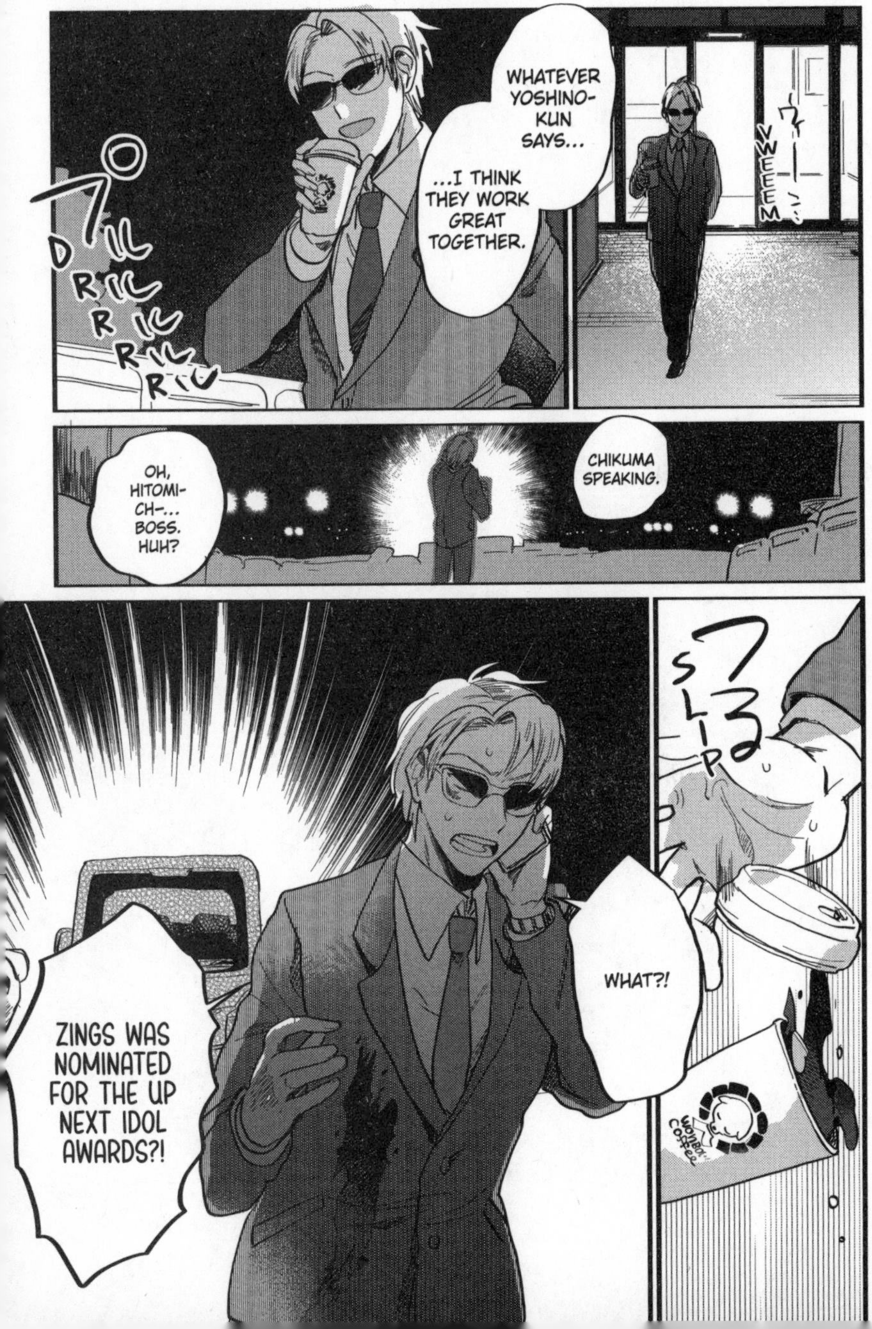
VWEEEM
WHATEVER YOSHINO-KUN SAYS...
...I THINK THEY WORK GREAT TOGETHER.
CHIKUMA SPEAKING.
OH, HITOMI-CH-... BOSS. HUH?
SLIP
WHAT?!
ZINGS WAS NOMINATED FOR THE UP NEXT IDOL AWARDS?!

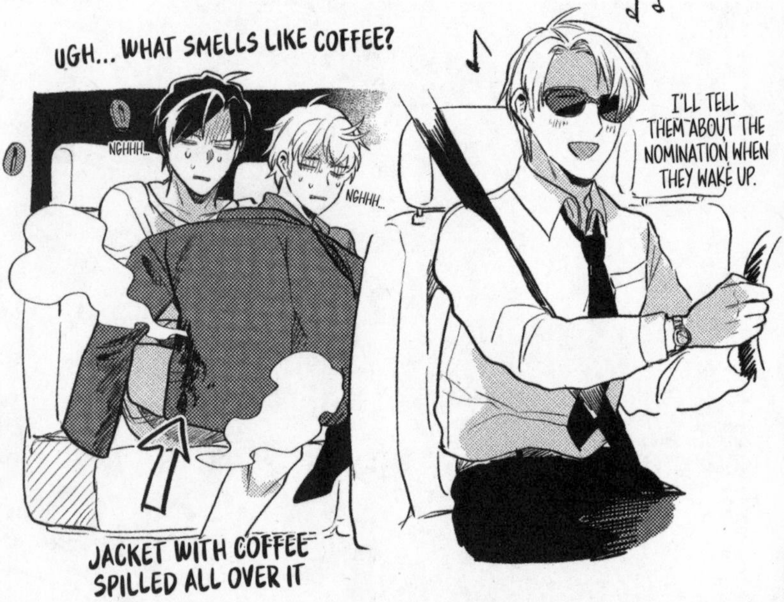
I'LL TELL THEM ABOUT THE NOMINATION WHEN THEY WAKE UP.
UGH... WHAT SMELLS LIKE COFFEE?
NGHHH...
NGHHH...
JACKET WITH COFFEE SPILLED ALL OVER IT

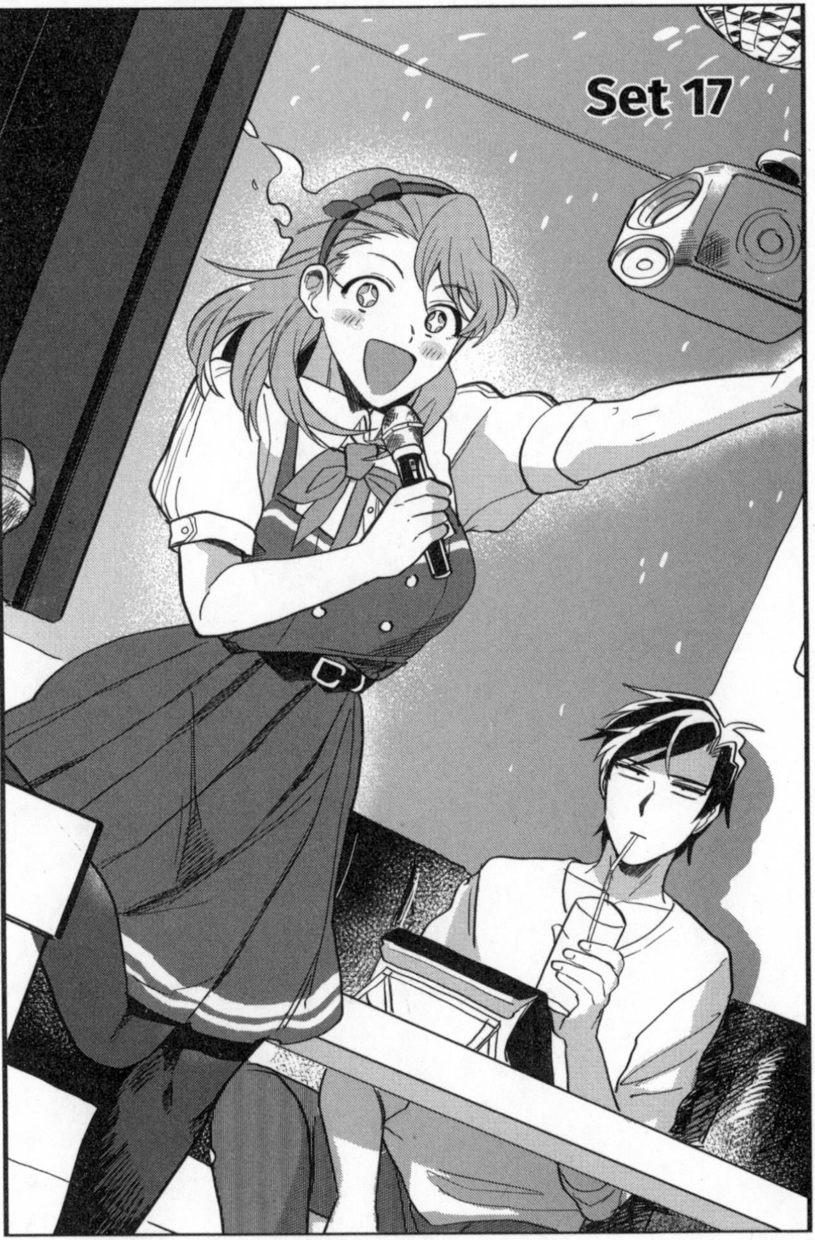
Set 17

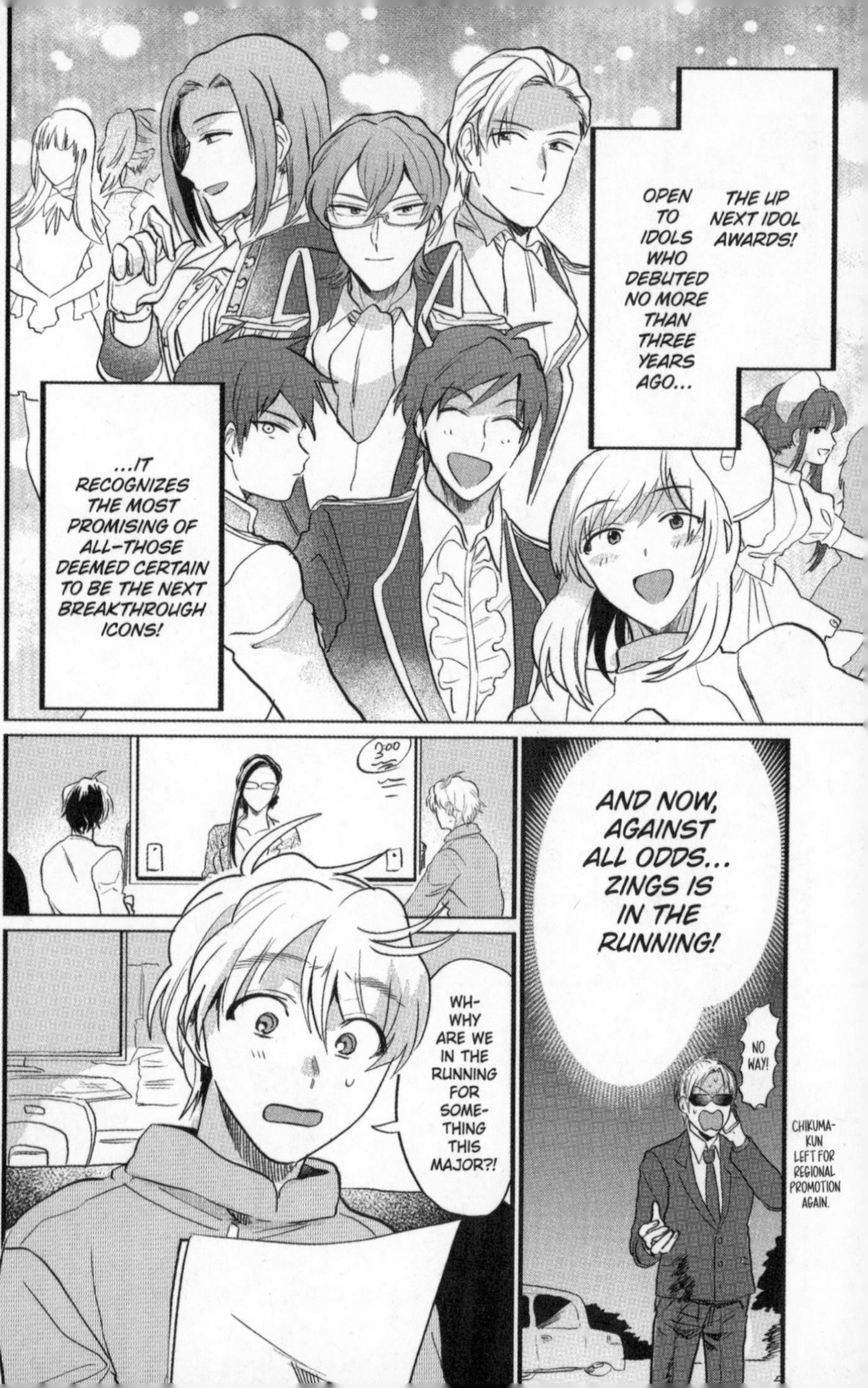
THE UP NEXT IDOL AWARDS!
OPEN TO IDOLS WHO DEBUTED NO MORE THAN THREE YEARS AGO...
...IT RECOGNIZES THE MOST PROMISING OF ALL—THOSE DEEMED CERTAIN TO BE THE NEXT BREAKTHROUGH ICONS!
AND NOW, AGAINST ALL ODDS... ZINGS IS IN THE RUNNING!
NO WAY!
CHIKUMA-KUN LEFT FOR REGIONAL PROMOTION AGAIN.
WH-WHY ARE WE IN THE RUNNING FOR SOMETHING THIS MAJOR?!

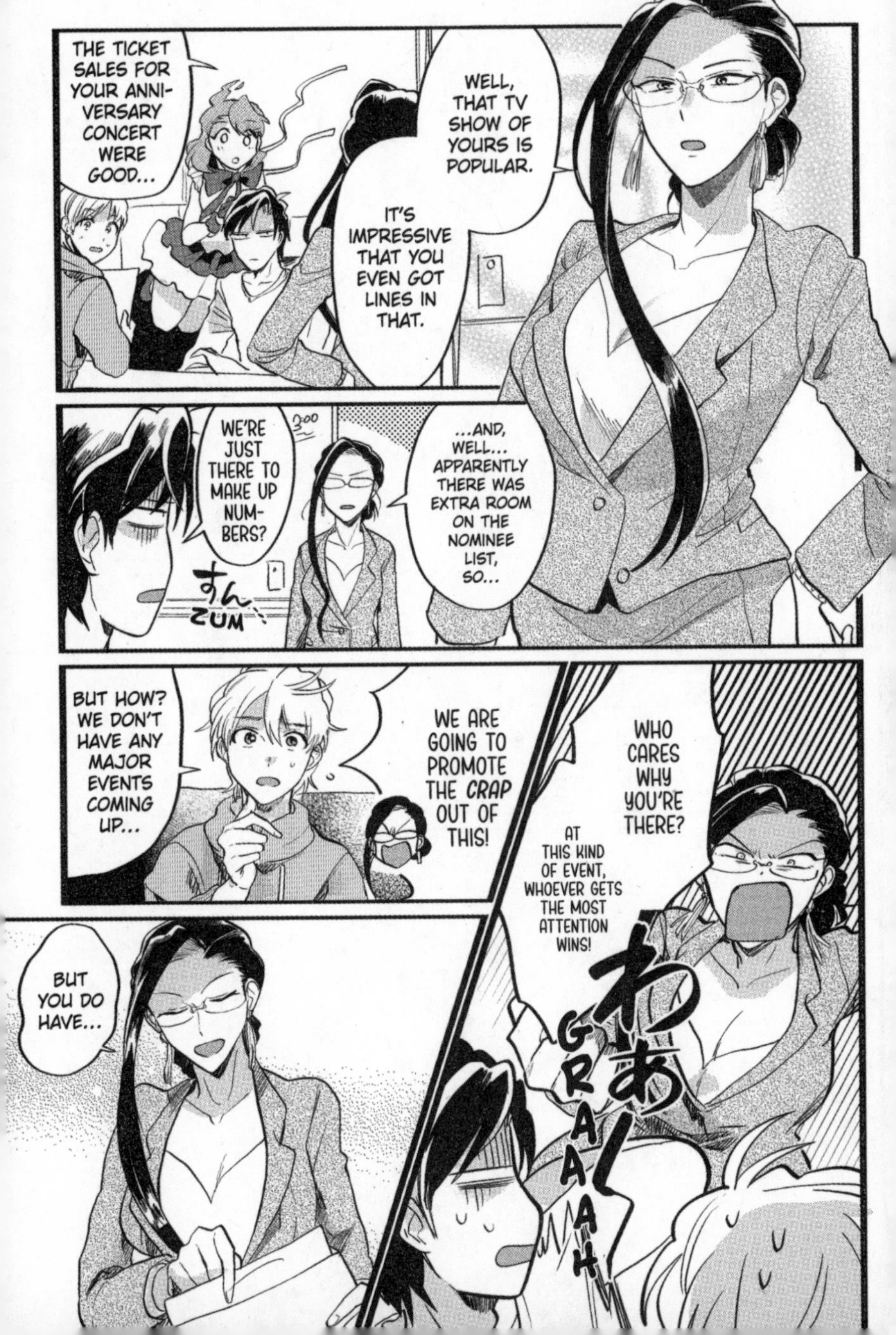
WELL, THAT TV SHOW OF YOURS IS POPULAR.
IT'S IMPRESSIVE THAT YOU EVEN GOT LINES IN THAT.
THE TICKET SALES FOR YOUR ANNI-VERSARY CONCERT WERE GOOD...
...AND, WELL... APPARENTLY THERE WAS EXTRA ROOM ON THE NOMINEE LIST, SO...
WE'RE JUST THERE TO MAKE UP NUM-BERS?
すん
ZUM
WHO CARES WHY YOU'RE THERE?
AT THIS KIND OF EVENT, WHOEVER GETS THE MOST ATTENTION WINS!
わあ
GRAAAAH
WE ARE GOING TO PROMOTE THE CRAP OUT OF THIS!
BUT HOW? WE DON'T HAVE ANY MAJOR EVENTS COMING UP...
BUT YOU DO HAVE...

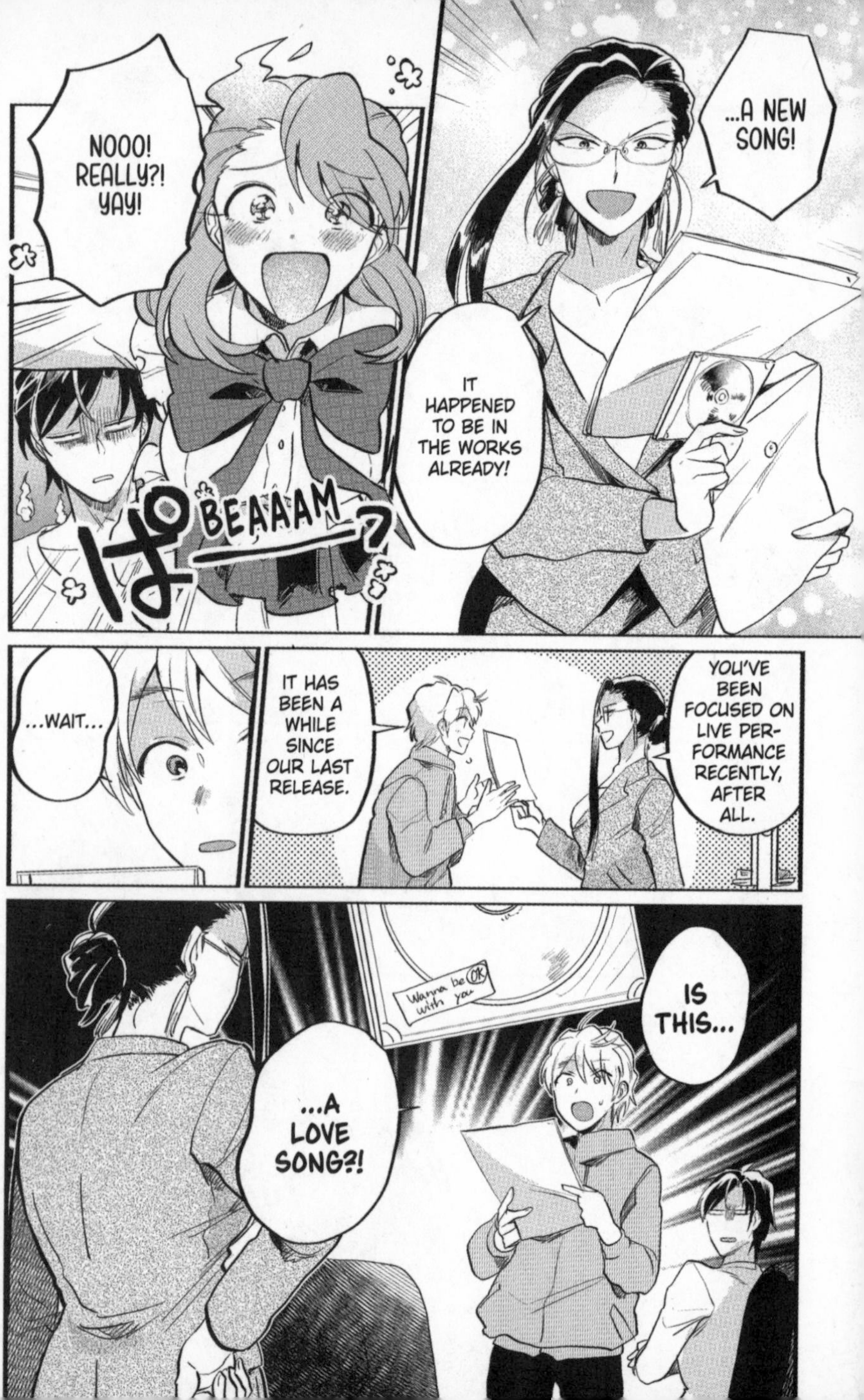
...A NEW SONG!
IT HAPPENED TO BE IN THE WORKS ALREADY!
NOOO! REALLY?! YAY!
ぱ BEAAAM
YOU'VE BEEN FOCUSED ON LIVE PER-FORMANCE RECENTLY, AFTER ALL.
IT HAS BEEN A WHILE SINCE OUR LAST RELEASE.
...WAIT...
Wanna be with you OK
IS THIS...
...A LOVE SONG?!

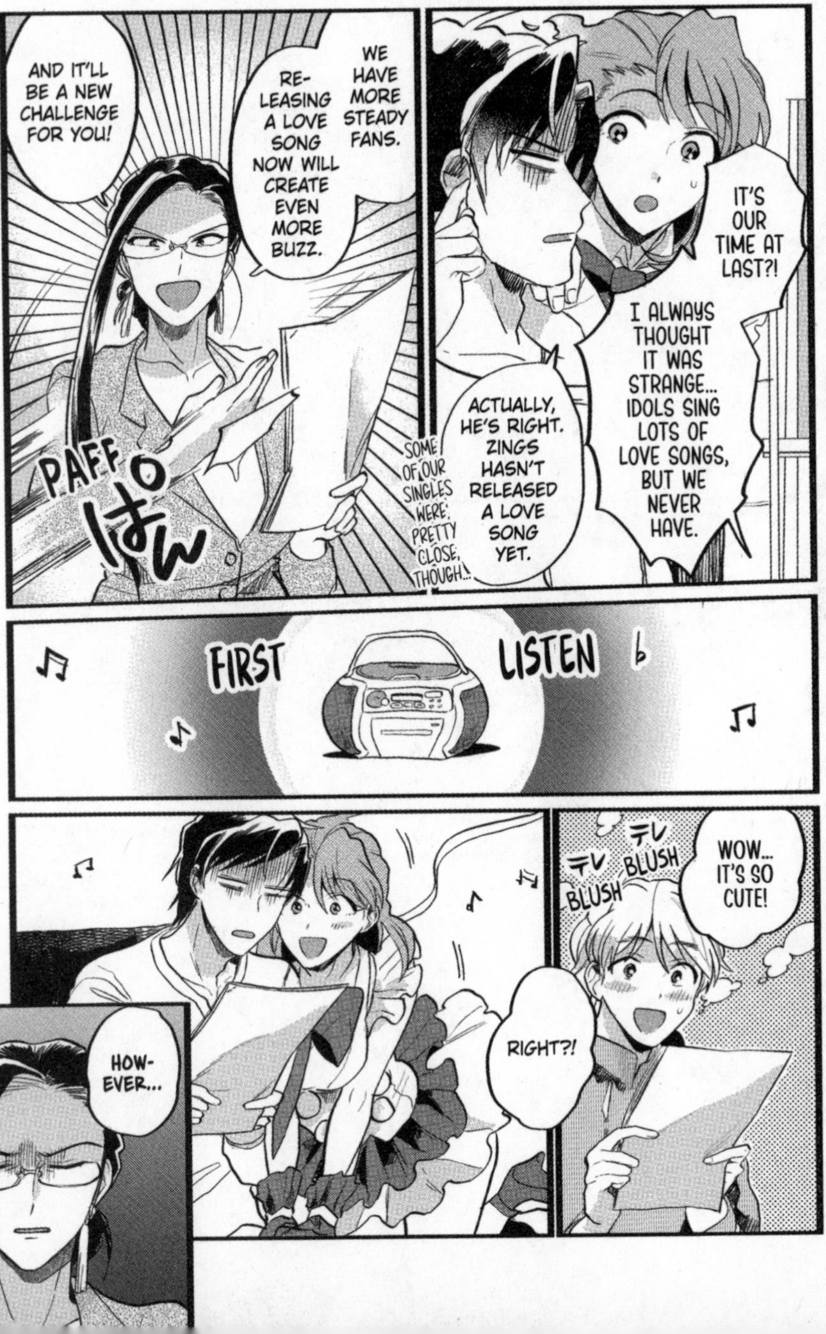
IT'S OUR TIME AT LAST?!
I ALWAYS THOUGHT IT WAS STRANGE... IDOLS SING LOTS OF LOVE SONGS, BUT WE NEVER HAVE.
ACTUALLY, HE'S RIGHT. ZINGS HASN'T RELEASED A LOVE SONG YET.
SOME OF OUR SINGLES WERE PRETTY CLOSE, THOUGH...
WE HAVE MORE STEADY FANS.
RE-LEASING A LOVE SONG NOW WILL CREATE EVEN MORE BUZZ.
AND IT'LL BE A NEW CHALLENGE FOR YOU!
PAFF
ぱん
FIRST LISTEN
WOW... IT'S SO CUTE!
テレ BLUSH
テレ BLUSH
RIGHT?!
HOW-EVER...

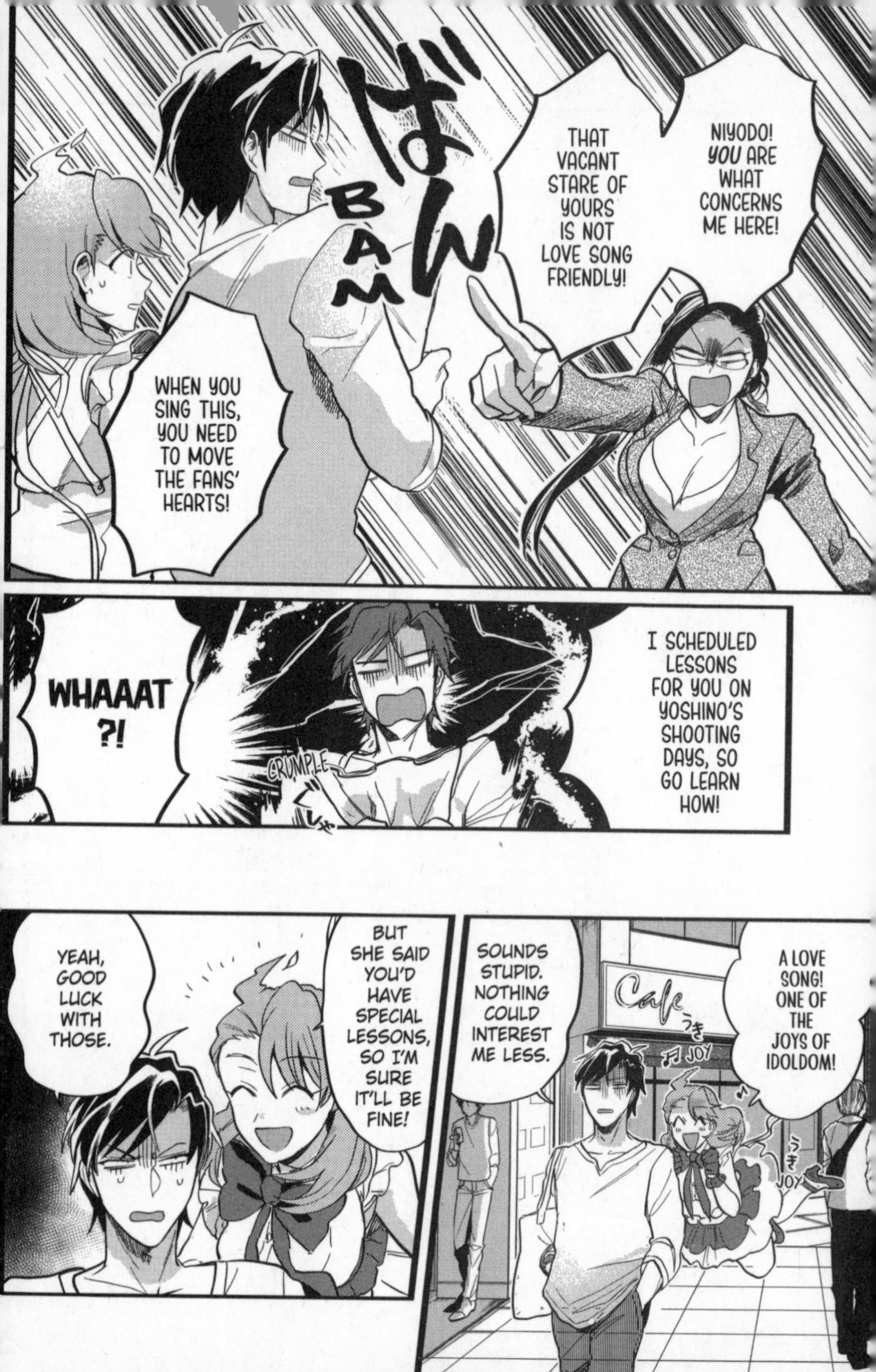
NIYODO! YOU ARE WHAT CONCERNS ME HERE!
THAT VACANT STARE OF YOURS IS NOT LOVE SONG FRIENDLY!
ばん
BAM
WHEN YOU SING THIS, YOU NEED TO MOVE THE FANS' HEARTS!
I SCHEDULED LESSONS FOR YOU ON YOSHINO'S SHOOTING DAYS, SO GO LEARN HOW!
CRUMPLE
ぐしゃ
WHAAAT ?!
A LOVE SONG! ONE OF THE JOYS OF IDOLDOM!
うき
JOY
うき
JOY
Cafe
SOUNDS STUPID. NOTHING COULD INTEREST ME LESS.
BUT SHE SAID YOU'D HAVE SPECIAL LESSONS, SO I'M SURE IT'LL BE FINE!
YEAH, GOOD LUCK WITH THOSE.

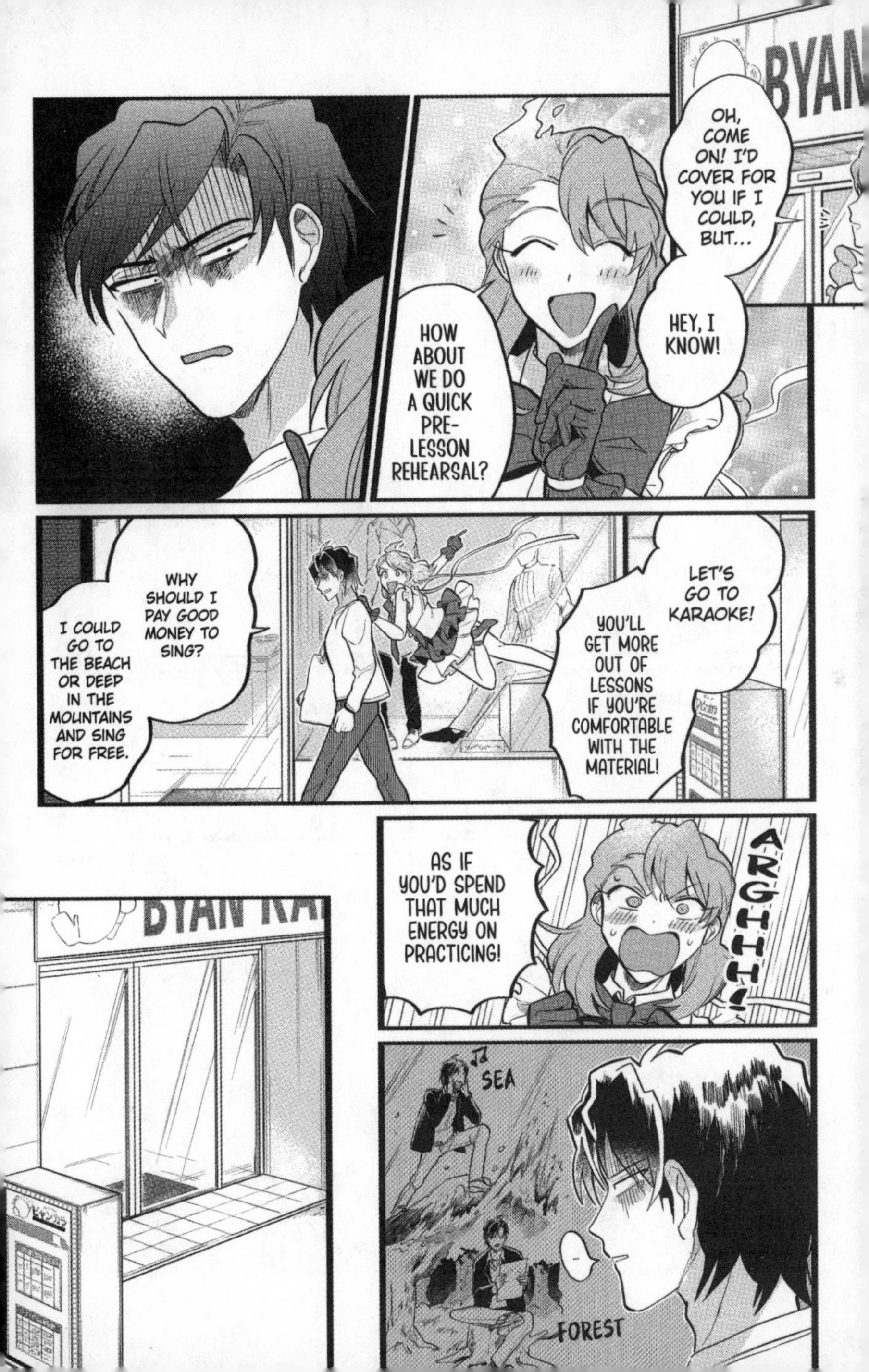
BYAN
OH, COME ON! I'D COVER FOR YOU IF I COULD, BUT...
HEY, I KNOW!
HOW ABOUT WE DO A QUICK PRE-LESSON REHEARSAL?
LET'S GO TO KARAOKE!
YOU'LL GET MORE OUT OF LESSONS IF YOU'RE COMFORTABLE WITH THE MATERIAL!
WHY SHOULD I PAY GOOD MONEY TO SING?
I COULD GO TO THE BEACH OR DEEP IN THE MOUNTAINS AND SING FOR FREE.
ARGHHH!
AS IF YOU'D SPEND THAT MUCH ENERGY ON PRACTICING!
SEA
...
FOREST
BYAN

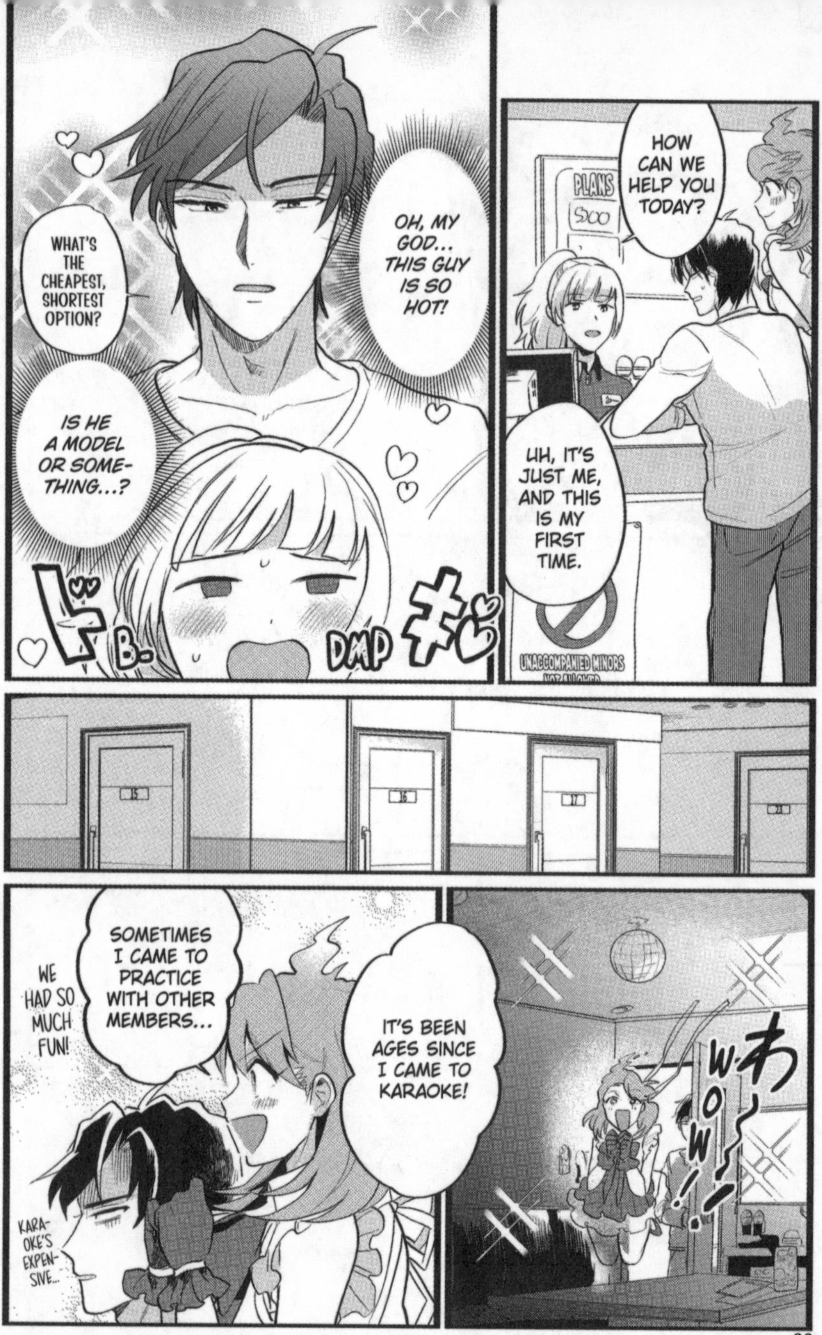
HOW CAN WE HELP YOU TODAY?
PLANS
UH, IT'S JUST ME, AND THIS IS MY FIRST TIME.
UNACCOMPANIED MINORS
OH, MY GOD... THIS GUY IS SO HOT!
WHAT'S THE CHEAPEST, SHORTEST OPTION?
IS HE A MODEL OR SOME-THING...?
B-
DMP
WOW~!!
IT'S BEEN AGES SINCE I CAME TO KARAOKE!
SOMETIMES I CAME TO PRACTICE WITH OTHER MEMBERS...
WE HAD SO MUCH FUN!
KARA-OKE'S EXPEN-SIVE...

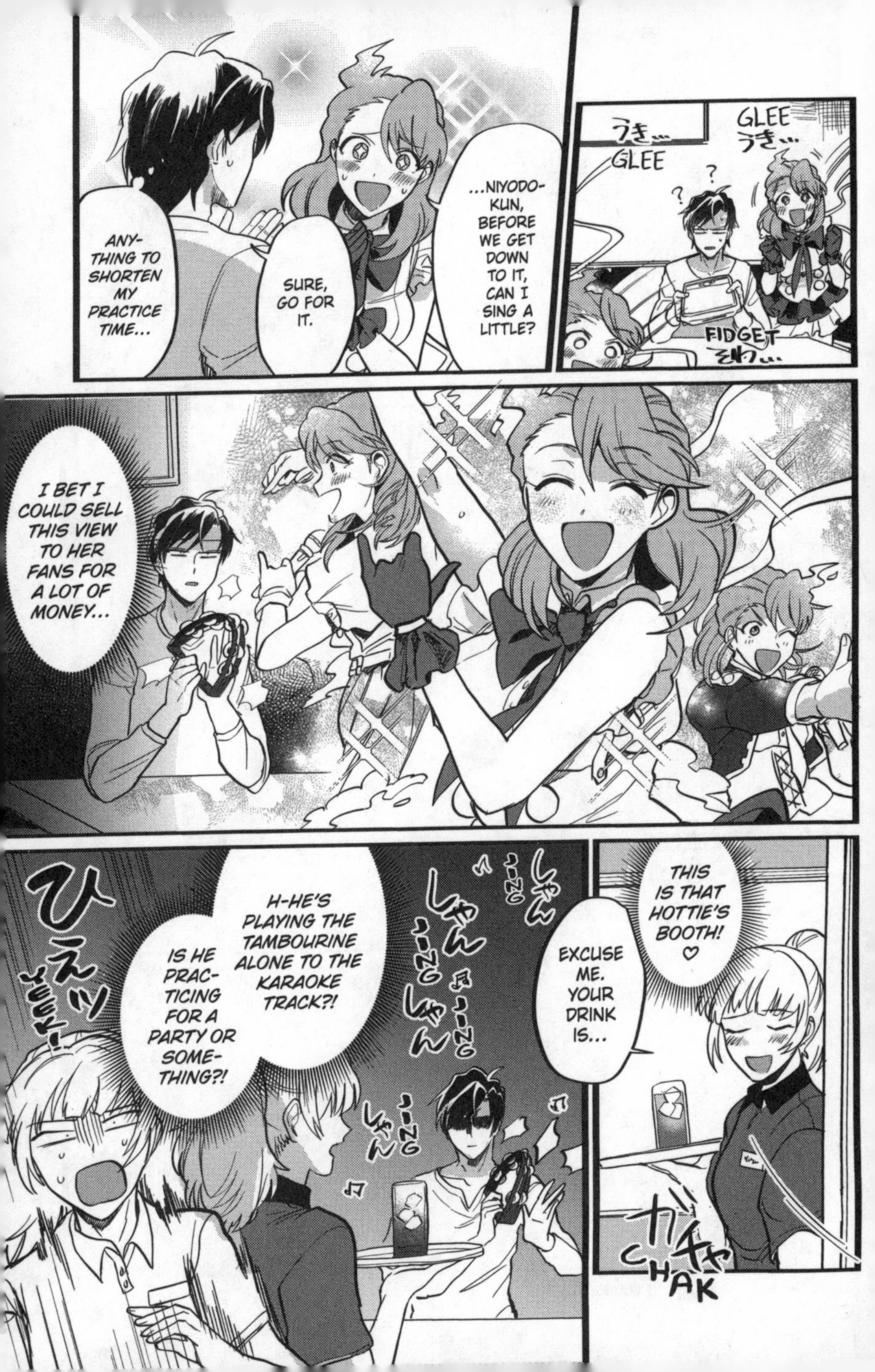
GLEE
うき…
うき…
GLEE
FIDGET
そわ…
...NIYODO-KUN, BEFORE WE GET DOWN TO IT, CAN I SING A LITTLE?
SURE, GO FOR IT.
ANY-THING TO SHORTEN MY PRACTICE TIME...
I BET I COULD SELL THIS VIEW TO HER FANS FOR A LOT OF MONEY...
THIS IS THAT HOTTIE'S BOOTH! ♡
EXCUSE ME. YOUR DRINK IS...
ガチャ
CHAK
しゃん
JING
しゃん
JING
しゃん
JING
しゃん
JING
H-HE'S PLAYING THE TAMBOURINE ALONE TO THE KARAOKE TRACK?!
IS HE PRAC-TICING FOR A PARTY OR SOME-THING?!
ひえッ
YEEK!

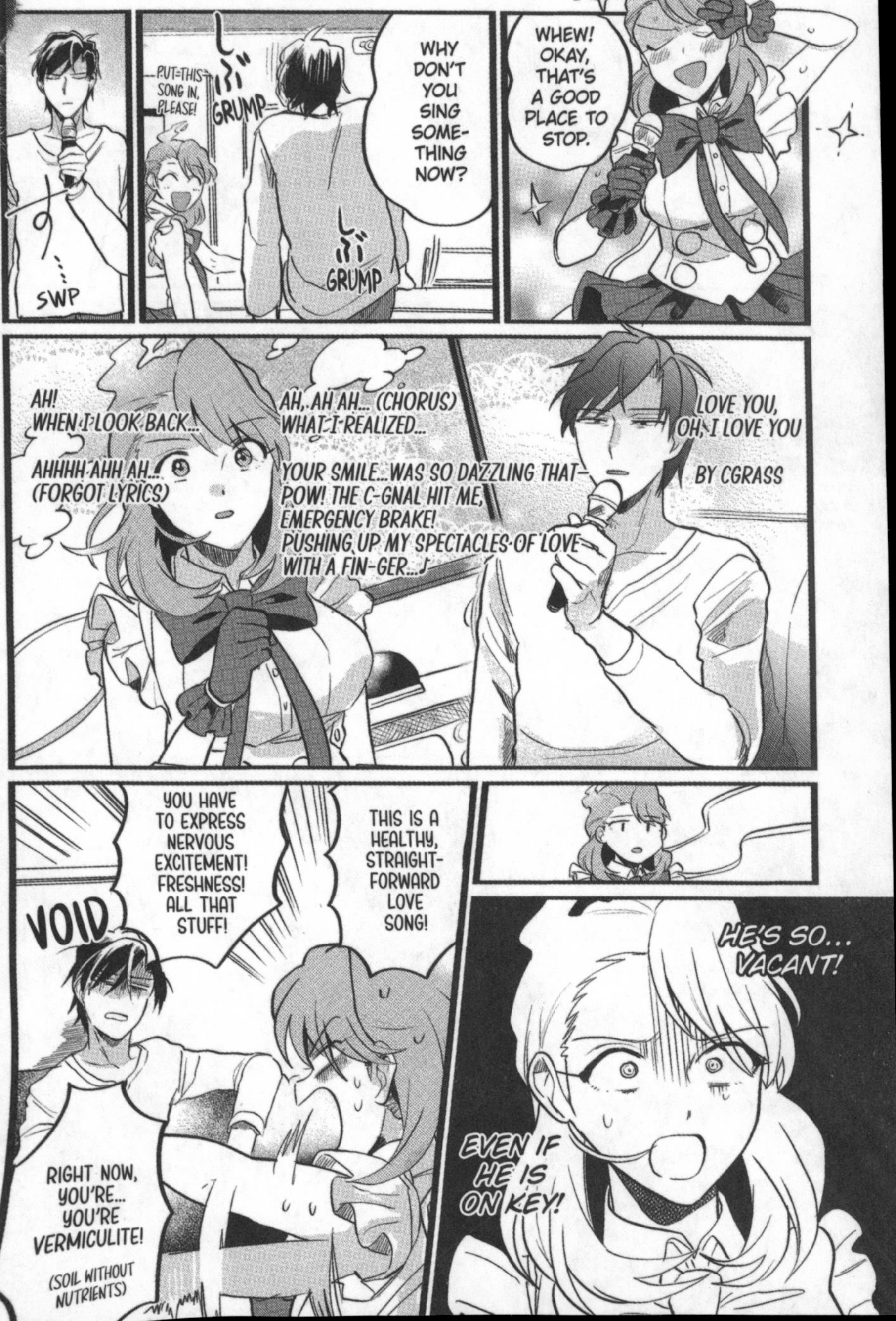
WHEW! OKAY, THAT'S A GOOD PLACE TO STOP.
WHY DON'T YOU SING SOME-THING NOW?
しぶ
GRUMP
しぶ
GRUMP
PUT=THIS=SONG IN, PLEASE!
SWP
LOVE YOU, OH, I LOVE YOU
BY CGRASS
AH, AH AH... (CHORUS) WHAT I REALIZED...
YOUR SMILE...WAS SO DAZZLING THAT—POW! THE C-GNAL HIT ME, EMERGENCY BRAKE! PUSHING UP MY SPECTACLES OF LOVE WITH A FIN-GER...♪
AH! WHEN I LOOK BACK...
AHHHH AHH AH... (FORGOT LYRICS)
HE'S SO... VACANT!
EVEN IF HE IS ON KEY!
THIS IS A HEALTHY, STRAIGHT-FORWARD LOVE SONG!
YOU HAVE TO EXPRESS NERVOUS EXCITEMENT! FRESHNESS! ALL THAT STUFF!
VOID
RIGHT NOW, YOU'RE... YOU'RE VERMICULITE!
(SOIL WITHOUT NUTRIENTS)

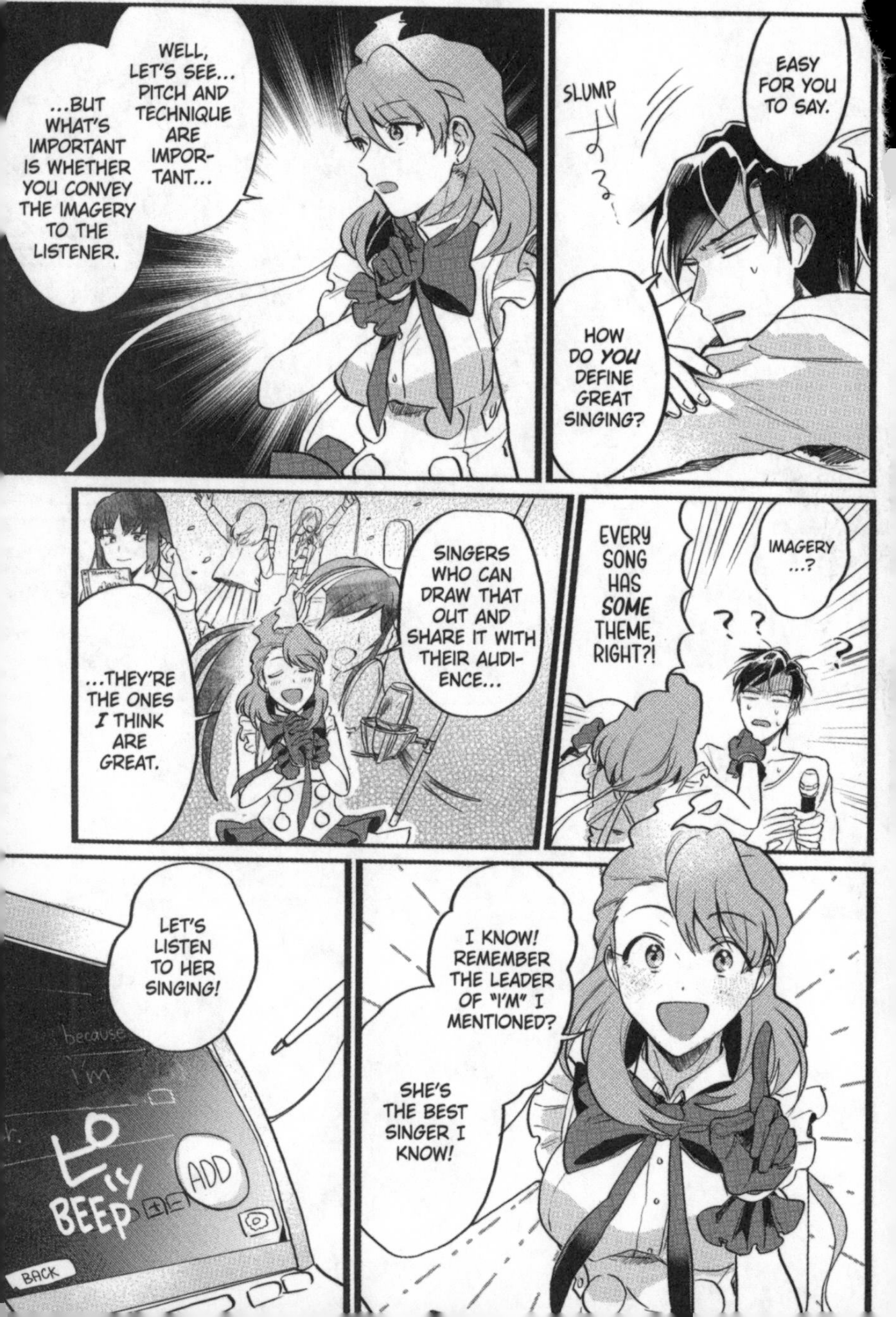
EASY FOR YOU TO SAY.
SLUMP
HOW DO *YOU* DEFINE GREAT SINGING?
WELL, LET'S SEE... PITCH AND TECHNIQUE ARE IMPOR-TANT...
...BUT WHAT'S IMPORTANT IS WHETHER YOU CONVEY THE IMAGERY TO THE LISTENER.
IMAGERY ...?
EVERY SONG HAS *SOME* THEME, RIGHT?!
SINGERS WHO CAN DRAW THAT OUT AND SHARE IT WITH THEIR AUDI-ENCE...
...THEY'RE THE ONES *I* THINK ARE GREAT.
I KNOW! REMEMBER THE LEADER OF "I'M" I MENTIONED?
SHE'S THE BEST SINGER I KNOW!
LET'S LISTEN TO HER SINGING!
ADD
BEEP
BACK

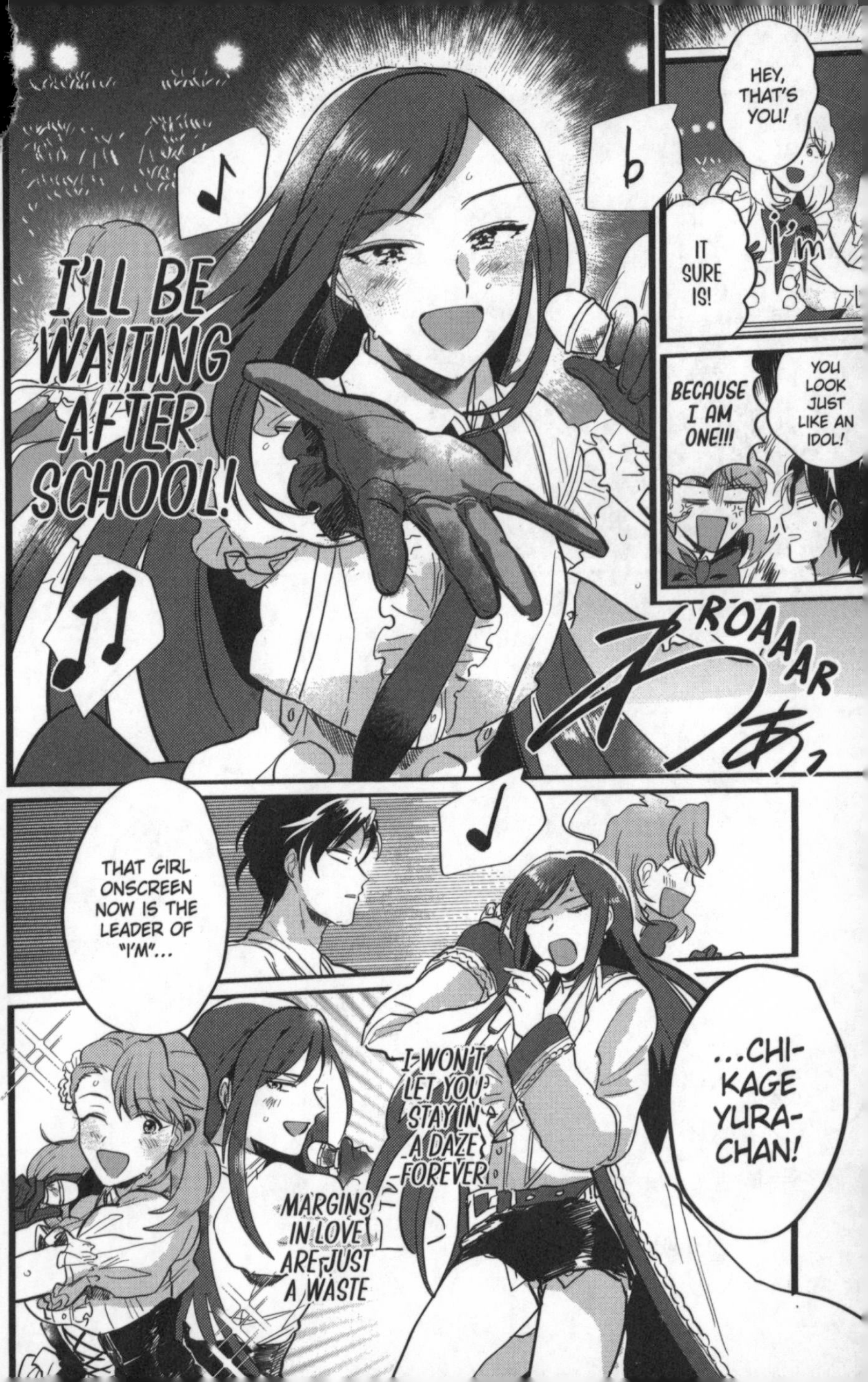
HEY, THAT'S YOU!
IT SURE IS!
i'm
YOU LOOK JUST LIKE AN IDOL!
BECAUSE I AM ONE!!!
I'LL BE WAITING AFTER SCHOOL!
ROAAAAR
わっあっ
THAT GIRL ONSCREEN NOW IS THE LEADER OF "I'M"...
...CHI-KAGE YURA-CHAN!
I WON'T LET YOU STAY IN A DAZE FOREVER
MARGINS IN LOVE ARE JUST A WASTE

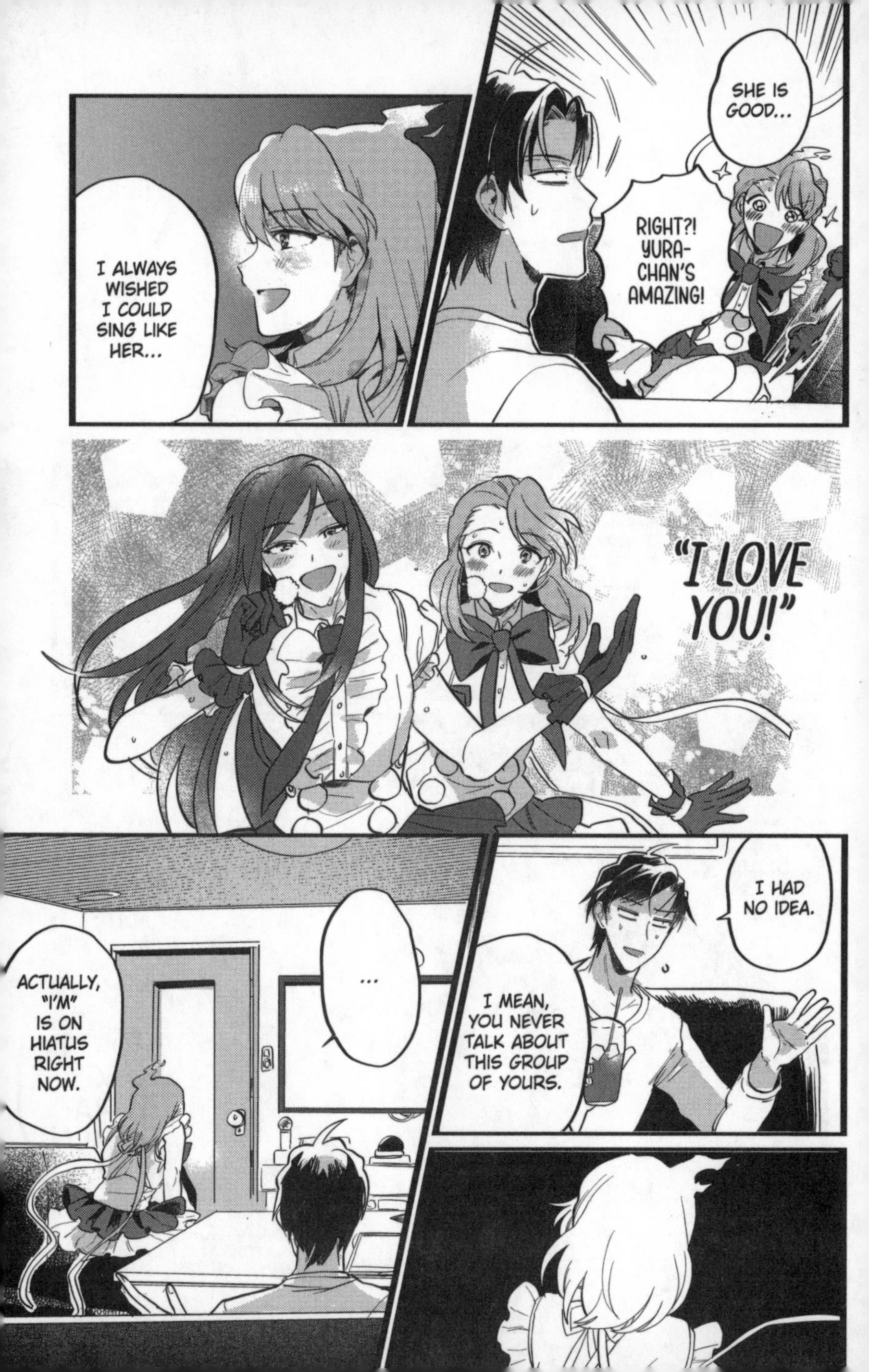
SHE IS GOOD...
RIGHT?! YURA-CHAN'S AMAZING!
I ALWAYS WISHED I COULD SING LIKE HER...
"I LOVE YOU!"
I HAD NO IDEA.
I MEAN, YOU NEVER TALK ABOUT THIS GROUP OF YOURS.
...
ACTUALLY, "I'M" IS ON HIATUS RIGHT NOW.

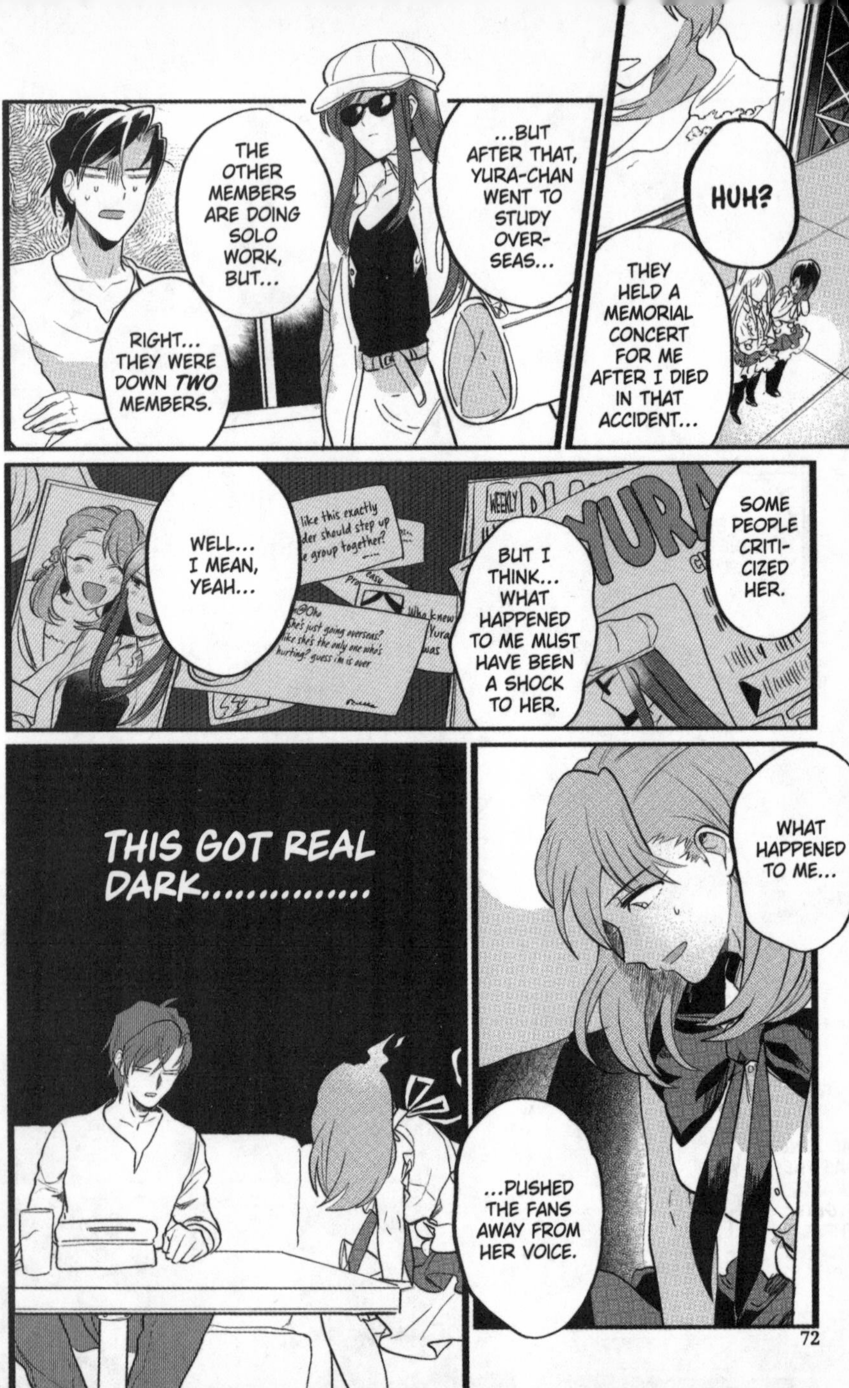
HUH?
THEY HELD A MEMORIAL CONCERT FOR ME AFTER I DIED IN THAT ACCIDENT...
...BUT AFTER THAT, YURA-CHAN WENT TO STUDY OVER-SEAS...
THE OTHER MEMBERS ARE DOING SOLO WORK, BUT...
RIGHT... THEY WERE DOWN *TWO* MEMBERS.
SOME PEOPLE CRITI-CIZED HER.
BUT I THINK... WHAT HAPPENED TO ME MUST HAVE BEEN A SHOCK TO HER.
WELL... I MEAN, YEAH...
WHAT HAPPENED TO ME...
...PUSHED THE FANS AWAY FROM HER VOICE.
THIS GOT REAL DARK..............

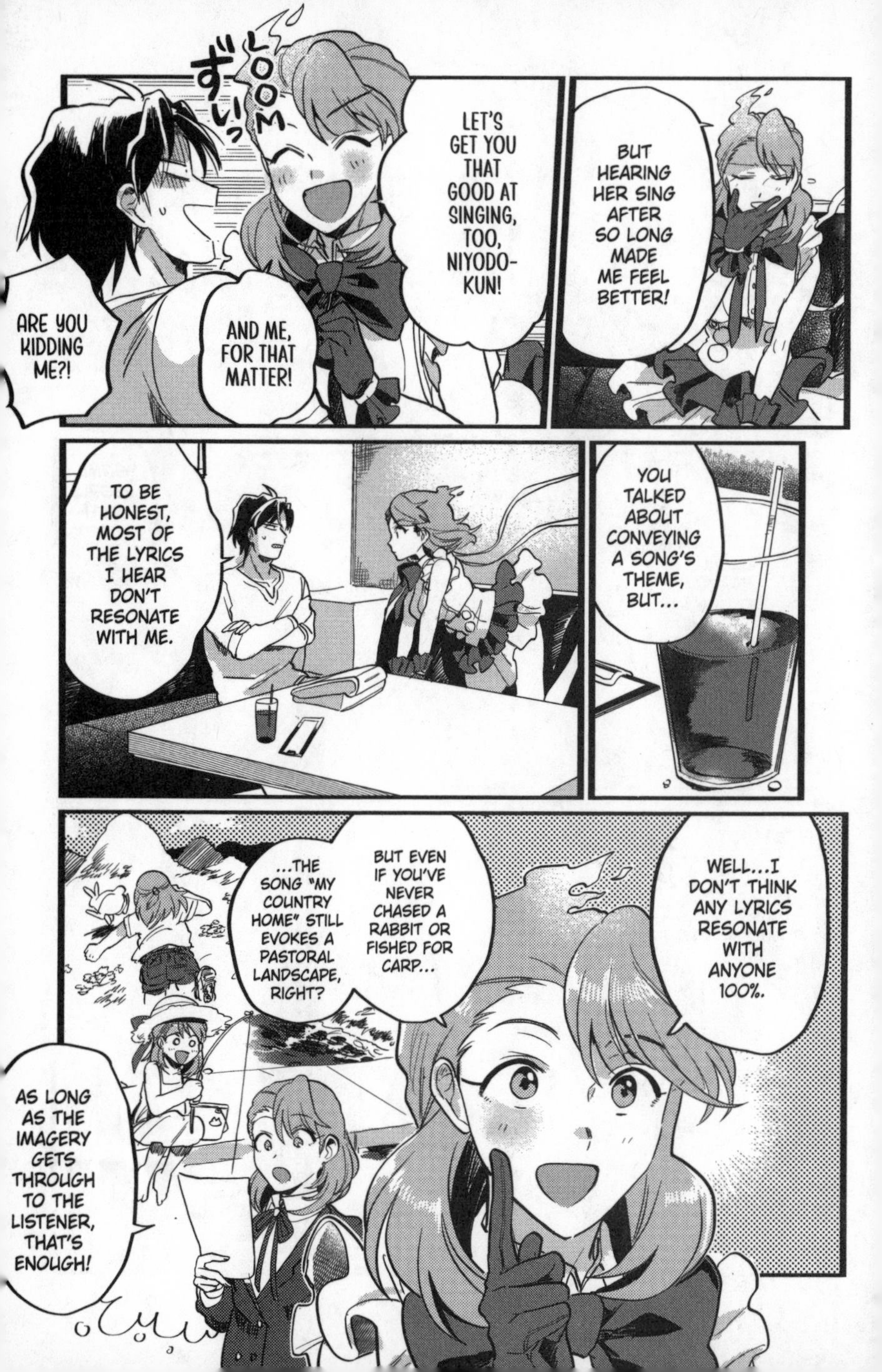
BUT HEARING HER SING AFTER SO LONG MADE ME FEEL BETTER!
LET'S GET YOU THAT GOOD AT SINGING, TOO, NIYODO-KUN!
ずいっ LOOM
AND ME, FOR THAT MATTER!
ARE YOU KIDDING ME?!
YOU TALKED ABOUT CONVEYING A SONG'S THEME, BUT...
TO BE HONEST, MOST OF THE LYRICS I HEAR DON'T RESONATE WITH ME.
WELL...I DON'T THINK ANY LYRICS RESONATE WITH ANYONE 100%.
BUT EVEN IF YOU'VE NEVER CHASED A RABBIT OR FISHED FOR CARP...
...THE SONG "MY COUNTRY HOME" STILL EVOKES A PASTORAL LANDSCAPE, RIGHT?
AS LONG AS THE IMAGERY GETS THROUGH TO THE LISTENER, THAT'S ENOUGH!

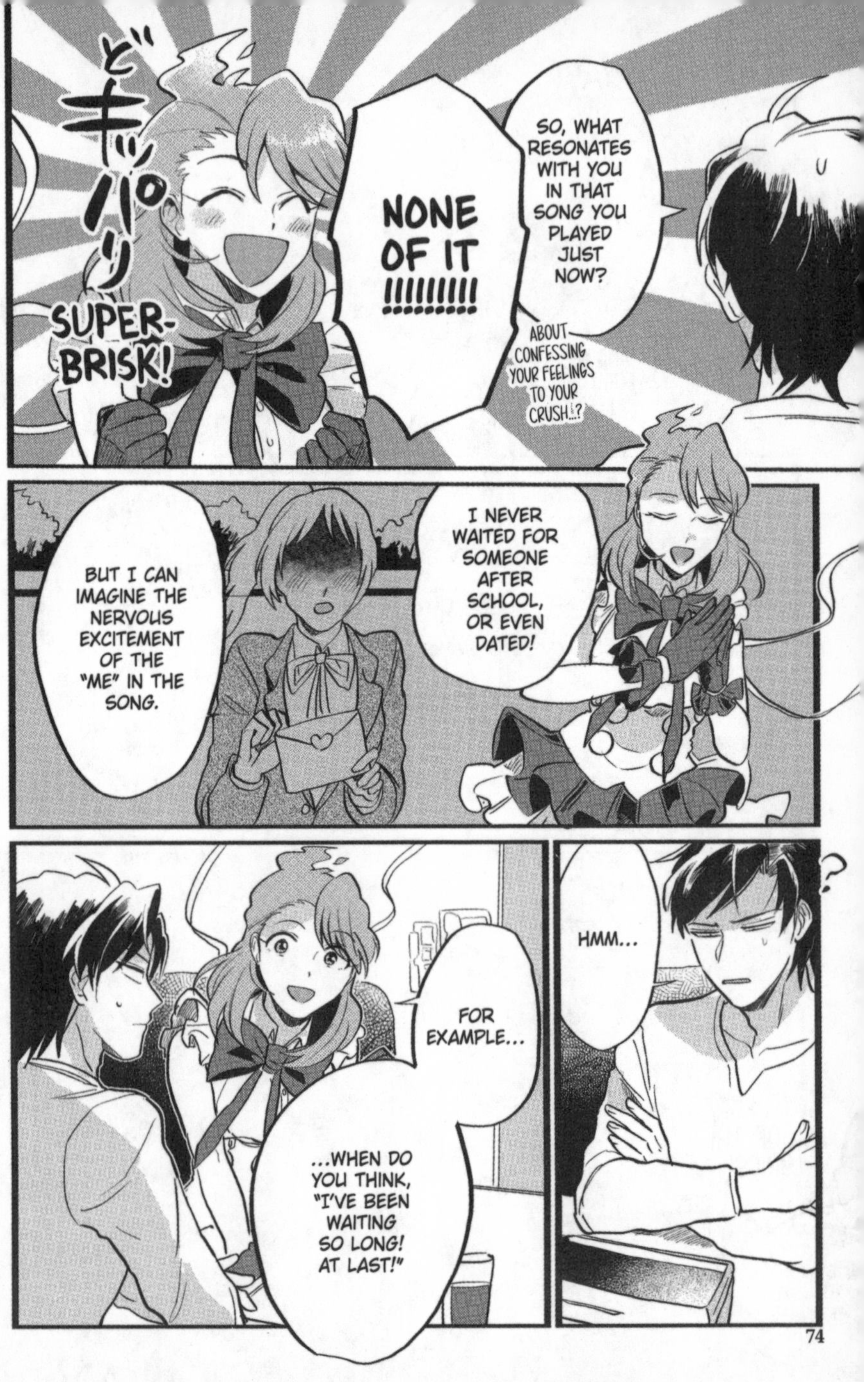
SO, WHAT RESONATES WITH YOU IN THAT SONG YOU PLAYED JUST NOW?
ABOUT CONFESSING YOUR FEELINGS TO YOUR CRUSH...?
NONE OF IT!!!!!!!!!!
ドギッパリ
SUPER-BRISK!
I NEVER WAITED FOR SOMEONE AFTER SCHOOL, OR EVEN DATED!
BUT I CAN IMAGINE THE NERVOUS EXCITEMENT OF THE "ME" IN THE SONG.
HMM...
FOR EXAMPLE...
...WHEN DO YOU THINK, "I'VE BEEN WAITING SO LONG! AT LAST!"

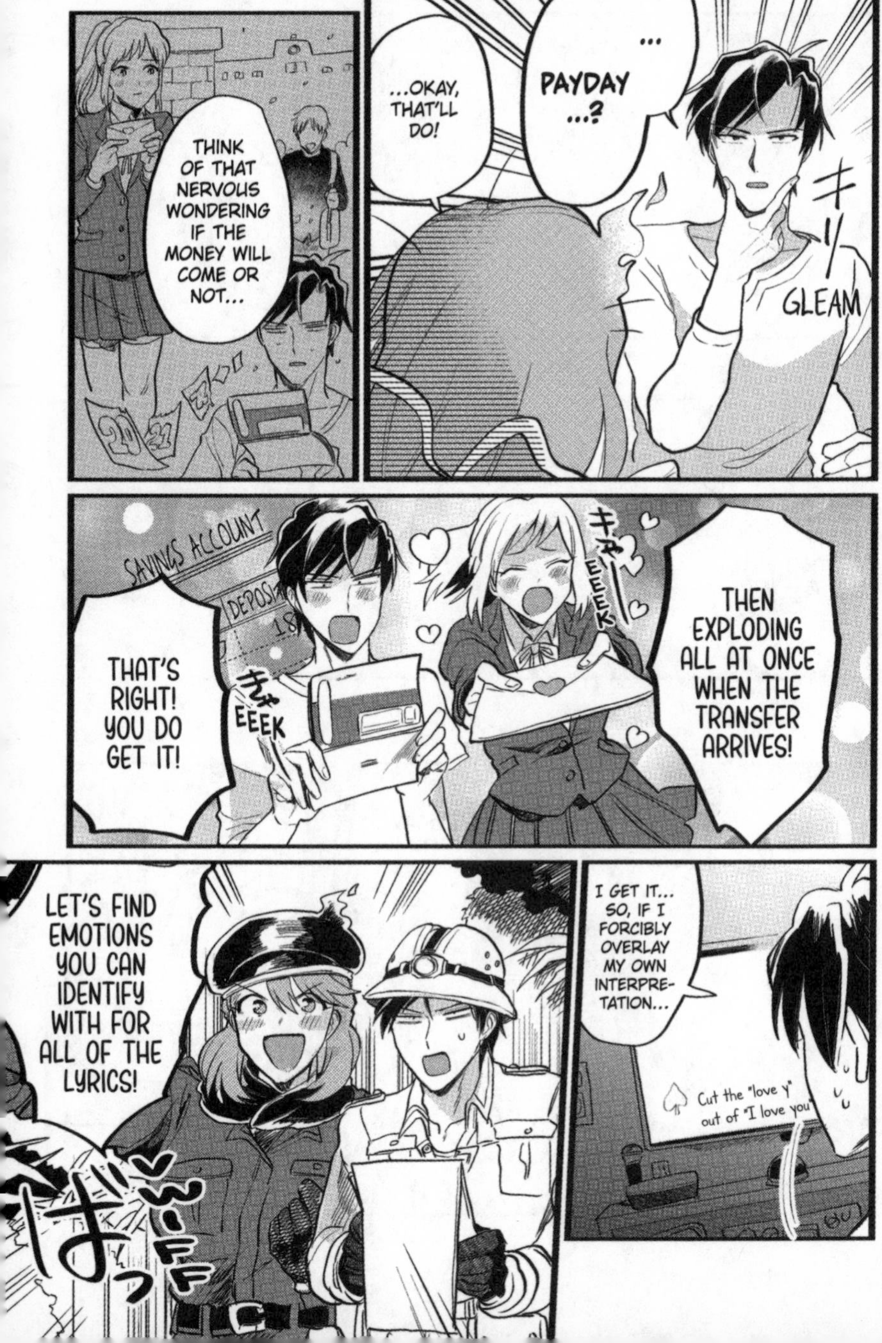
...
PAYDAY ...?
...OKAY, THAT'LL DO!
GLEAM
THINK OF THAT NERVOUS WONDERING IF THE MONEY WILL COME OR NOT...
THEN EXPLODING ALL AT ONCE WHEN THE TRANSFER ARRIVES!
EEEK
SAVINGS ACCOUNT
DEPOSI
18
THAT'S RIGHT! YOU DO GET IT!
EEEK
I GET IT... SO, IF I FORCIBLY OVERLAY MY OWN INTERPRETATION...
Cut the "love y" out of "I love you"
LET'S FIND EMOTIONS YOU CAN IDENTIFY WITH FOR ALL OF THE LYRICS!
WHIFF

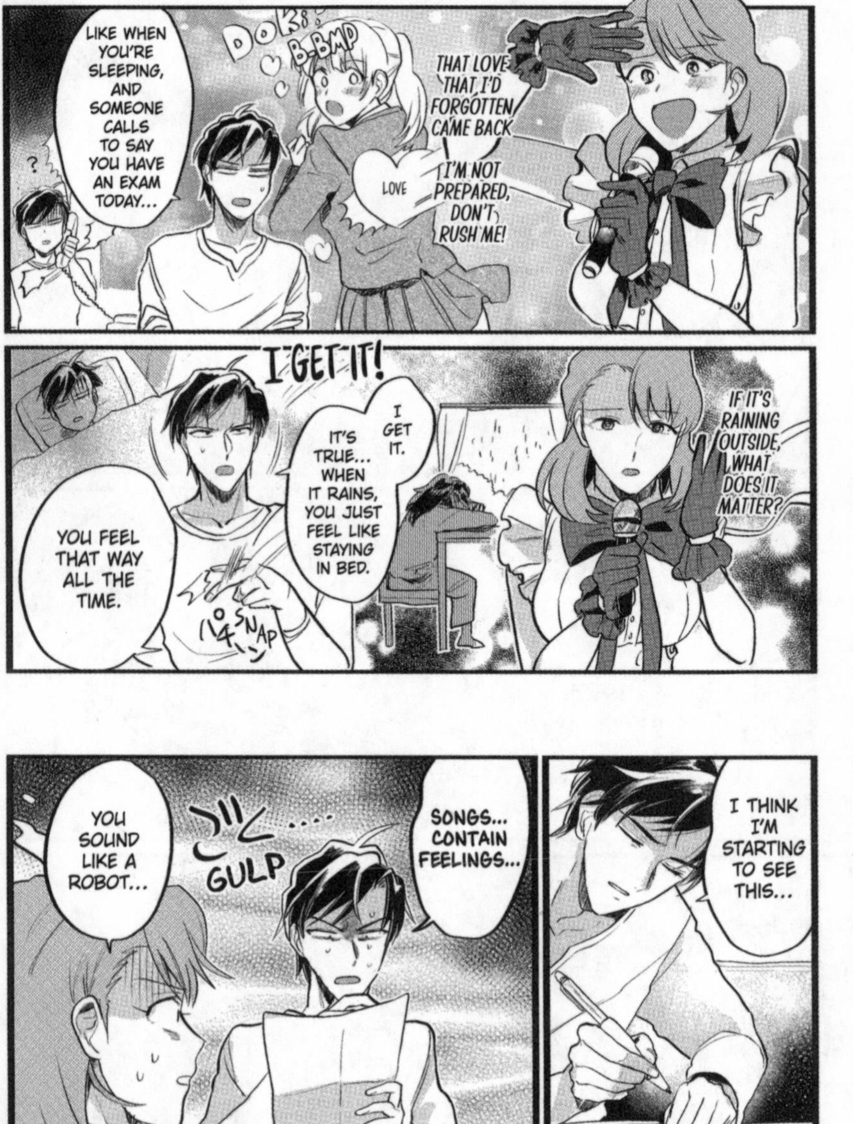
THAT LOVE THAT I'D FORGOTTEN CAME BACK
I'M NOT PREPARED, DON'T RUSH ME!
LOVE
DOKI B-BMP
LIKE WHEN YOU'RE SLEEPING, AND SOMEONE CALLS TO SAY YOU HAVE AN EXAM TODAY...
?
IF IT'S RAINING OUTSIDE, WHAT DOES IT MATTER?
I GET IT!
I GET IT.
IT'S TRUE... WHEN IT RAINS, YOU JUST FEEL LIKE STAYING IN BED.
SNAP
YOU FEEL THAT WAY ALL THE TIME.
I THINK I'M STARTING TO SEE THIS...
SONGS... CONTAIN FEELINGS...
GULP
...
YOU SOUND LIKE A ROBOT...

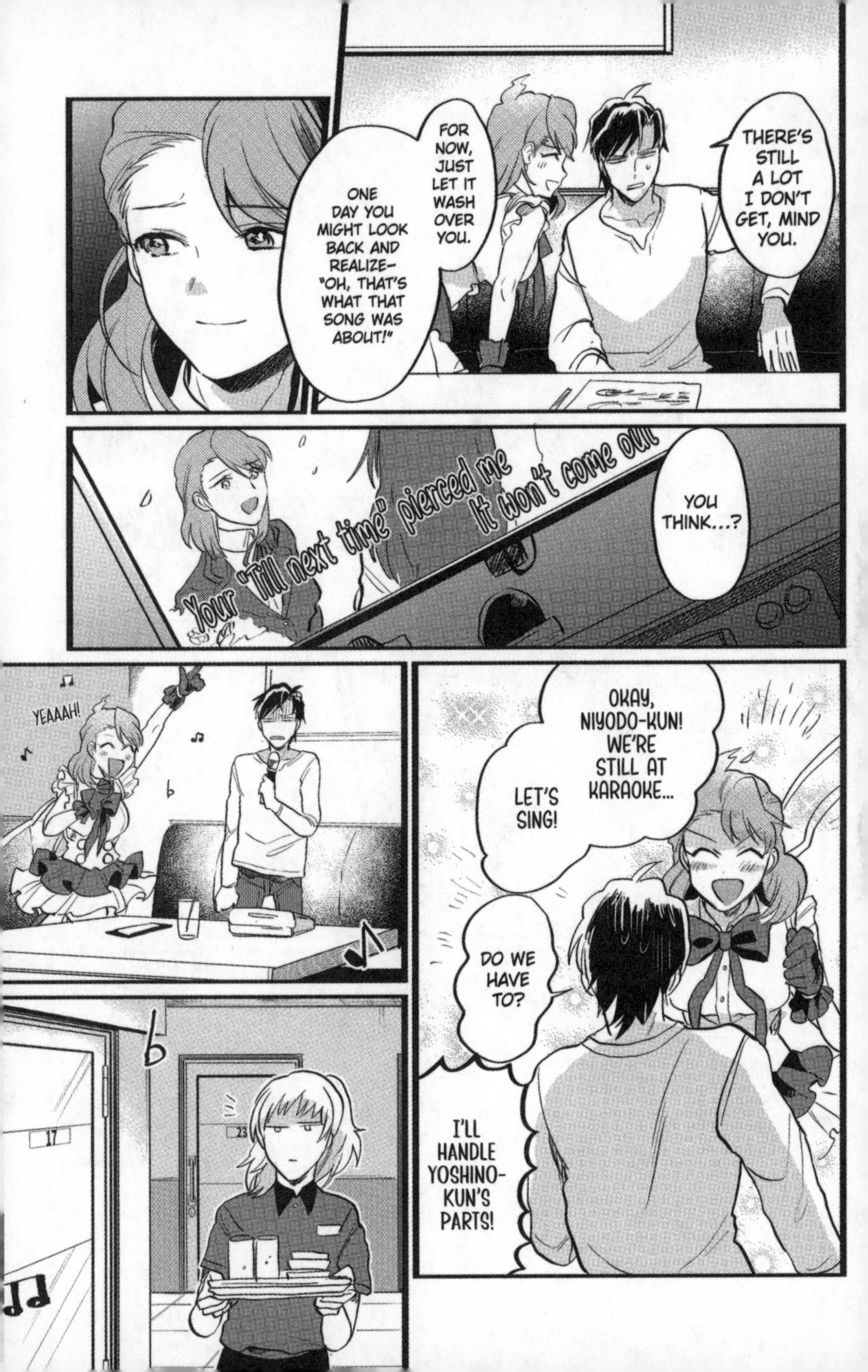
THERE'S STILL A LOT I DON'T GET, MIND YOU.
FOR NOW, JUST LET IT WASH OVER YOU.
ONE DAY YOU MIGHT LOOK BACK AND REALIZE— "OH, THAT'S WHAT THAT SONG WAS ABOUT!"
YOU THINK...?
Your "Till next time" pierced me
It won't come out
OKAY, NIYODO-KUN! WE'RE STILL AT KARAOKE...
LET'S SING!
DO WE HAVE TO?
I'LL HANDLE YOSHINO-KUN'S PARTS!
YEAAAH!
23
17

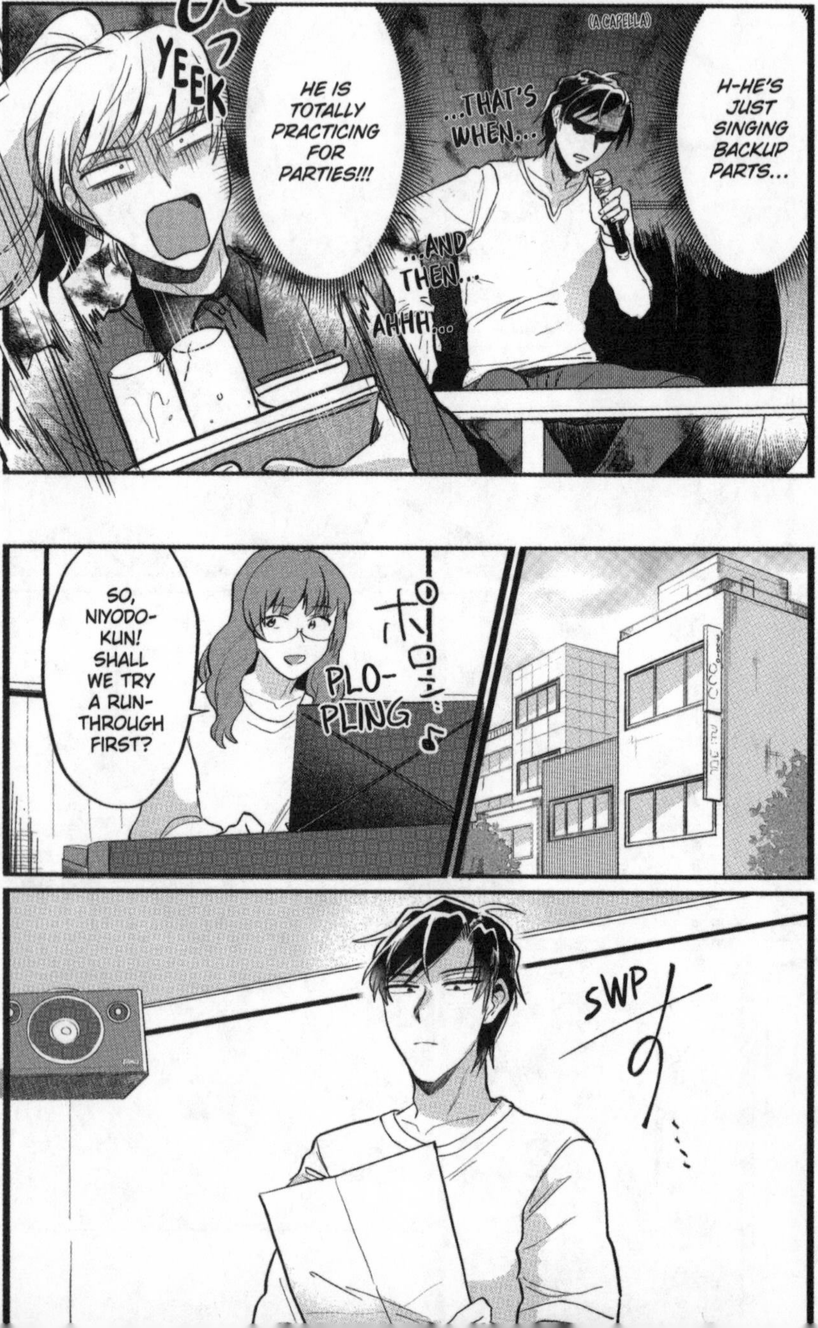
(A CAPELLA)
H-HE'S JUST SINGING BACKUP PARTS...
...THAT'S WHEN...
...AND THEN...
AHHH...
HE IS TOTALLY PRACTICING FOR PARTIES!!!
YEEK
PLO-PLING
SO, NIYODO-KUN! SHALL WE TRY A RUN-THROUGH FIRST?
SWP

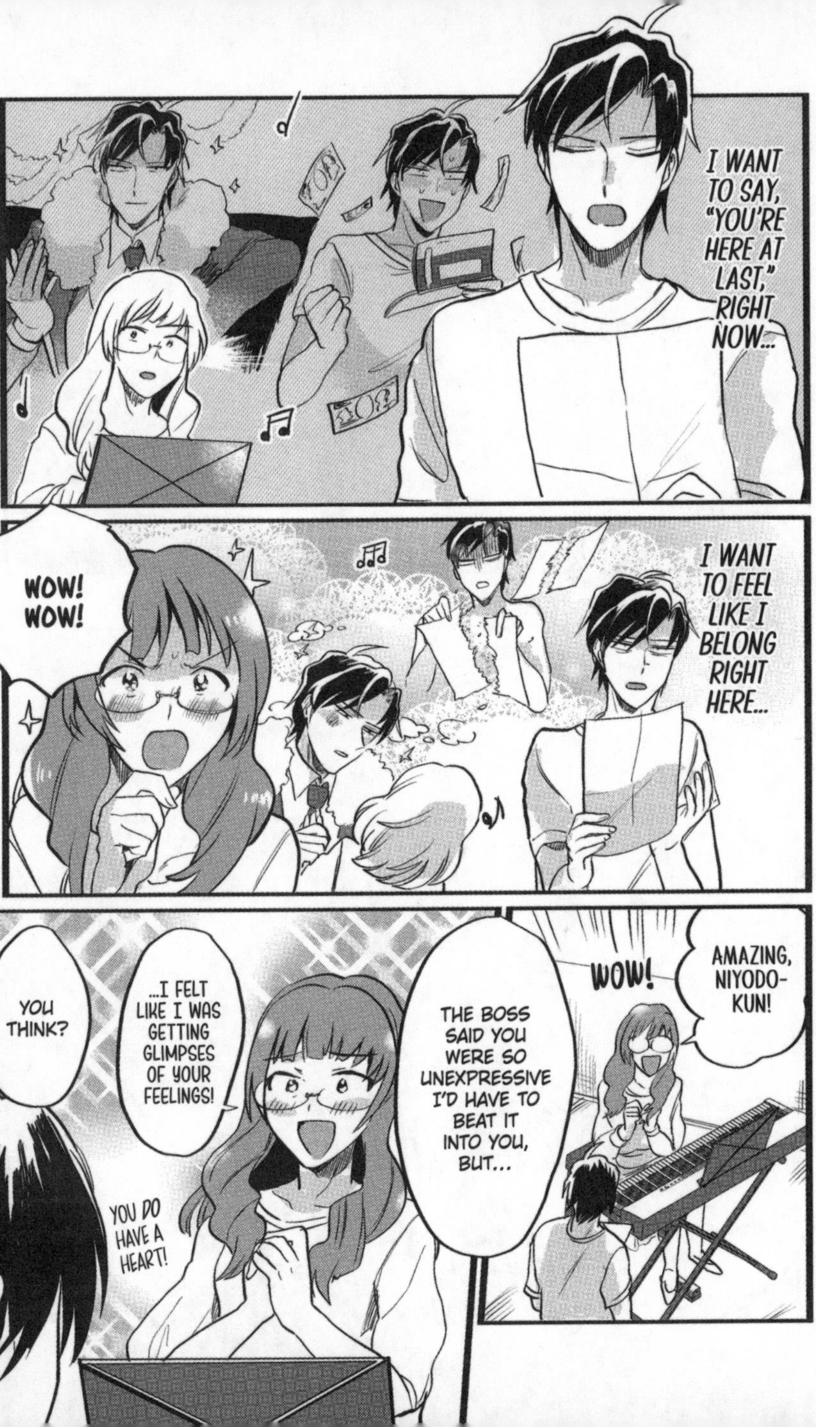
I WANT TO SAY, "YOU'RE HERE AT LAST," RIGHT NOW...
I WANT TO FEEL LIKE I BELONG RIGHT HERE...
WOW! WOW!
WOW!
AMAZING, NIYODO-KUN!
THE BOSS SAID YOU WERE SO UNEXPRESSIVE I'D HAVE TO BEAT IT INTO YOU, BUT...
...I FELT LIKE I WAS GETTING GLIMPSES OF YOUR FEELINGS!
YOU THINK?
YOU DO HAVE A HEART!

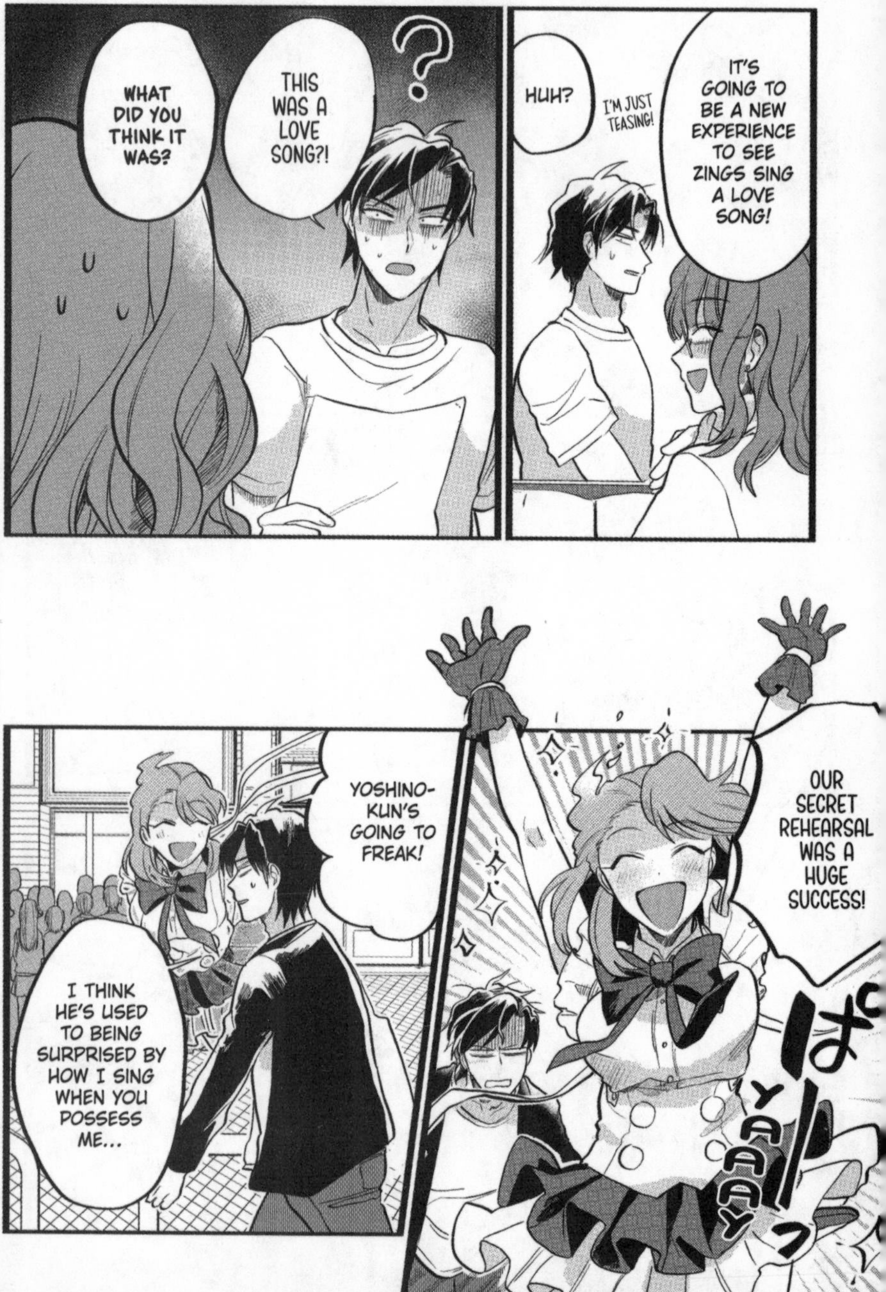
IT'S GOING TO BE A NEW EXPERIENCE TO SEE ZINGS SING A LOVE SONG!
I'M JUST TEASING!
HUH?
THIS WAS A LOVE SONG?!
WHAT DID YOU THINK IT WAS?
OUR SECRET REHEARSAL WAS A HUGE SUCCESS!
ぱーっ
YAAAAY
YOSHINO-KUN'S GOING TO FREAK!
I THINK HE'S USED TO BEING SURPRISED BY HOW I SING WHEN YOU POSSESS ME...

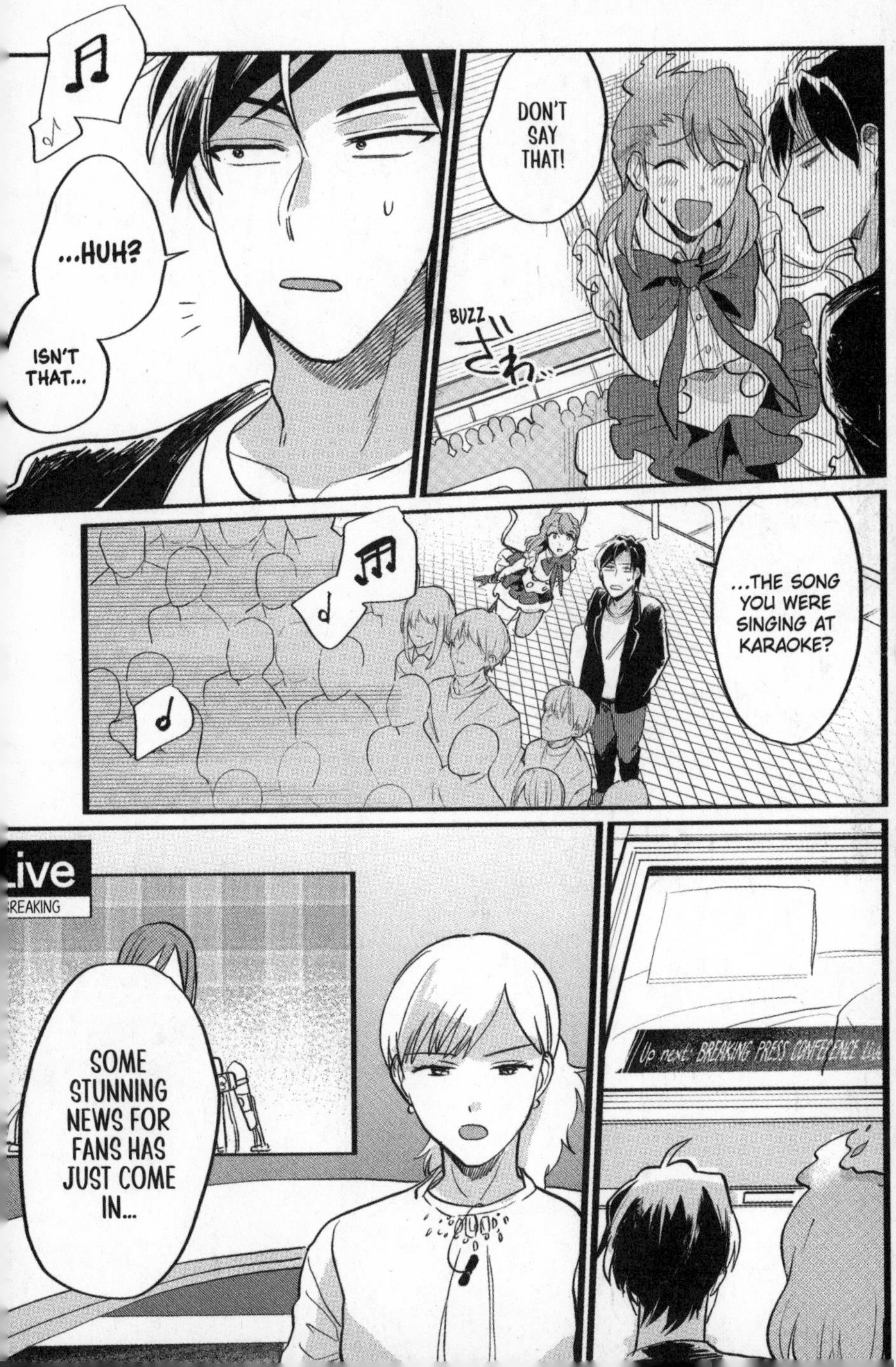
DON'T SAY THAT!
BUZZ
ざわ
...HUH?
ISN'T THAT...
...THE SONG YOU WERE SINGING AT KARAOKE?
Up next: BREAKING PRESS CONFERENCE Live
Live
BREAKING
SOME STUNNING NEWS FOR FANS HAS JUST COME IN...

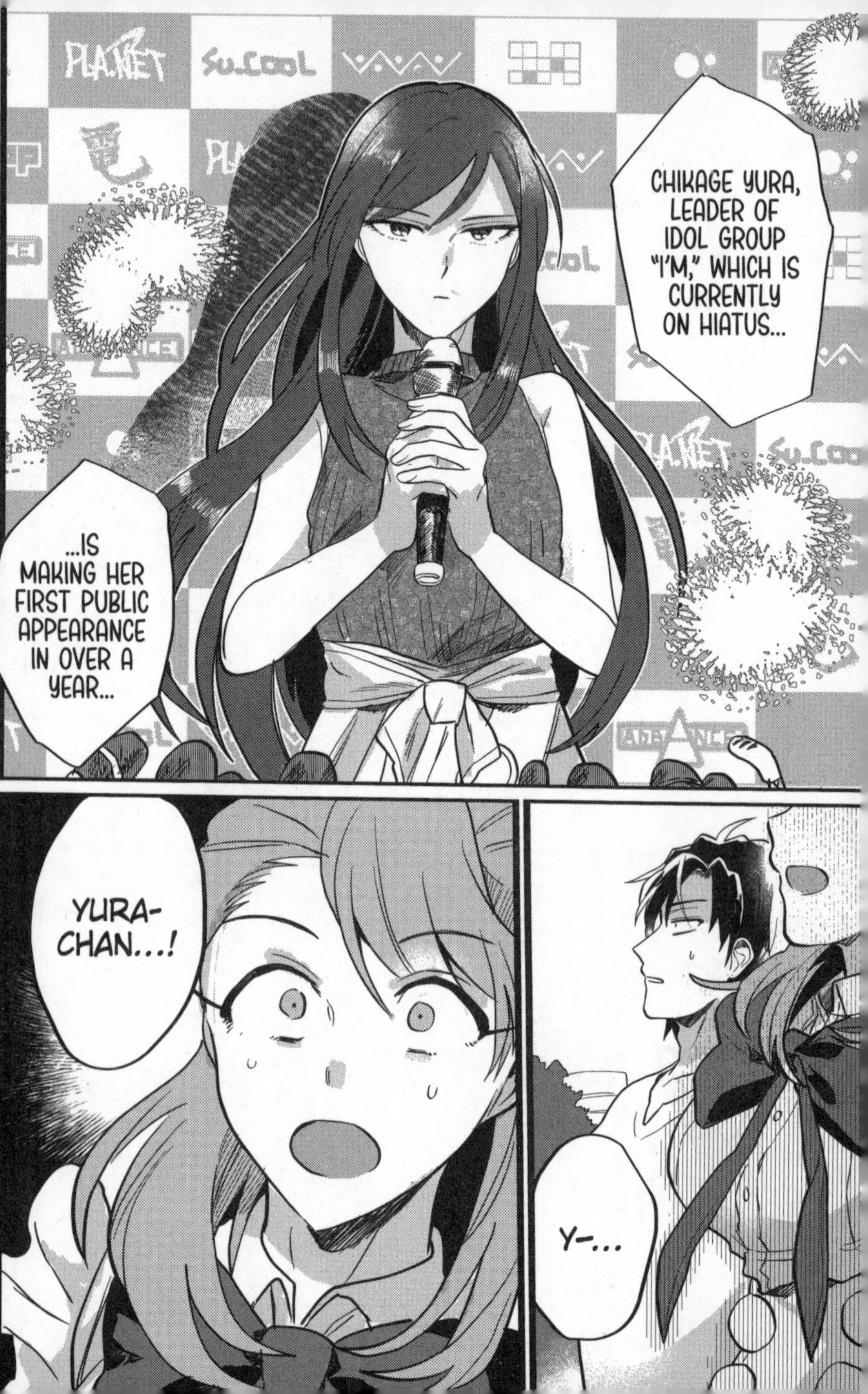
CHIKAGE YURA, LEADER OF IDOL GROUP "I'M," WHICH IS CURRENTLY ON HIATUS...
...IS MAKING HER FIRST PUBLIC APPEARANCE IN OVER A YEAR...
Y-...
YURA-CHAN...!

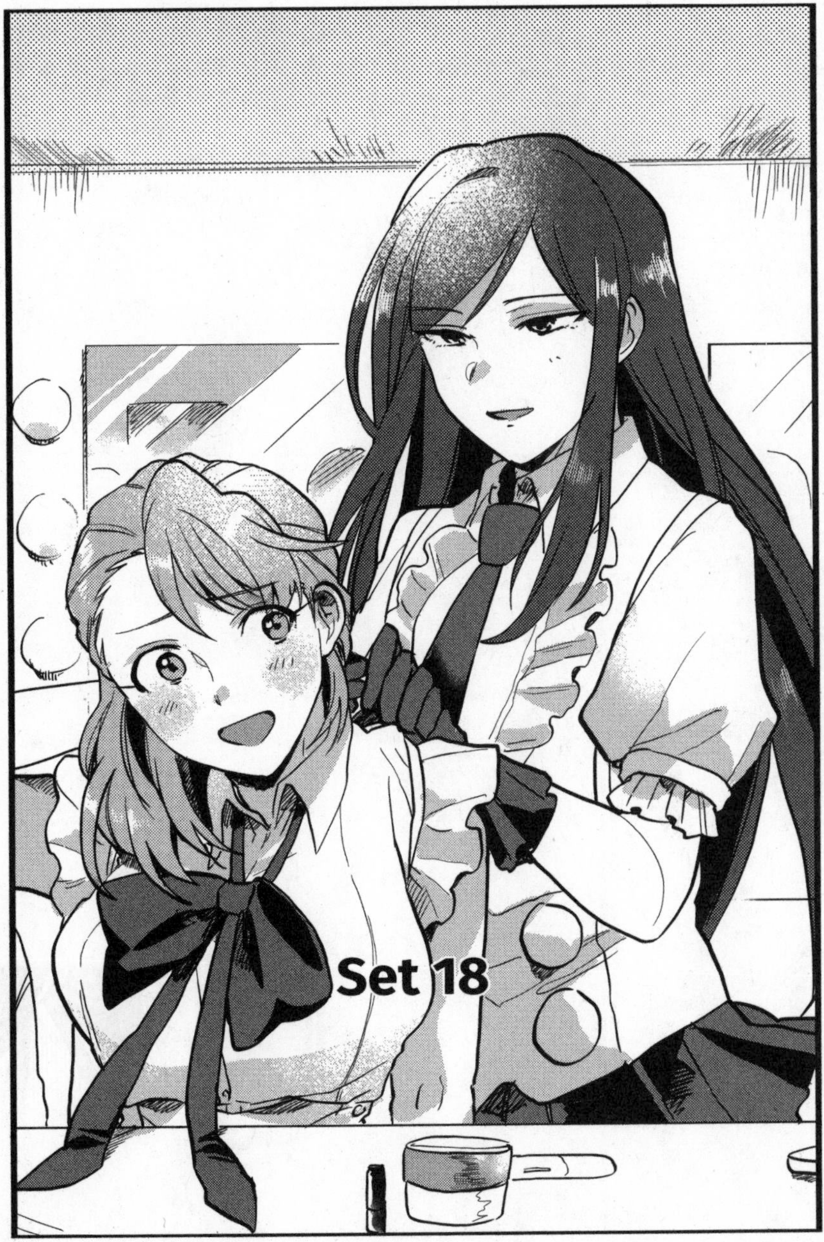
Set 18

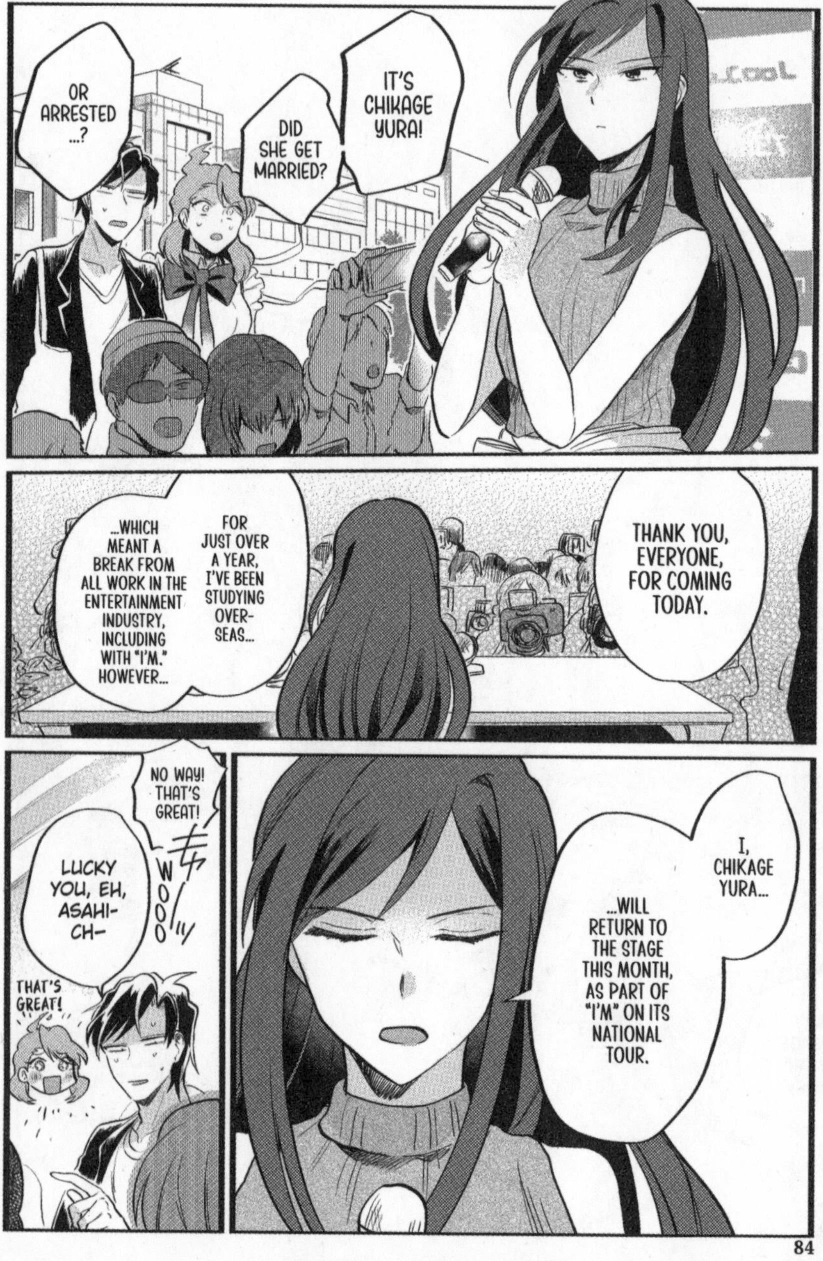
IT'S CHIKAGE YURA!
DID SHE GET MARRIED?
OR ARRESTED ...?
THANK YOU, EVERYONE, FOR COMING TODAY.
FOR JUST OVER A YEAR, I'VE BEEN STUDYING OVER-SEAS...
...WHICH MEANT A BREAK FROM ALL WORK IN THE ENTERTAINMENT INDUSTRY, INCLUDING WITH "I'M." HOWEVER...
I, CHIKAGE YURA...
...WILL RETURN TO THE STAGE THIS MONTH, AS PART OF "I'M" ON ITS NATIONAL TOUR.
NO WAY! THAT'S GREAT!
WOOOO!!
LUCKY YOU, EH, ASAHI-CH-
THAT'S GREAT!

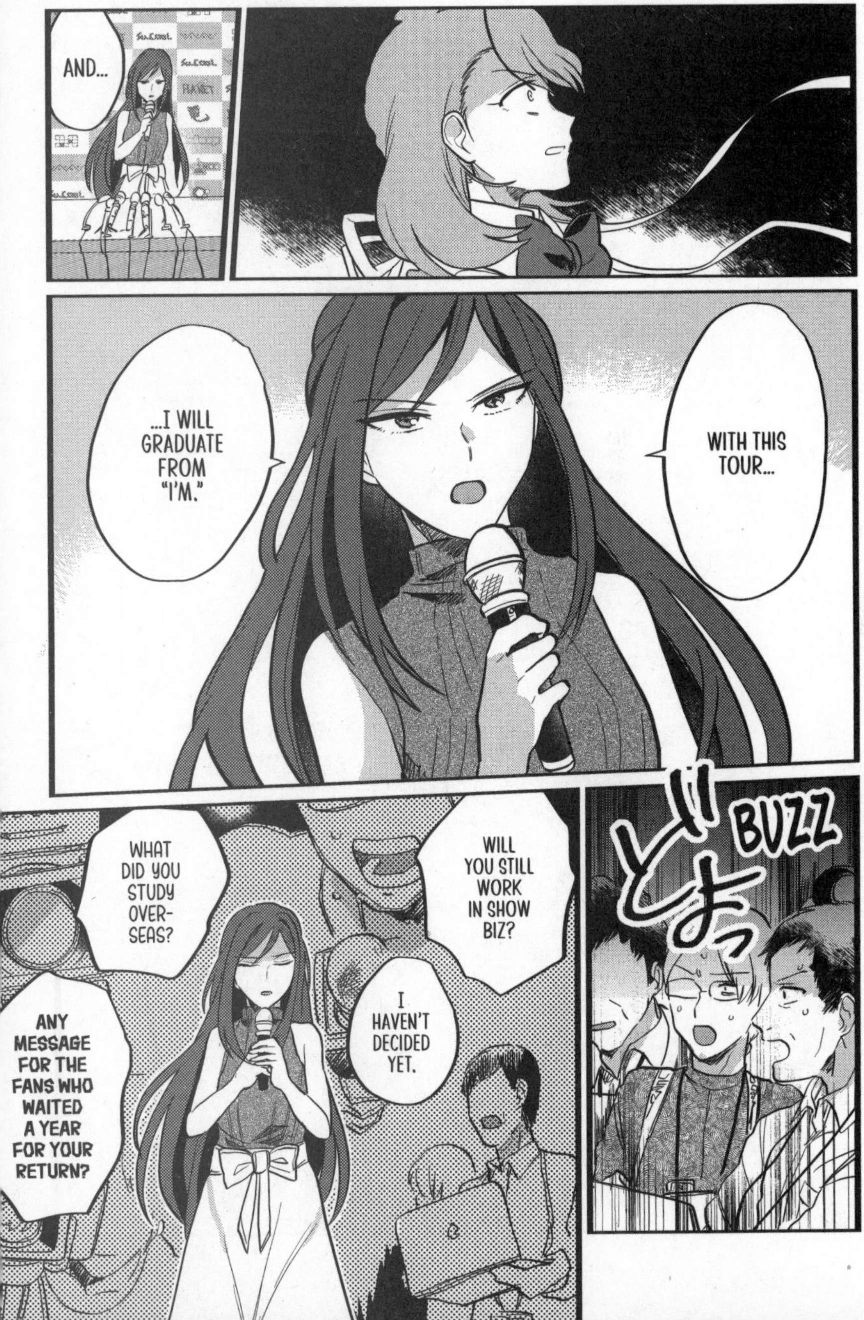
AND...
WITH THIS TOUR...
...I WILL GRADUATE FROM "I'M."
どよっ
BUZZ
WILL YOU STILL WORK IN SHOW BIZ?
WHAT DID YOU STUDY OVERSEAS?
I HAVEN'T DECIDED YET.
ANY MESSAGE FOR THE FANS WHO WAITED A YEAR FOR YOUR RETURN?

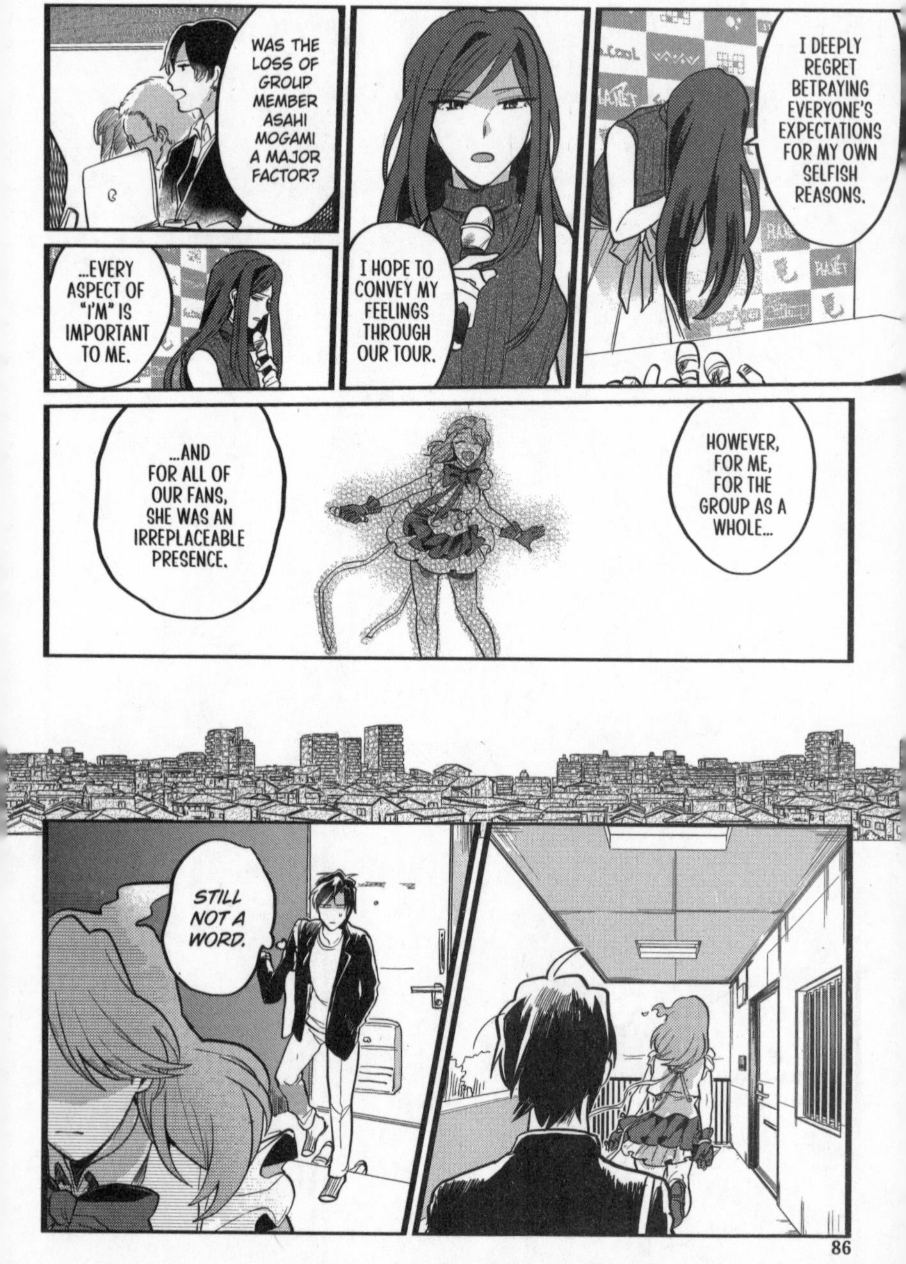
I DEEPLY REGRET BETRAYING EVERYONE'S EXPECTATIONS FOR MY OWN SELFISH REASONS.
I HOPE TO CONVEY MY FEELINGS THROUGH OUR TOUR.
WAS THE LOSS OF GROUP MEMBER ASAHI MOGAMI A MAJOR FACTOR?
...EVERY ASPECT OF "I'M" IS IMPORTANT TO ME.
HOWEVER, FOR ME, FOR THE GROUP AS A WHOLE...
...AND FOR ALL OF OUR FANS, SHE WAS AN IRREPLACEABLE PRESENCE.
STILL NOT A WORD.

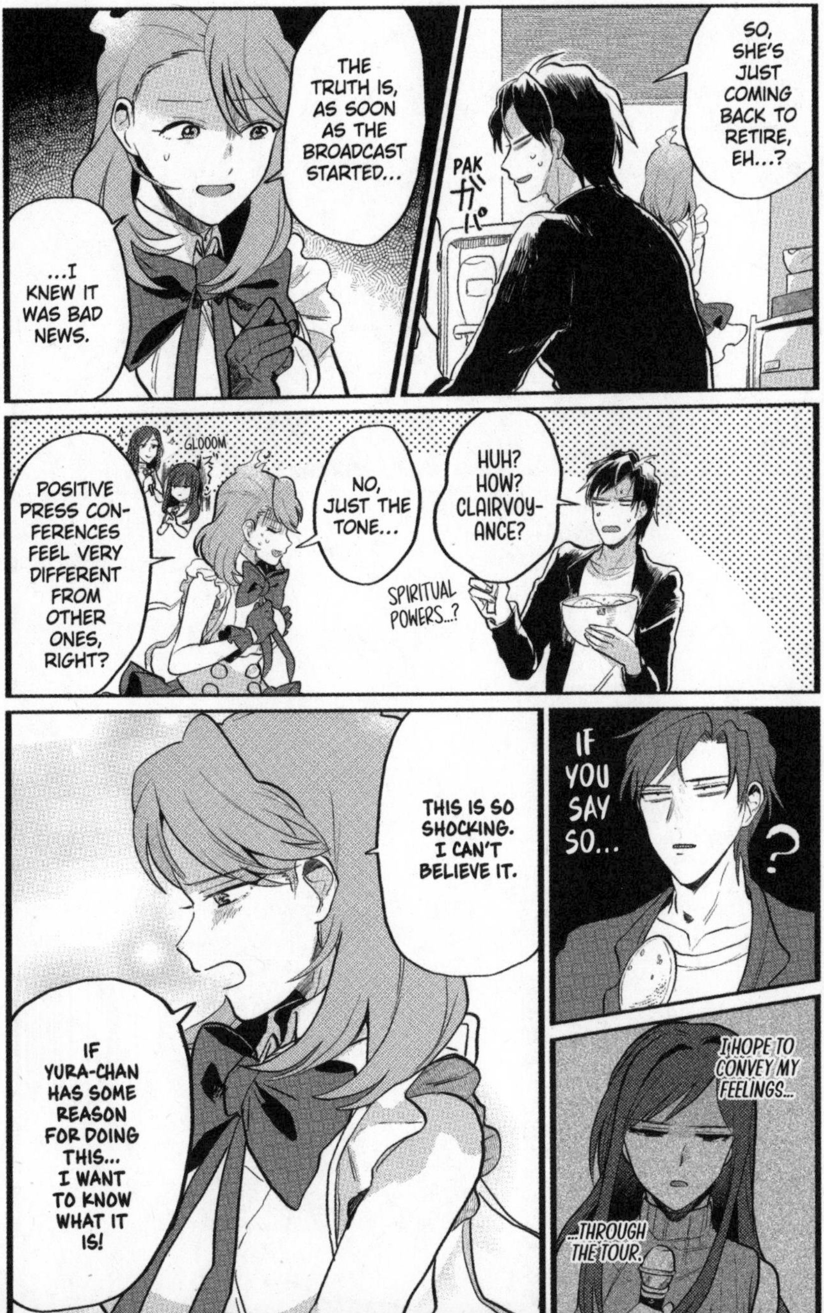
SO, SHE'S JUST COMING BACK TO RETIRE, EH...?
PAK
THE TRUTH IS, AS SOON AS THE BROADCAST STARTED...
...I KNEW IT WAS BAD NEWS.
HUH? HOW? CLAIRVOY-ANCE?
SPIRITUAL POWERS...?
NO, JUST THE TONE...
GLOOOM
POSITIVE PRESS CON-FERENCES FEEL VERY DIFFERENT FROM OTHER ONES, RIGHT?
IF YOU SAY SO...
?
I HOPE TO CONVEY MY FEELINGS...
...THROUGH THE TOUR.
THIS IS SO SHOCKING. I CAN'T BELIEVE IT.
IF YURA-CHAN HAS SOME REASON FOR DOING THIS... I WANT TO KNOW WHAT IT IS!

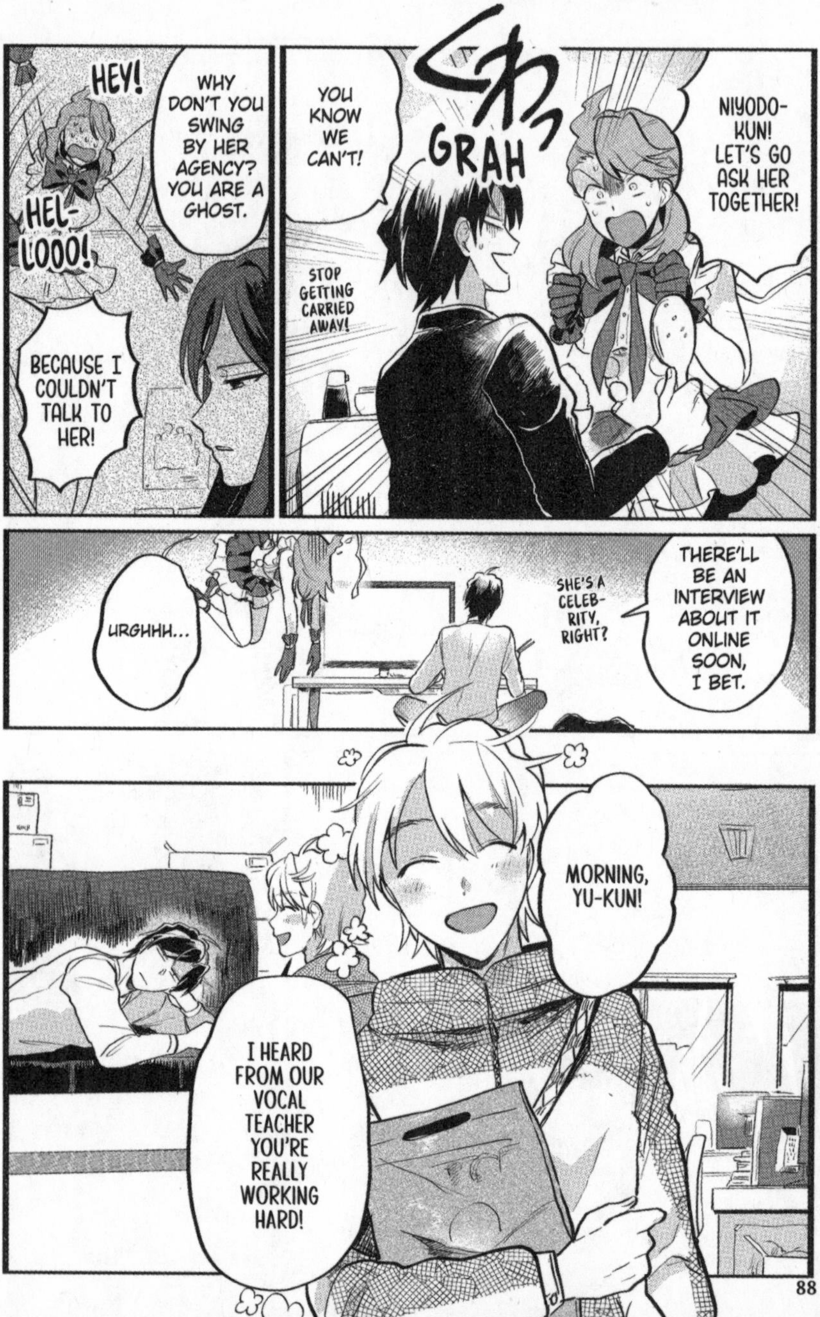
NIYODO-KUN! LET'S GO ASK HER TOGETHER!
くわっ
GRAH
YOU KNOW WE CAN'T!
STOP GETTING CARRIED AWAY!
WHY DON'T YOU SWING BY HER AGENCY? YOU ARE A GHOST.
HEY!
HEL-LOOO!
BECAUSE I COULDN'T TALK TO HER!
THERE'LL BE AN INTERVIEW ABOUT IT ONLINE SOON, I BET.
SHE'S A CELEB-RITY, RIGHT?
URGHHH...
MORNING, YU-KUN!
I HEARD FROM OUR VOCAL TEACHER YOU'RE REALLY WORKING HARD!

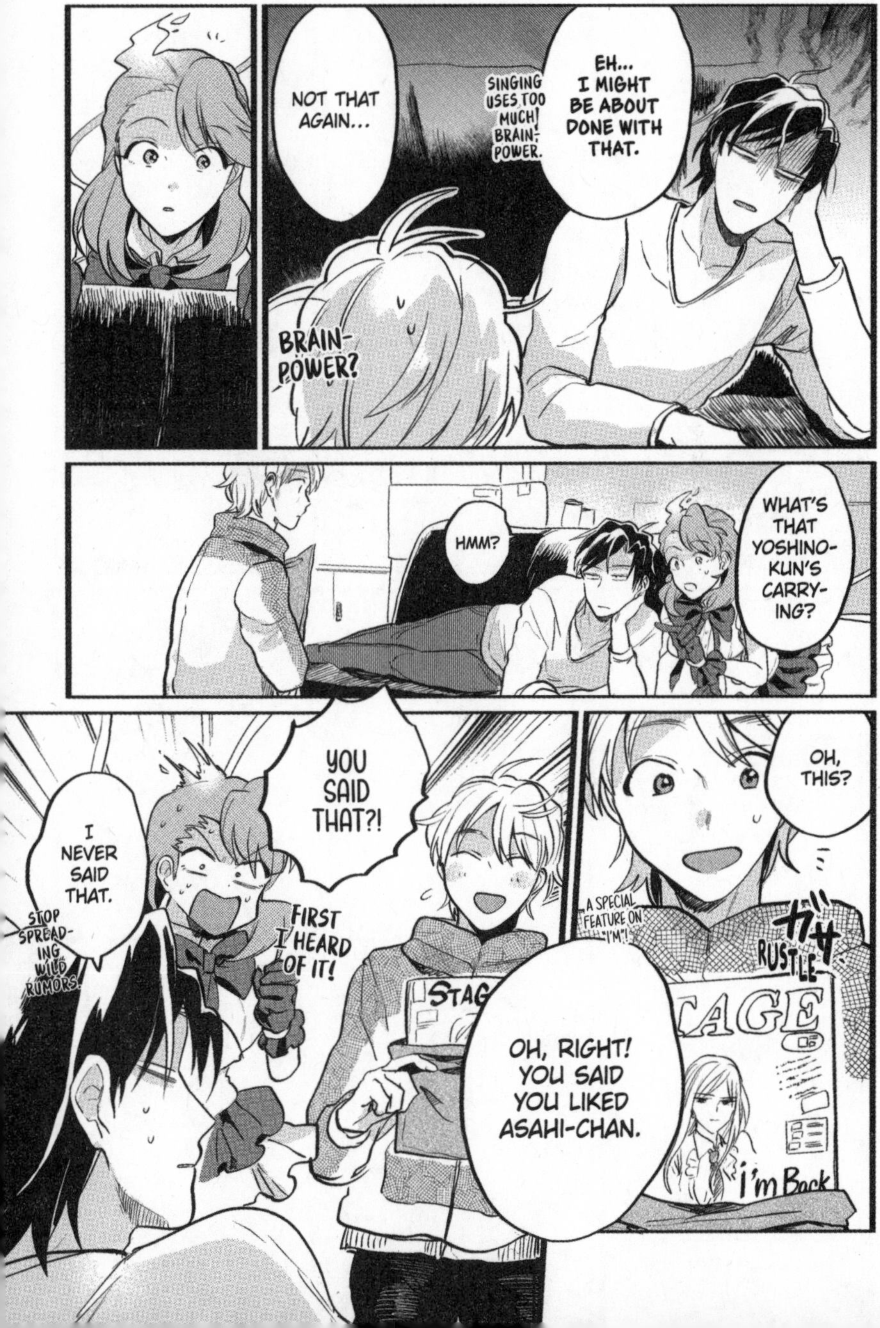
EH... I MIGHT BE ABOUT DONE WITH THAT.
SINGING USES TOO MUCH! BRAIN-POWER.
NOT THAT AGAIN...
BRAIN-POWER?
WHAT'S THAT YOSHINO-KUN'S CARRYING?
HMM?
OH, THIS?
A SPECIAL FEATURE ON "I'M"!
RUSTLE
I'm Back
OH, RIGHT! YOU SAID YOU LIKED ASAHI-CHAN.
YOU SAID THAT?!
FIRST I HEARD OF IT!
I NEVER SAID THAT.
STOP SPREADING WILD RUMORS.

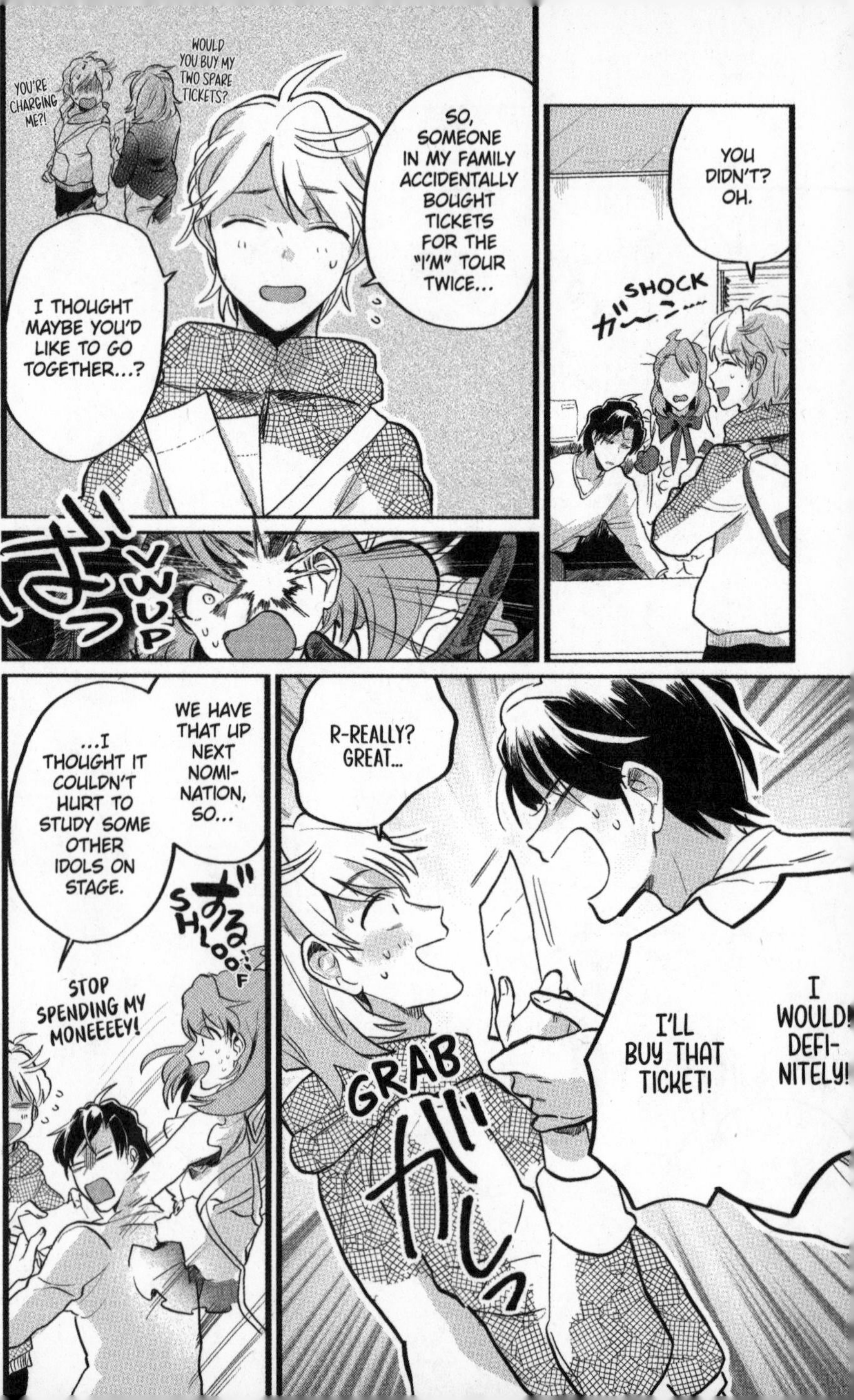
YOU DIDN'T? OH.
SHOCK
SO, SOMEONE IN MY FAMILY ACCIDENTALLY BOUGHT TICKETS FOR THE "I'M" TOUR TWICE...
WOULD YOU BUY MY TWO SPARE TICKETS?
YOU'RE CHARGING ME?!
I THOUGHT MAYBE YOU'D LIKE TO GO TOGETHER...?
VWUP
I WOULD! DEFI-NITELY!
I'LL BUY THAT TICKET!
R-REALLY? GREAT...
GRAB
WE HAVE THAT UP NEXT NOMI-NATION, SO...
...I THOUGHT IT COULDN'T HURT TO STUDY SOME OTHER IDOLS ON STAGE.
SHLOOF
STOP SPENDING MY MONEEEEY!

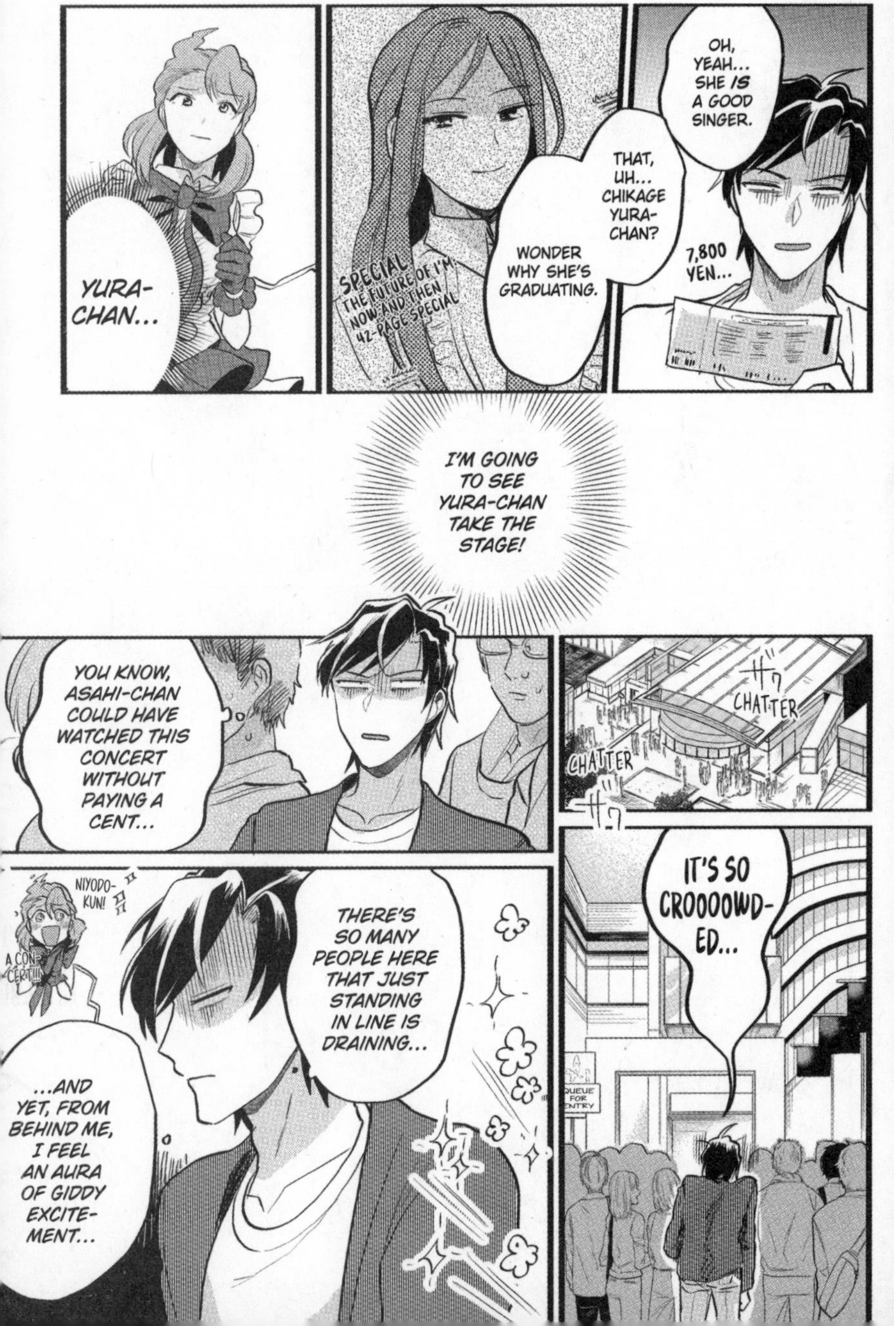
OH, YEAH... SHE *IS* A GOOD SINGER.
THAT, UH... CHIKAGE YURA-CHAN?
7,800 YEN...
WONDER WHY SHE'S GRADUATING.
SPECIAL THE FUTURE OF I'M NOW AND THEN 42-PAGE SPECIAL
YURA-CHAN...
I'M GOING TO SEE YURA-CHAN TAKE THE STAGE!
CHATTER
CHATTER
YOU KNOW, ASAHI-CHAN COULD HAVE WATCHED THIS CONCERT WITHOUT PAYING A CENT...
IT'S SO CROOOOWD-ED...
QUEUE FOR ENTRY
THERE'S SO MANY PEOPLE HERE THAT JUST STANDING IN LINE IS DRAINING...
NIYODO-KUN!
A CON-CERT!!!
...AND YET, FROM BEHIND ME, I FEEL AN AURA OF GIDDY EXCITE-MENT...

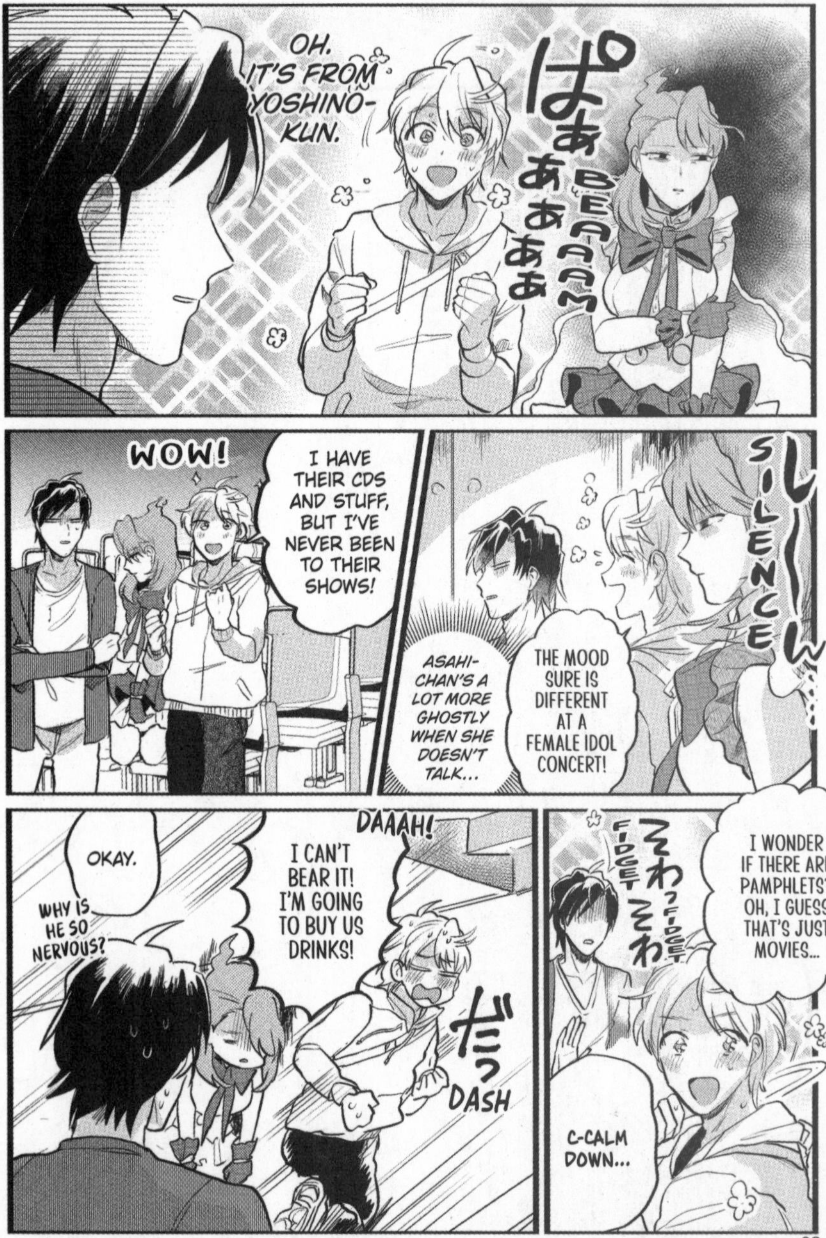
OH. IT'S FROM YOSHINO-KUN.
ぱあああああ
BEAAAM
しーん
SILENCE
THE MOOD SURE IS DIFFERENT AT A FEMALE IDOL CONCERT!
ASAHI-CHAN'S A LOT MORE GHOSTLY WHEN SHE DOESN'T TALK...
I HAVE THEIR CDS AND STUFF, BUT I'VE NEVER BEEN TO THEIR SHOWS!
WOW!
I WONDER IF THERE ARE PAMPHLETS? OH, I GUESS THAT'S JUST MOVIES...
そわっそわ
FIDGET FIDGET
C-CALM DOWN...
DAAAH!
I CAN'T BEAR IT! I'M GOING TO BUY US DRINKS!
だっ
DASH
OKAY.
WHY IS HE SO NERVOUS?

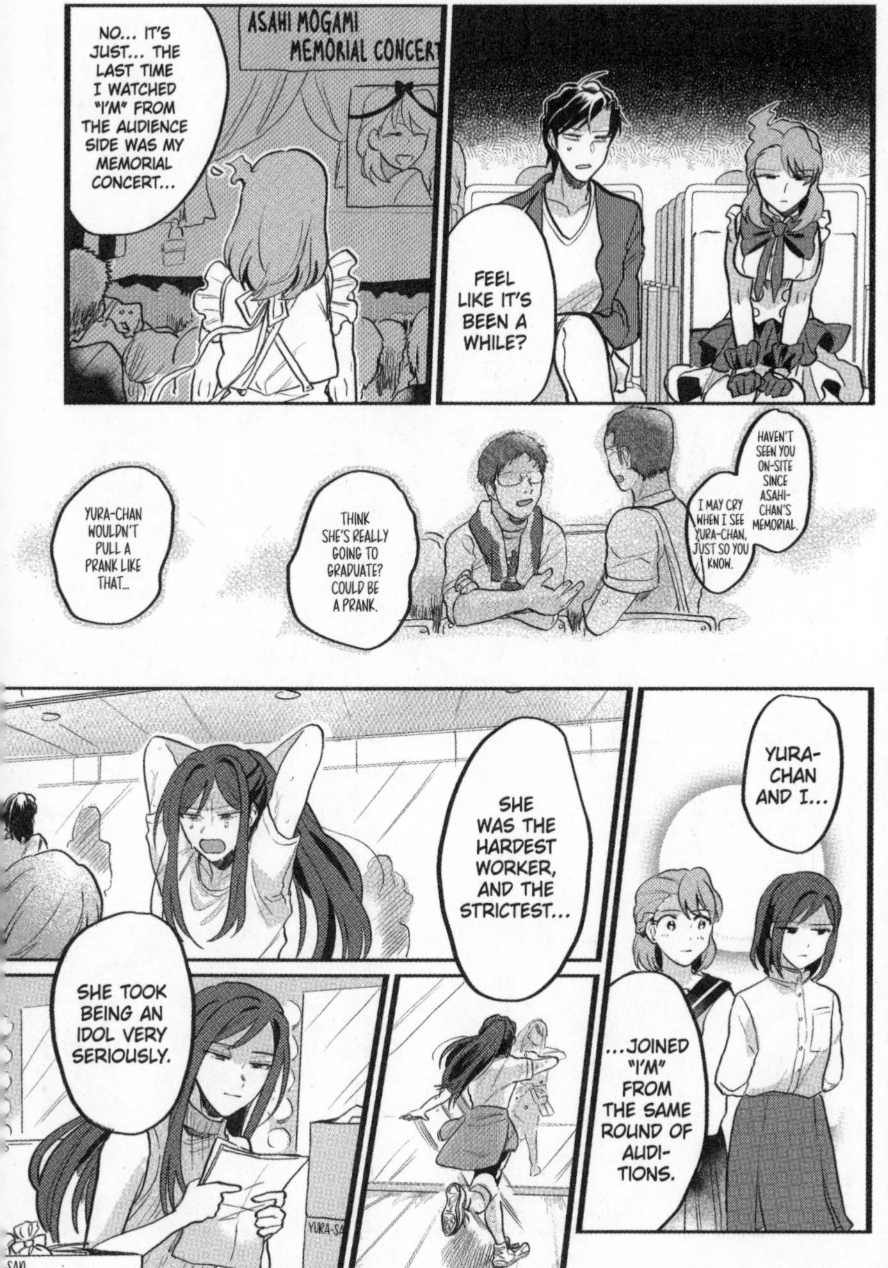

FEEL LIKE IT'S BEEN A WHILE?
ASAHI MOGAMI MEMORIAL CONCERT
NO... IT'S JUST... THE LAST TIME I WATCHED "I'M" FROM THE AUDIENCE SIDE WAS MY MEMORIAL CONCERT...
HAVEN'T SEEN YOU ON-SITE SINCE ASAHI-CHAN'S MEMORIAL.
I MAY CRY WHEN I SEE YURA-CHAN, JUST SO YOU KNOW.
THINK SHE'S REALLY GOING TO GRADUATE? COULD BE A PRANK.
YURA-CHAN WOULDN'T PULL A PRANK LIKE THAT...
YURA-CHAN AND I...
...JOINED "I'M" FROM THE SAME ROUND OF AUDI-TIONS.
SHE WAS THE HARDEST WORKER, AND THE STRICTEST...
SHE TOOK BEING AN IDOL VERY SERIOUSLY.

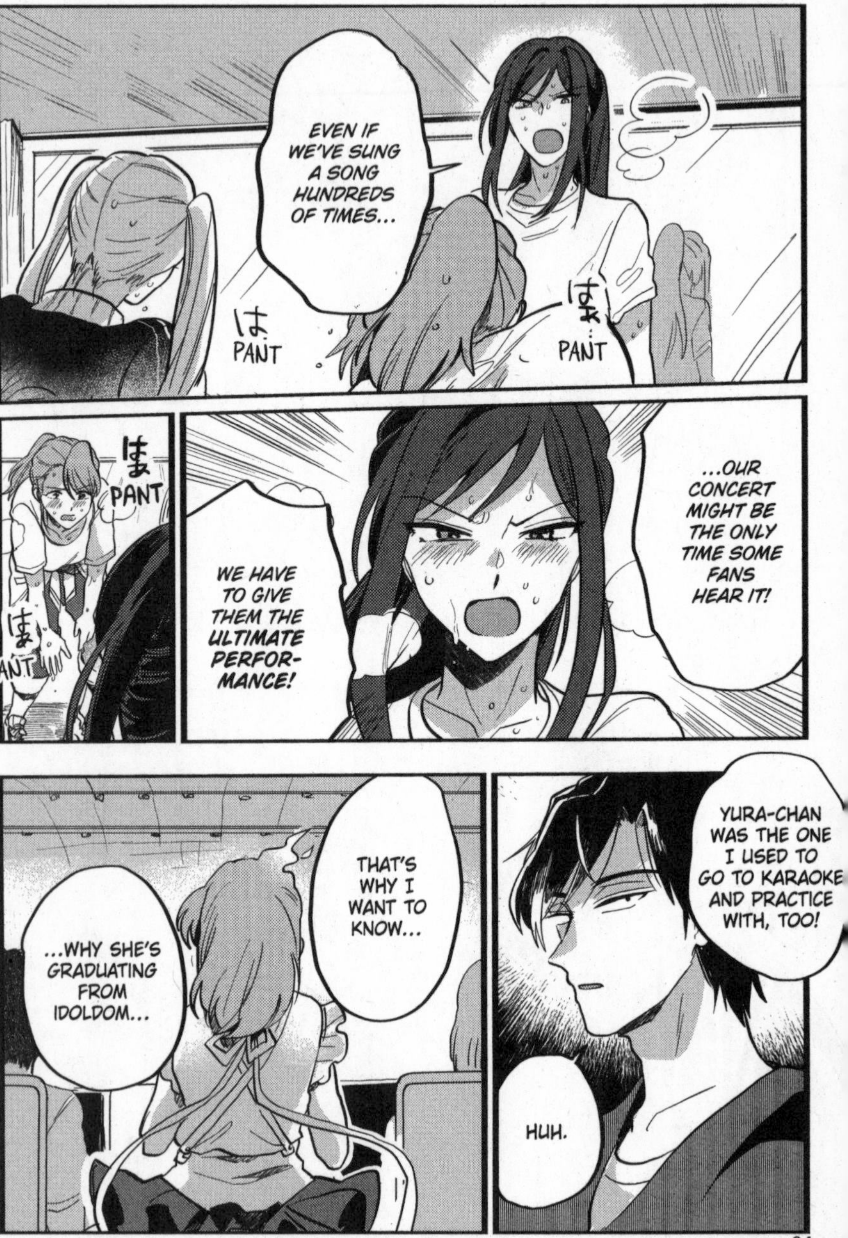
EVEN IF WE'VE SUNG A SONG HUNDREDS OF TIMES...
はぁ PANT
は PANT
...OUR CONCERT MIGHT BE THE ONLY TIME SOME FANS HEAR IT!
WE HAVE TO GIVE THEM THE ULTIMATE PERFORMANCE!
はぁ PANT
はぁ PANT
YURA-CHAN WAS THE ONE I USED TO GO TO KARAOKE AND PRACTICE WITH, TOO!
HUH.
THAT'S WHY I WANT TO KNOW...
...WHY SHE'S GRADUATING FROM IDOLDOM...

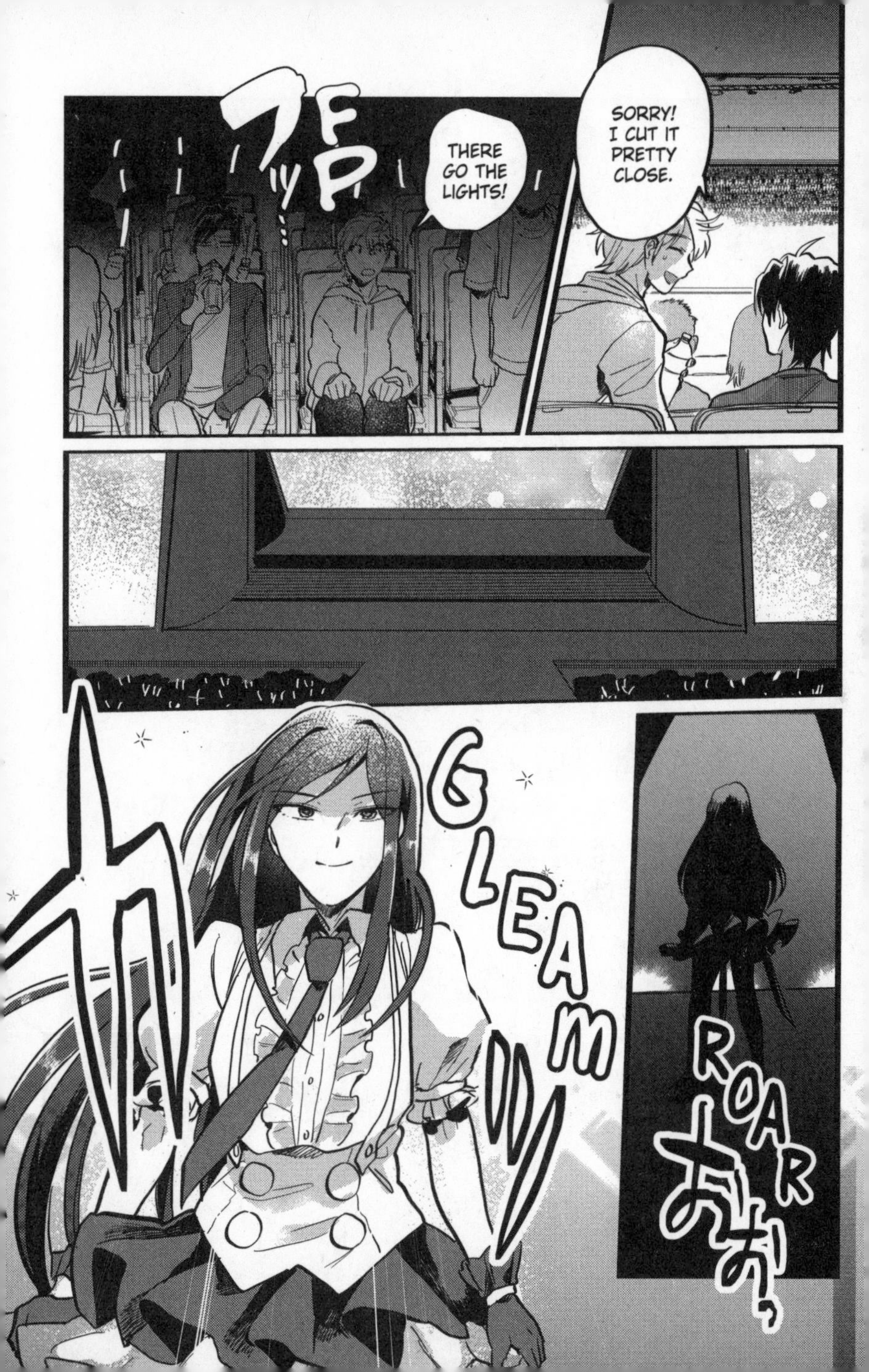
SORRY! I CUT IT PRETTY CLOSE.
FP
THERE GO THE LIGHTS!
ROAR
GLEAM

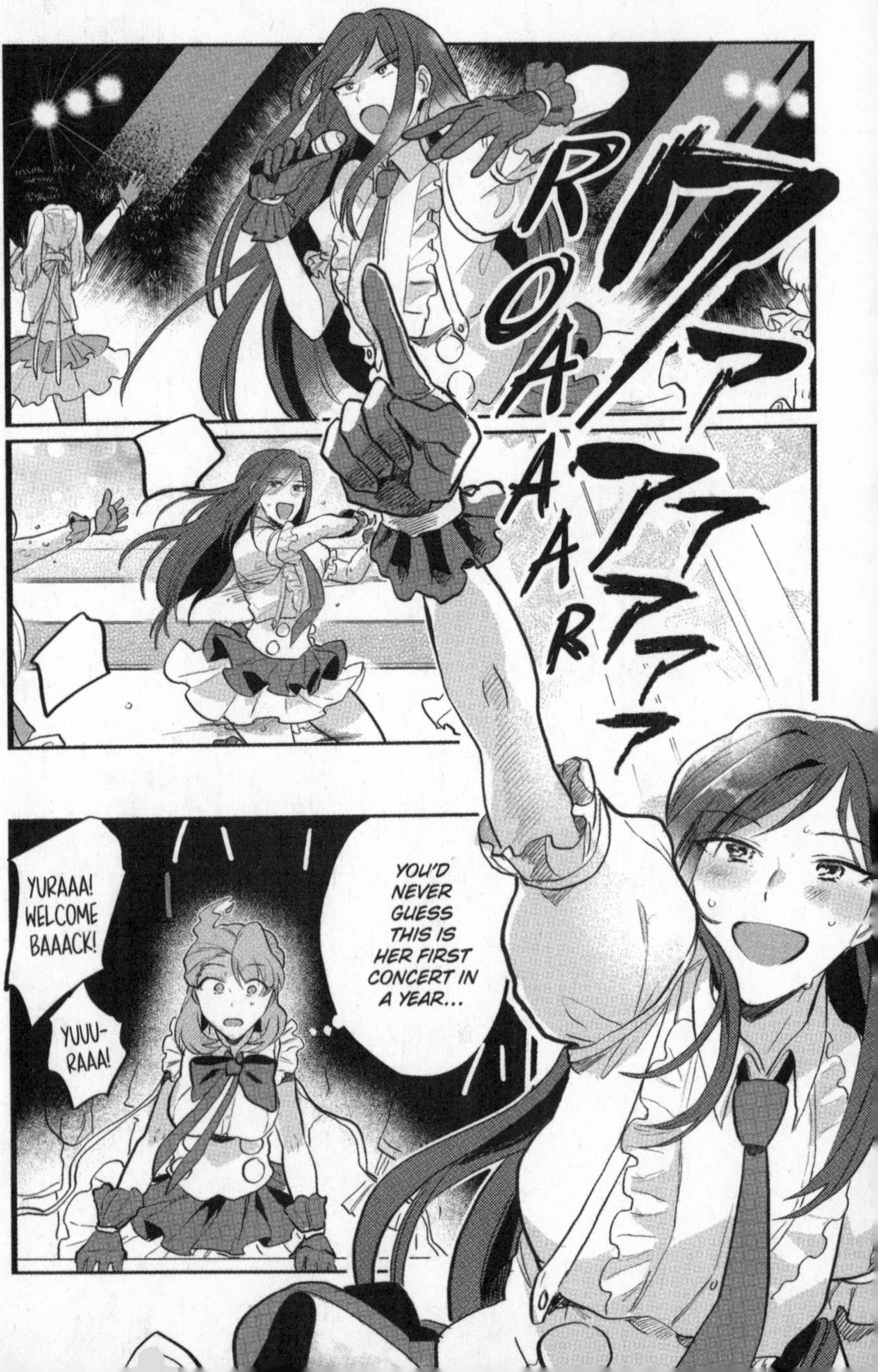
ROAAAR
YOU'D NEVER GUESS THIS IS HER FIRST CONCERT IN A YEAR...
YURAAA! WELCOME BAAACK!
YUUU-RAAA!

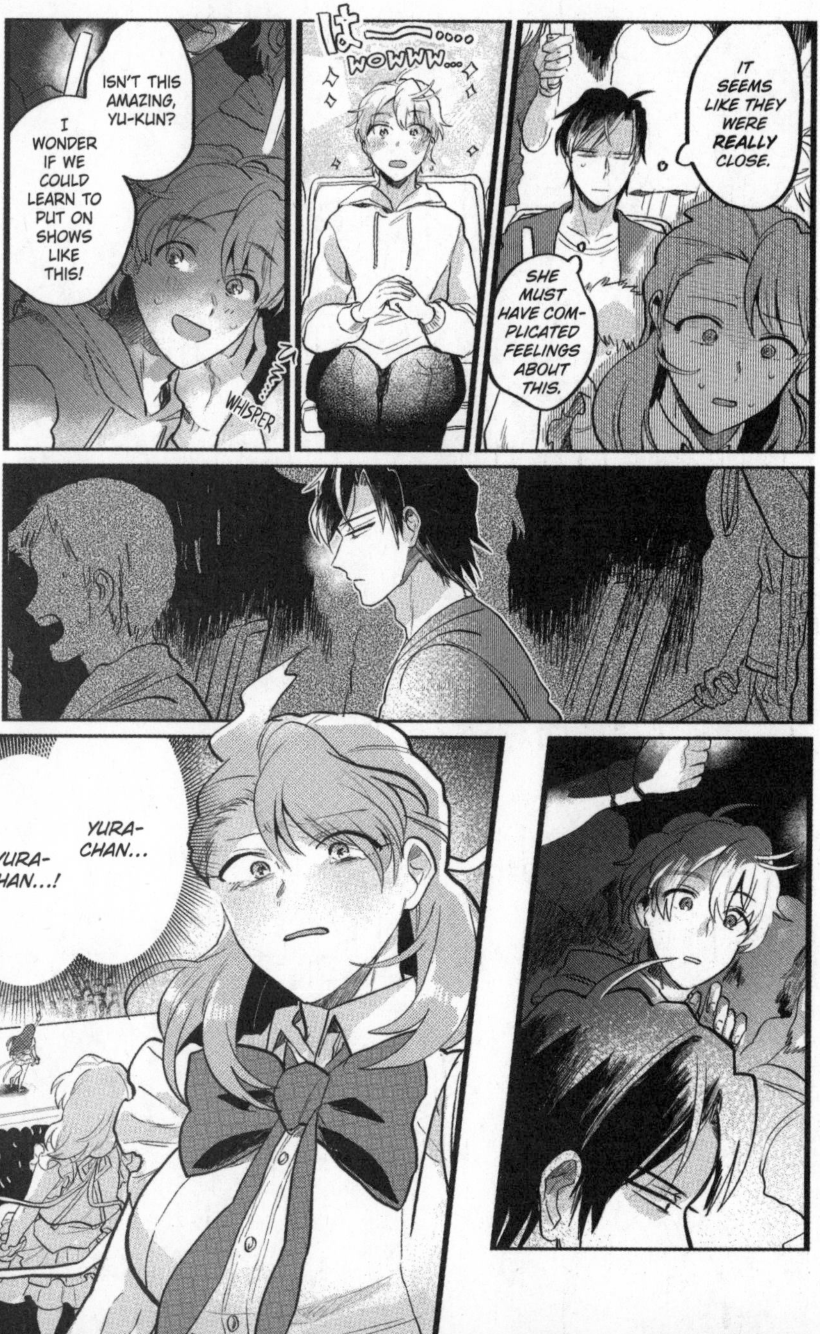
IT SEEMS LIKE THEY WERE **REALLY** CLOSE.
SHE MUST HAVE COMPLICATED FEELINGS ABOUT THIS.
はーーoooo
WOWWW...
ISN'T THIS AMAZING, YU-KUN?
I WONDER IF WE COULD LEARN TO PUT ON SHOWS LIKE THIS!
WHISPER
YURA-CHAN...
YURA-CHAN...!

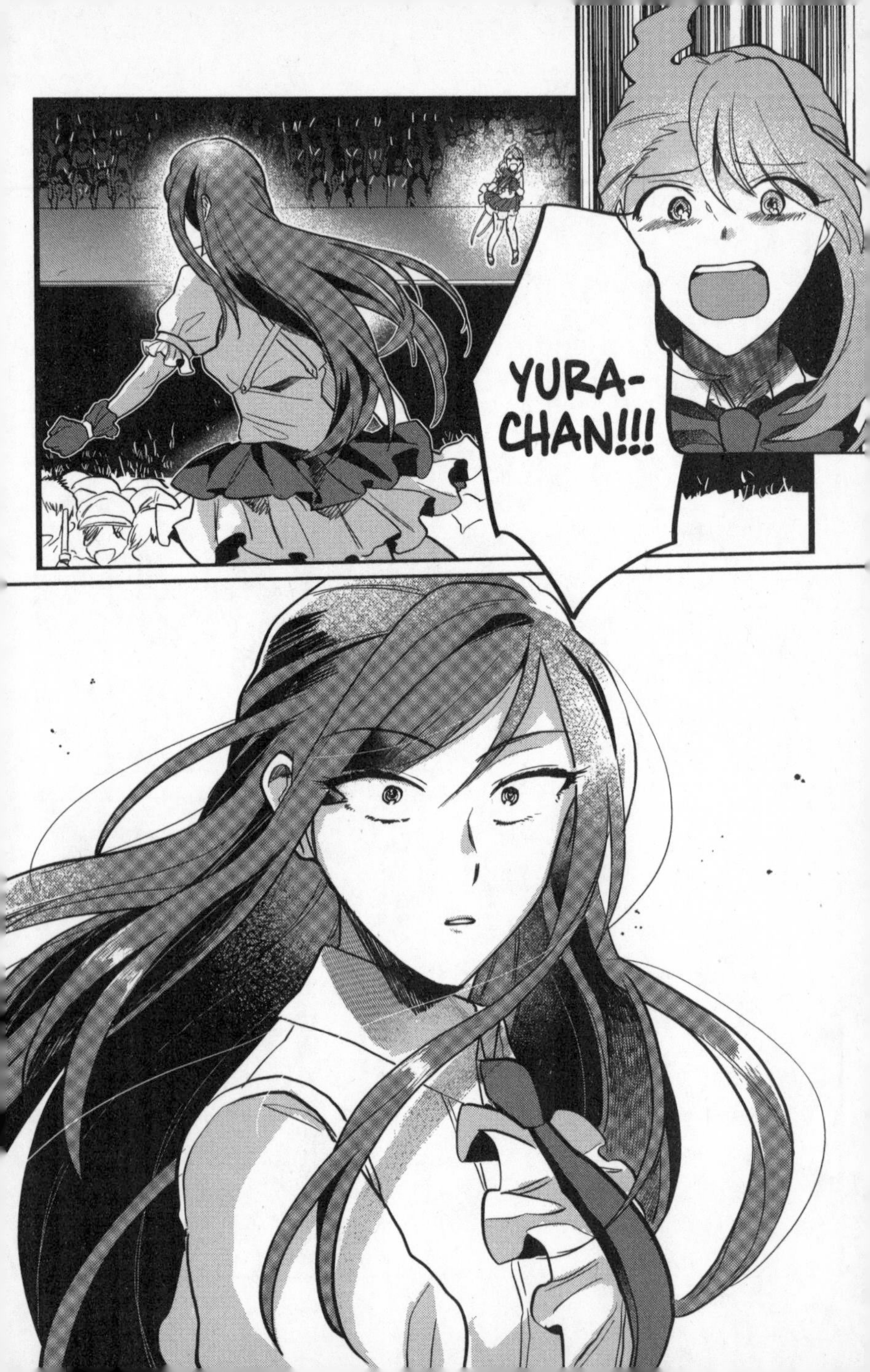
YURA-
CHAN!!!!

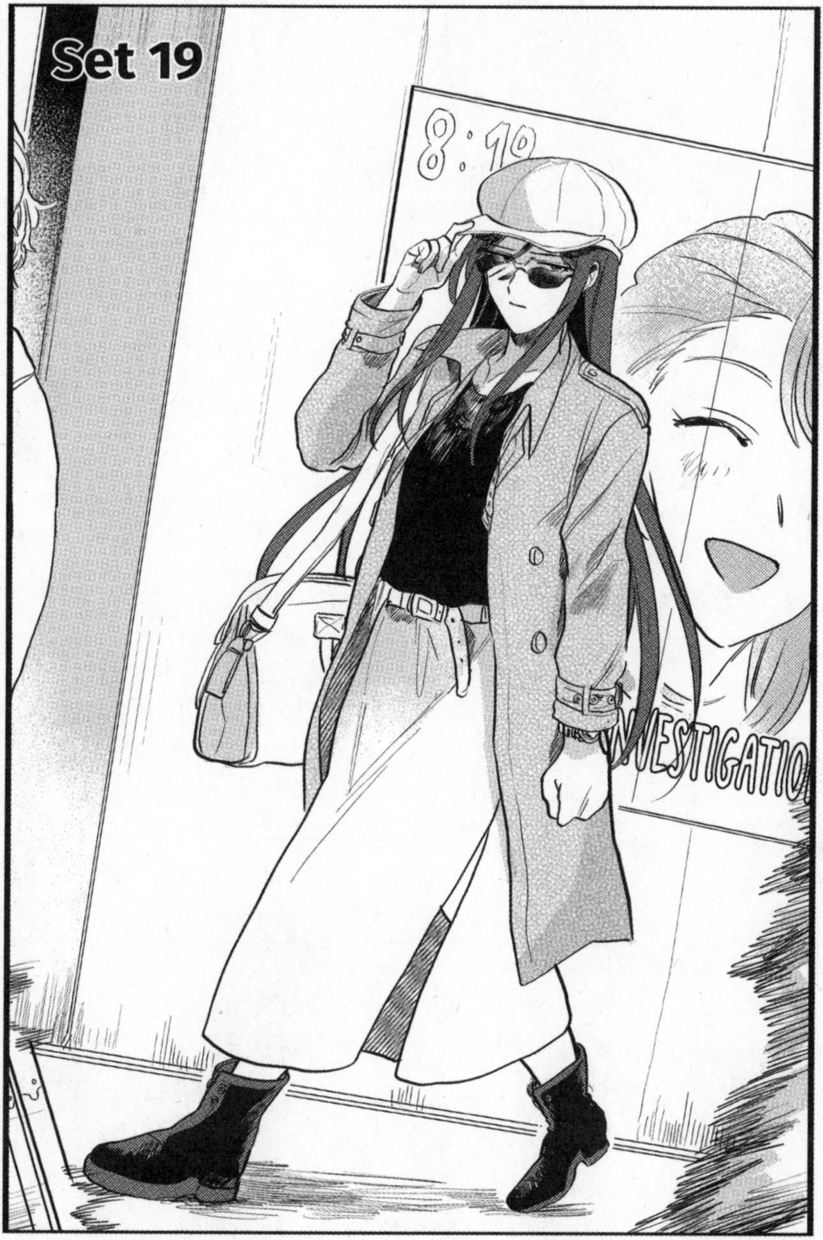
Set 19

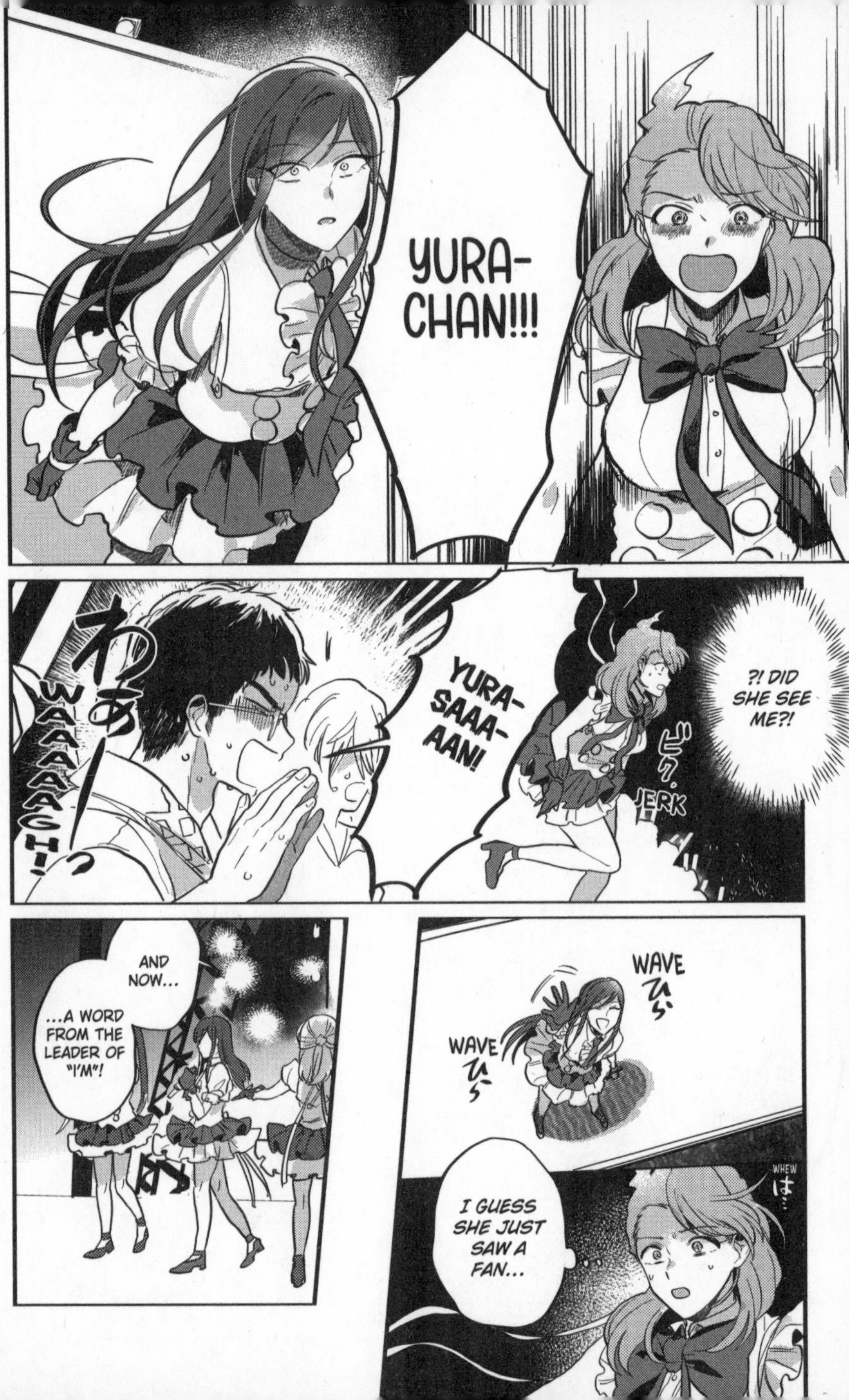
YURA-CHAN!!!
?! DID SHE SEE ME?!
ビク。
JERK
YURA-SAAAA-AAN!
わあ！！
WAAAAAAAGH!!
WAVE ひら
WAVE ひら
はぁ…
WHEW
I GUESS SHE JUST SAW A FAN...
AND NOW...
...A WORD FROM THE LEADER OF "I'M"!

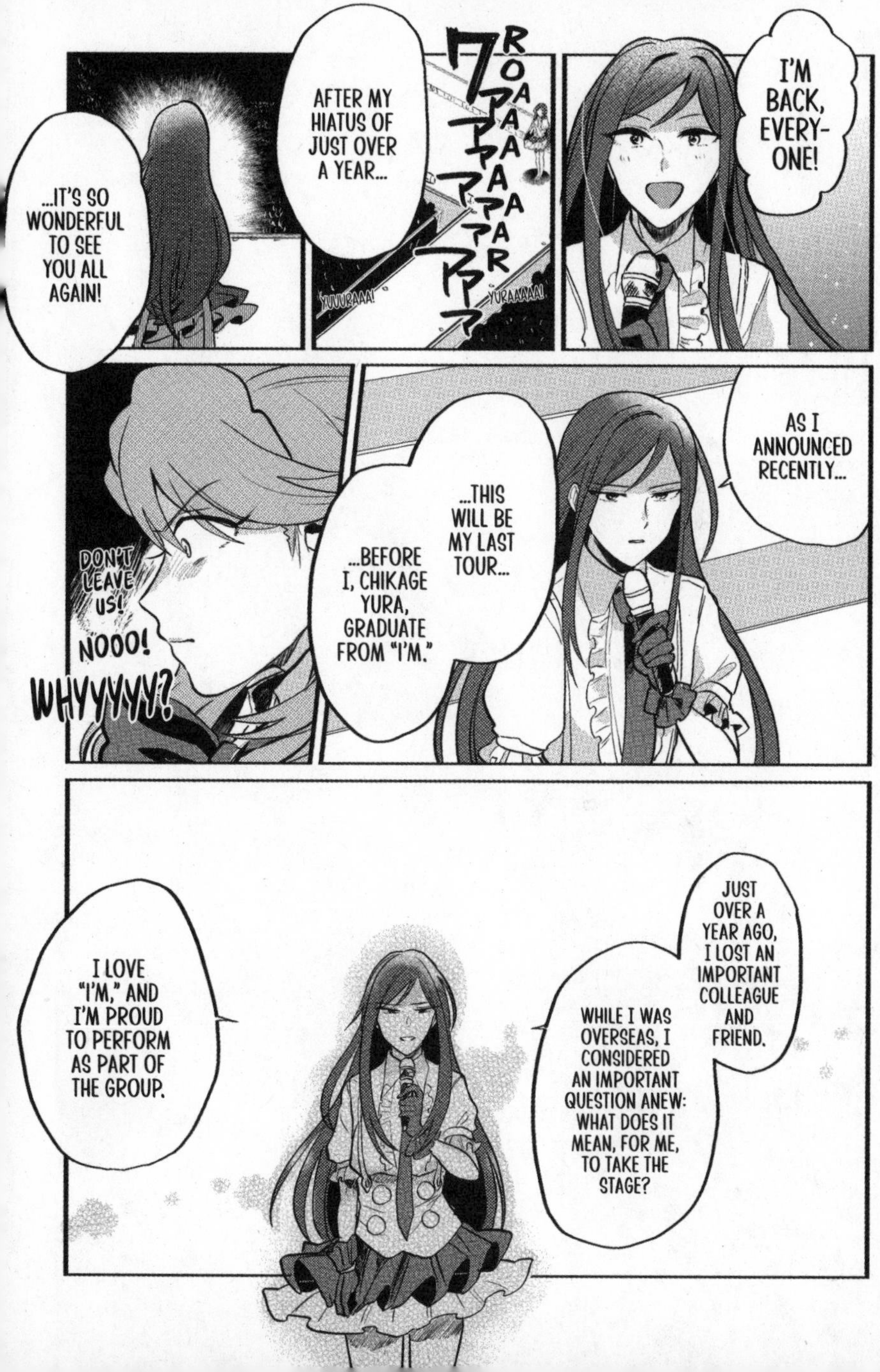
I'M BACK, EVERY-ONE!
ROAAAAAAR
AFTER MY HIATUS OF JUST OVER A YEAR...
YURAAAAA!
YUUURAAA!
...IT'S SO WONDERFUL TO SEE YOU ALL AGAIN!
AS I ANNOUNCED RECENTLY...
...THIS WILL BE MY LAST TOUR...
...BEFORE I, CHIKAGE YURA, GRADUATE FROM "I'M."
DON'T LEAVE US!
NOOO!
WHYYYYY?
JUST OVER A YEAR AGO, I LOST AN IMPORTANT COLLEAGUE AND FRIEND.
WHILE I WAS OVERSEAS, I CONSIDERED AN IMPORTANT QUESTION ANEW: WHAT DOES IT MEAN, FOR ME, TO TAKE THE STAGE?
I LOVE "I'M," AND I'M PROUD TO PERFORM AS PART OF THE GROUP.

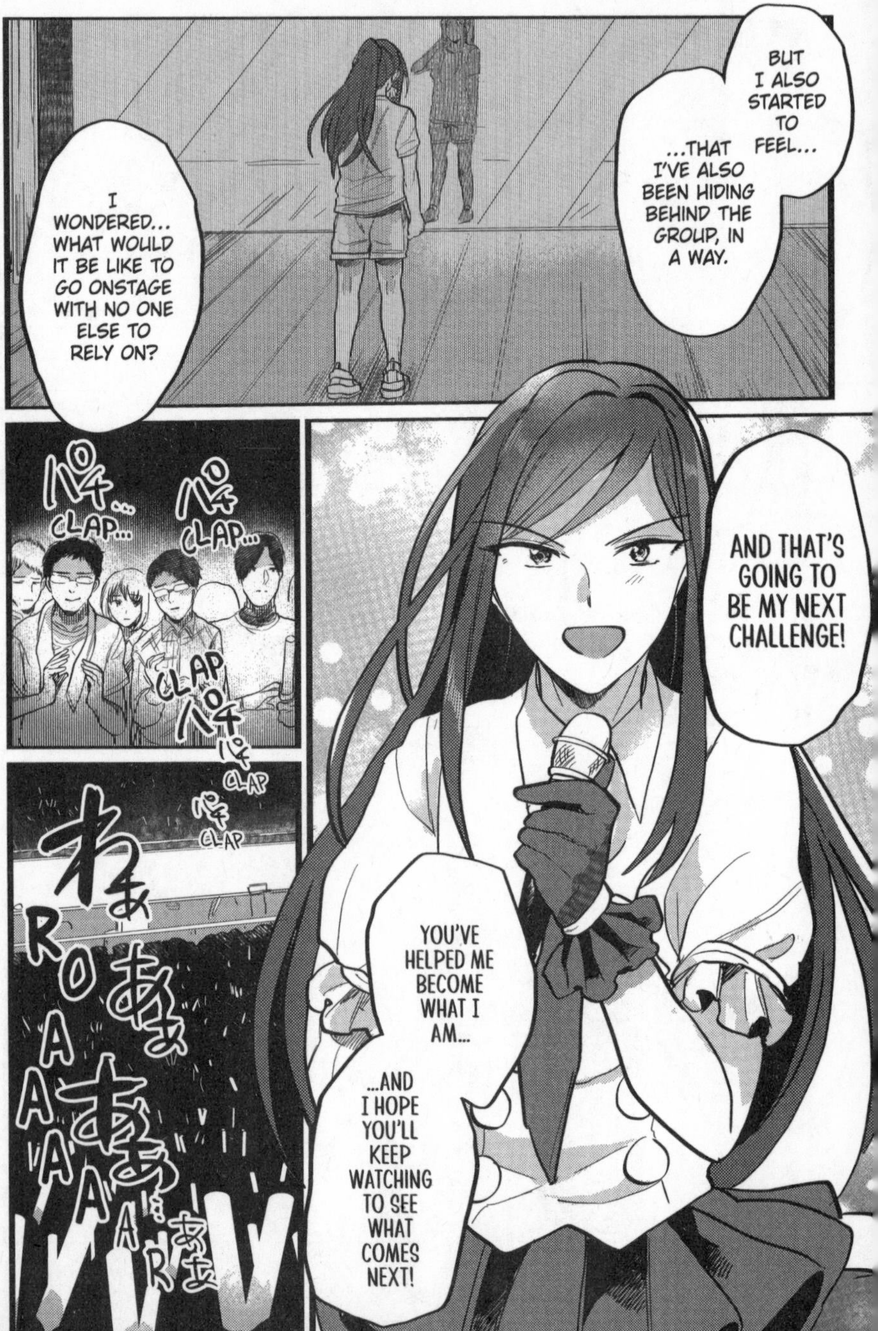
BUT I ALSO STARTED TO FEEL...
...THAT I'VE ALSO BEEN HIDING BEHIND THE GROUP, IN A WAY.
I WONDERED... WHAT WOULD IT BE LIKE TO GO ONSTAGE WITH NO ONE ELSE TO RELY ON?
AND THAT'S GOING TO BE MY NEXT CHALLENGE!
YOU'VE HELPED ME BECOME WHAT I AM...
...AND I HOPE YOU'LL KEEP WATCHING TO SEE WHAT COMES NEXT!
パチ… CLAP...
パチ… CLAP...
パチ CLAP
パチ CLAP
パチ CLAP
わあああ ROAAAAAR

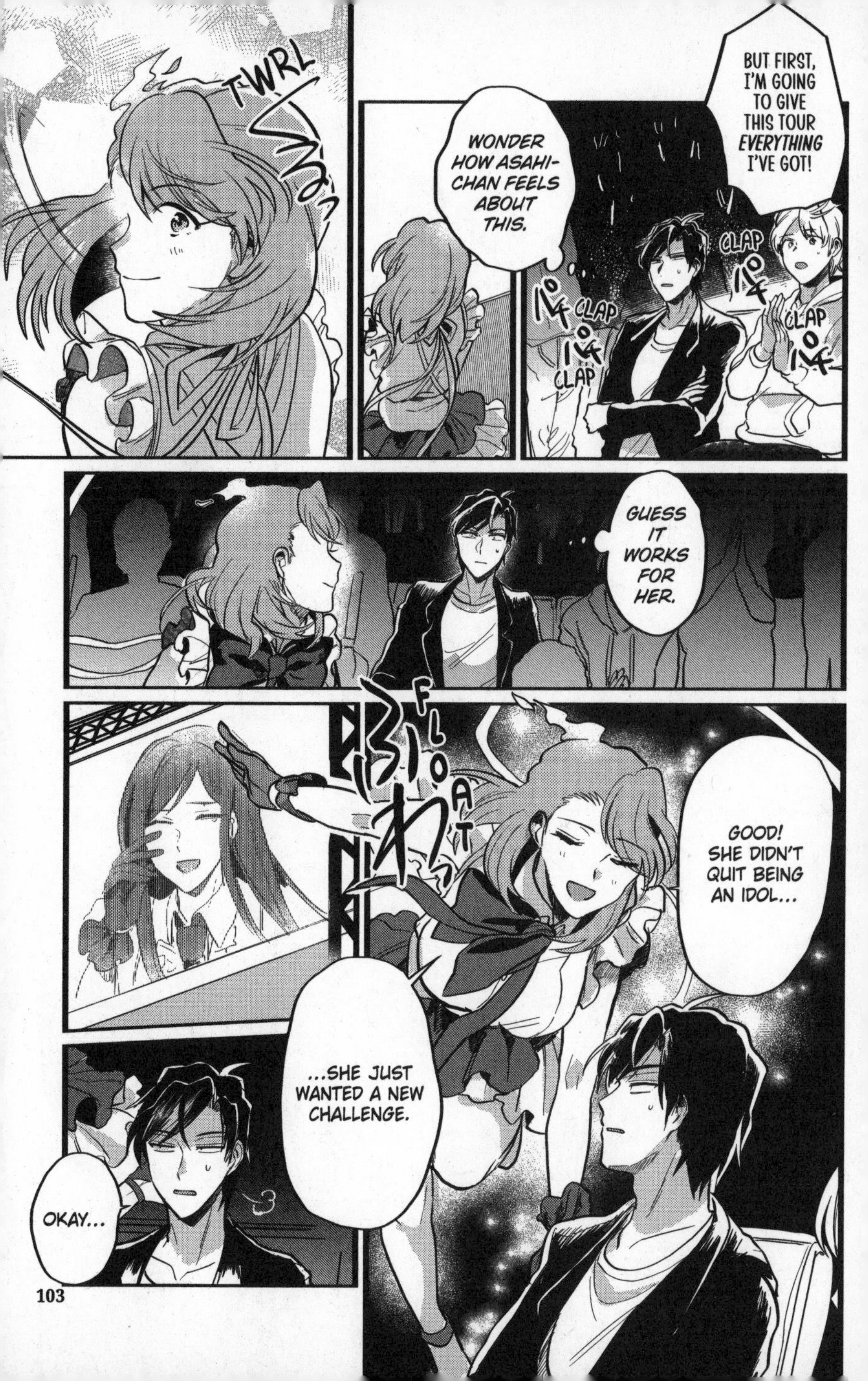
BUT FIRST, I'M GOING TO GIVE THIS TOUR *EVERYTHING* I'VE GOT!
CLAP CLAP
CLAP CLAP
WONDER HOW ASAHI-CHAN FEELS ABOUT THIS.
TWRL
GUESS IT WORKS FOR HER.
FLOAT
GOOD! SHE DIDN'T QUIT BEING AN IDOL...
...SHE JUST WANTED A NEW CHALLENGE.
OKAY...

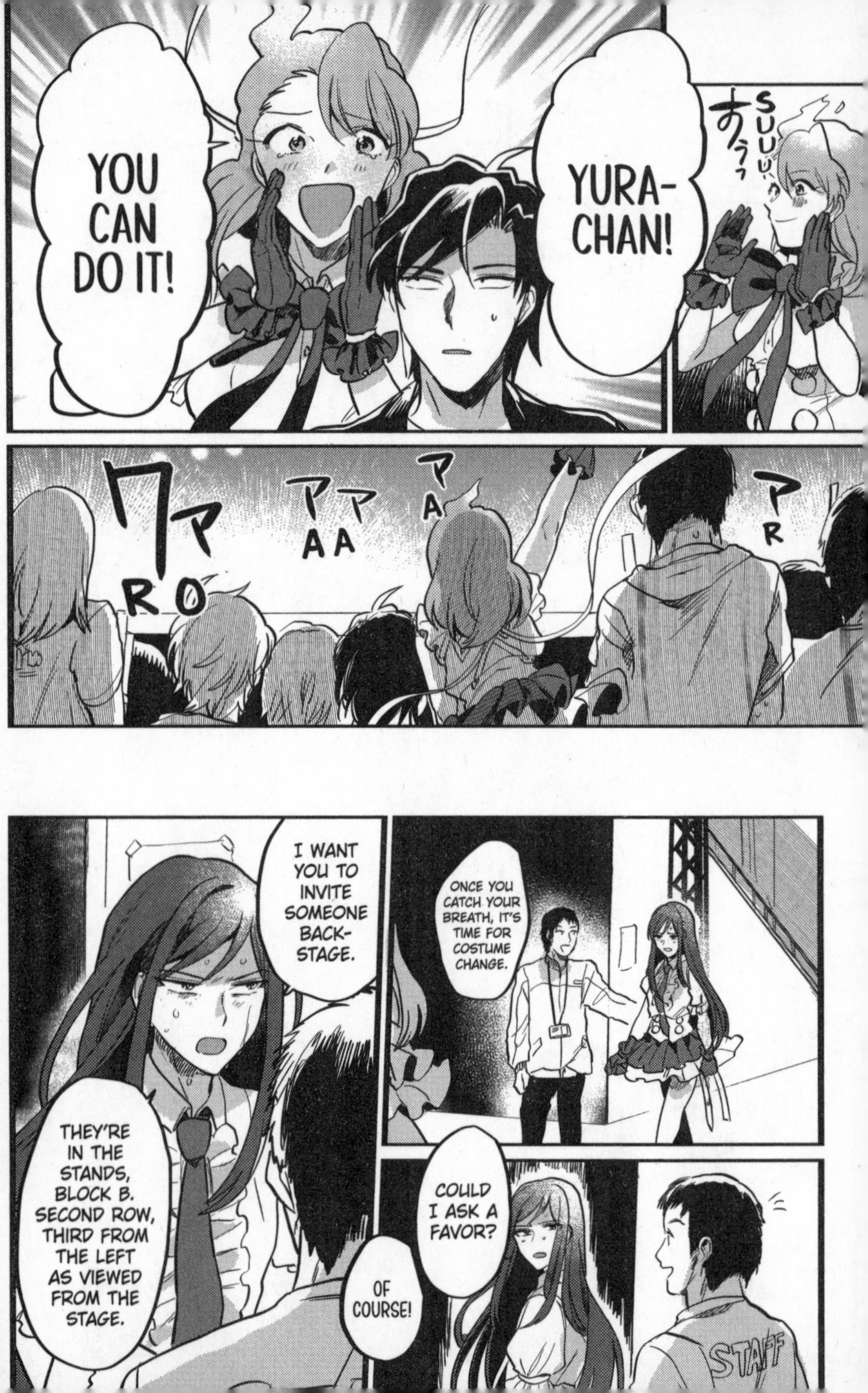
SUUU
YURA-CHAN!
YOU CAN DO IT!
R
A
AA
RO
ONCE YOU CATCH YOUR BREATH, IT'S TIME FOR COSTUME CHANGE.
COULD I ASK A FAVOR?
OF COURSE!
STAFF
I WANT YOU TO INVITE SOMEONE BACK-STAGE.
THEY'RE IN THE STANDS, BLOCK B. SECOND ROW, THIRD FROM THE LEFT AS VIEWED FROM THE STAGE.

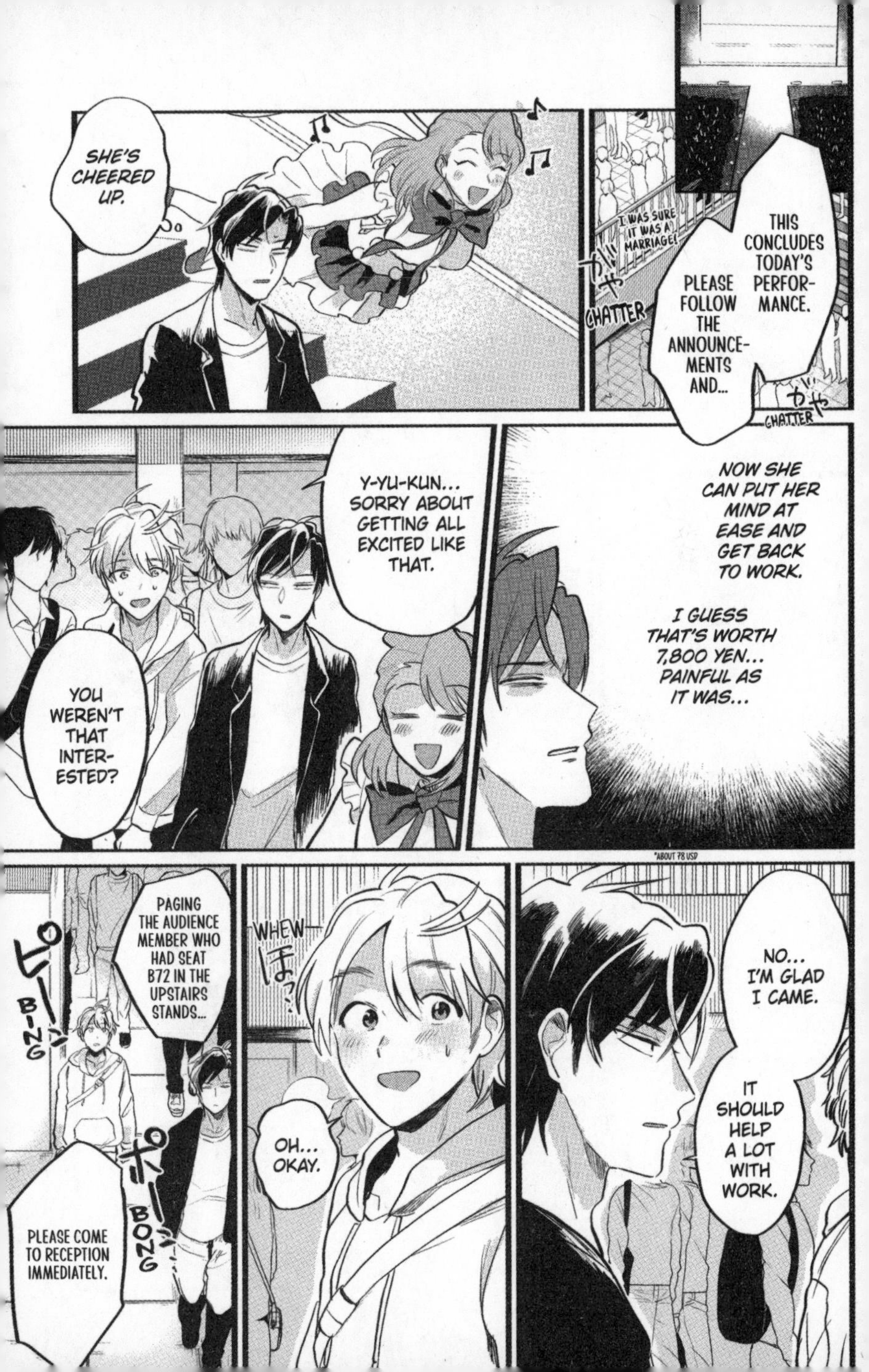
THIS CONCLUDES TODAY'S PERFORMANCE. PLEASE FOLLOW THE ANNOUNCEMENTS AND...
I WAS SURE IT WAS A MARRIAGE!
CHATTER
CHATTER
SHE'S CHEERED UP.
NOW SHE CAN PUT HER MIND AT EASE AND GET BACK TO WORK.
I GUESS THAT'S WORTH 7,800 YEN... PAINFUL AS IT WAS...
*ABOUT 78 USD
Y-YU-KUN... SORRY ABOUT GETTING ALL EXCITED LIKE THAT.
YOU WEREN'T THAT INTERESTED?
NO... I'M GLAD I CAME.
IT SHOULD HELP A LOT WITH WORK.
WHEW
OH... OKAY.
PAGING THE AUDIENCE MEMBER WHO HAD SEAT B72 IN THE UPSTAIRS STANDS...
BING
BONG
PLEASE COME TO RECEPTION IMMEDIATELY.

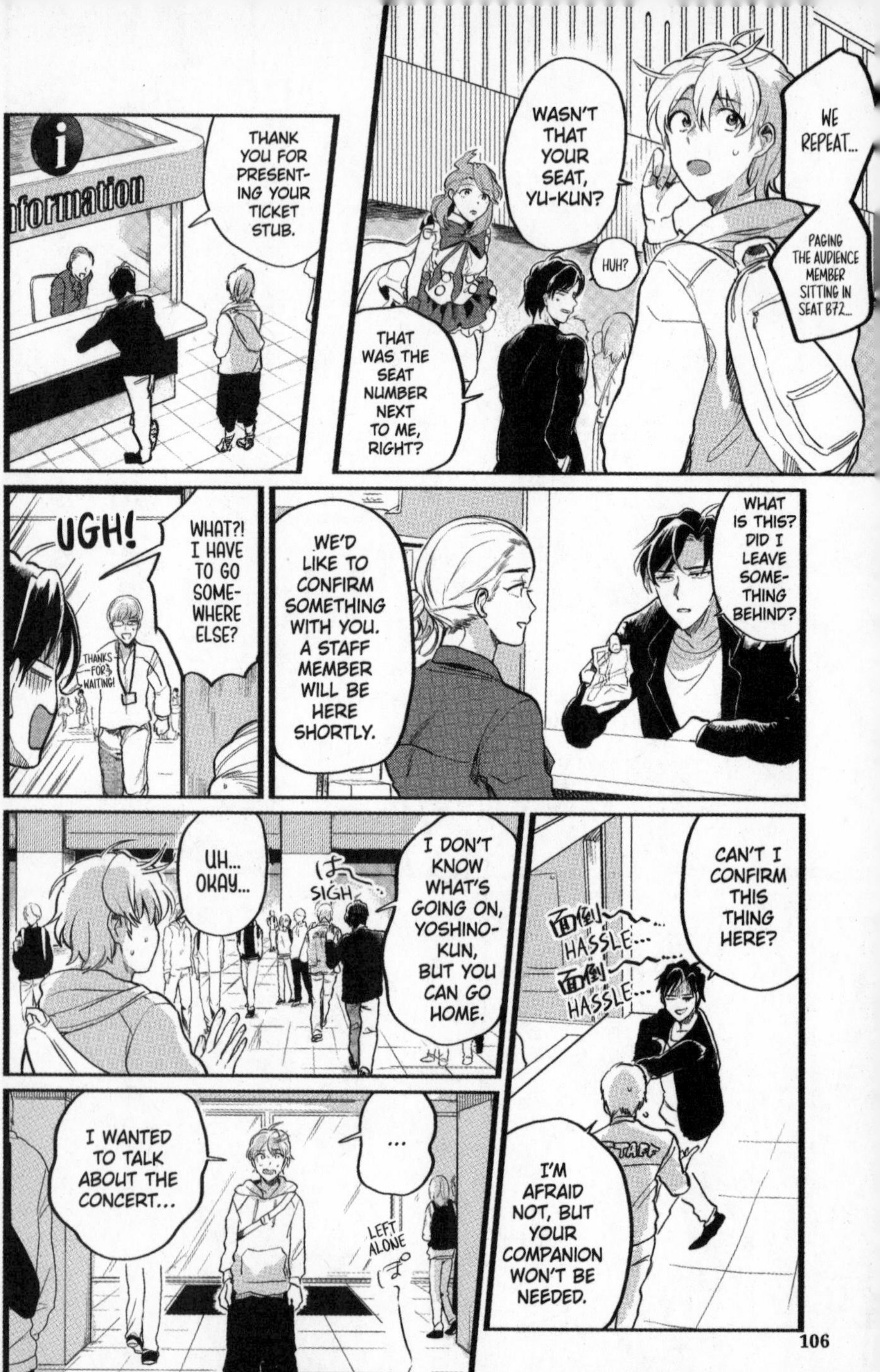
WE REPEAT...
PAGING THE AUDIENCE MEMBER SITTING IN SEAT B72...
WASN'T THAT YOUR SEAT, YU-KUN?
HUH?
THAT WAS THE SEAT NUMBER NEXT TO ME, RIGHT?
nformation
THANK YOU FOR PRESENTING YOUR TICKET STUB.
WHAT IS THIS? DID I LEAVE SOMETHING BEHIND?
WE'D LIKE TO CONFIRM SOMETHING WITH YOU. A STAFF MEMBER WILL BE HERE SHORTLY.
UGH!
WHAT?! I HAVE TO GO SOMEWHERE ELSE?
THANKS FOR WAITING!
CAN'T I CONFIRM THIS THING HERE?
面倒 HASSLE...
面倒 HASSLE...
STAFF
I'M AFRAID NOT, BUT YOUR COMPANION WON'T BE NEEDED.
I DON'T KNOW WHAT'S GOING ON, YOSHINO-KUN, BUT YOU CAN GO HOME.
は SIGH
UH... OKAY...
...
I WANTED TO TALK ABOUT THE CONCERT...
LEFT ALONE

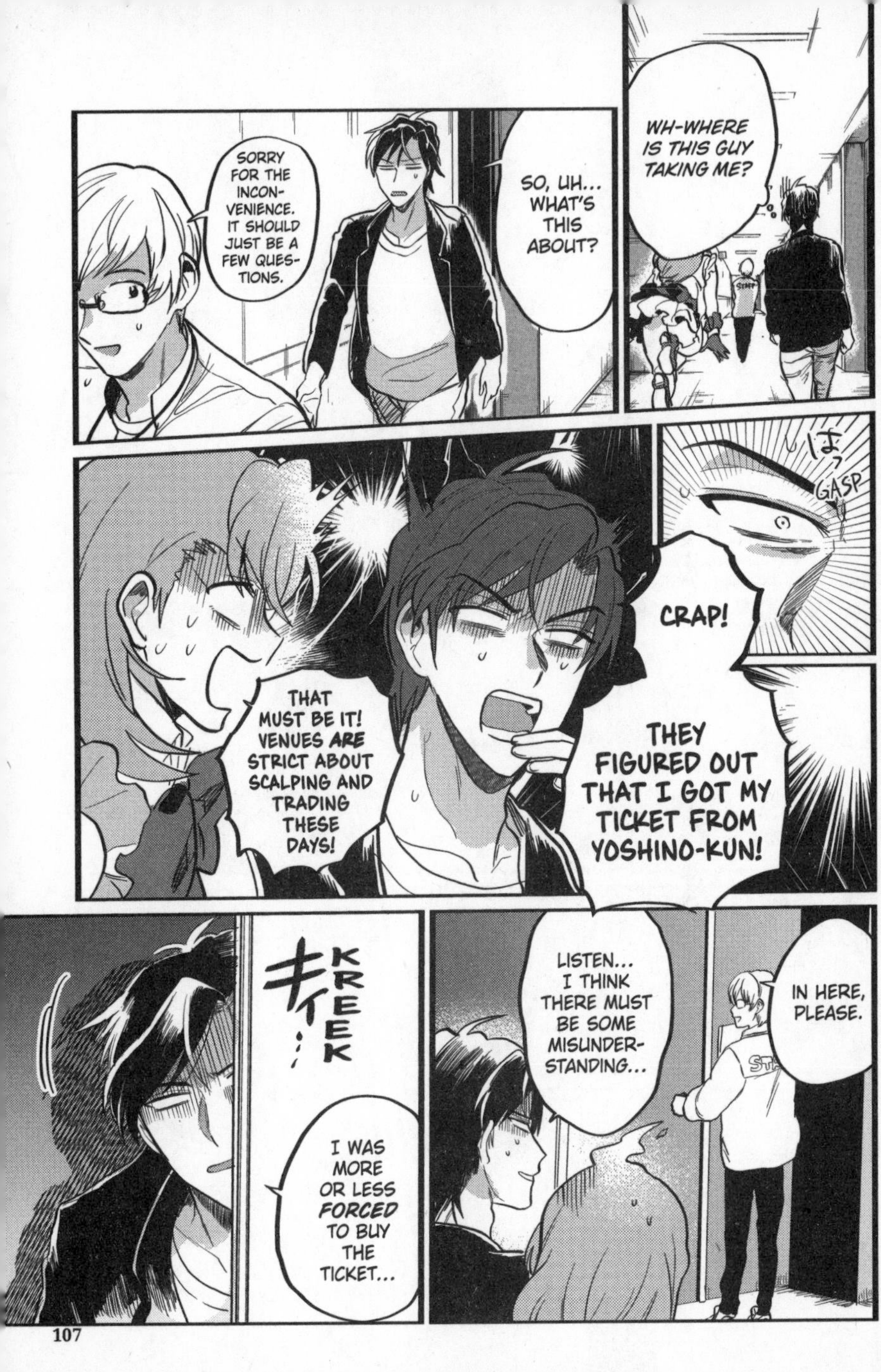
WH-WHERE IS THIS GUY TAKING ME?
SO, UH... WHAT'S THIS ABOUT?
SORRY FOR THE INCONVENIENCE. IT SHOULD JUST BE A FEW QUESTIONS.
はっ
GASP
CRAP!
THEY FIGURED OUT THAT I GOT MY TICKET FROM YOSHINO-KUN!
THAT MUST BE IT! VENUES *ARE* STRICT ABOUT SCALPING AND TRADING THESE DAYS!
IN HERE, PLEASE.
LISTEN... I THINK THERE MUST BE SOME MISUNDERSTANDING...
キイ…
KREEK
I WAS MORE OR LESS *FORCED* TO BUY THE TICKET...

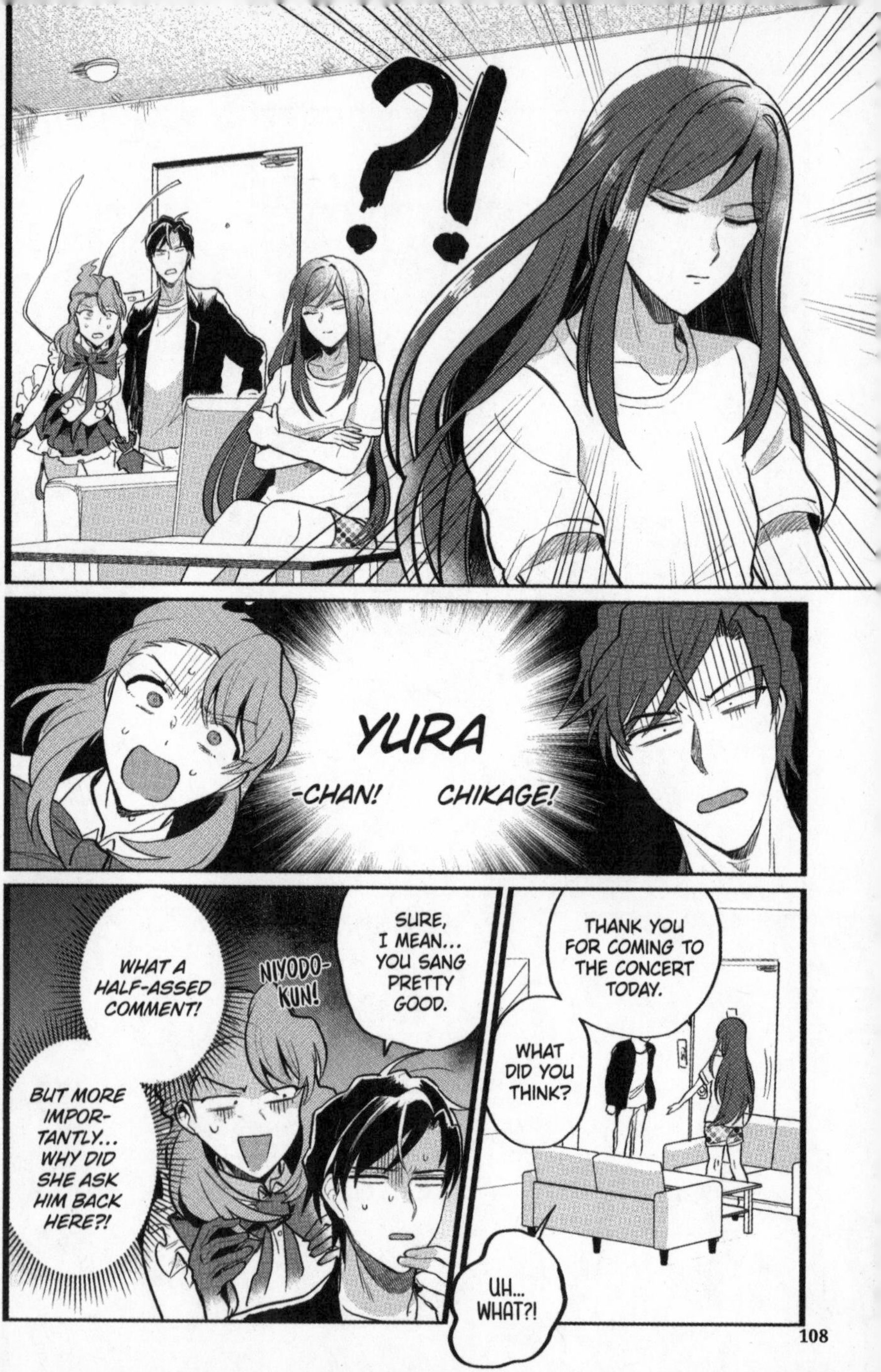
?!
YURA
-CHAN!
CHIKAGE!
THANK YOU FOR COMING TO THE CONCERT TODAY.
WHAT DID YOU THINK?
UH... WHAT?!
SURE, I MEAN... YOU SANG PRETTY GOOD.
NIYODO-KUN!
WHAT A HALF-ASSED COMMENT!
BUT MORE IMPORTANTLY... WHY DID SHE ASK HIM BACK HERE?!

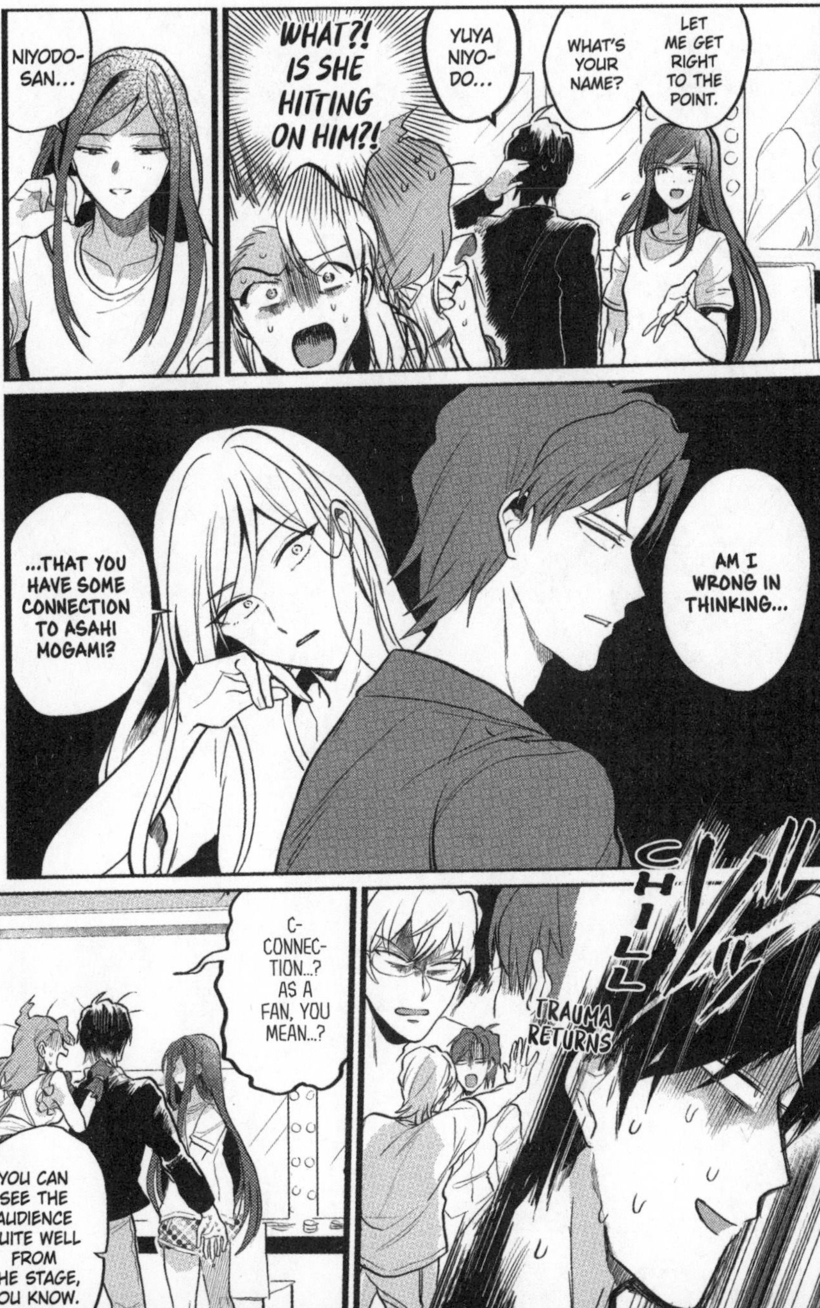
LET ME GET RIGHT TO THE POINT.
WHAT'S YOUR NAME?
YUYA NIYODO...
WHAT?! IS SHE HITTING ON HIM?!
NIYODO-SAN...
AM I WRONG IN THINKING...
...THAT YOU HAVE SOME CONNECTION TO ASAHI MOGAMI?
CHILL
TRAUMA RETURNS
C-CONNECTION...? AS A FAN, YOU MEAN...?
YOU CAN SEE THE AUDIENCE QUITE WELL FROM THE STAGE, YOU KNOW.

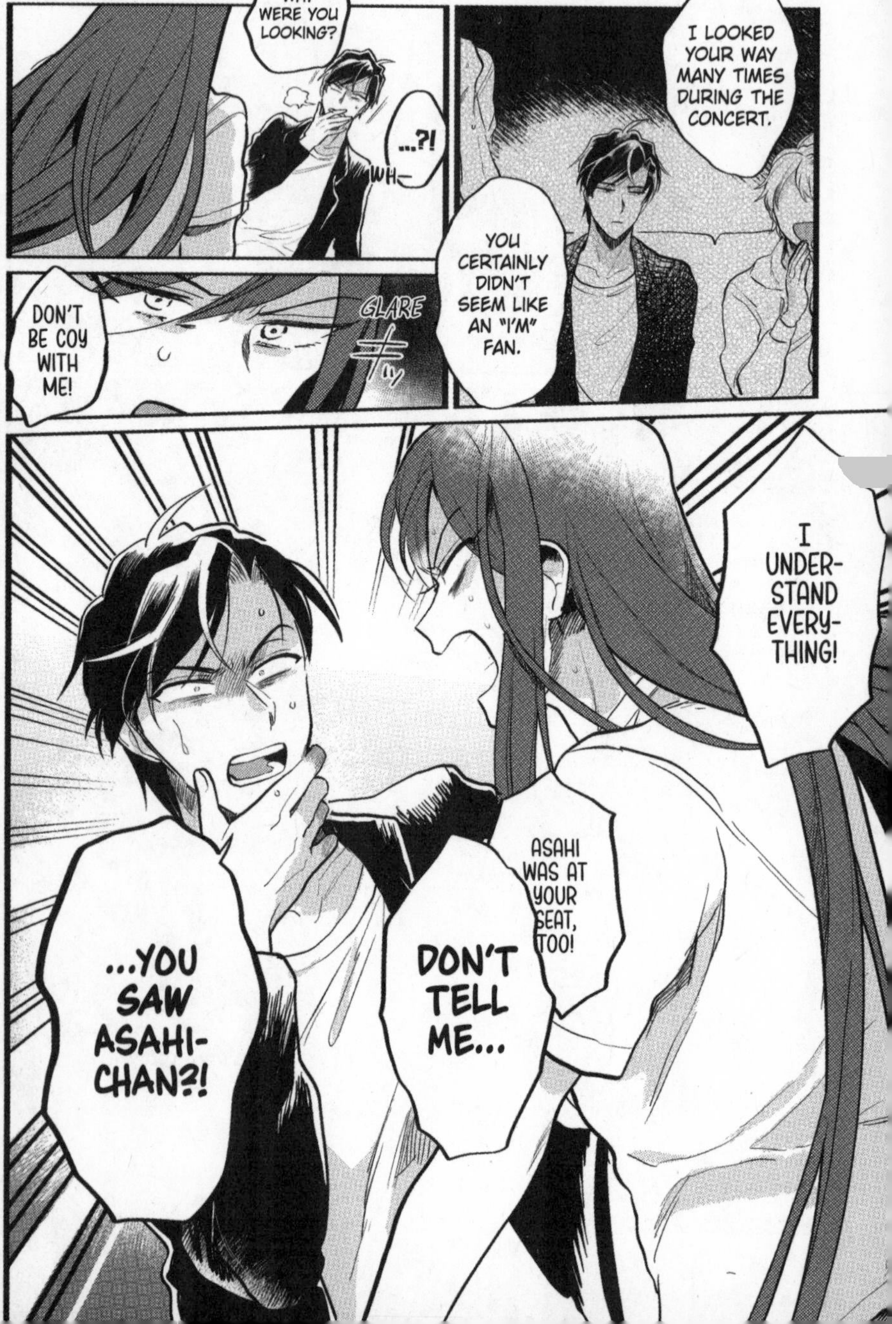
I LOOKED YOUR WAY MANY TIMES DURING THE CONCERT.
YOU CERTAINLY DIDN'T SEEM LIKE AN "I'M" FAN.
WHY WERE YOU LOOKING?
...?!
WH—
GLARE
DON'T BE COY WITH ME!
I UNDERSTAND EVERYTHING!
ASAHI WAS AT YOUR SEAT, TOO!
DON'T TELL ME...
...YOU SAW ASAHI-CHAN?!

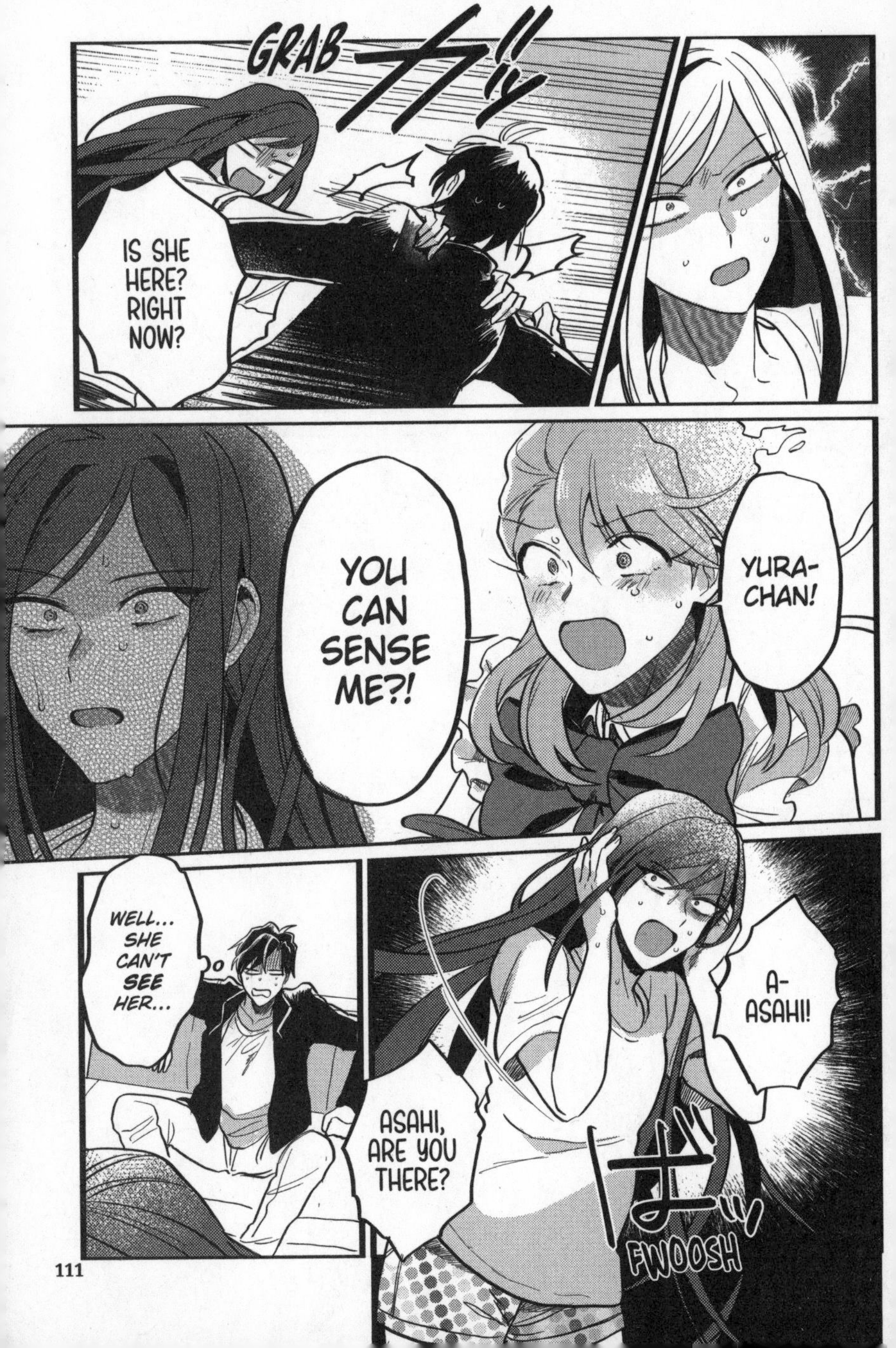
GRAB
IS SHE HERE? RIGHT NOW?
YURA-CHAN!
YOU CAN SENSE ME?!
A-ASAHI!
ASAHI, ARE YOU THERE?
FWOOSH
WELL... SHE CAN'T SEE HER...

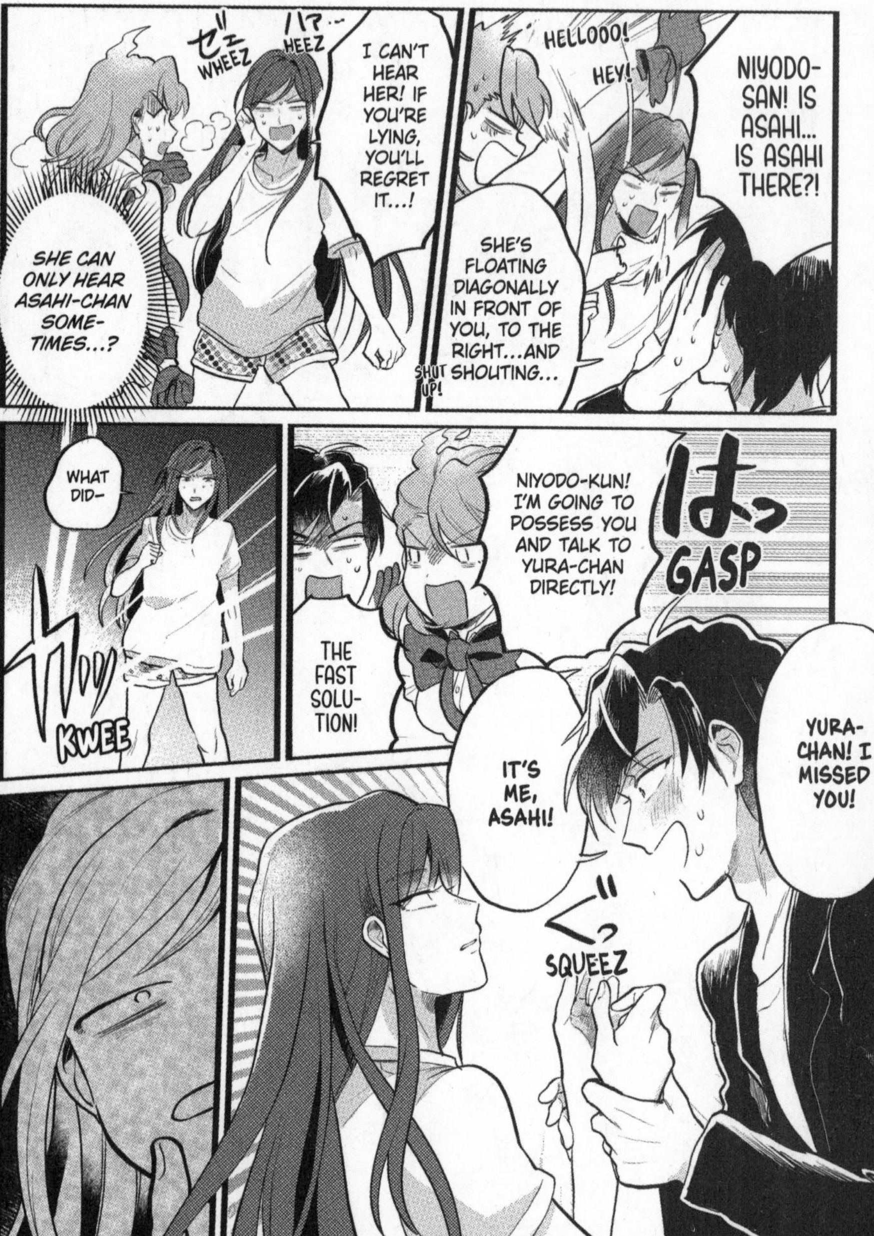
HELLOOO!
HEY!
NIYODO-SAN! IS ASAHI... IS ASAHI THERE?!
SHE'S FLOATING DIAGONALLY IN FRONT OF YOU, TO THE RIGHT...AND SHOUTING...
SHUT UP!
ゼェ WHEEZ
ハァ… HEEZ
I CAN'T HEAR HER! IF YOU'RE LYING, YOU'LL REGRET IT...!
SHE CAN ONLY HEAR ASAHI-CHAN SOME-TIMES...?
はっ GASP
NIYODO-KUN! I'M GOING TO POSSESS YOU AND TALK TO YURA-CHAN DIRECTLY!
THE FAST SOLUTION!
WHAT DID-
KWEE
YURA-CHAN! I MISSED YOU!
IT'S ME, ASAHI!
ぐっ SQUEEZ

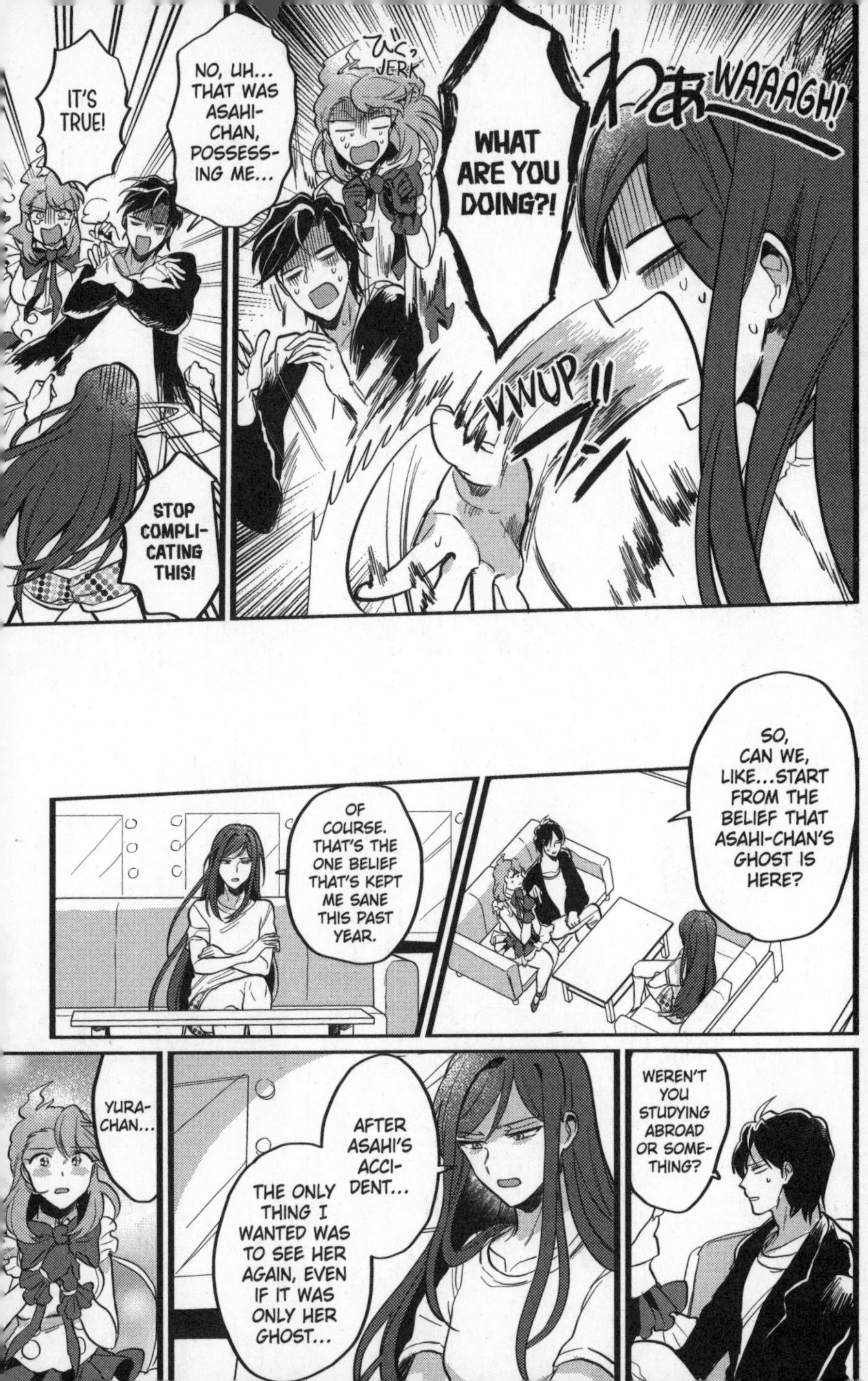
わあ WAAAGH!
WHAT ARE YOU DOING?!
VWUP
びくっ JERK
NO, UH... THAT WAS ASAHI-CHAN, POSSESSING ME...
IT'S TRUE!
STOP COMPLICATING THIS!
SO, CAN WE, LIKE...START FROM THE BELIEF THAT ASAHI-CHAN'S GHOST IS HERE?
OF COURSE. THAT'S THE ONE BELIEF THAT'S KEPT ME SANE THIS PAST YEAR.
WEREN'T YOU STUDYING ABROAD OR SOMETHING?
AFTER ASAHI'S ACCIDENT...
THE ONLY THING I WANTED WAS TO SEE HER AGAIN, EVEN IF IT WAS ONLY HER GHOST...
YURA-CHAN...

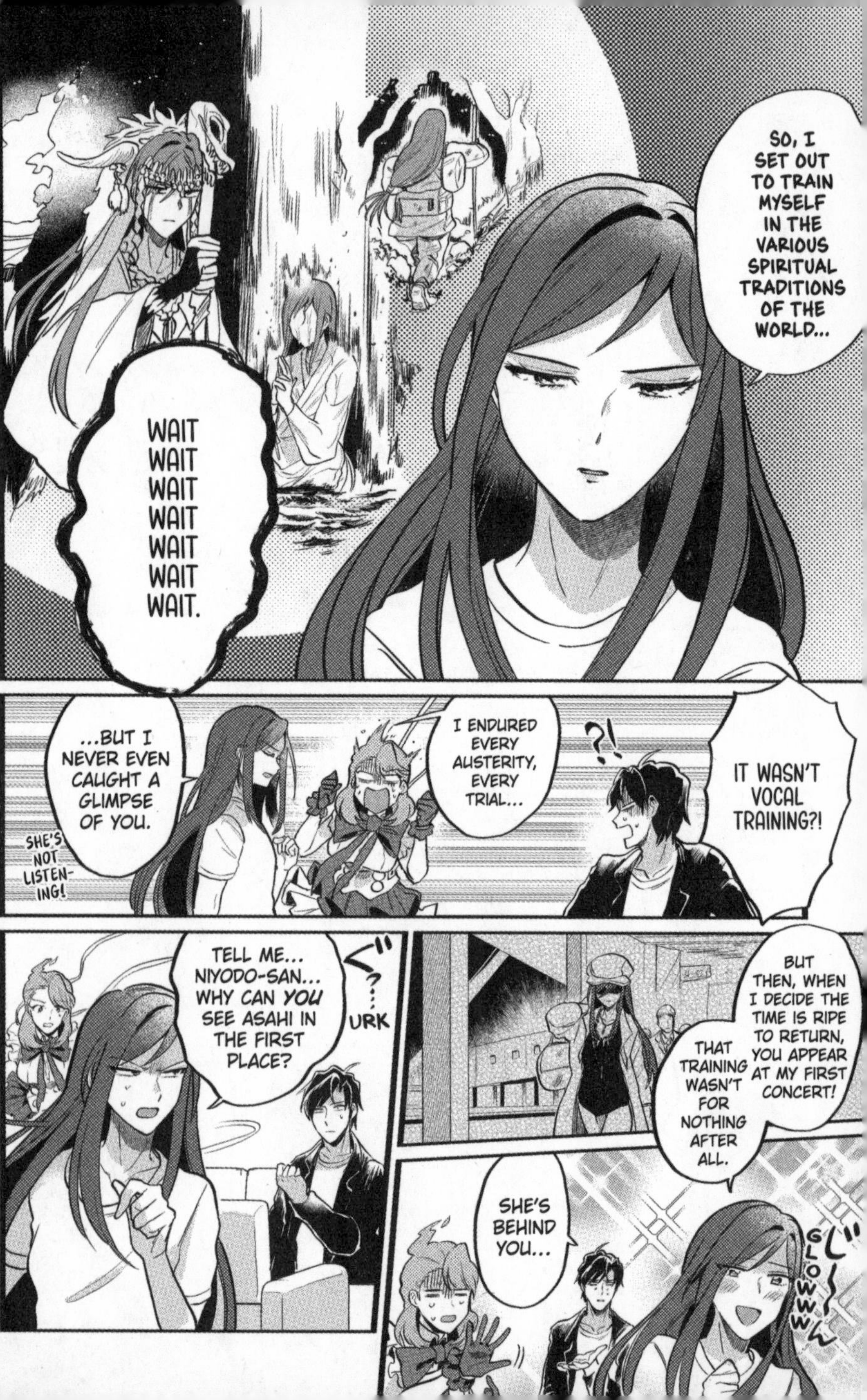
SO, I SET OUT TO TRAIN MYSELF IN THE VARIOUS SPIRITUAL TRADITIONS OF THE WORLD...
WAIT WAIT WAIT WAIT WAIT WAIT WAIT.
IT WASN'T VOCAL TRAINING?!
?!
I ENDURED EVERY AUSTERITY, EVERY TRIAL...
...BUT I NEVER EVEN CAUGHT A GLIMPSE OF YOU.
SHE'S NOT LISTENING!
BUT THEN, WHEN I DECIDE THE TIME IS RIPE TO RETURN, YOU APPEAR AT MY FIRST CONCERT!
THAT TRAINING WASN'T FOR NOTHING AFTER ALL.
SHE'S BEHIND YOU...
GLOWWW
TELL ME... NIYODO-SAN... WHY CAN *YOU* SEE ASAHI IN THE FIRST PLACE?
URK

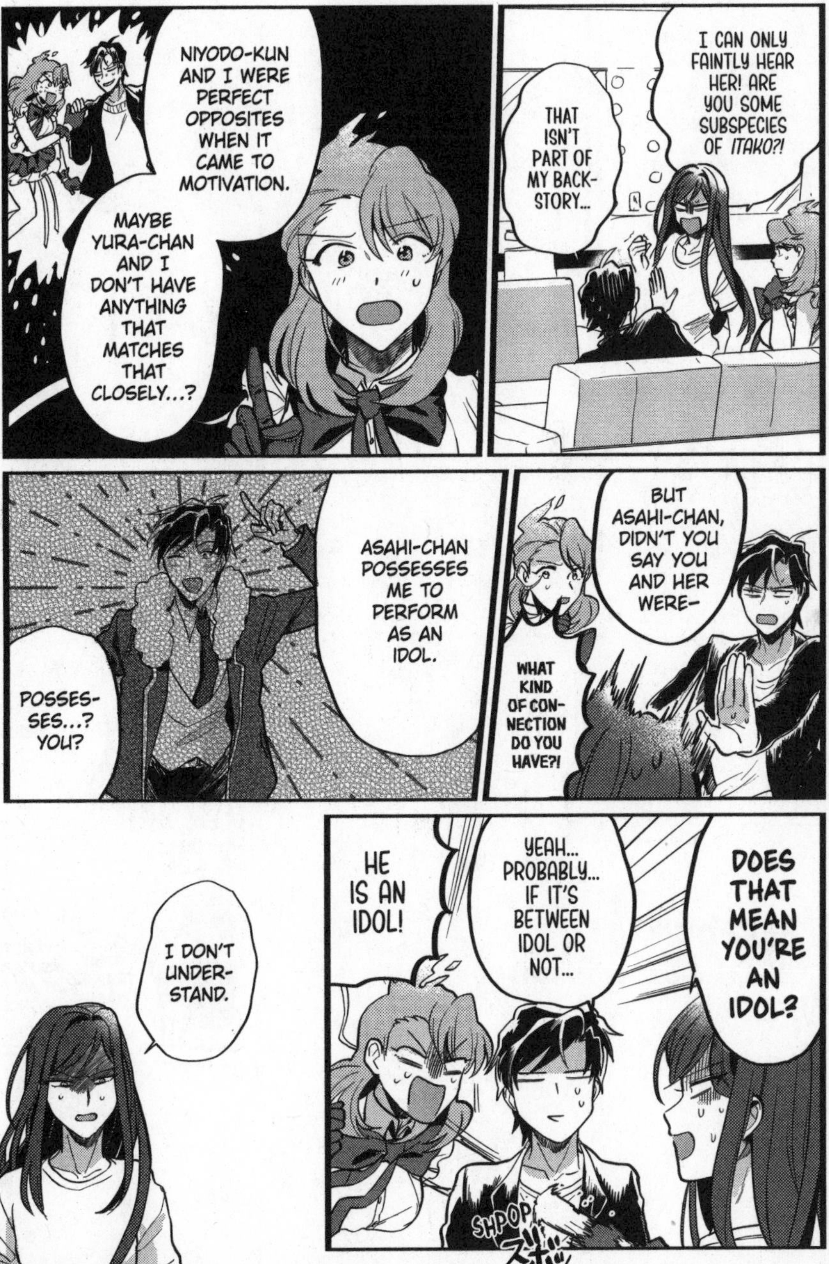
I CAN ONLY FAINTLY HEAR HER! ARE YOU SOME SUBSPECIES OF *ITAKO*?!
THAT ISN'T PART OF MY BACK-STORY...
NIYODO-KUN AND I WERE PERFECT OPPOSITES WHEN IT CAME TO MOTIVATION.
MAYBE YURA-CHAN AND I DON'T HAVE ANYTHING THAT MATCHES THAT CLOSELY...?
BUT ASAHI-CHAN, DIDN'T YOU SAY YOU AND HER WERE–
WHAT KIND OF CONNECTION DO YOU HAVE?!
ASAHI-CHAN POSSESSES ME TO PERFORM AS AN IDOL.
POSSES-SES...? YOU?
DOES THAT MEAN YOU'RE AN IDOL?
YEAH... PROBABLY... IF IT'S BETWEEN IDOL OR NOT...
HE IS AN IDOL!
SHPOP
I DON'T UNDER-STAND.

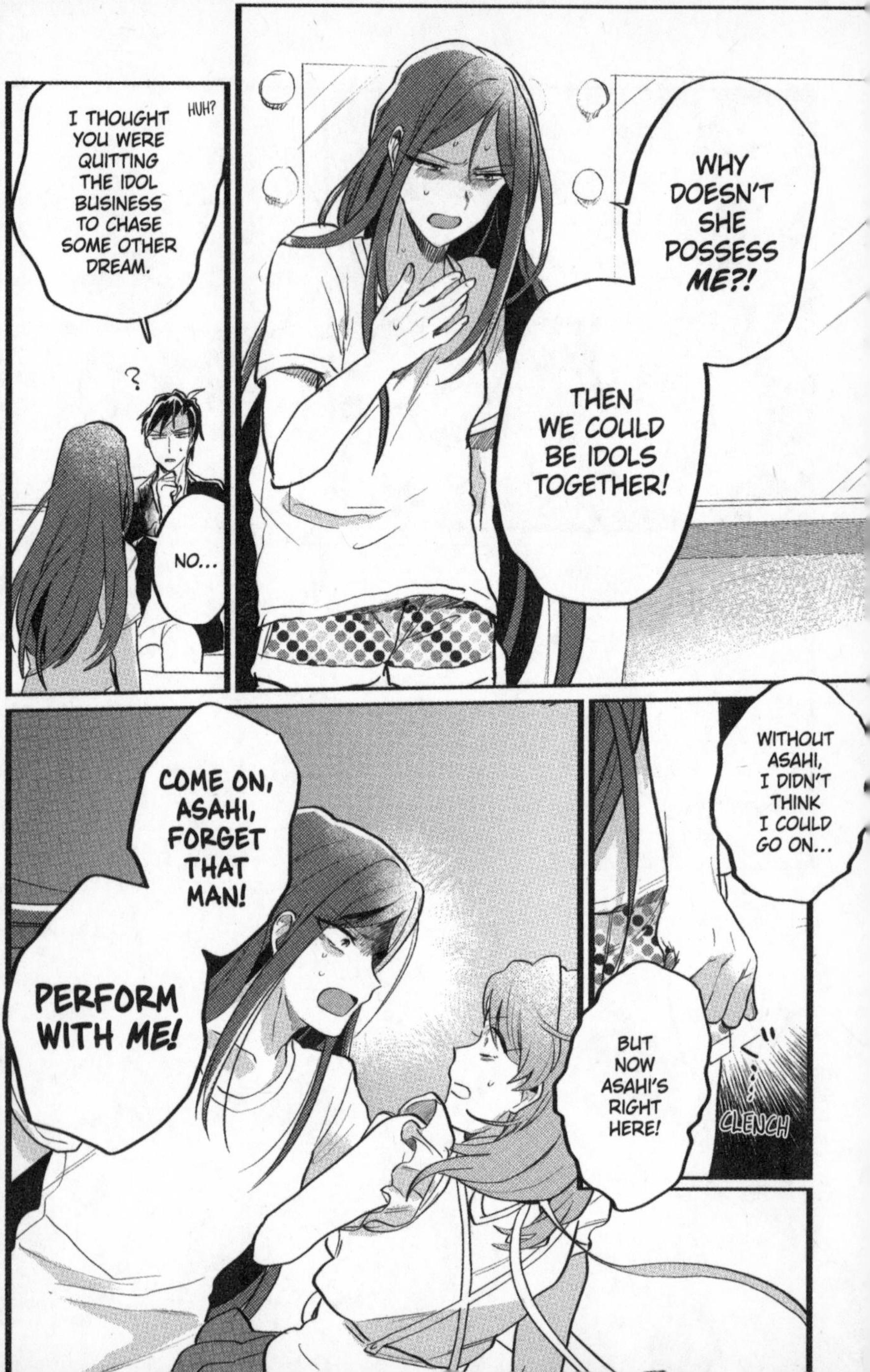
WHY DOESN'T SHE POSSESS ME?!
THEN WE COULD BE IDOLS TOGETHER!
HUH?
I THOUGHT YOU WERE QUITTING THE IDOL BUSINESS TO CHASE SOME OTHER DREAM.
?
NO...
WITHOUT ASAHI, I DIDN'T THINK I COULD GO ON...
BUT NOW ASAHI'S RIGHT HERE!
CLENCH
COME ON, ASAHI, FORGET THAT MAN!
PERFORM WITH ME!

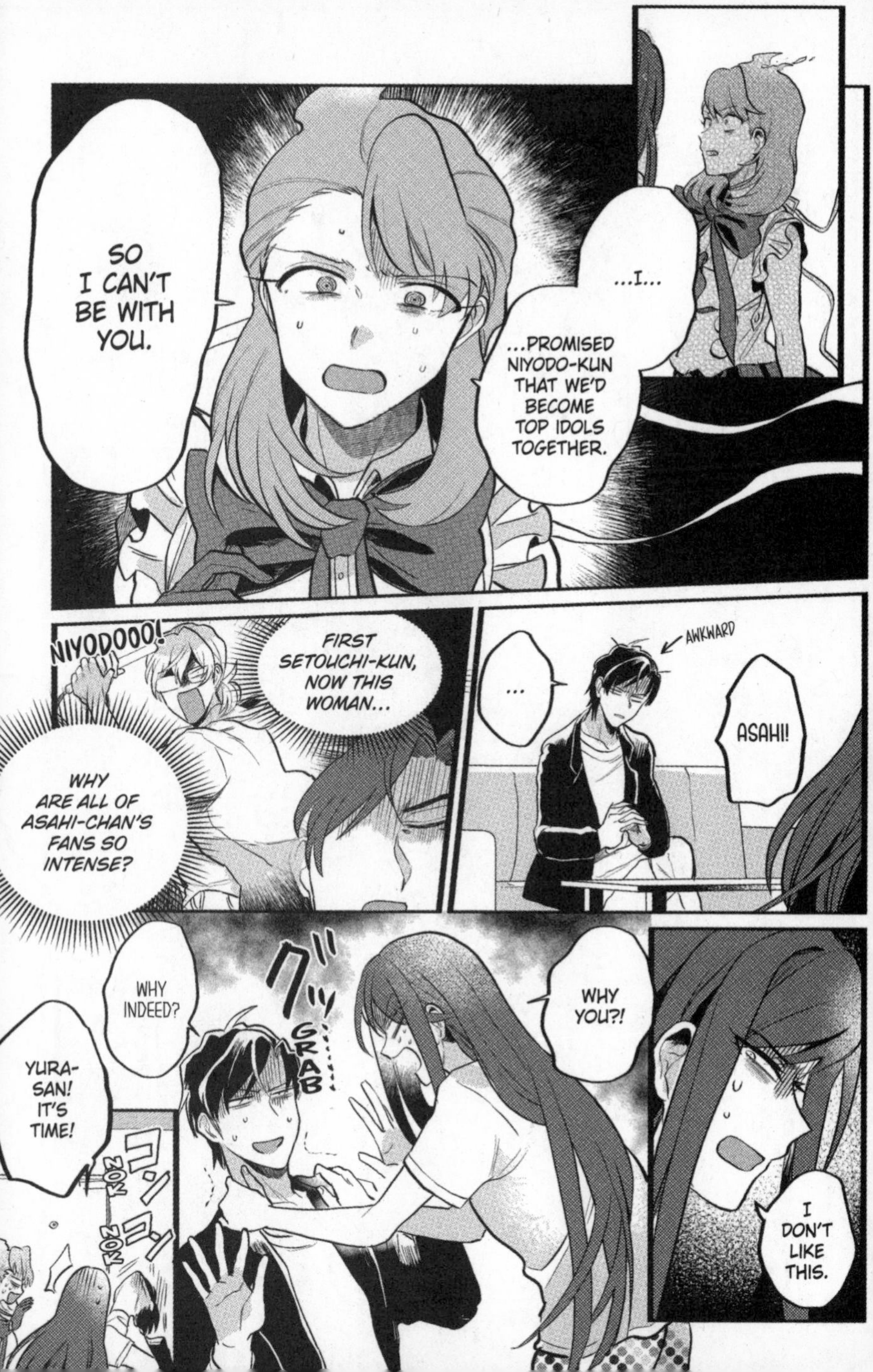
...I...
...PROMISED NIYODO-KUN THAT WE'D BECOME TOP IDOLS TOGETHER.
SO I CAN'T BE WITH YOU.
AWKWARD
ASAHI!
...
FIRST SETOUCHI-KUN, NOW THIS WOMAN...
NIYODOOO!
WHY ARE ALL OF ASAHI-CHAN'S FANS SO INTENSE?
I DON'T LIKE THIS.
WHY YOU?!
GRAB
WHY INDEED?
YURA-SAN! IT'S TIME!
NOK NOK

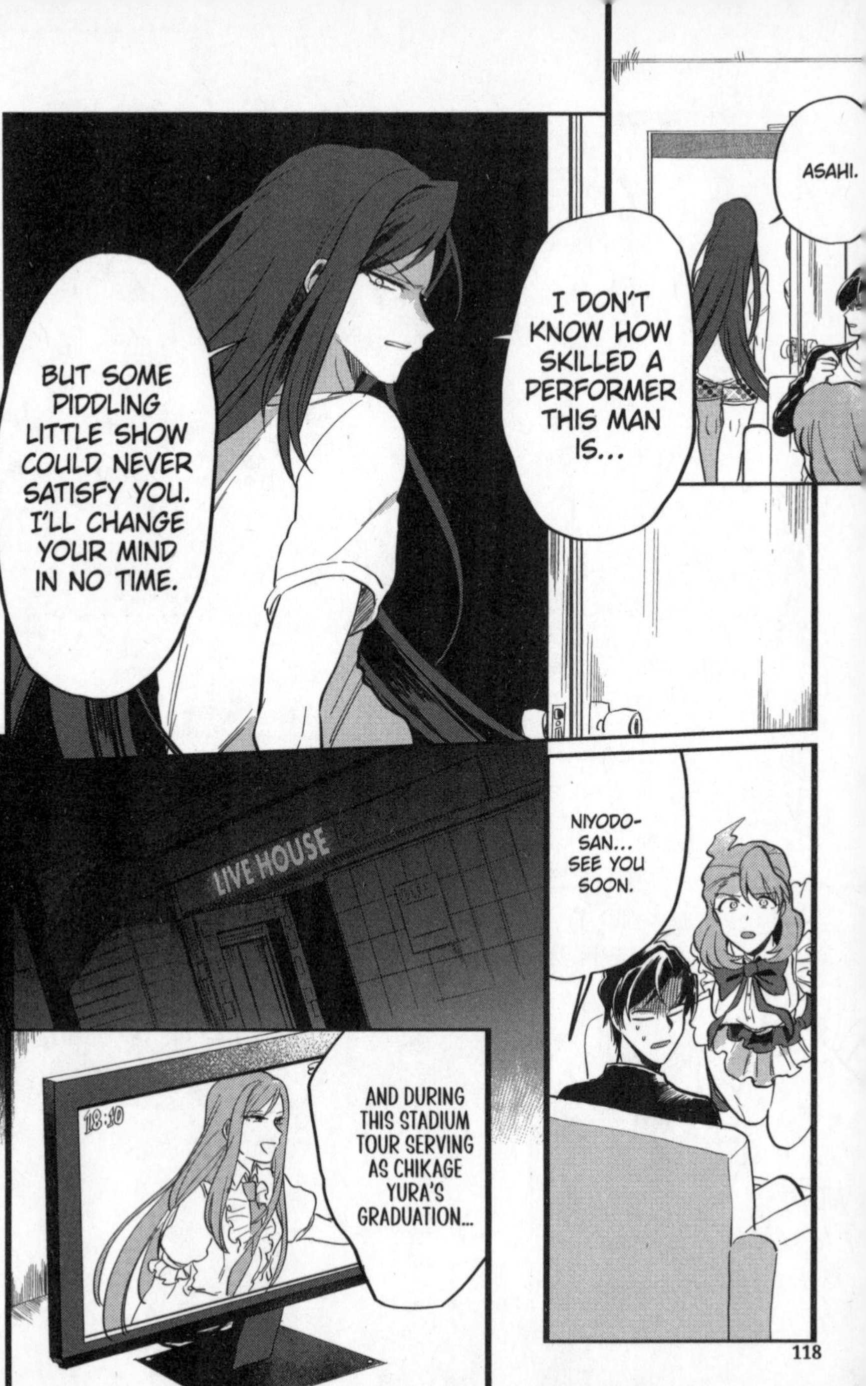
ASAHI.
I DON'T KNOW HOW SKILLED A PERFORMER THIS MAN IS...
BUT SOME PIDDLING LITTLE SHOW COULD NEVER SATISFY YOU. I'LL CHANGE YOUR MIND IN NO TIME.
NIYODO-SAN... SEE YOU SOON.
LIVE HOUSE
18:10
AND DURING THIS STADIUM TOUR SERVING AS CHIKAGE YURA'S GRADUATION...

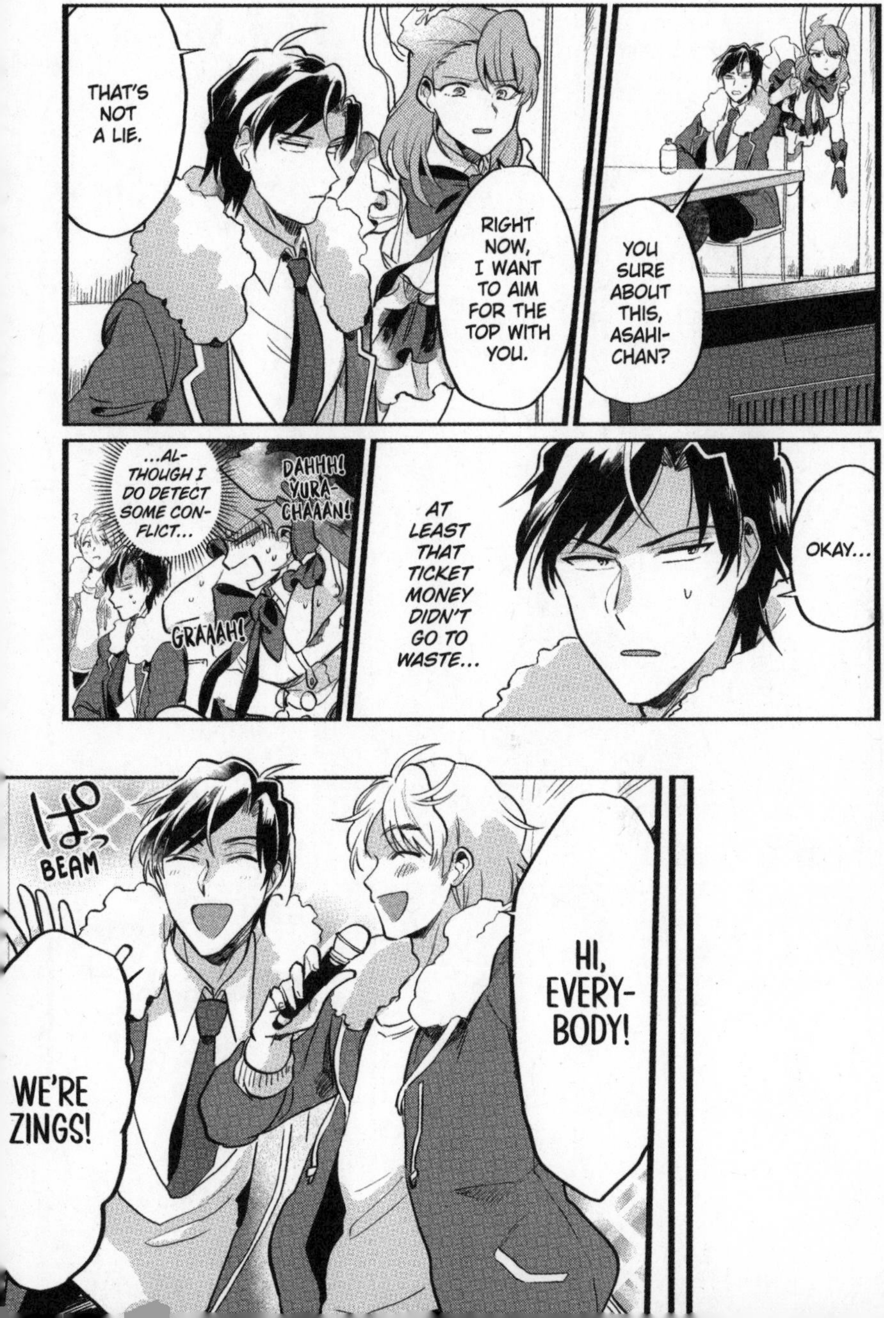
YOU SURE ABOUT THIS, ASAHI-CHAN?
RIGHT NOW, I WANT TO AIM FOR THE TOP WITH YOU.
THAT'S NOT A LIE.
OKAY...
AT LEAST THAT TICKET MONEY DIDN'T GO TO WASTE...
DAHHH! YURA-CHAAAN!
...AL-THOUGH I DO DETECT SOME CON-FLICT...
GRAAAH!
HI, EVERY-BODY!
ぱっ
BEAM
WE'RE ZINGS!

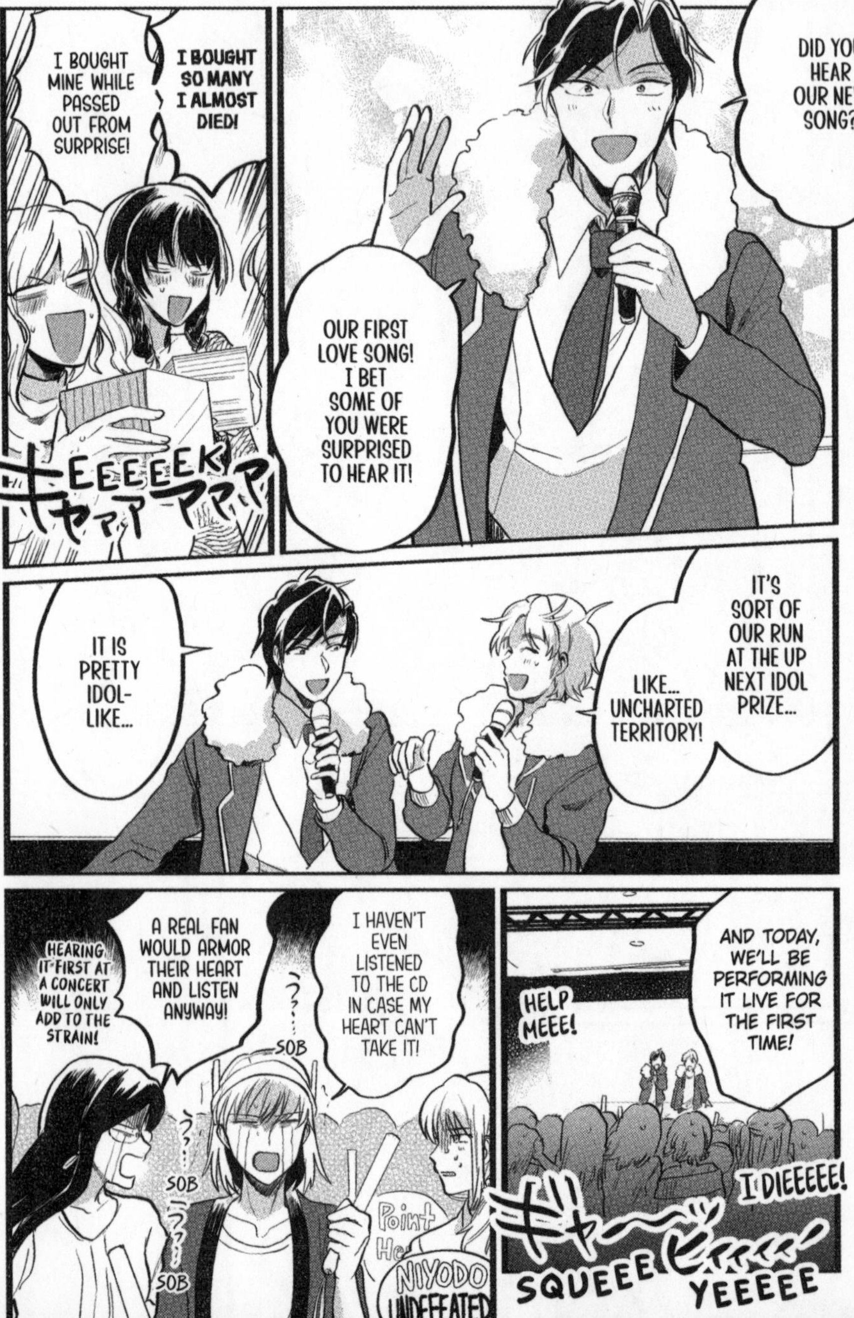
DID YOU HEAR OUR NEW SONG?
OUR FIRST LOVE SONG! I BET SOME OF YOU WERE SURPRISED TO HEAR IT!
I BOUGHT SO MANY I ALMOST DIED!
I BOUGHT MINE WHILE PASSED OUT FROM SURPRISE!
EEEEEEK
IT'S SORT OF OUR RUN AT THE UP NEXT IDOL PRIZE...
LIKE... UNCHARTED TERRITORY!
IT IS PRETTY IDOL-LIKE...
AND TODAY, WE'LL BE PERFORMING IT LIVE FOR THE FIRST TIME!
HELP MEEE!
I DIEEEEEE!
SQUEEE YEEEEE
I HAVEN'T EVEN LISTENED TO THE CD IN CASE MY HEART CAN'T TAKE IT!
SOB
A REAL FAN WOULD ARMOR THEIR HEART AND LISTEN ANYWAY!
HEARING IT FIRST AT A CONCERT WILL ONLY ADD TO THE STRAIN!
SOB
SOB
NIYODO UNDEFEATED

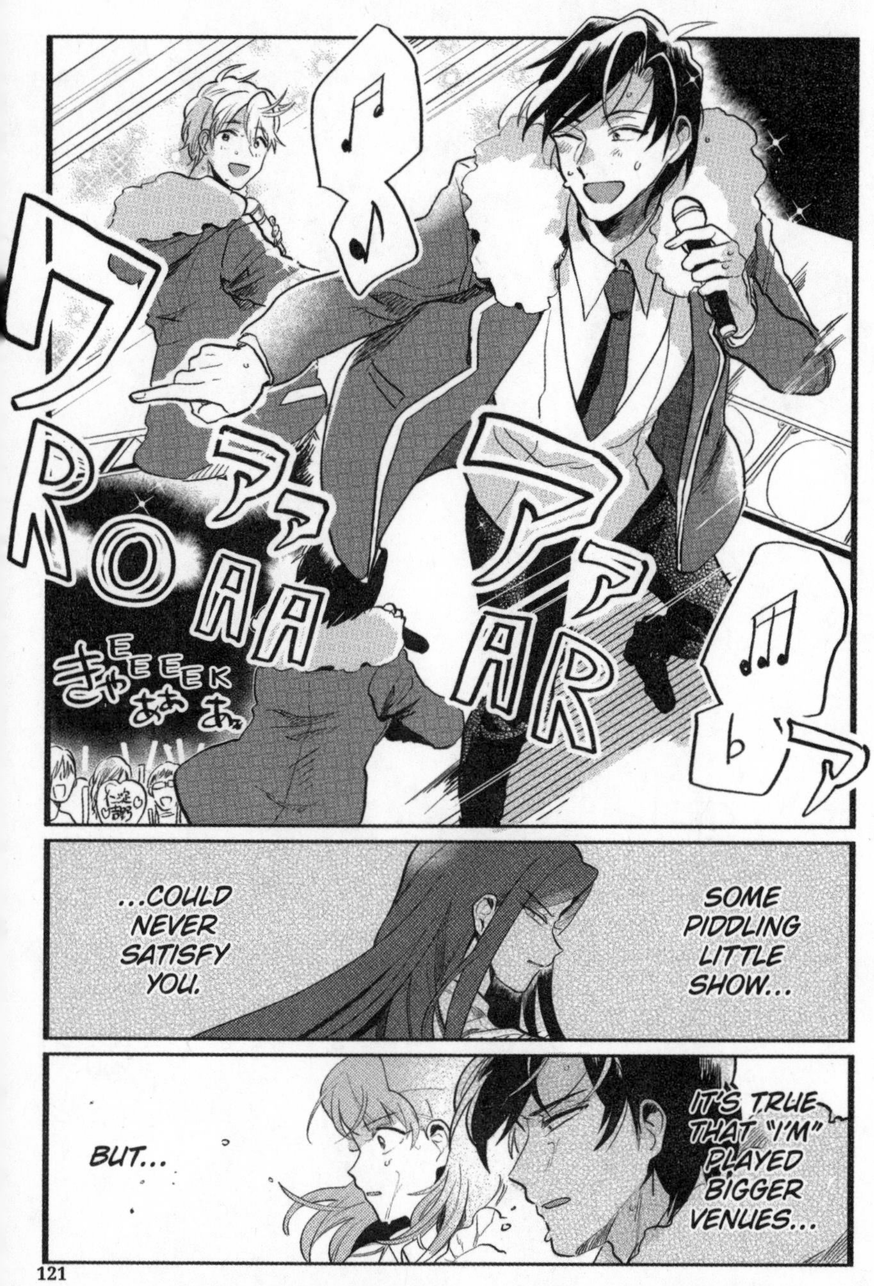
ROAARR
EEEEK
SOME PIDDLING LITTLE SHOW...
...COULD NEVER SATISFY YOU.
IT'S TRUE THAT "I'M" PLAYED BIGGER VENUES...
BUT...

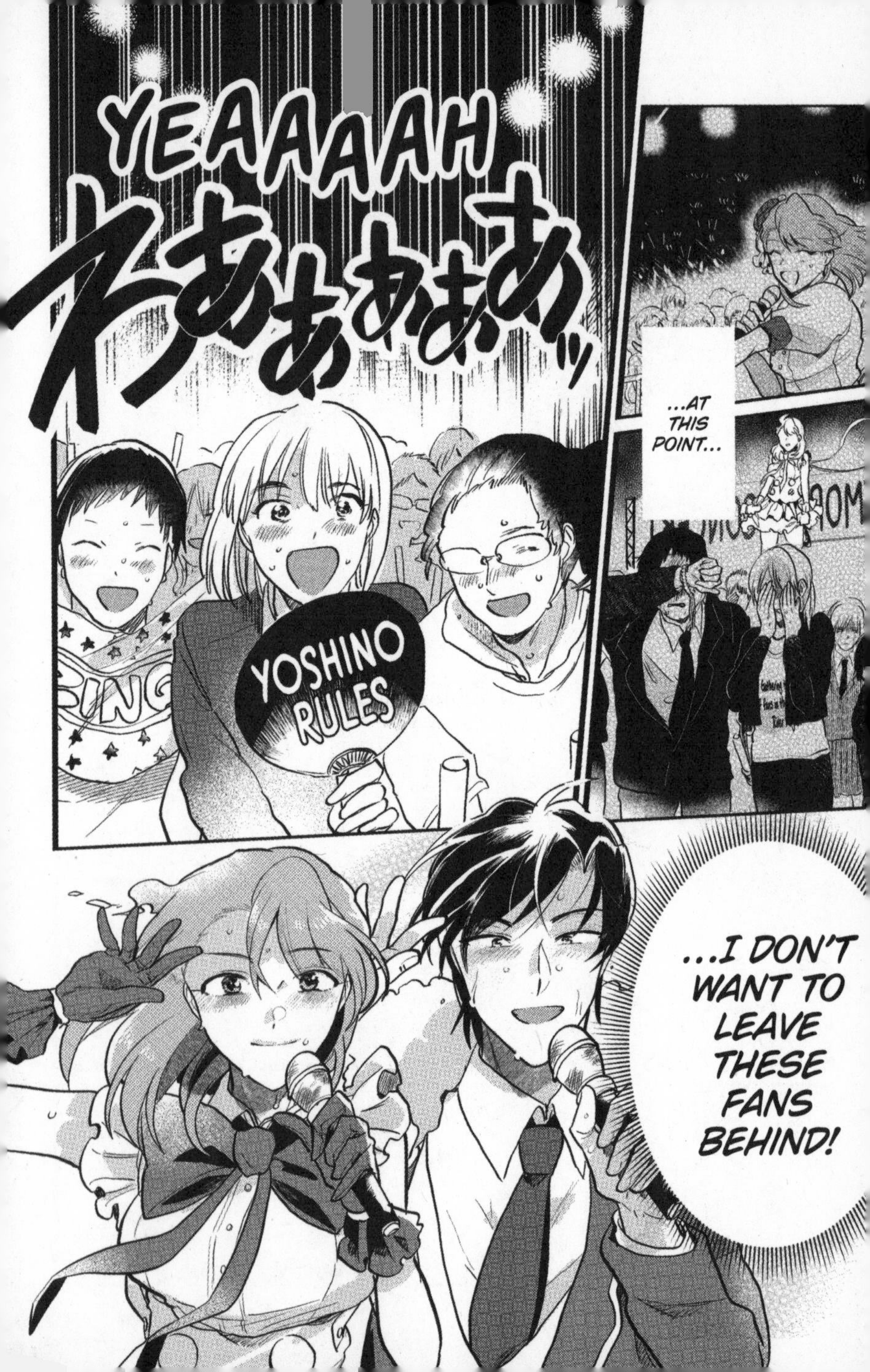
...AT THIS POINT...
YEAAAAH
わああああッ
YOSHINO RULES
...I DON'T WANT TO LEAVE THESE FANS BEHIND!

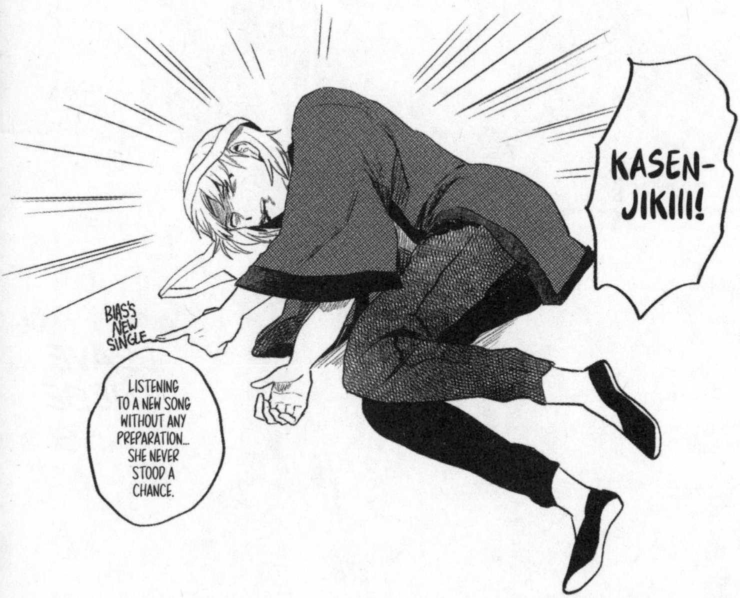
KASEN-JIKIII!
BIAS'S NEW SINGLE
LISTENING TO A NEW SONG WITHOUT ANY PREPARATION... SHE NEVER STOOD A CHANCE.

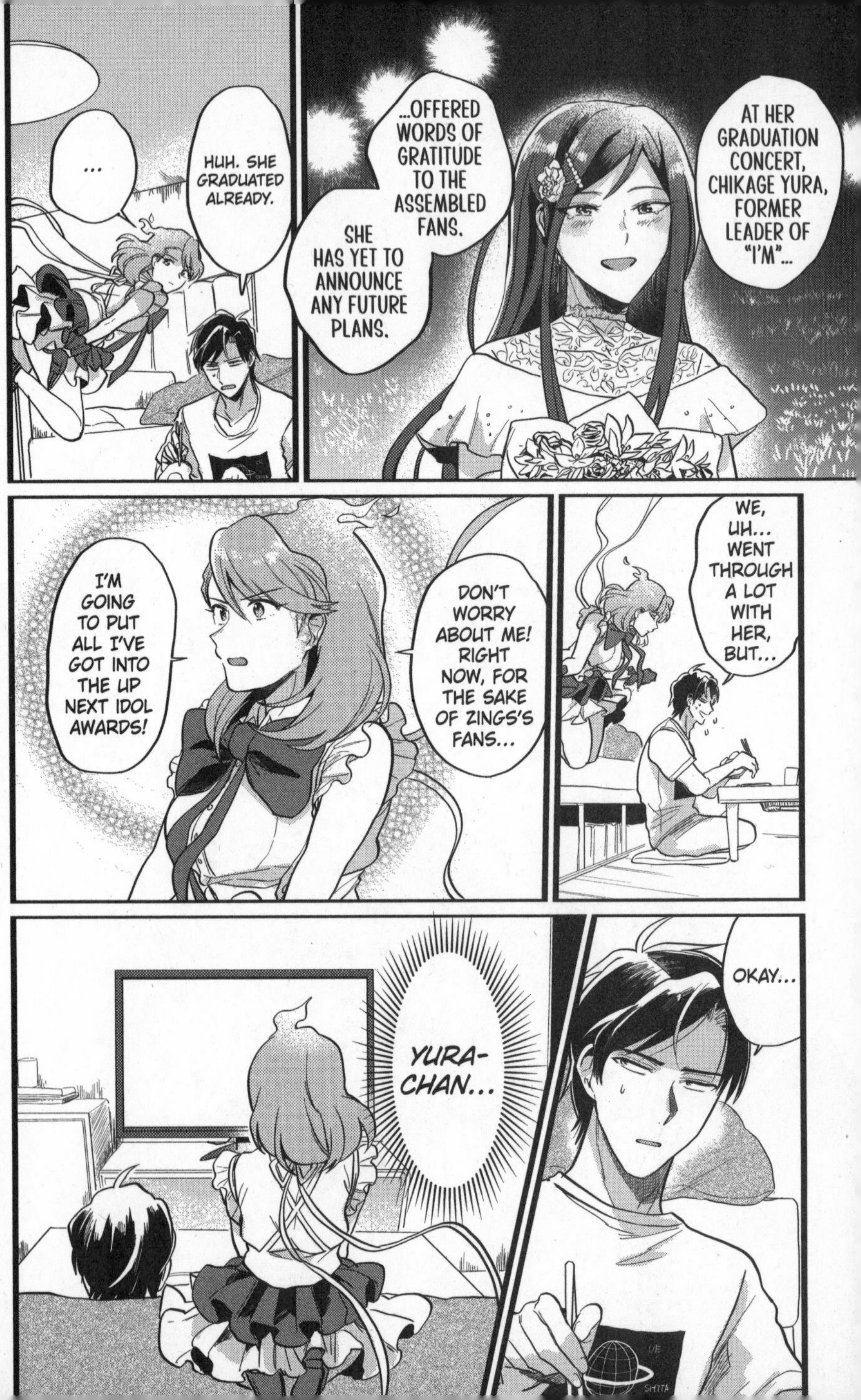
AT HER GRADUATION CONCERT, CHIKAGE YURA, FORMER LEADER OF "I'M"...
...OFFERED WORDS OF GRATITUDE TO THE ASSEMBLED FANS.
SHE HAS YET TO ANNOUNCE ANY FUTURE PLANS.
HUH. SHE GRADUATED ALREADY.
...
WE, UH... WENT THROUGH A LOT WITH HER, BUT...
DON'T WORRY ABOUT ME! RIGHT NOW, FOR THE SAKE OF ZINGS'S FANS...
I'M GOING TO PUT ALL I'VE GOT INTO THE UP NEXT IDOL AWARDS!
OKAY...
YURA-CHAN...

# Set 20

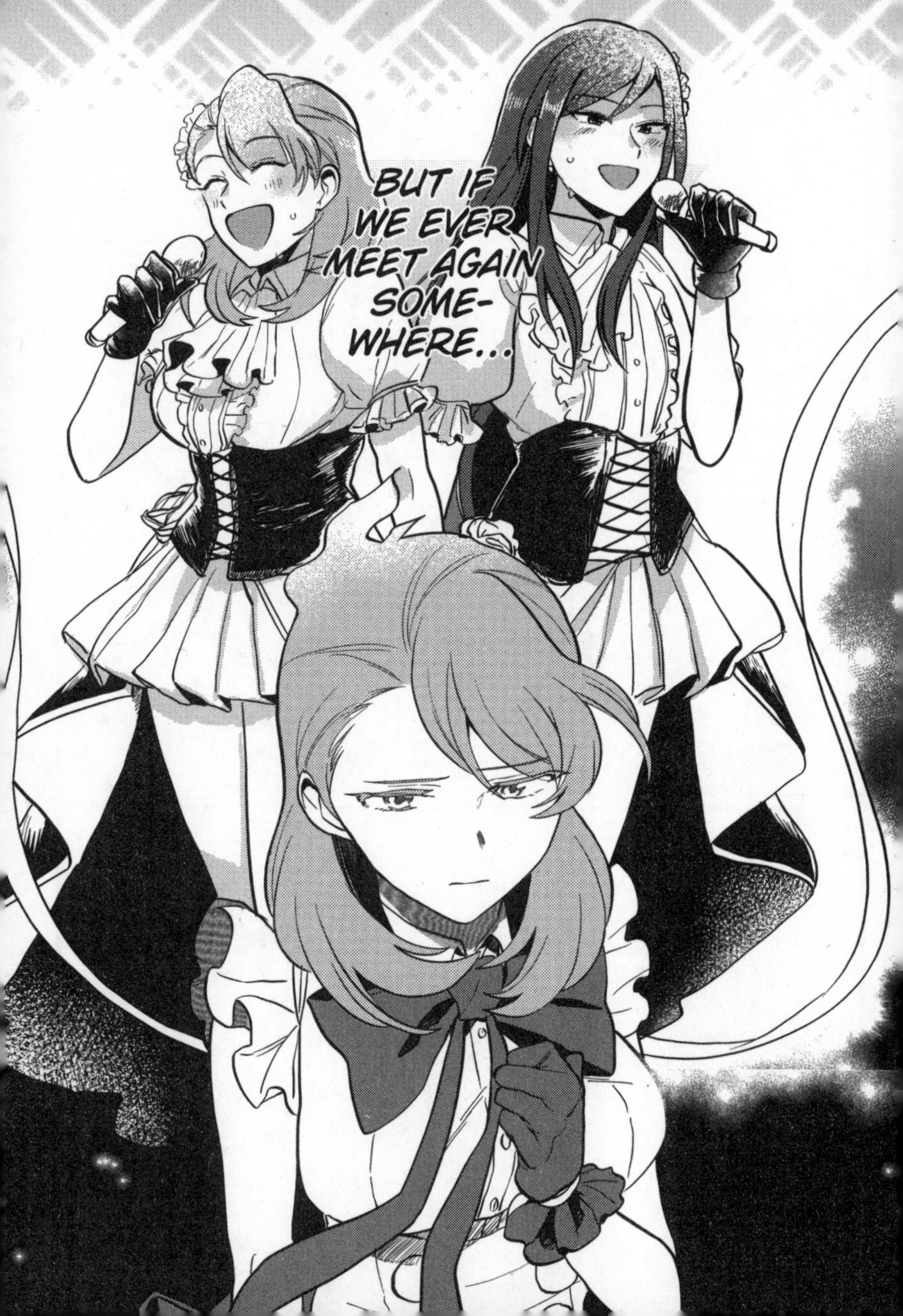
BUT IF WE EVER MEET AGAIN SOME-WHERE...

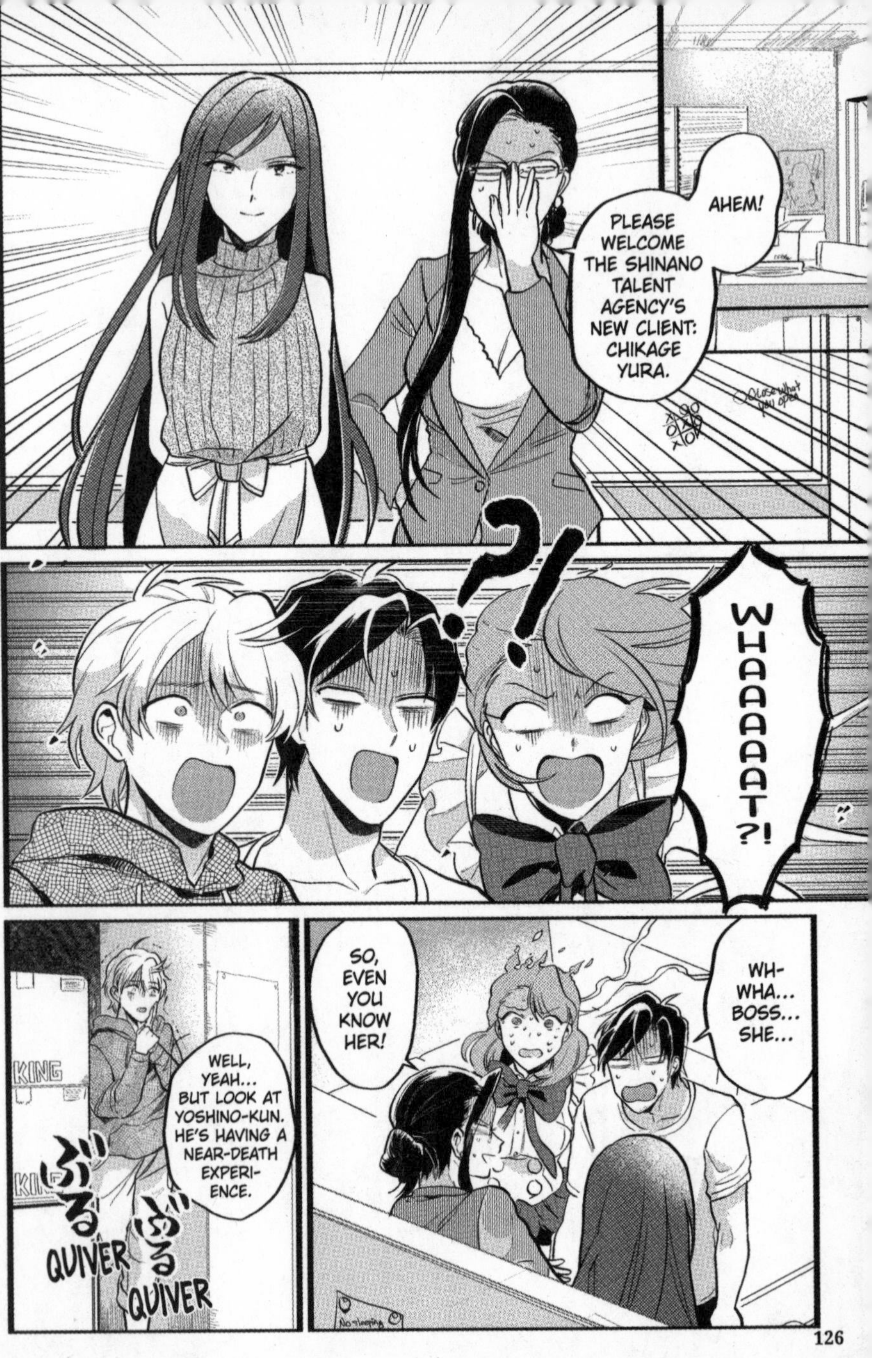
AHEM!
PLEASE WELCOME THE SHINANO TALENT AGENCY'S NEW CLIENT: CHIKAGE YURA.
Close what you open
?!
WHAAAAAT?!
WH- WHA... BOSS... SHE...
SO, EVEN YOU KNOW HER!
WELL, YEAH... BUT LOOK AT YOSHINO-KUN. HE'S HAVING A NEAR-DEATH EXPERI- ENCE.
ぶるぶる
QUIVER QUIVER
No sleeping

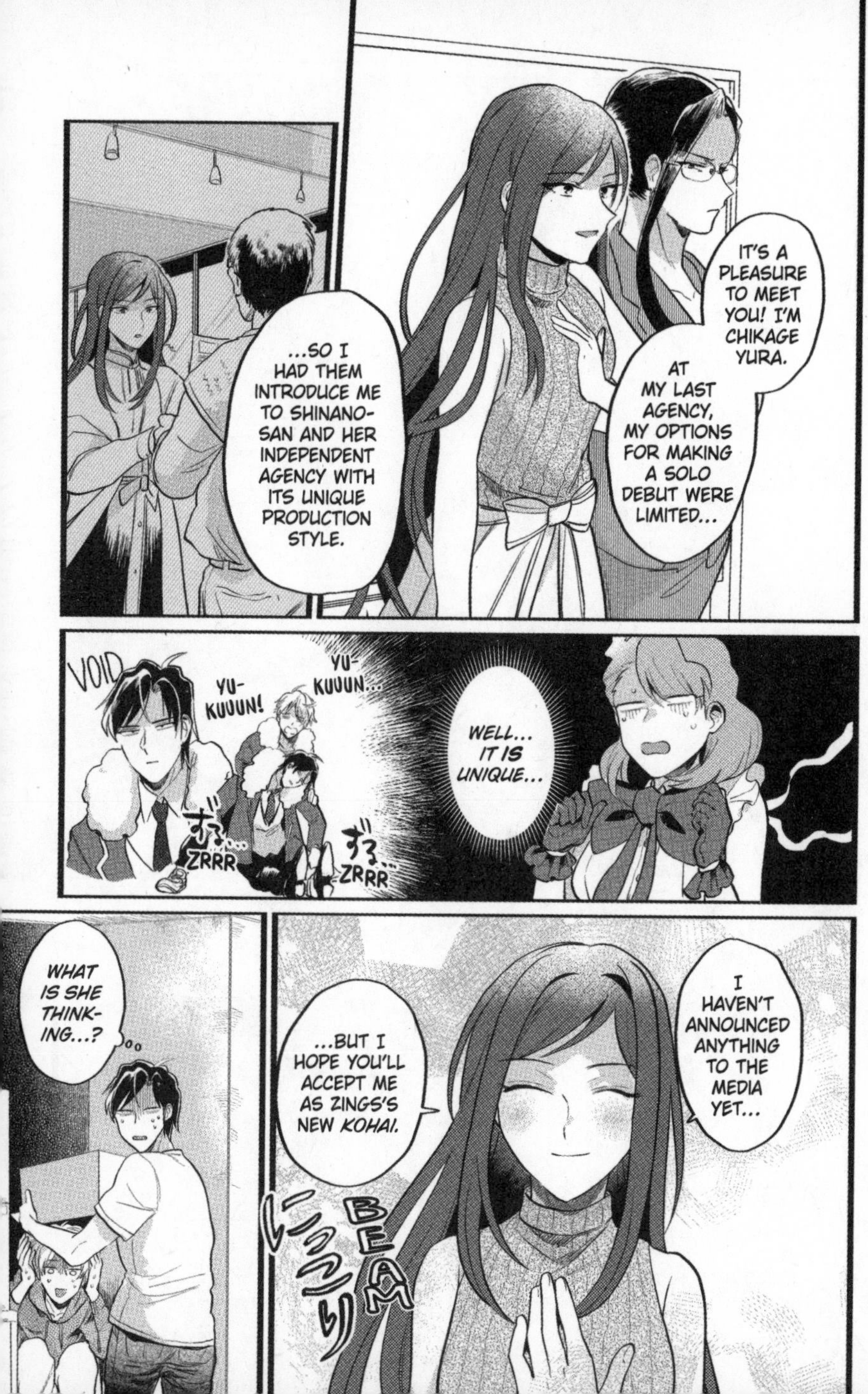
IT'S A PLEASURE TO MEET YOU! I'M CHIKAGE YURA.
AT MY LAST AGENCY, MY OPTIONS FOR MAKING A SOLO DEBUT WERE LIMITED...
...SO I HAD THEM INTRODUCE ME TO SHINANO-SAN AND HER INDEPENDENT AGENCY WITH ITS UNIQUE PRODUCTION STYLE.
WELL... IT IS UNIQUE...
YU-KUUUN...
YU-KUUUN!
VOID
ずる... ZRRR
ずる... ZRRR
I HAVEN'T ANNOUNCED ANYTHING TO THE MEDIA YET...
...BUT I HOPE YOU'LL ACCEPT ME AS ZINGS'S NEW KOHAI.
にっこり BEAM
WHAT IS SHE THINKING...?

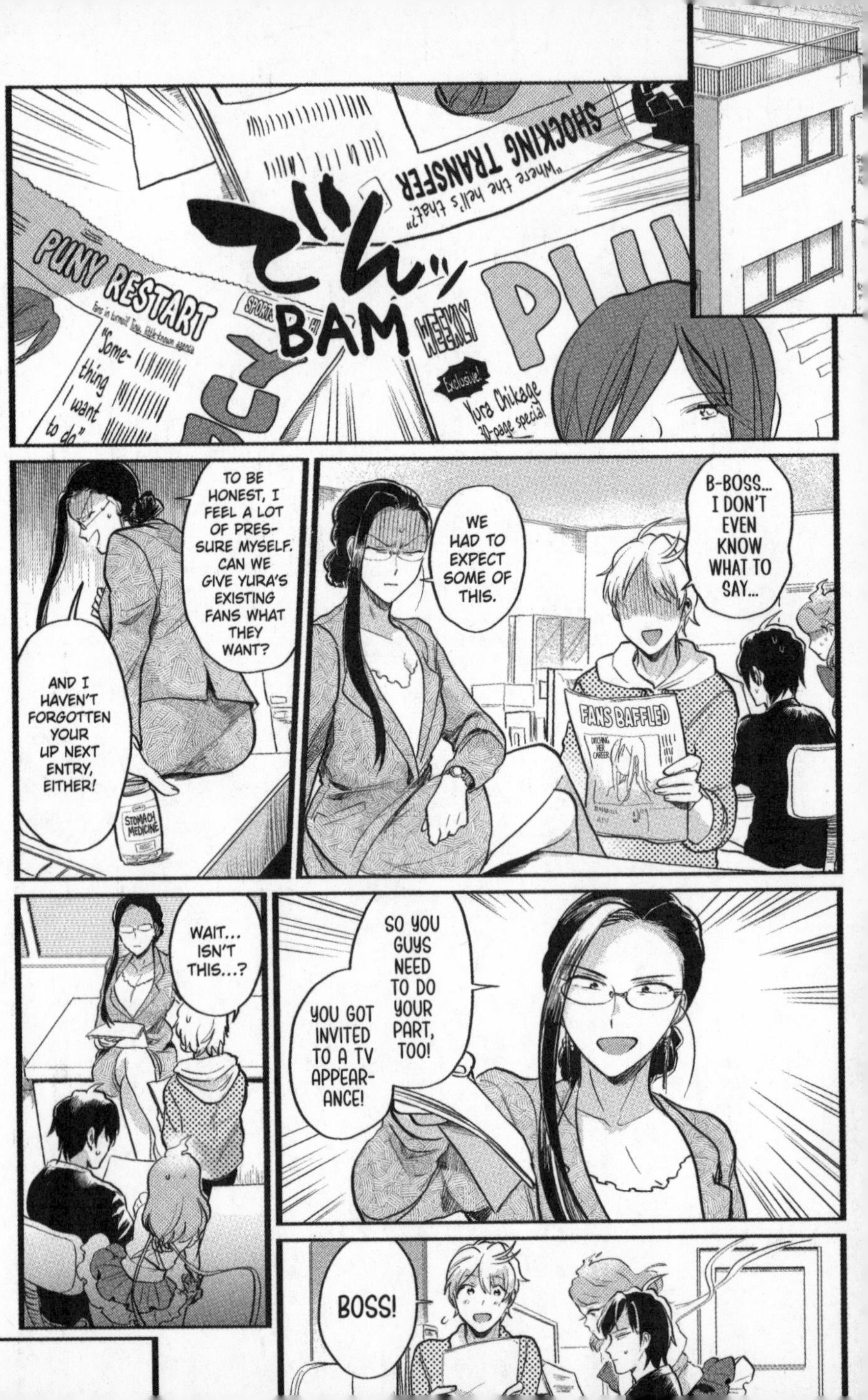
SHOCKING TRANSFER
"Where the hell's that?"
BAM
WEEKLY
Exclusive!
Yura Chikage 30-page special
PUNY RESTART
Fans in turmoil! Tiny, little-known agency
"Something I want to do"
B-BOSS... I DON'T EVEN KNOW WHAT TO SAY...
WE HAD TO EXPECT SOME OF THIS.
FANS BAFFLED
DITCHING HER CAREER
TO BE HONEST, I FEEL A LOT OF PRESSURE MYSELF. CAN WE GIVE YURA'S EXISTING FANS WHAT THEY WANT?
AND I HAVEN'T FORGOTTEN YOUR UP NEXT ENTRY, EITHER!
STOMACH MEDICINE
SO YOU GUYS NEED TO DO YOUR PART, TOO!
YOU GOT INVITED TO A TV APPEARANCE!
BOSS!
WAIT... ISN'T THIS...?

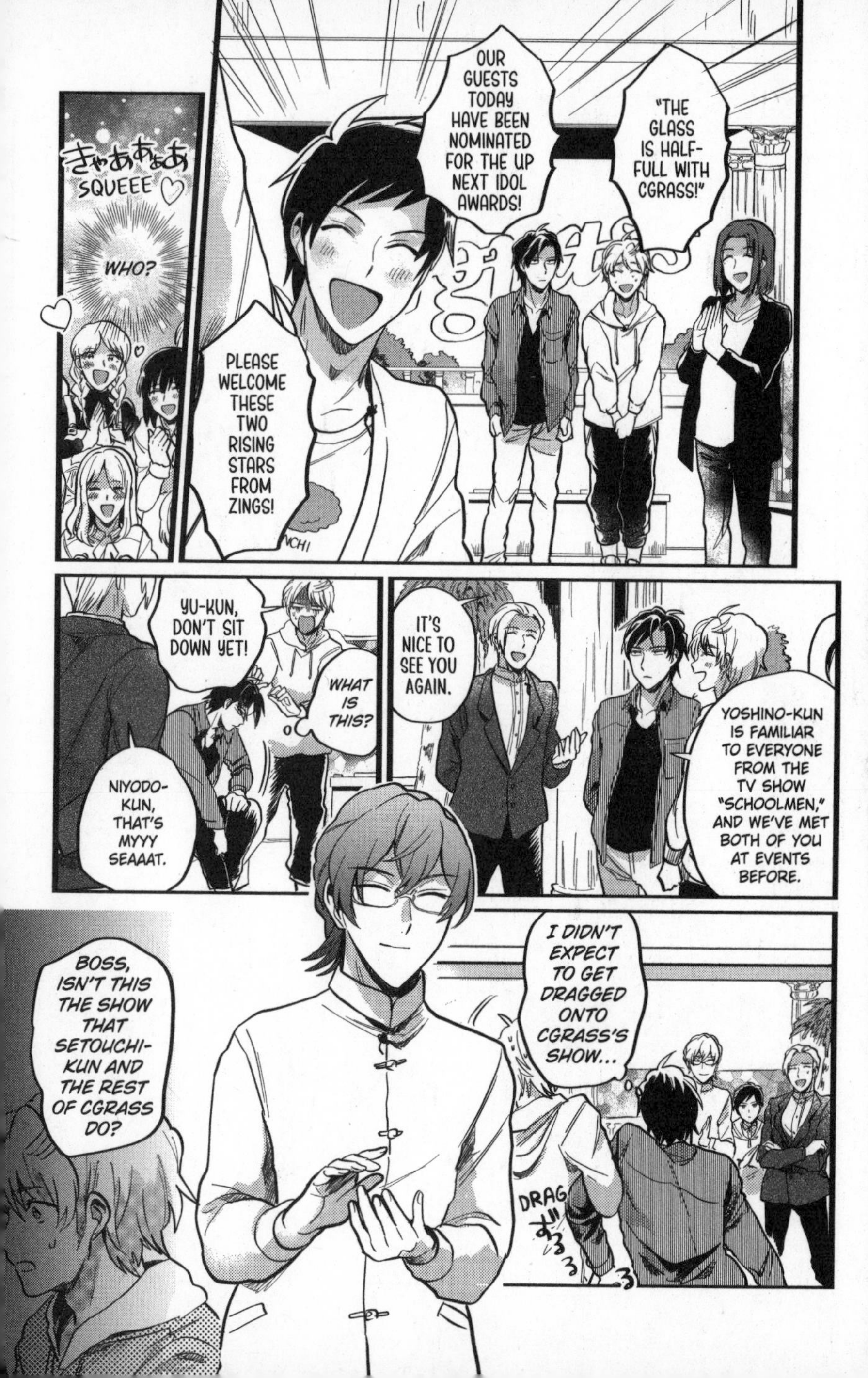
"THE GLASS IS HALF-FULL WITH CGRASS!"
OUR GUESTS TODAY HAVE BEEN NOMINATED FOR THE UP NEXT IDOL AWARDS!
PLEASE WELCOME THESE TWO RISING STARS FROM ZINGS!
きゃあぁぁあ
SQUEEE ♡
WHO?
IT'S NICE TO SEE YOU AGAIN.
YOSHINO-KUN IS FAMILIAR TO EVERYONE FROM THE TV SHOW "SCHOOLMEN," AND WE'VE MET BOTH OF YOU AT EVENTS BEFORE.
YU-KUN, DON'T SIT DOWN YET!
WHAT IS THIS?
NIYODO-KUN, THAT'S MYYY SEAAAT.
I DIDN'T EXPECT TO GET DRAGGED ONTO CGRASS'S SHOW...
DRAG
ずるるる
BOSS, ISN'T THIS THE SHOW THAT SETOUCHI-KUN AND THE REST OF CGRASS DO?

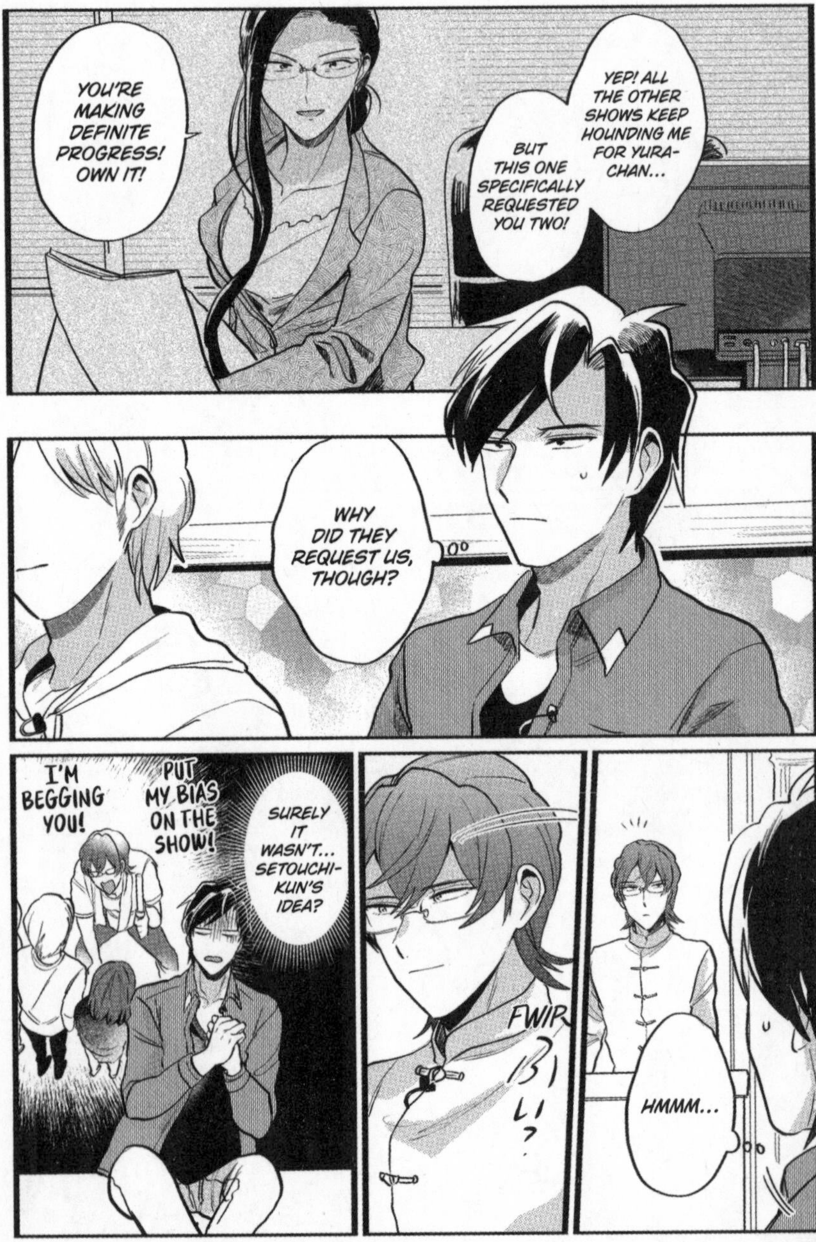
YEP! ALL THE OTHER SHOWS KEEP HOUNDING ME FOR YURA-CHAN…
BUT THIS ONE SPECIFICALLY REQUESTED YOU TWO!
YOU'RE MAKING DEFINITE PROGRESS! OWN IT!
WHY DID THEY REQUEST US, THOUGH?
HMMM…
FWIP
SURELY IT WASN'T… SETOUCHI-KUN'S IDEA?
PUT MY BIAS ON THE SHOW!
I'M BEGGING YOU!

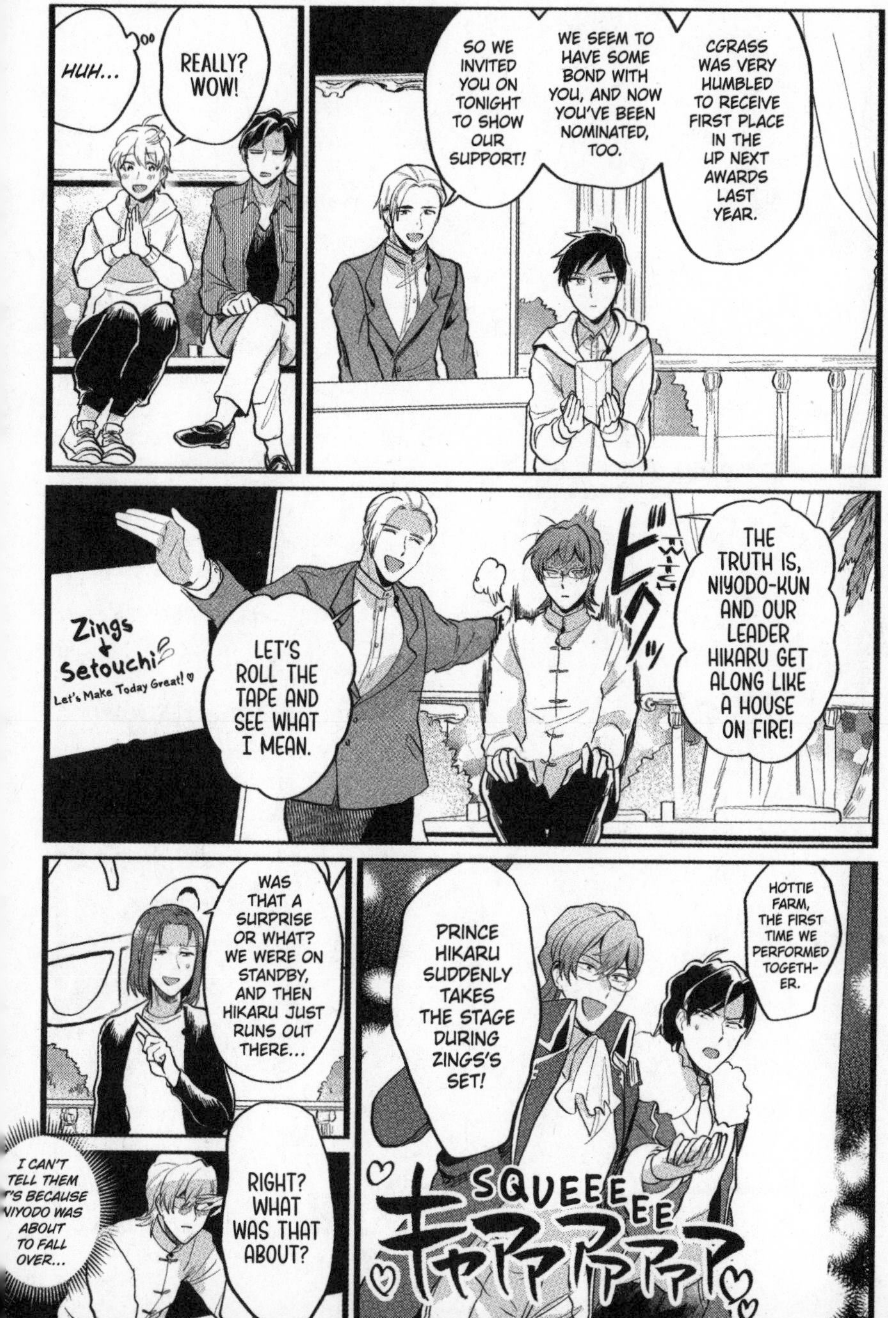
CGRASS WAS VERY HUMBLED TO RECEIVE FIRST PLACE IN THE UP NEXT AWARDS LAST YEAR.
WE SEEM TO HAVE SOME BOND WITH YOU, AND NOW YOU'VE BEEN NOMINATED, TOO.
SO WE INVITED YOU ON TONIGHT TO SHOW OUR SUPPORT!
REALLY? WOW!
HUH...
THE TRUTH IS, NIYODO-KUN AND OUR LEADER HIKARU GET ALONG LIKE A HOUSE ON FIRE!
ビクッ
TWITCH
LET'S ROLL THE TAPE AND SEE WHAT I MEAN.
Zings + Setouchi
Let's Make Today Great!
HOTTIE FARM, THE FIRST TIME WE PERFORMED TOGETH-ER.
PRINCE HIKARU SUDDENLY TAKES THE STAGE DURING ZINGS'S SET!
SQUEEEEEE
キャアアアアア
WAS THAT A SURPRISE OR WHAT? WE WERE ON STANDBY, AND THEN HIKARU JUST RUNS OUT THERE...
RIGHT? WHAT WAS THAT ABOUT?
I CAN'T TELL THEM 'S BECAUSE IYODO WAS ABOUT TO FALL OVER...

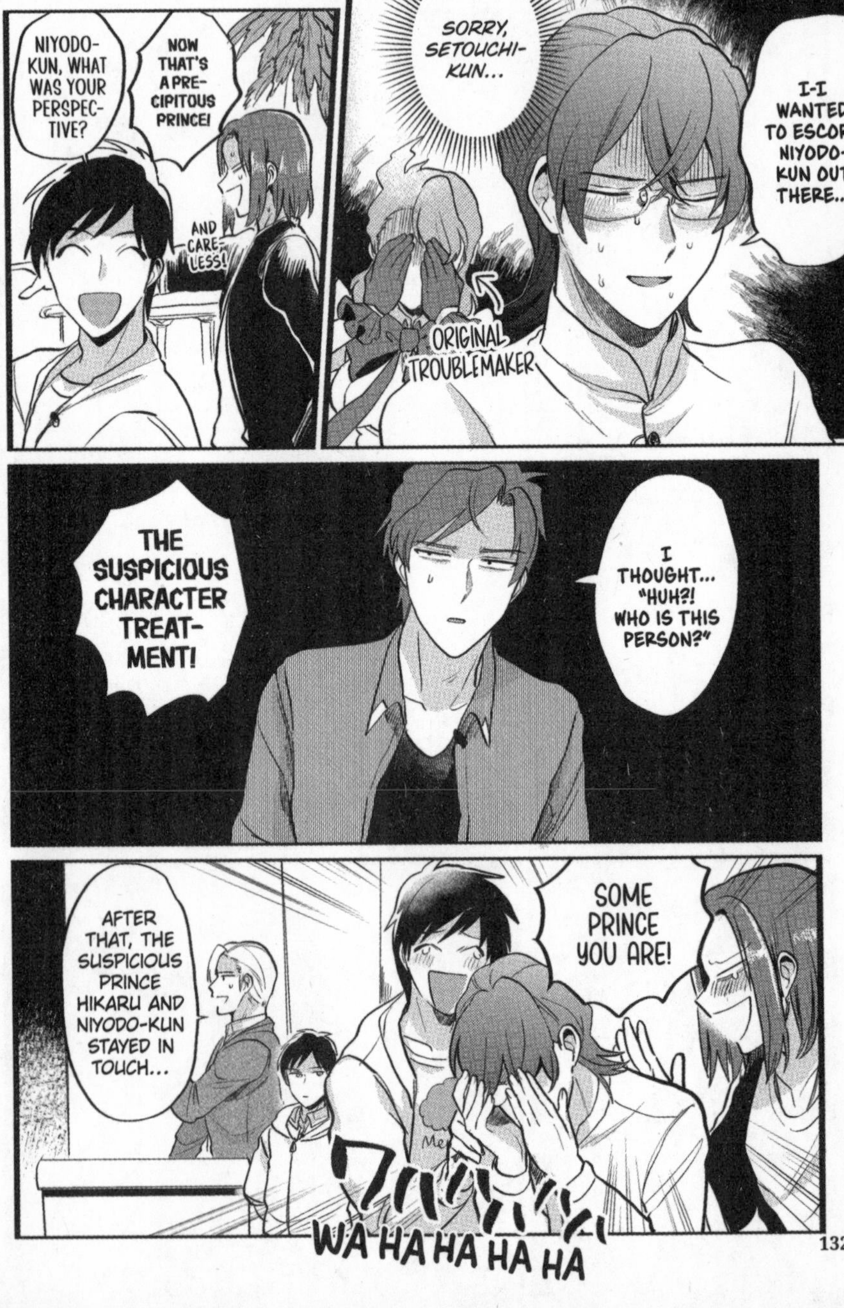
I-I WANTED TO ESCORT NIYODO-KUN OUT THERE...
SORRY, SETOUCHI-KUN...
ORIGINAL TROUBLEMAKER
NOW THAT'S A PRECIPITOUS PRINCE!
NIYODO-KUN, WHAT WAS YOUR PERSPECTIVE?
AND CARELESS!
I THOUGHT... "HUH?! WHO IS THIS PERSON?"
THE SUSPICIOUS CHARACTER TREATMENT!
SOME PRINCE YOU ARE!
AFTER THAT, THE SUSPICIOUS PRINCE HIKARU AND NIYODO-KUN STAYED IN TOUCH...
WA HA HA HA HA

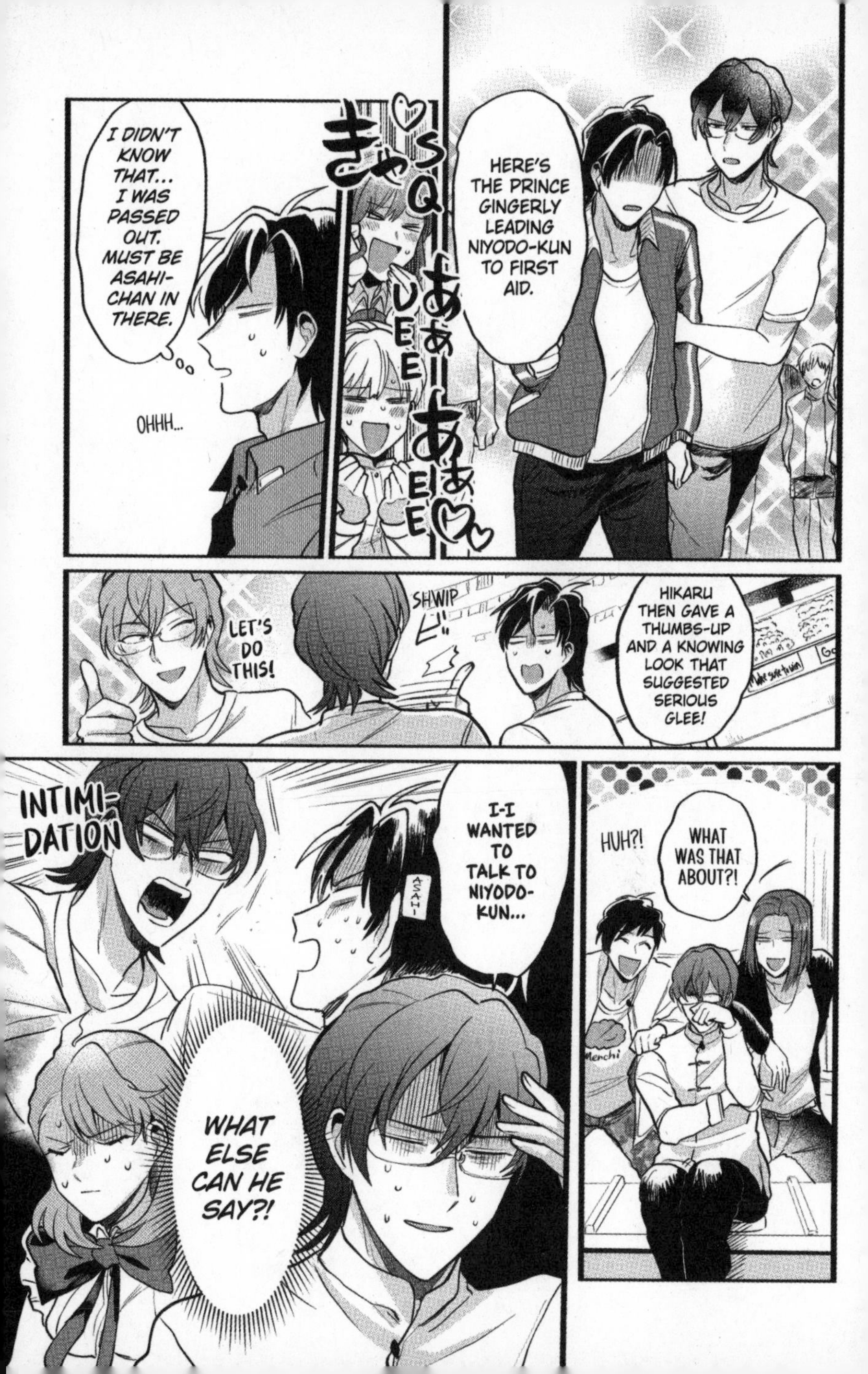
HERE'S THE PRINCE GINGERLY LEADING NIYODO-KUN TO FIRST AID.
きゃああああ
SQUEEEE
I DIDN'T KNOW THAT... I WAS PASSED OUT. MUST BE ASAHI-CHAN IN THERE.
OHHH...
HIKARU THEN GAVE A THUMBS-UP AND A KNOWING LOOK THAT SUGGESTED SERIOUS GLEE!
SHWIP
ビ
LET'S DO THIS!
WHAT WAS THAT ABOUT?!
HUH?!
I-I WANTED TO TALK TO NIYODO-KUN...
ASAHI
INTIMI-DATION
WHAT ELSE CAN HE SAY?!

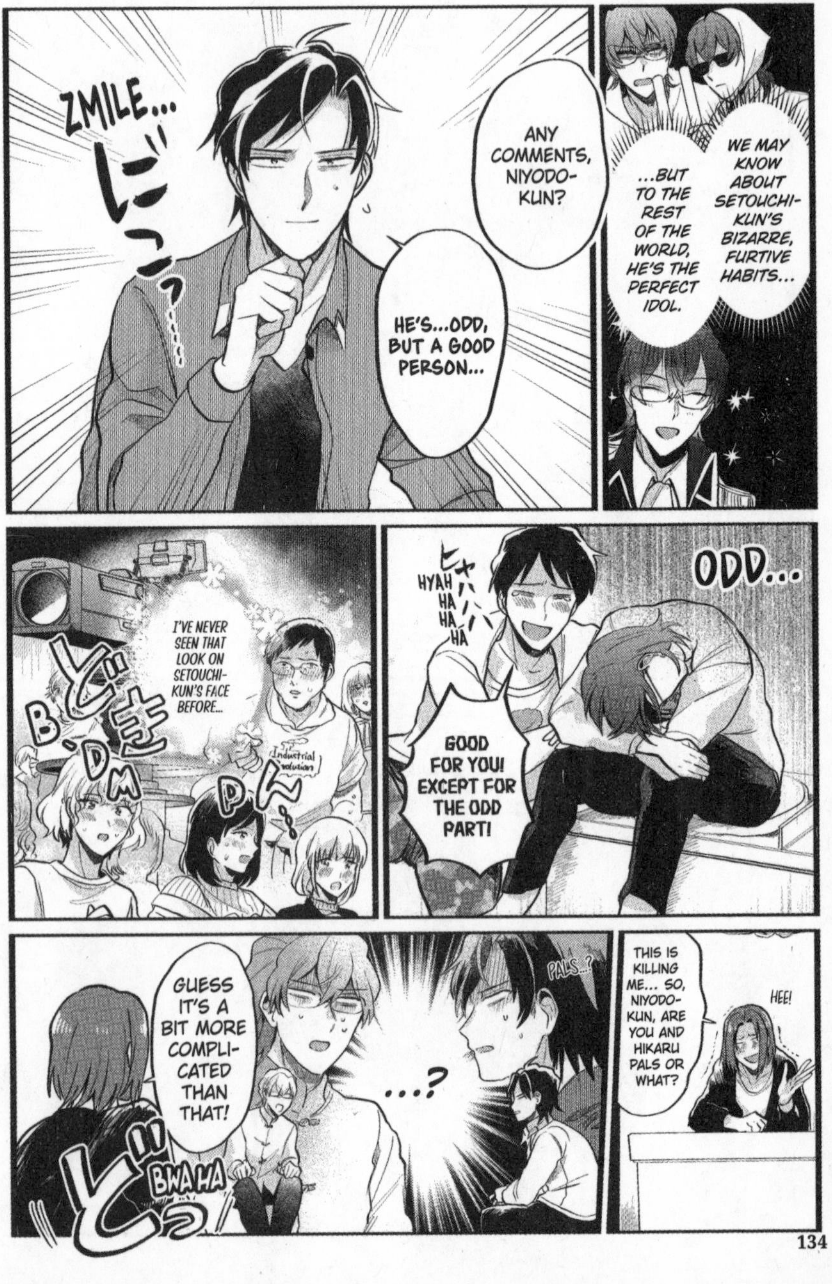
WE MAY KNOW ABOUT SETOUCHI-KUN'S BIZARRE, FURTIVE HABITS...
...BUT TO THE REST OF THE WORLD, HE'S THE PERFECT IDOL.
ANY COMMENTS, NIYODO-KUN?
ZMILE...
HE'S...ODD, BUT A GOOD PERSON...
ODD...
HYAH HA HA HA
GOOD FOR YOU! EXCEPT FOR THE ODD PART!
I'VE NEVER SEEN THAT LOOK ON SETOUCHI-KUN'S FACE BEFORE...
BDMP
THIS IS KILLING ME... SO, NIYODO-KUN, ARE YOU AND HIKARU PALS OR WHAT?
HEE!
PALS...?
GUESS IT'S A BIT MORE COMPLICATED THAN THAT!
...?
BWAHA

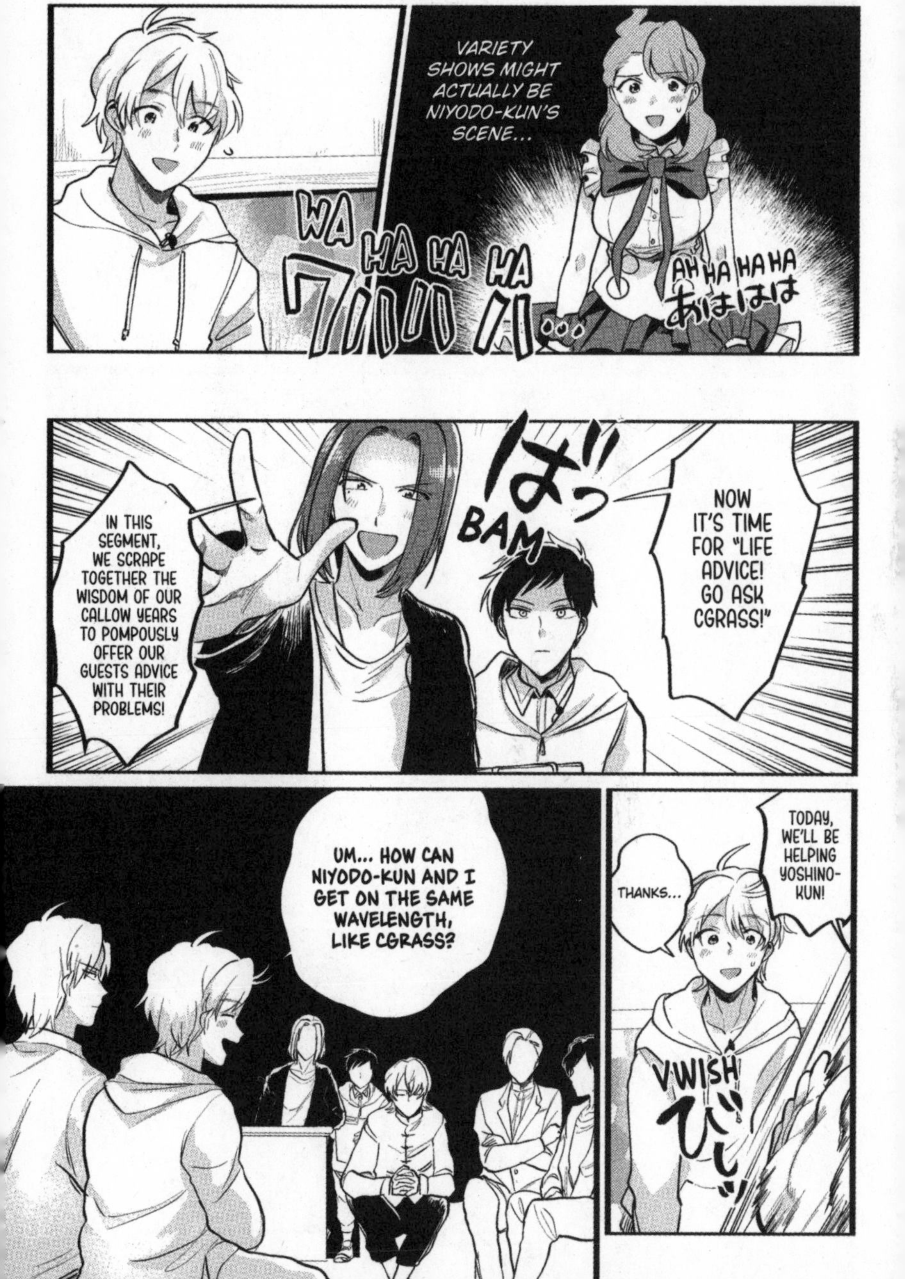

VARIETY SHOWS MIGHT ACTUALLY BE NIYODO-KUN'S SCENE...
AH HA HA HA
あははは
WA HA HA HA
NOW IT'S TIME FOR "LIFE ADVICE! GO ASK CGRASS!"
ばっ
BAM
IN THIS SEGMENT, WE SCRAPE TOGETHER THE WISDOM OF OUR CALLOW YEARS TO POMPOUSLY OFFER OUR GUESTS ADVICE WITH THEIR PROBLEMS!
TODAY, WE'LL BE HELPING YOSHINO-KUN!
THANKS...
VWISH
びしっ
UM... HOW CAN NIYODO-KUN AND I GET ON THE SAME WAVELENGTH, LIKE CGRASS?

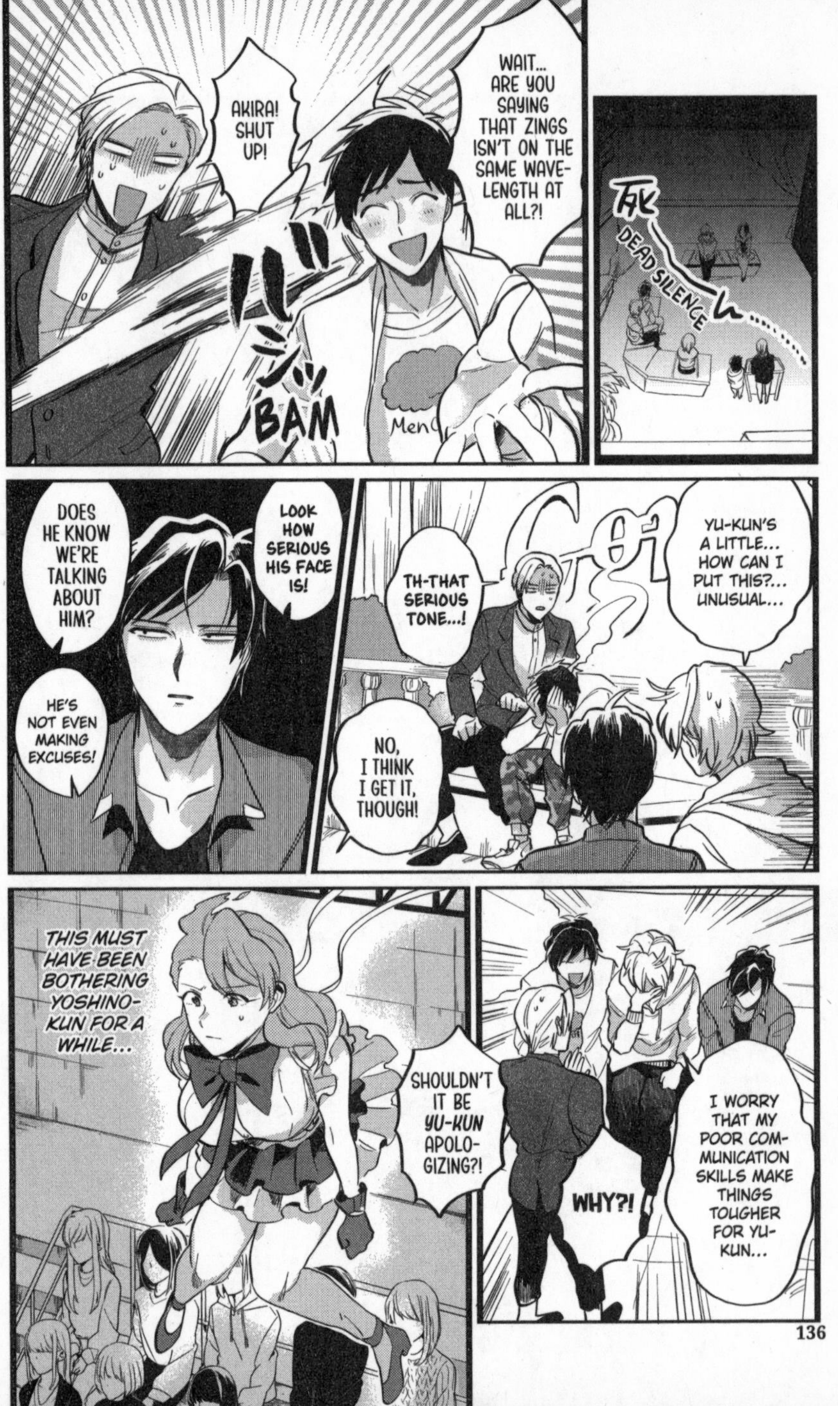
DEAD SILENCE
WAIT... ARE YOU SAYING THAT ZINGS ISN'T ON THE SAME WAVE-LENGTH AT ALL?!
AKIRA! SHUT UP!
BAM
Men
YU-KUN'S A LITTLE... HOW CAN I PUT THIS?... UNUSUAL...
TH-THAT SERIOUS TONE...!
NO, I THINK I GET IT, THOUGH!
LOOK HOW SERIOUS HIS FACE IS!
DOES HE KNOW WE'RE TALKING ABOUT HIM?
HE'S NOT EVEN MAKING EXCUSES!
I WORRY THAT MY POOR COM-MUNICATION SKILLS MAKE THINGS TOUGHER FOR YU-KUN...
SHOULDN'T IT BE YU-KUN APOLO-GIZING?!
WHY?!
THIS MUST HAVE BEEN BOTHERING YOSHINO-KUN FOR A WHILE...

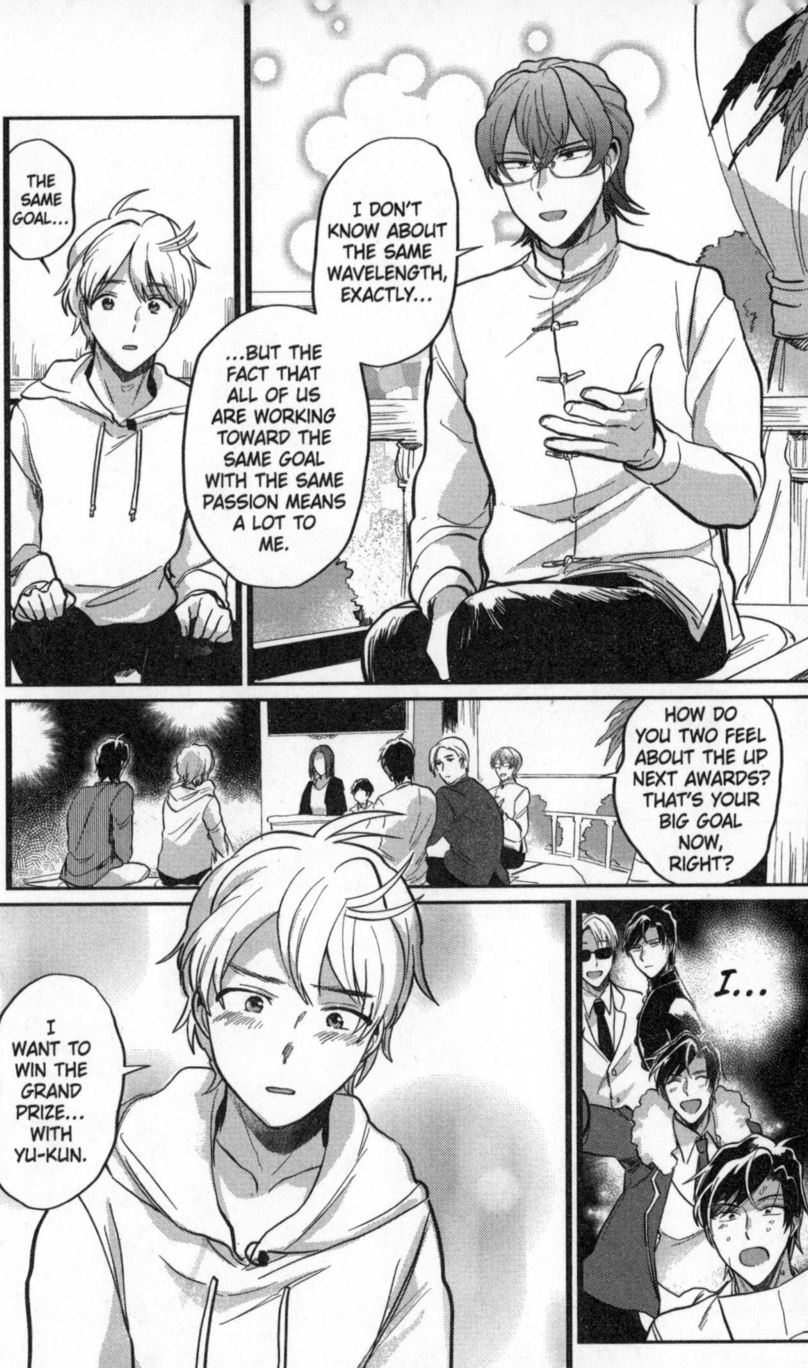
I DON'T KNOW ABOUT THE SAME WAVELENGTH, EXACTLY...
...BUT THE FACT THAT ALL OF US ARE WORKING TOWARD THE SAME GOAL WITH THE SAME PASSION MEANS A LOT TO ME.
THE SAME GOAL...
HOW DO YOU TWO FEEL ABOUT THE UP NEXT AWARDS? THAT'S YOUR BIG GOAL NOW, RIGHT?
I...
I WANT TO WIN THE GRAND PRIZE... WITH YU-KUN.

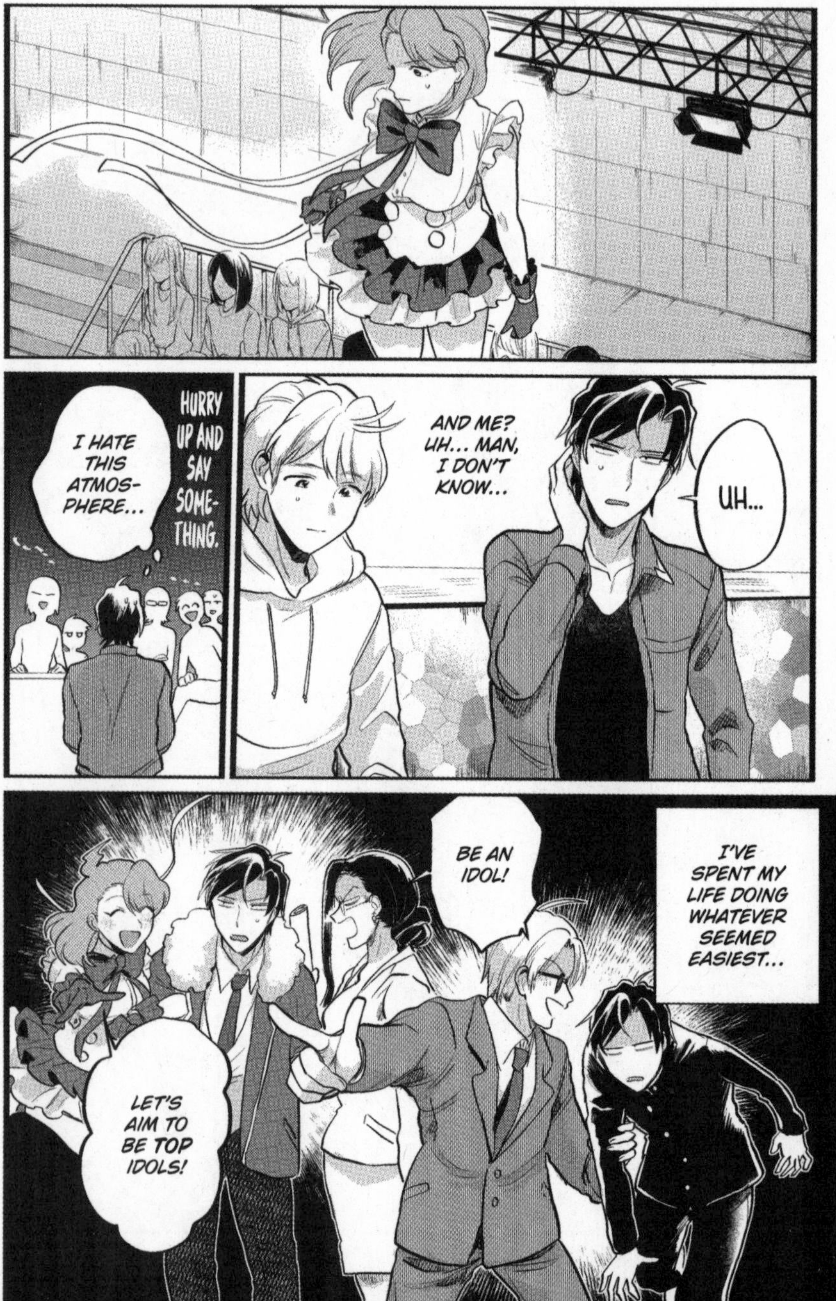
UH...
AND ME? UH... MAN, I DON'T KNOW...
HURRY UP AND SAY SOMETHING.
I HATE THIS ATMOSPHERE...
I'VE SPENT MY LIFE DOING WHATEVER SEEMED EASIEST...
BE AN IDOL!
LET'S AIM TO BE TOP IDOLS!

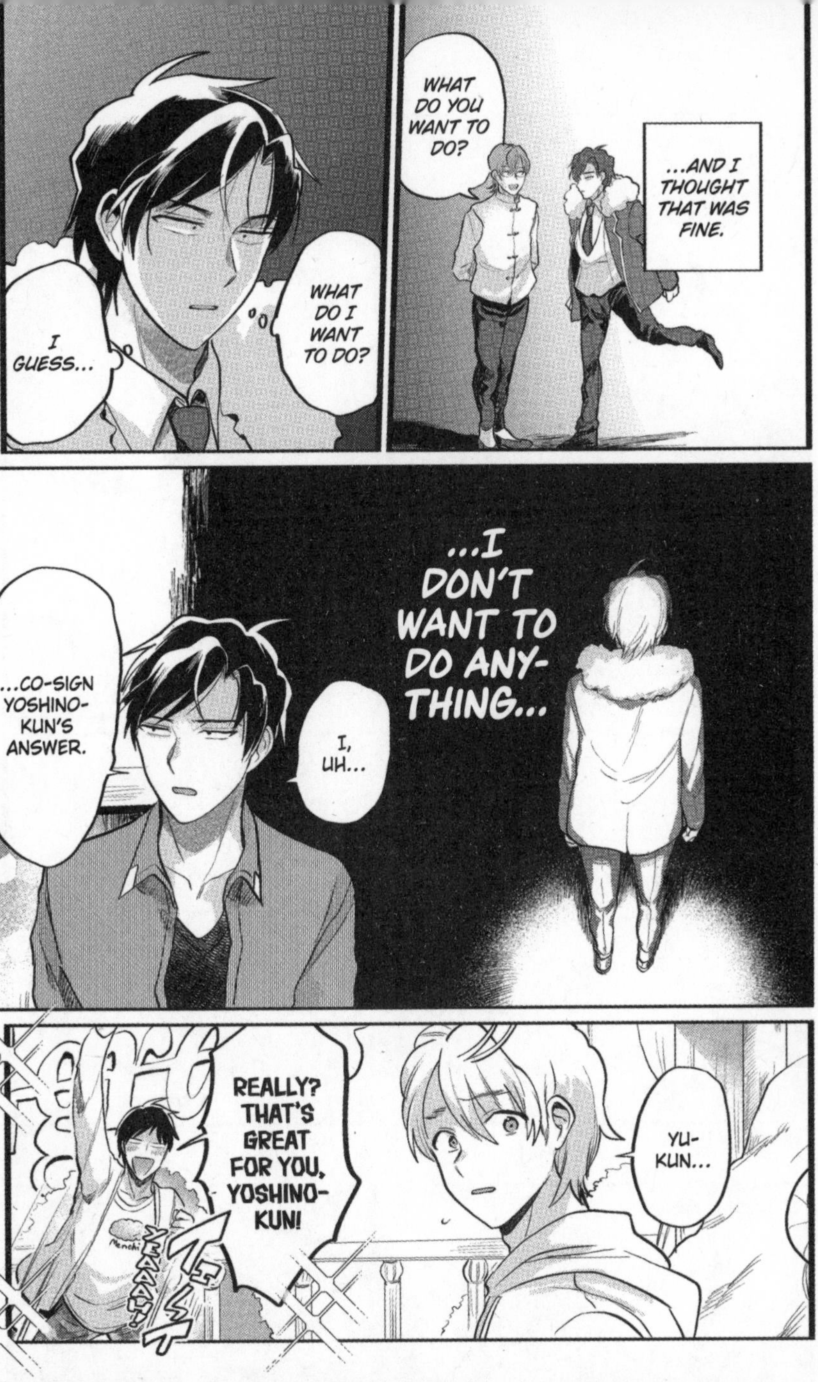
WHAT DO YOU WANT TO DO?
...AND I THOUGHT THAT WAS FINE.
WHAT DO I WANT TO DO?
I GUESS...
...I DON'T WANT TO DO ANY-THING...
I, UH...
...CO-SIGN YOSHINO-KUN'S ANSWER.
YU-KUN...
REALLY? THAT'S GREAT FOR YOU, YOSHINO-KUN!
YEAAAH!
Menchi

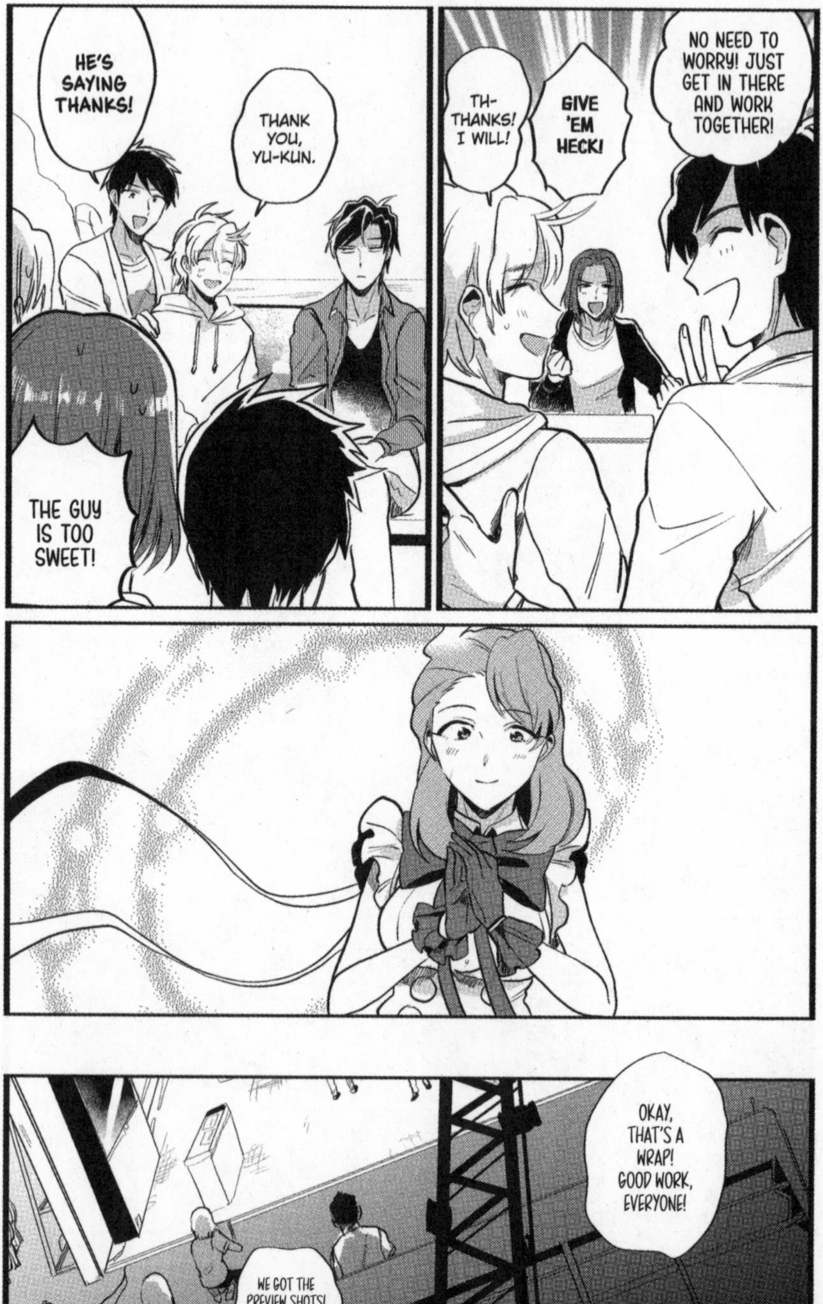
NO NEED TO WORRY! JUST GET IN THERE AND WORK TOGETHER!
GIVE 'EM HECK!
TH-THANKS! I WILL!
THANK YOU, YU-KUN.
HE'S SAYING THANKS!
THE GUY IS TOO SWEET!
OKAY, THAT'S A WRAP! GOOD WORK, EVERYONE!
WE GOT THE PREVIEW SHOTS!

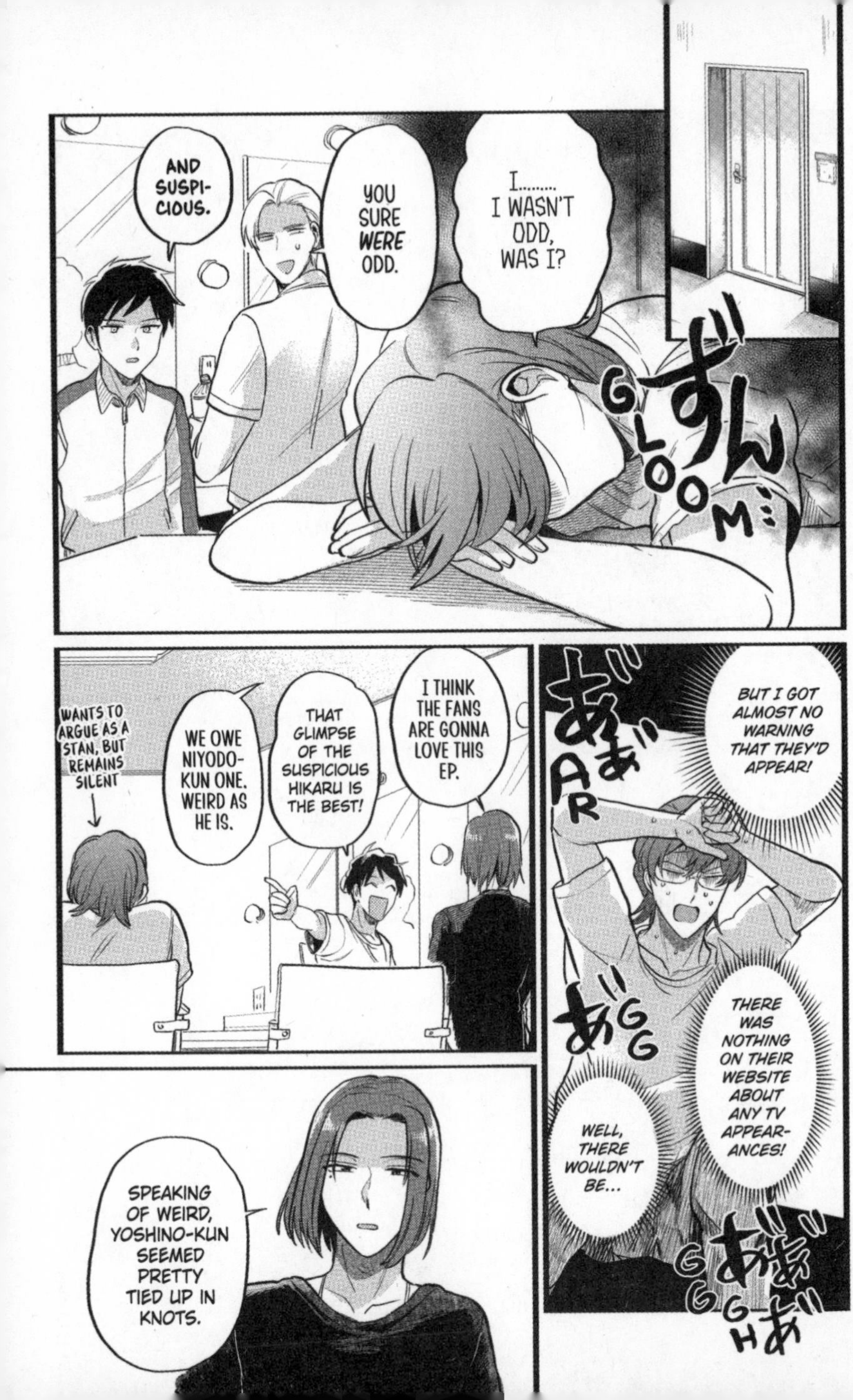
I........ I WASN'T ODD, WAS I?
YOU SURE WERE ODD.
AND SUSPICIOUS.
ずん
GLOOM
ああ
AR
BUT I GOT ALMOST NO WARNING THAT THEY'D APPEAR!
ああ
GG
THERE WAS NOTHING ON THEIR WEBSITE ABOUT ANY TV APPEARANCES!
WELL, THERE WOULDN'T BE...
ああ
GGGH
I THINK THE FANS ARE GONNA LOVE THIS EP.
THAT GLIMPSE OF THE SUSPICIOUS HIKARU IS THE BEST!
WE OWE NIYODO-KUN ONE. WEIRD AS HE IS.
WANTS TO ARGUE AS A STAN, BUT REMAINS SILENT
SPEAKING OF WEIRD, YOSHINO-KUN SEEMED PRETTY TIED UP IN KNOTS.

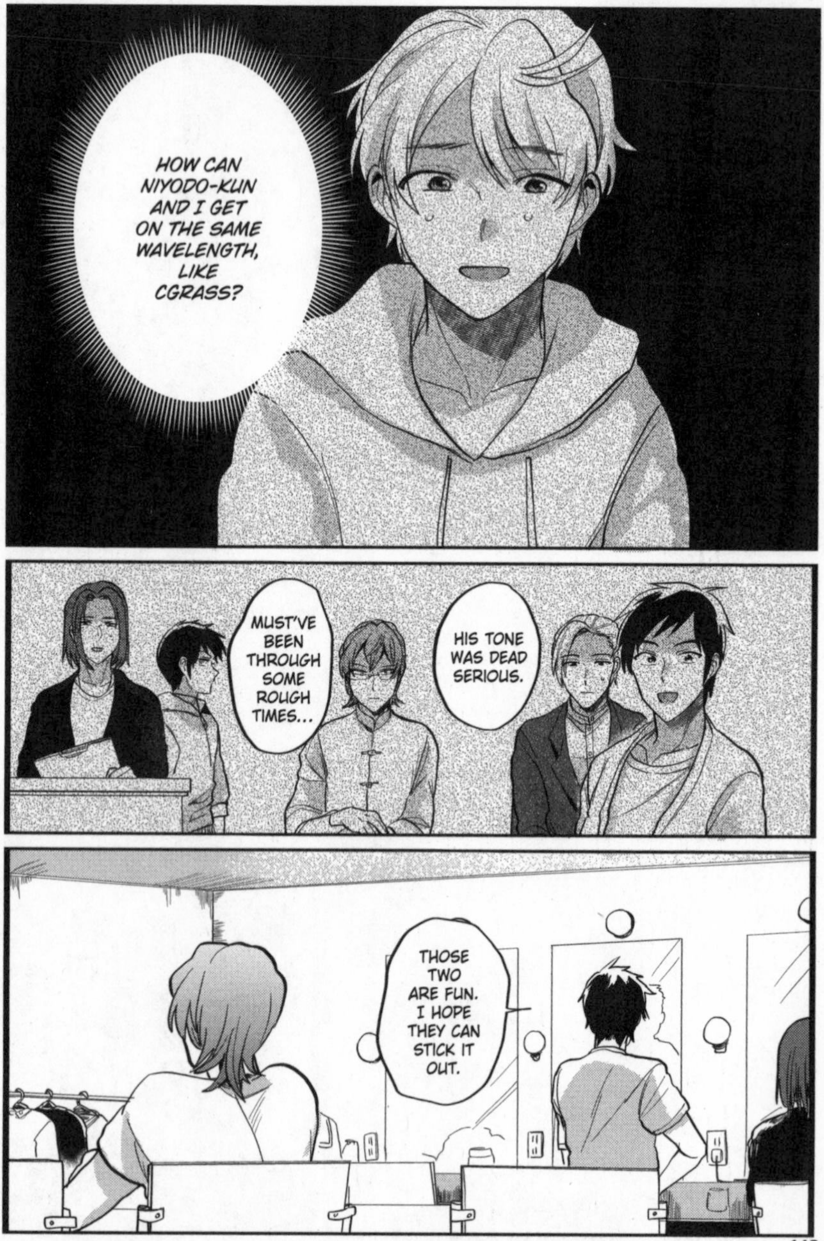
HOW CAN NIYODO-KUN AND I GET ON THE SAME WAVELENGTH, LIKE CGRASS?
HIS TONE WAS DEAD SERIOUS.
MUST'VE BEEN THROUGH SOME ROUGH TIMES...
THOSE TWO ARE FUN. I HOPE THEY CAN STICK IT OUT.

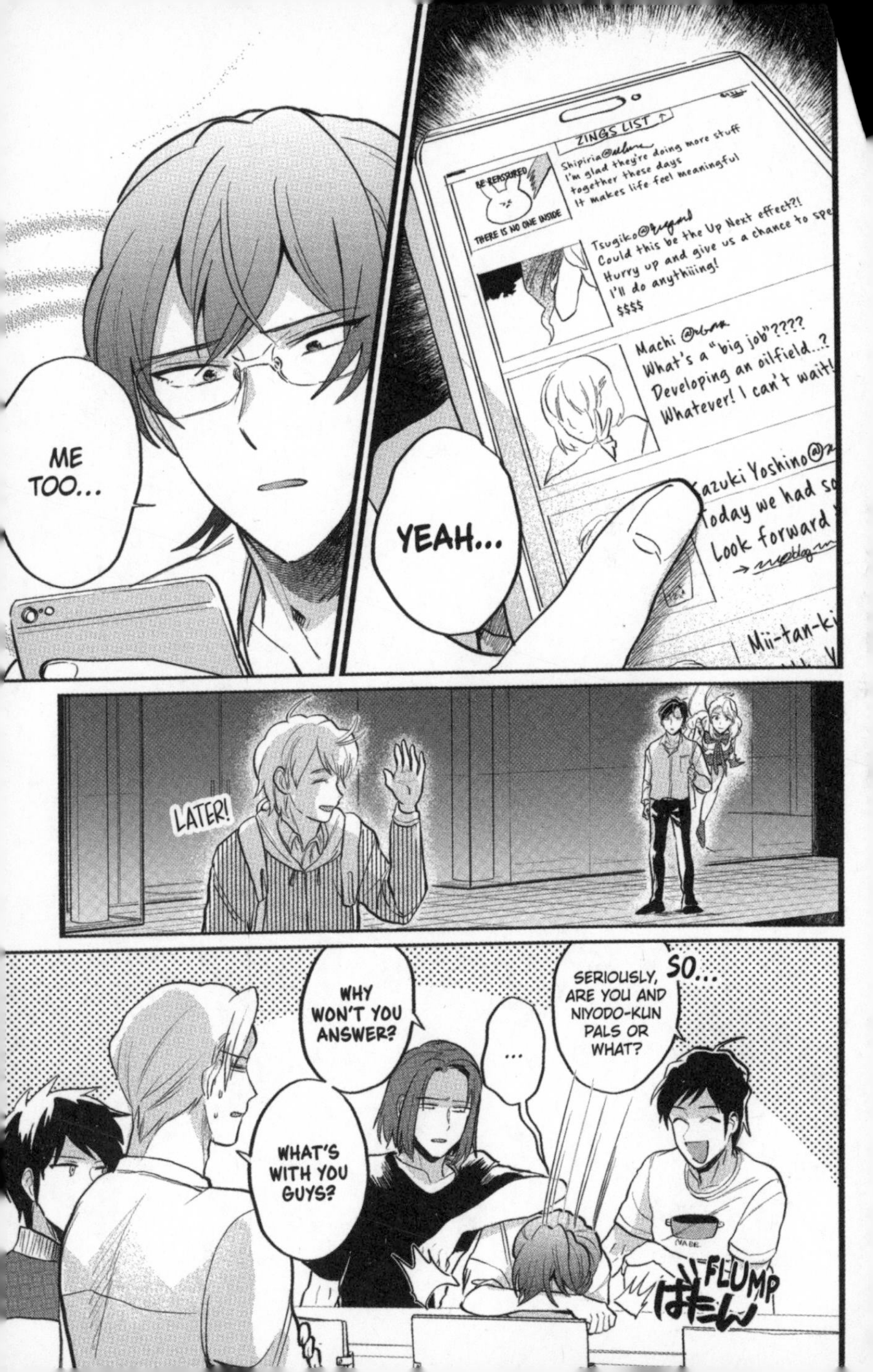
ZINGS LIST
Shipiria@
I'm glad they're doing more stuff
together these days
It makes life feel meaningful
BE REASSURED
THERE IS NO ONE INSIDE
Tsugiko@
Could this be the Up Next effect?!
Hurry up and give us a chance to spe
I'll do anythiiing!
$$$$
Machi @
What's a "big job"????
What's a "big job"????
Developing an oilfield...?
Whatever! I can't wait!
Kazuki Yoshino@
Today we had so
Look forward
Mii-tan-ki
YEAH...
ME TOO...
LATER!
SO...
SERIOUSLY, ARE YOU AND NIYODO-KUN PALS OR WHAT?
...
WHY WON'T YOU ANSWER?
WHAT'S WITH YOU GUYS?
NABE
FLUMP
ばたん

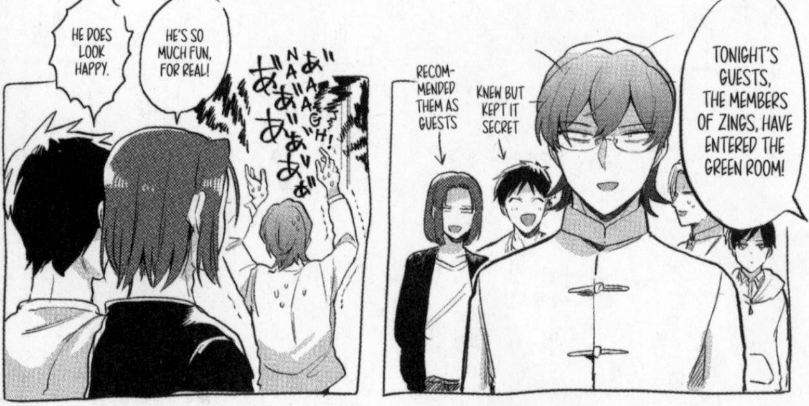
TONIGHT'S GUESTS, THE MEMBERS OF ZINGS, HAVE ENTERED THE GREEN ROOM!
KNEW BUT KEPT IT SECRET
RECOM-MENDED THEM AS GUESTS
HE'S SO MUCH FUN, FOR REAL!
HE DOES LOOK HAPPY.
NAAAGH!

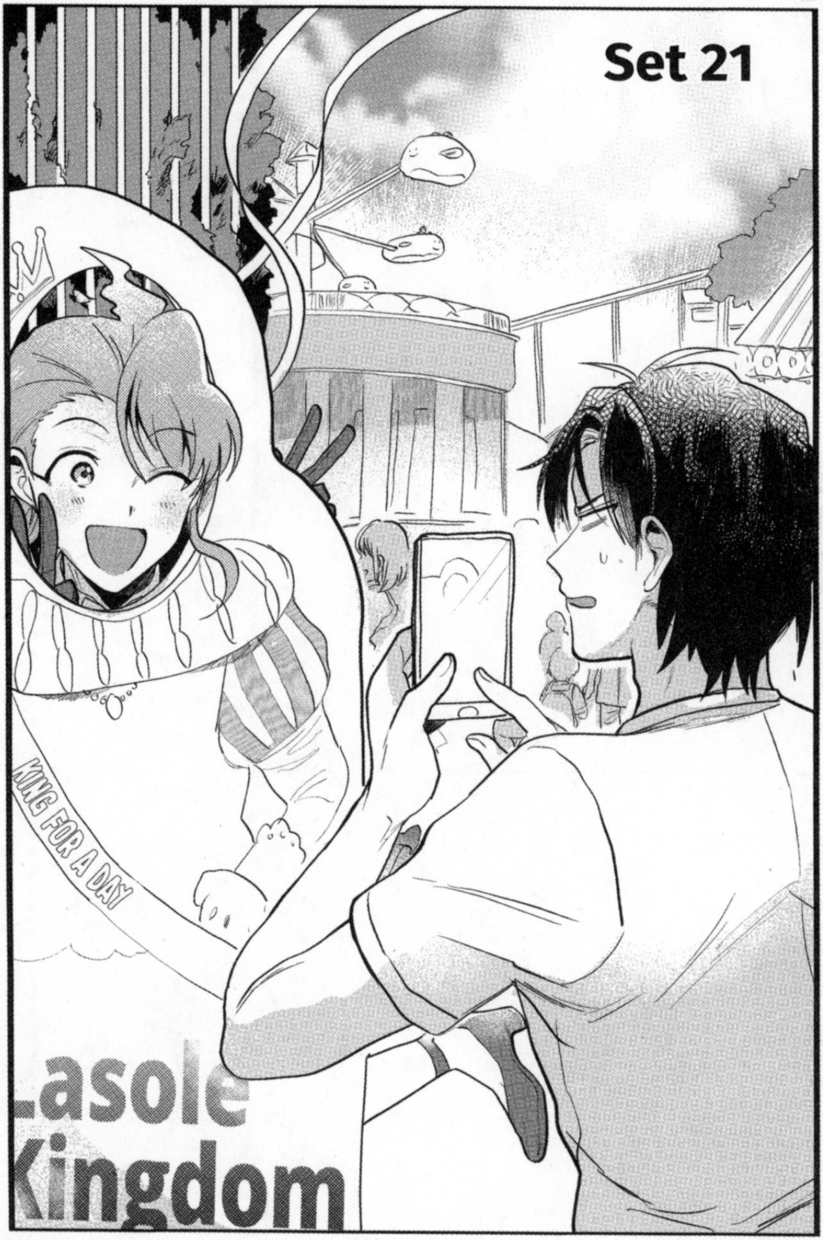
Set 21
KING FOR A DAY
Lasole Kingdom

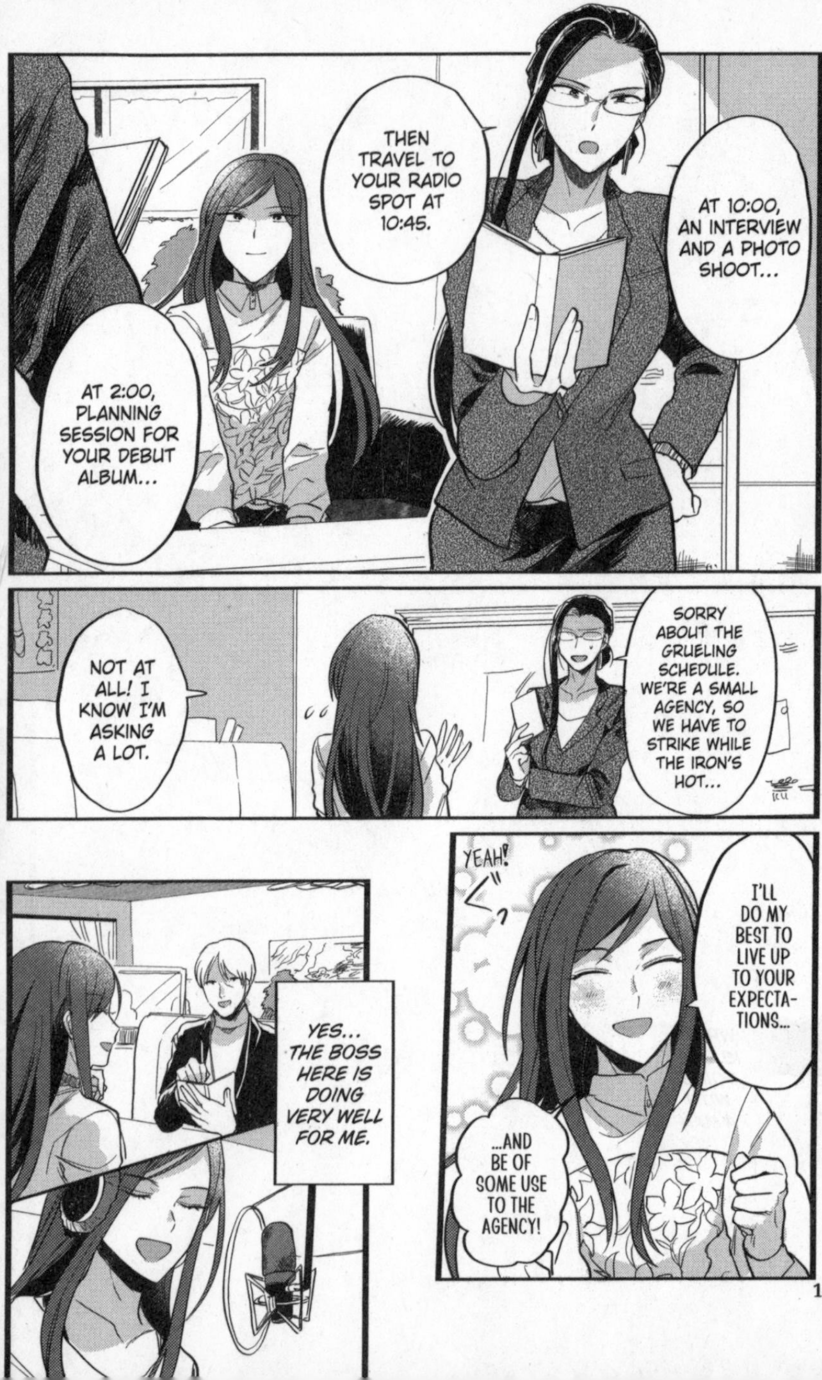
AT 10:00, AN INTERVIEW AND A PHOTO SHOOT...
THEN TRAVEL TO YOUR RADIO SPOT AT 10:45.
AT 2:00, PLANNING SESSION FOR YOUR DEBUT ALBUM...
SORRY ABOUT THE GRUELING SCHEDULE. WE'RE A SMALL AGENCY, SO WE HAVE TO STRIKE WHILE THE IRON'S HOT...
NOT AT ALL! I KNOW I'M ASKING A LOT.
I'LL DO MY BEST TO LIVE UP TO YOUR EXPECTATIONS...
YEAH!
...AND BE OF SOME USE TO THE AGENCY!
YES... THE BOSS HERE IS DOING VERY WELL FOR ME.

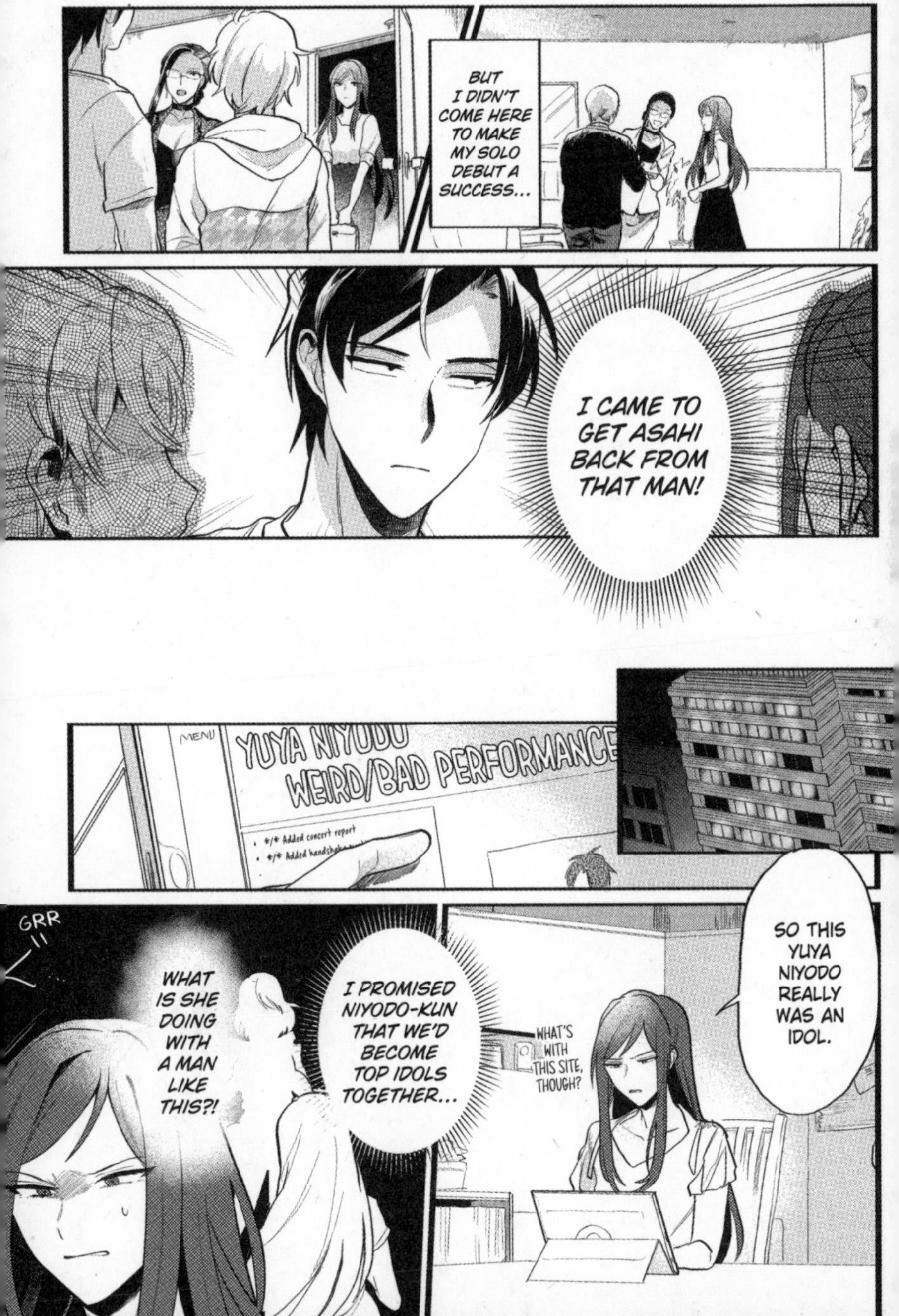
BUT I DIDN'T COME HERE TO MAKE MY SOLO DEBUT A SUCCESS…
I CAME TO GET ASAHI BACK FROM THAT MAN!
MENU
YUYA NIYODO WEIRD/BAD PERFORMANCE
*/* Added concert report
SO THIS YUYA NIYODO REALLY WAS AN IDOL.
WHAT'S WITH THIS SITE, THOUGH?
I PROMISED NIYODO-KUN THAT WE'D BECOME TOP IDOLS TOGETHER…
WHAT IS SHE DOING WITH A MAN LIKE THIS?!
GRR

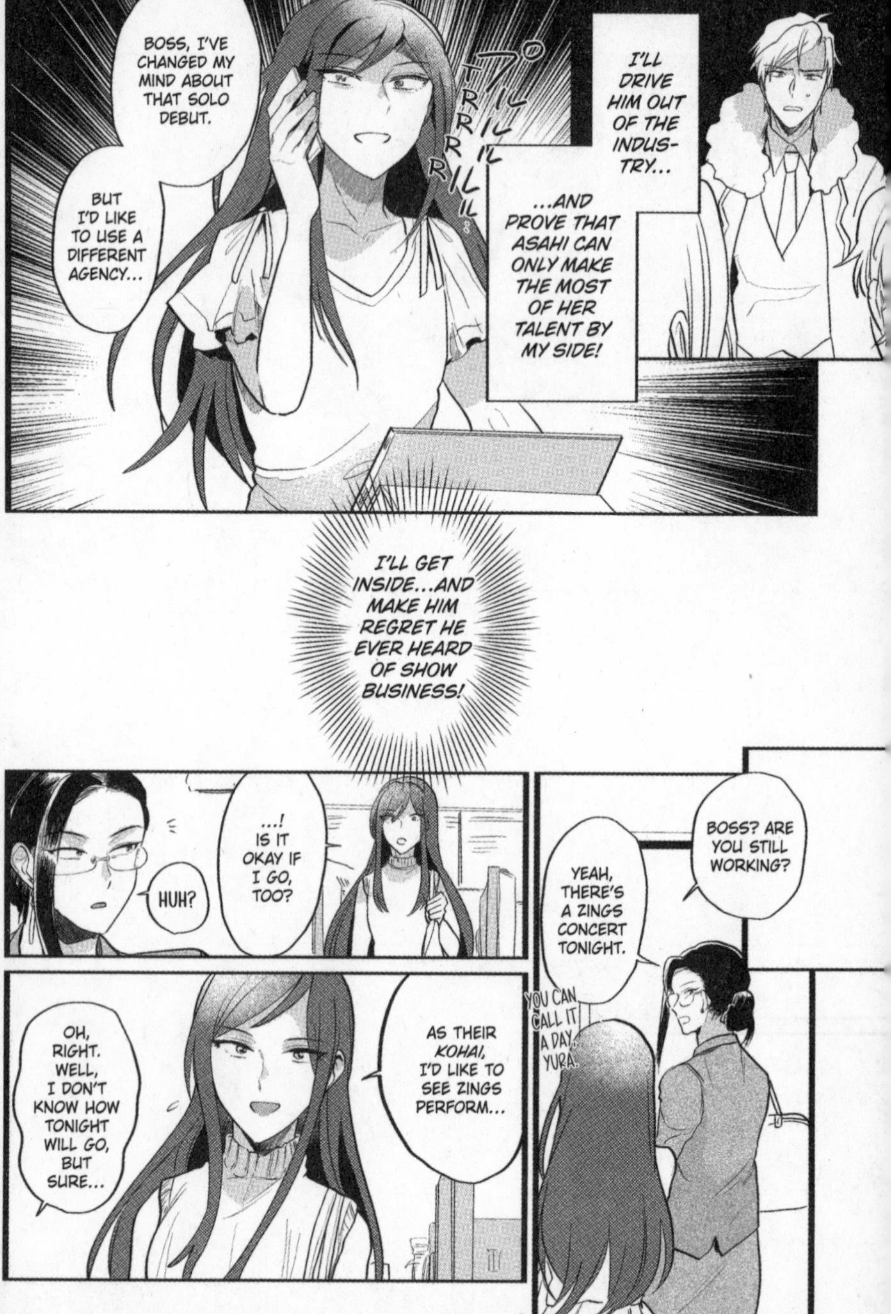
I'LL DRIVE HIM OUT OF THE INDUS-TRY...
...AND PROVE THAT ASAHI CAN ONLY MAKE THE MOST OF HER TALENT BY MY SIDE!
TRRRR
BOSS, I'VE CHANGED MY MIND ABOUT THAT SOLO DEBUT.
BUT I'D LIKE TO USE A DIFFERENT AGENCY...
I'LL GET INSIDE...AND MAKE HIM REGRET HE EVER HEARD OF SHOW BUSINESS!
BOSS? ARE YOU STILL WORKING?
YEAH, THERE'S A ZINGS CONCERT TONIGHT.
YOU CAN CALL IT A DAY, YURA.
...! IS IT OKAY IF I GO, TOO?
HUH?
AS THEIR *KOHAI*, I'D LIKE TO SEE ZINGS PERFORM...
OH, RIGHT. WELL, I DON'T KNOW HOW TONIGHT WILL GO, BUT SURE...

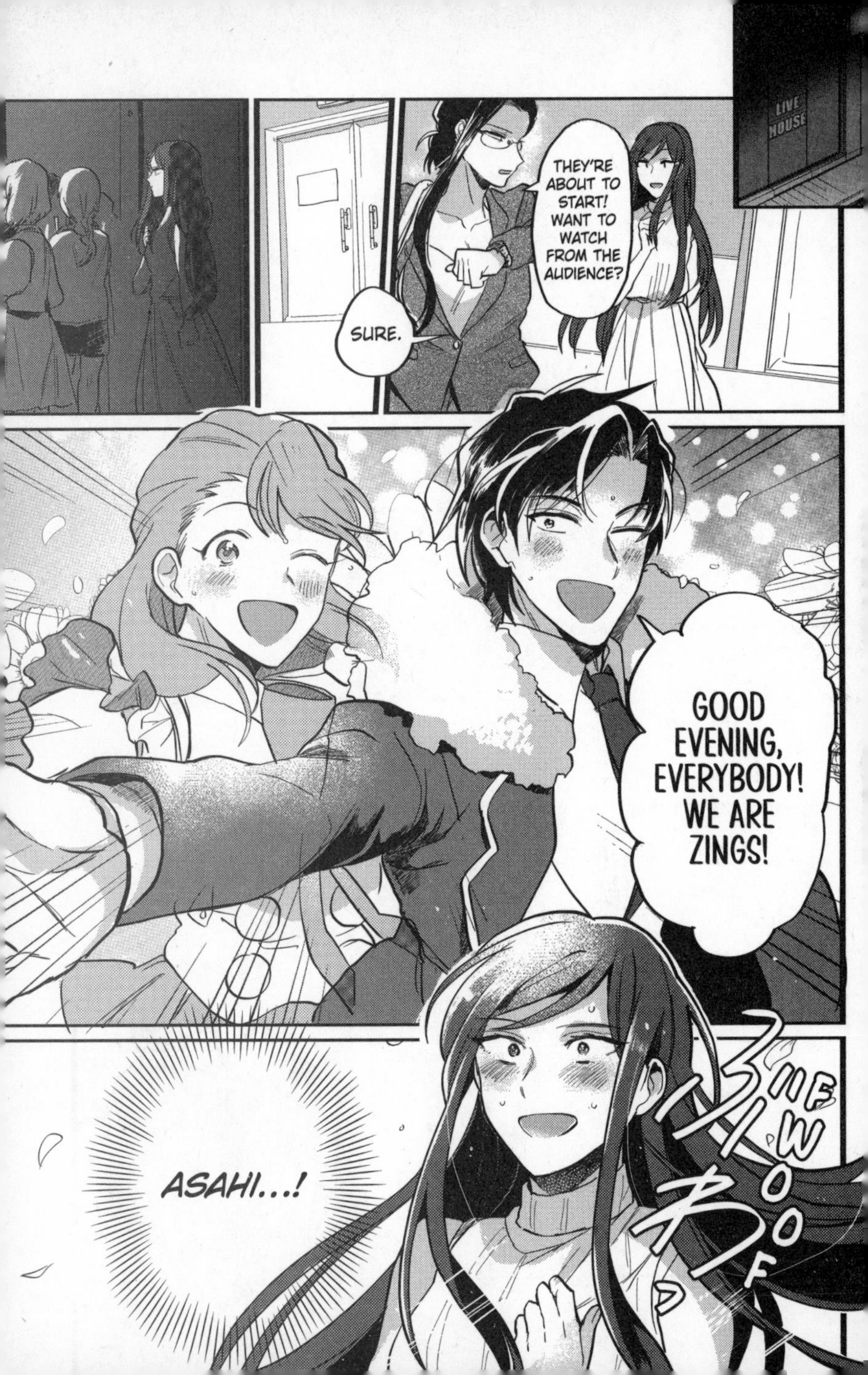
LIVE HOUSE
THEY'RE ABOUT TO START! WANT TO WATCH FROM THE AUDIENCE?
SURE.
GOOD EVENING, EVERYBODY! WE ARE ZINGS!
FWOOF
ASAHI...!

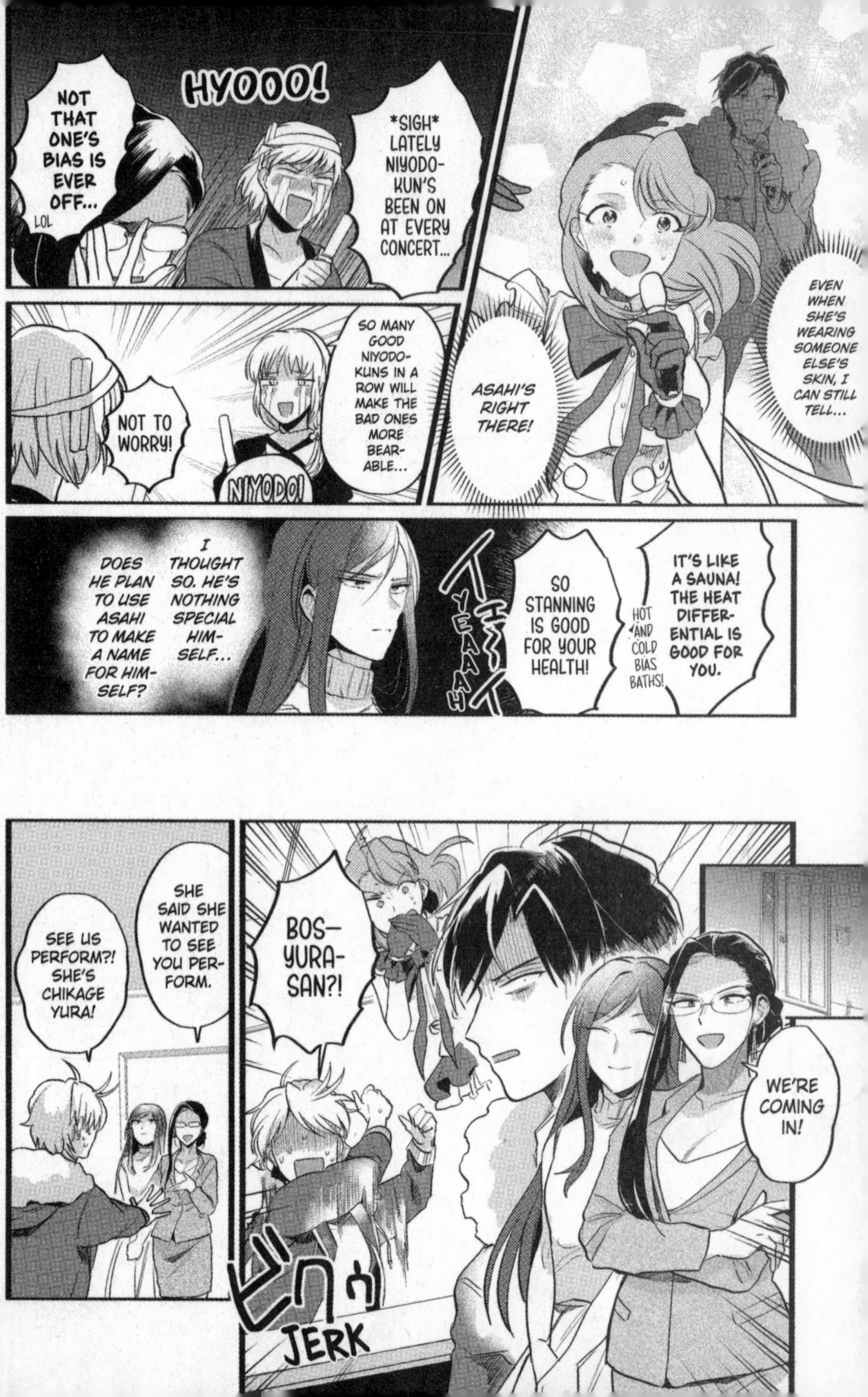
EVEN WHEN SHE'S WEARING SOMEONE ELSE'S SKIN, I CAN STILL TELL...
ASAHI'S RIGHT THERE!
*SIGH* LATELY NIYODO-KUN'S BEEN ON AT EVERY CONCERT...
HYOOO!
NOT THAT ONE'S BIAS IS EVER OFF...
LOL
SO MANY GOOD NIYODO-KUNS IN A ROW WILL MAKE THE BAD ONES MORE BEARABLE...
NIYODO!
NOT TO WORRY!
IT'S LIKE A SAUNA! THE HEAT DIFFER-ENTIAL IS GOOD FOR YOU.
HOT AND COLD BIAS BATHS!
SO STANNING IS GOOD FOR YOUR HEALTH!
YEAAAH
I THOUGHT SO. HE'S NOTHING SPECIAL HIM-SELF...
DOES HE PLAN TO USE ASAHI TO MAKE A NAME FOR HIM-SELF?
WE'RE COMING IN!
BOS-YURA-SAN?!
JERK
SHE SAID SHE WANTED TO SEE YOU PER-FORM.
SEE US PERFORM?! SHE'S CHIKAGE YURA!

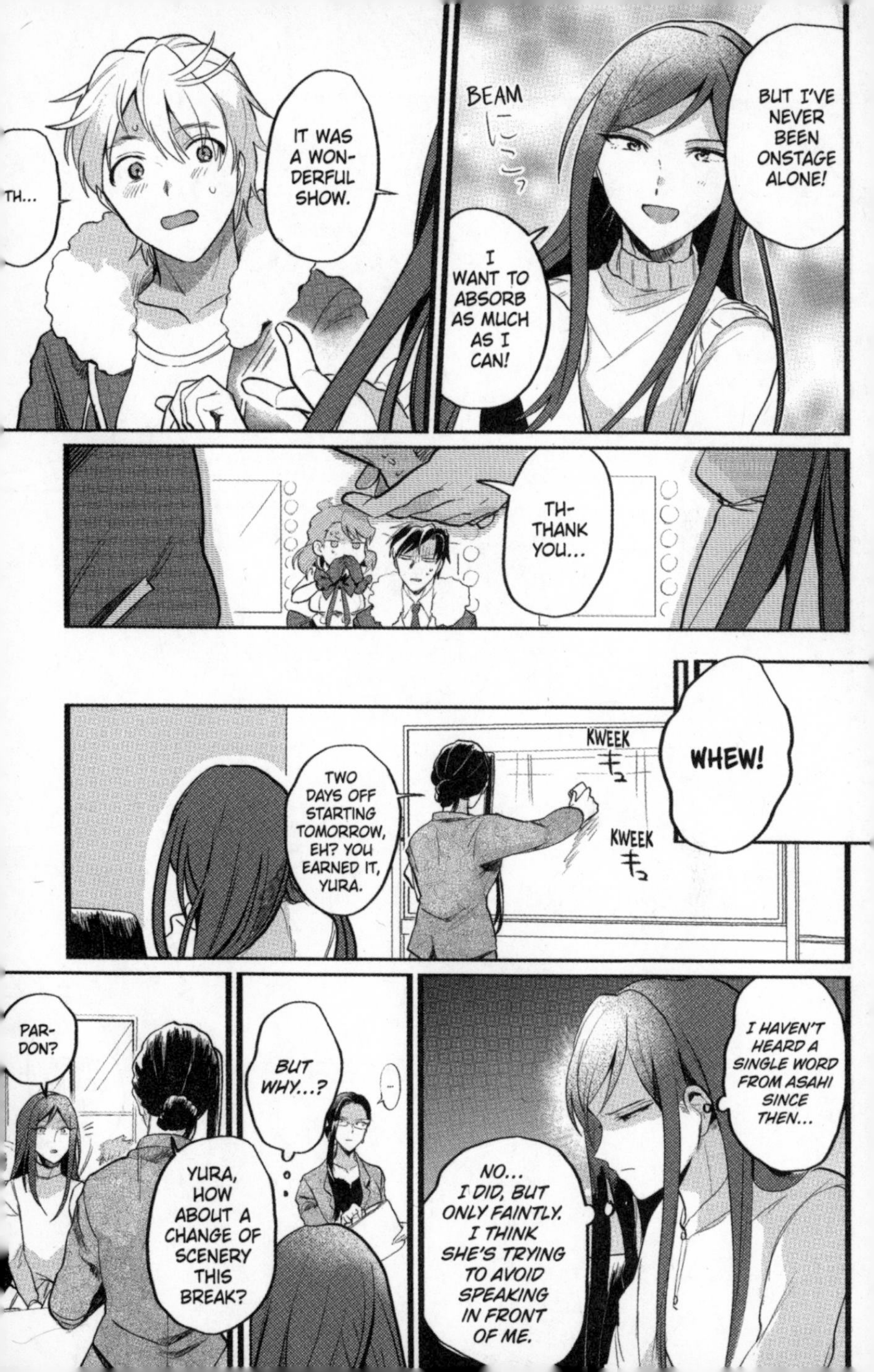
BUT I'VE NEVER BEEN ONSTAGE ALONE!
BEAM
I WANT TO ABSORB AS MUCH AS I CAN!
IT WAS A WON-DERFUL SHOW.
TH...
TH-THANK YOU...
WHEW!
KWEEK
KWEEK
TWO DAYS OFF STARTING TOMORROW, EH? YOU EARNED IT, YURA.
I HAVEN'T HEARD A SINGLE WORD FROM ASAHI SINCE THEN...
NO... I DID, BUT ONLY FAINTLY. I THINK SHE'S TRYING TO AVOID SPEAKING IN FRONT OF ME.
BUT WHY...?
...
YURA, HOW ABOUT A CHANGE OF SCENERY THIS BREAK?
PAR-DON?

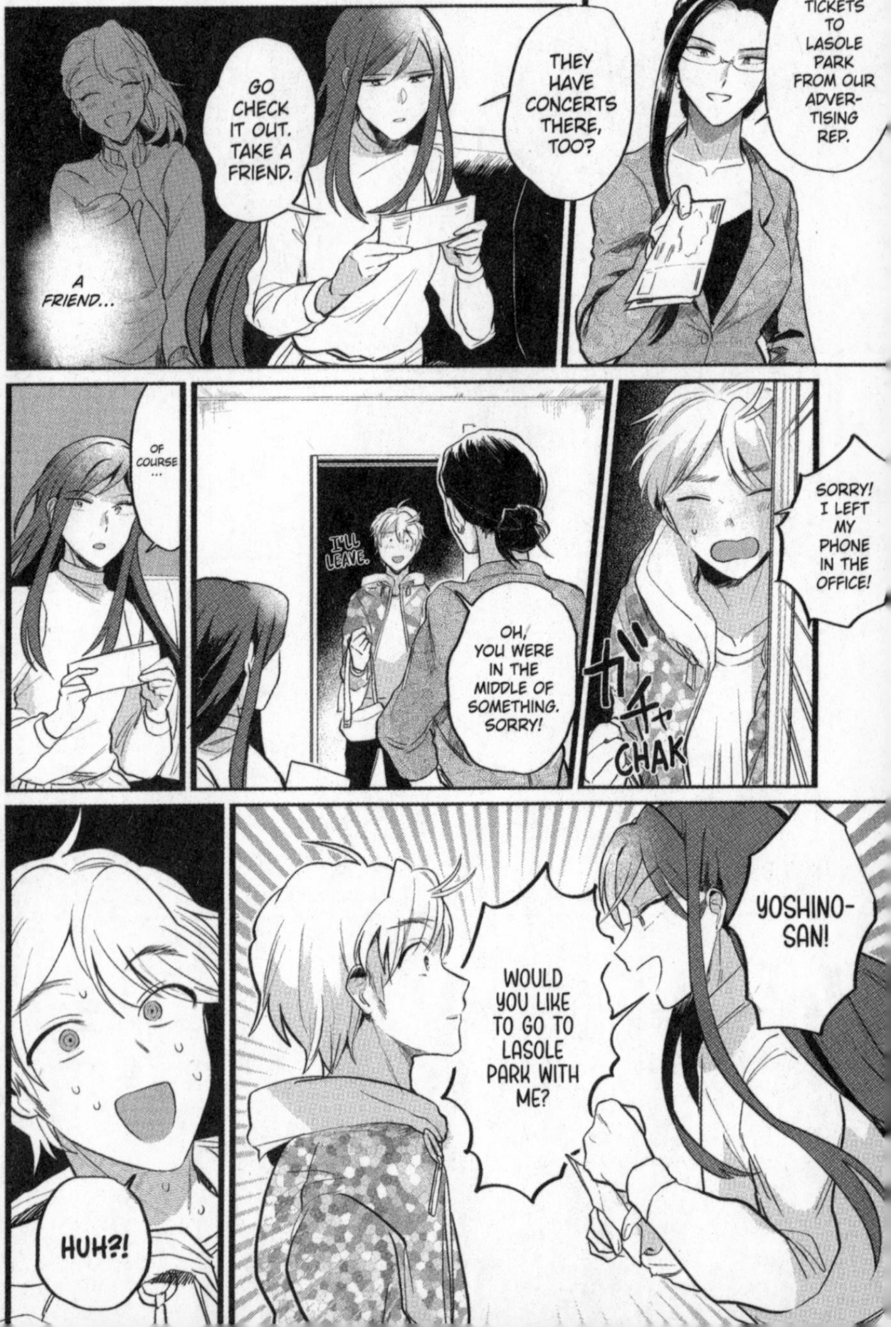
I GOT TICKETS TO LASOLE PARK FROM OUR ADVERTISING REP.
THEY HAVE CONCERTS THERE, TOO?
GO CHECK IT OUT. TAKE A FRIEND.
A FRIEND...
SORRY! I LEFT MY PHONE IN THE OFFICE!
CHAK
OH, YOU WERE IN THE MIDDLE OF SOMETHING. SORRY!
I'LL LEAVE.
OF COURSE...
YOSHINO-SAN!
WOULD YOU LIKE TO GO TO LASOLE PARK WITH ME?
HUH?!

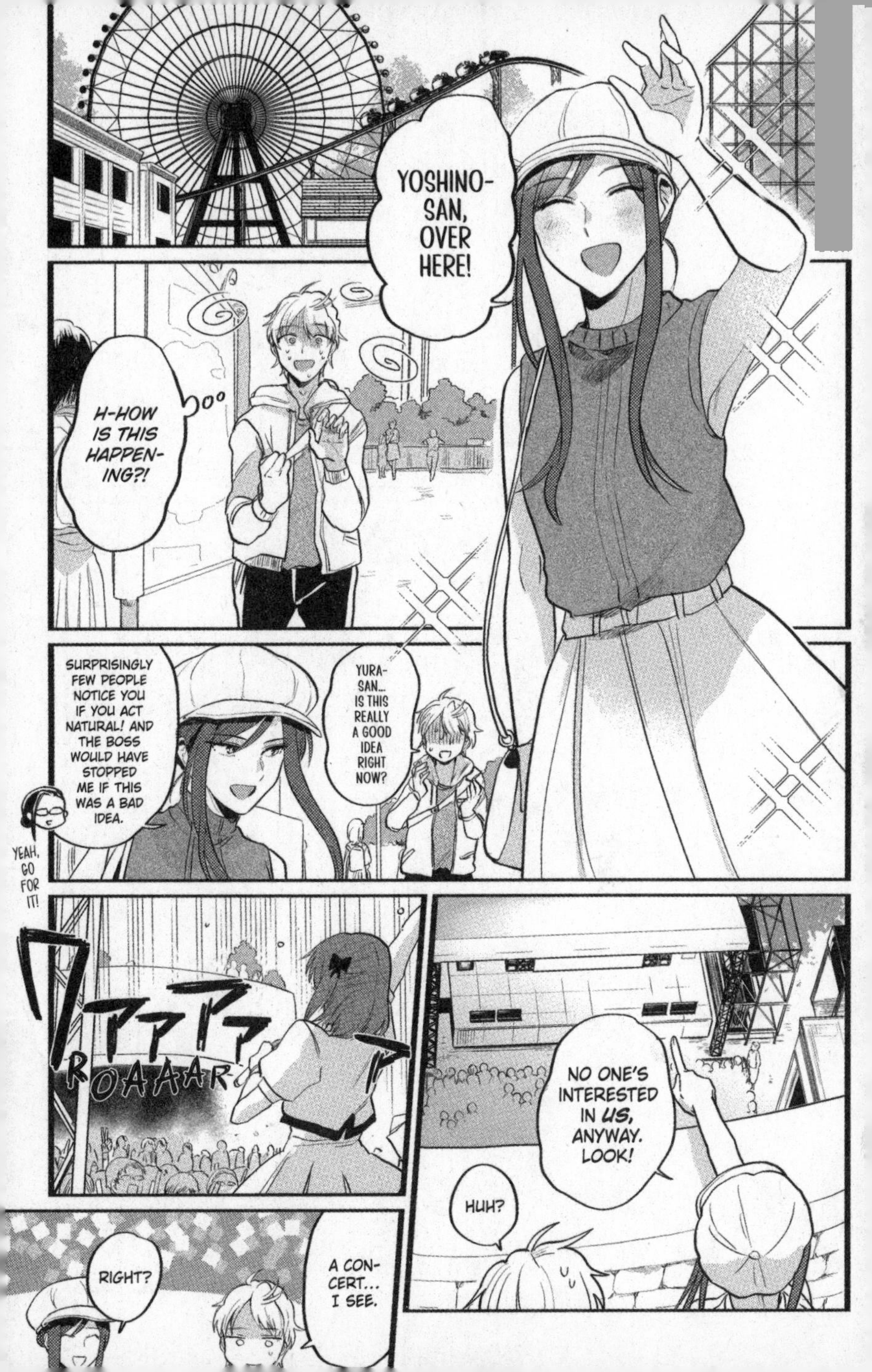
YOSHINO-SAN, OVER HERE!
H-HOW IS THIS HAPPENING?!
YURA-SAN... IS THIS REALLY A GOOD IDEA RIGHT NOW?
SURPRISINGLY FEW PEOPLE NOTICE YOU IF YOU ACT NATURAL! AND THE BOSS WOULD HAVE STOPPED ME IF THIS WAS A BAD IDEA.
YEAH, GO FOR IT!
NO ONE'S INTERESTED IN *US*, ANYWAY. LOOK!
HUH?
ROAAAR
A CON-CERT... I SEE.
RIGHT?

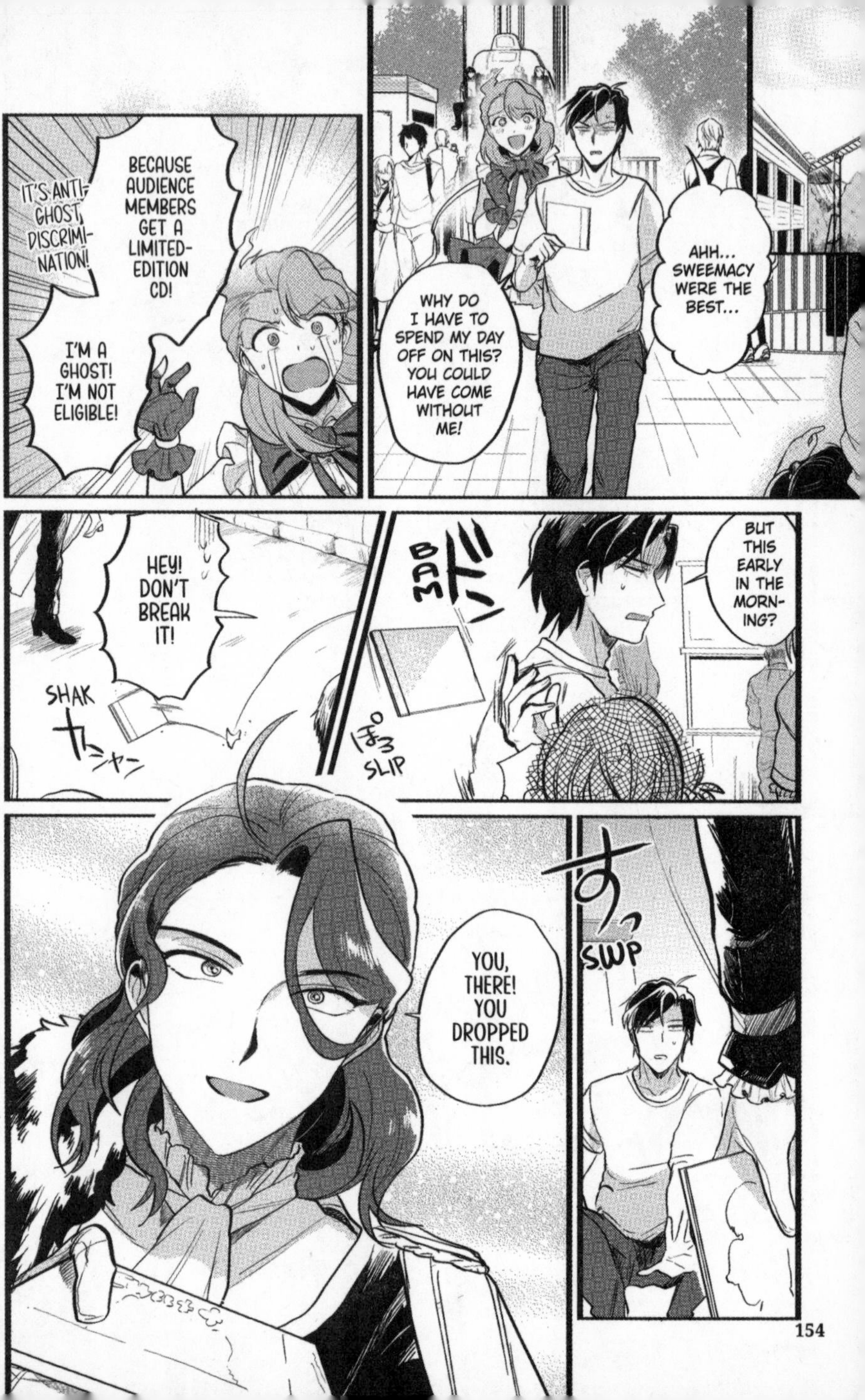
AHH... SWEEMACY WERE THE BEST...
WHY DO I HAVE TO SPEND MY DAY OFF ON THIS? YOU COULD HAVE COME WITHOUT ME!
BECAUSE AUDIENCE MEMBERS GET A LIMITED-EDITION CD!
IT'S ANTI-GHOST DISCRIMINATION!
I'M A GHOST! I'M NOT ELIGIBLE!
BUT THIS EARLY IN THE MORNING?
ドン
BAM
ぽろ
SLIP
HEY! DON'T BREAK IT!
SHAK
カシャン
すっ
SWP
YOU, THERE! YOU DROPPED THIS.

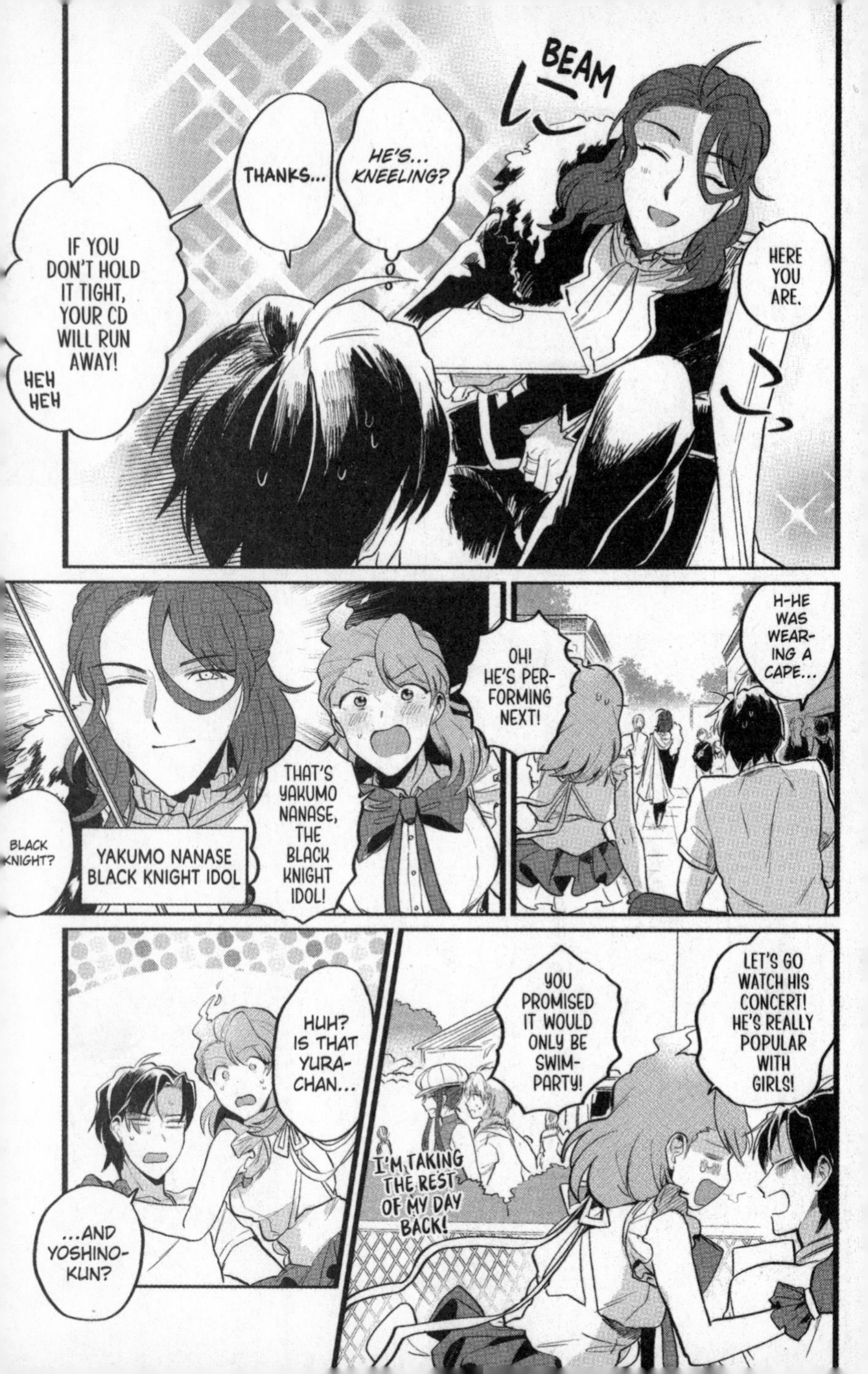
BEAM
HERE YOU ARE.
HE'S... KNEELING?
THANKS...
IF YOU DON'T HOLD IT TIGHT, YOUR CD WILL RUN AWAY!
HEH HEH
H-HE WAS WEARING A CAPE...
OH! HE'S PER-FORMING NEXT!
THAT'S YAKUMO NANASE, THE BLACK KNIGHT IDOL!
YAKUMO NANASE BLACK KNIGHT IDOL
BLACK KNIGHT?
LET'S GO WATCH HIS CONCERT! HE'S REALLY POPULAR WITH GIRLS!
YOU PROMISED IT WOULD ONLY BE SWIM-PARTY!
I'M TAKING THE REST OF MY DAY BACK!
HUH? IS THAT YURA-CHAN...
...AND YOSHINO-KUN?

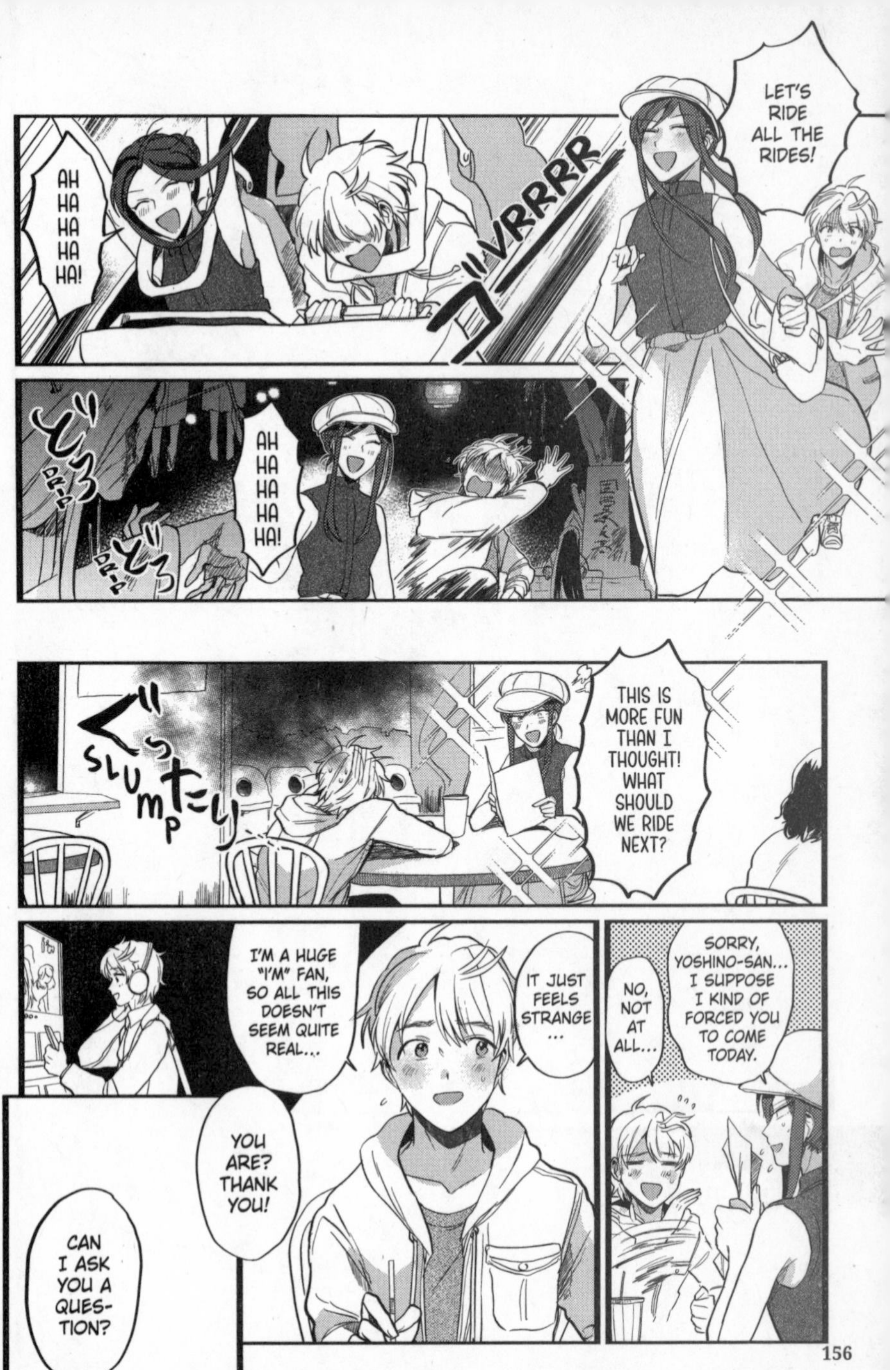
LET'S RIDE ALL THE RIDES!
VRRRR
AH HA HA HA HA!
AH HA HA HA HA!
DRIP
DRIP
THIS IS MORE FUN THAN I THOUGHT! WHAT SHOULD WE RIDE NEXT?
SLUMP
SORRY, YOSHINO-SAN... I SUPPOSE I KIND OF FORCED YOU TO COME TODAY.
NO, NOT AT ALL...
IT JUST FEELS STRANGE...
I'M A HUGE "I'M" FAN, SO ALL THIS DOESN'T SEEM QUITE REAL...
YOU ARE? THANK YOU!
CAN I ASK YOU A QUES-TION?

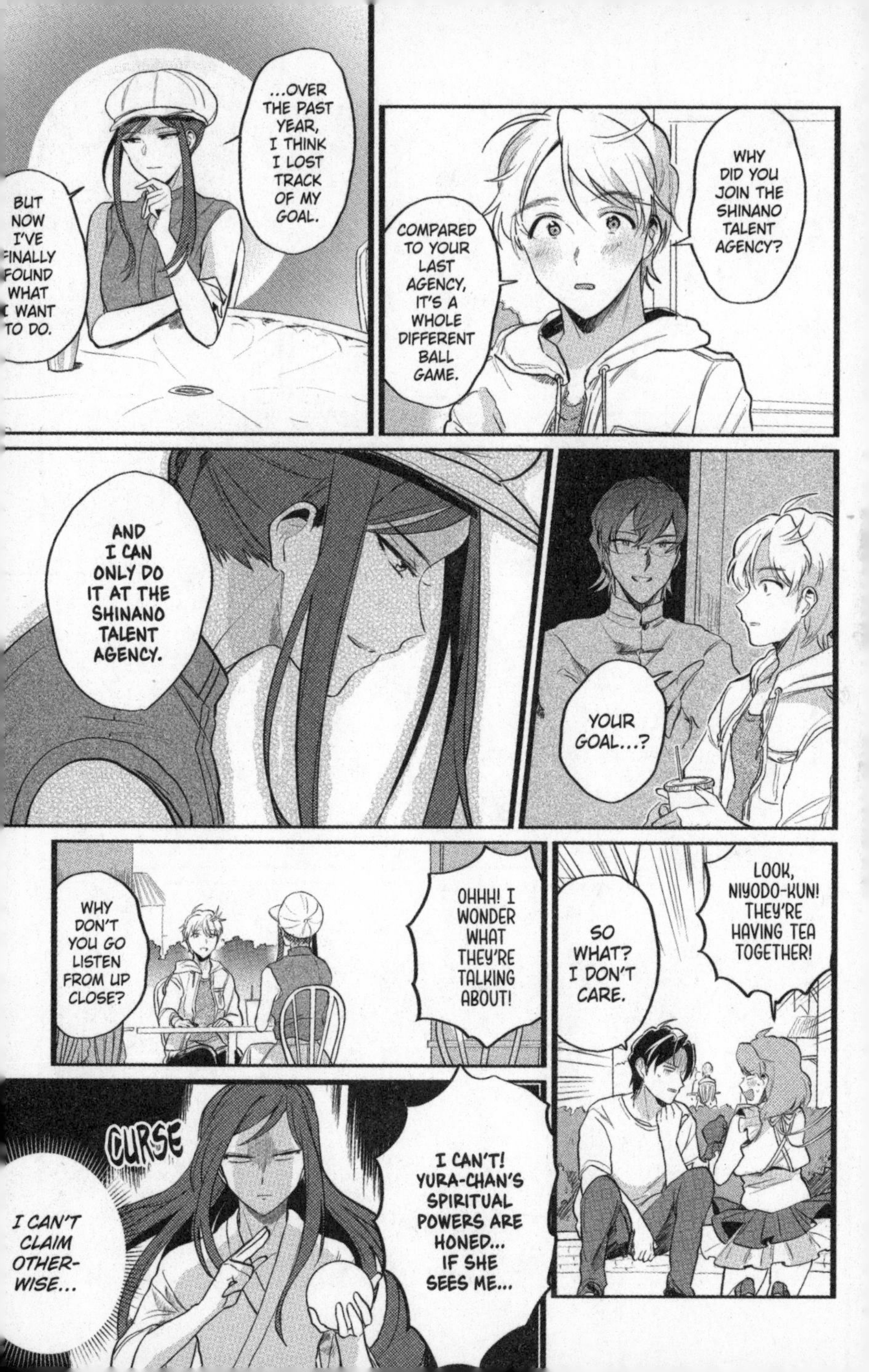
WHY DID YOU JOIN THE SHINANO TALENT AGENCY?
COMPARED TO YOUR LAST AGENCY, IT'S A WHOLE DIFFERENT BALL GAME.
...OVER THE PAST YEAR, I THINK I LOST TRACK OF MY GOAL.
BUT NOW I'VE FINALLY FOUND WHAT I WANT TO DO.
YOUR GOAL...?
AND I CAN ONLY DO IT AT THE SHINANO TALENT AGENCY.
LOOK, NIYODO-KUN! THEY'RE HAVING TEA TOGETHER!
SO WHAT? I DON'T CARE.
OHHH! I WONDER WHAT THEY'RE TALKING ABOUT!
WHY DON'T YOU GO LISTEN FROM UP CLOSE?
I CAN'T! YURA-CHAN'S SPIRITUAL POWERS ARE HONED... IF SHE SEES ME...
CURSE
I CAN'T CLAIM OTHER-WISE...

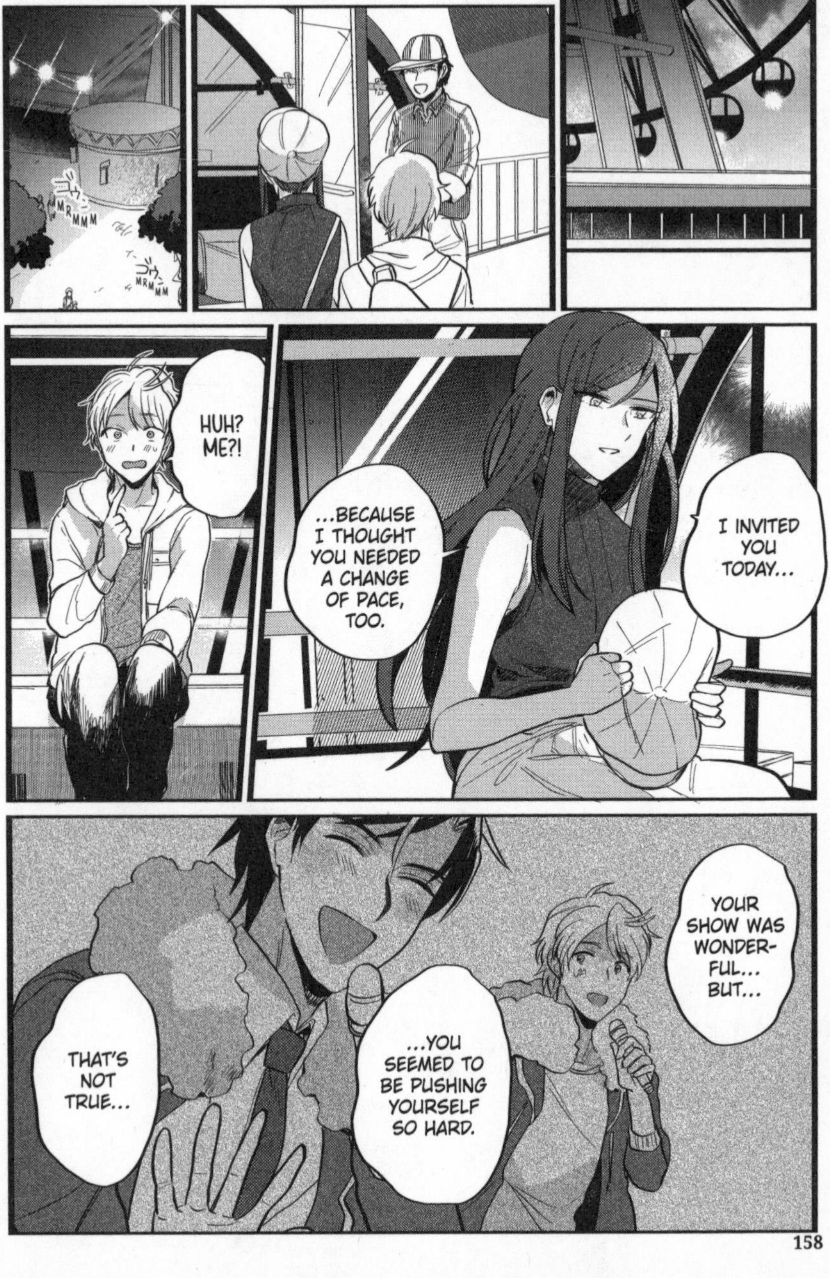
MRMMM
MRMMM
I INVITED YOU TODAY...
...BECAUSE I THOUGHT YOU NEEDED A CHANGE OF PACE, TOO.
HUH? ME?!
YOUR SHOW WAS WONDER-FUL... BUT...
...YOU SEEMED TO BE PUSHING YOURSELF SO HARD.
THAT'S NOT TRUE...

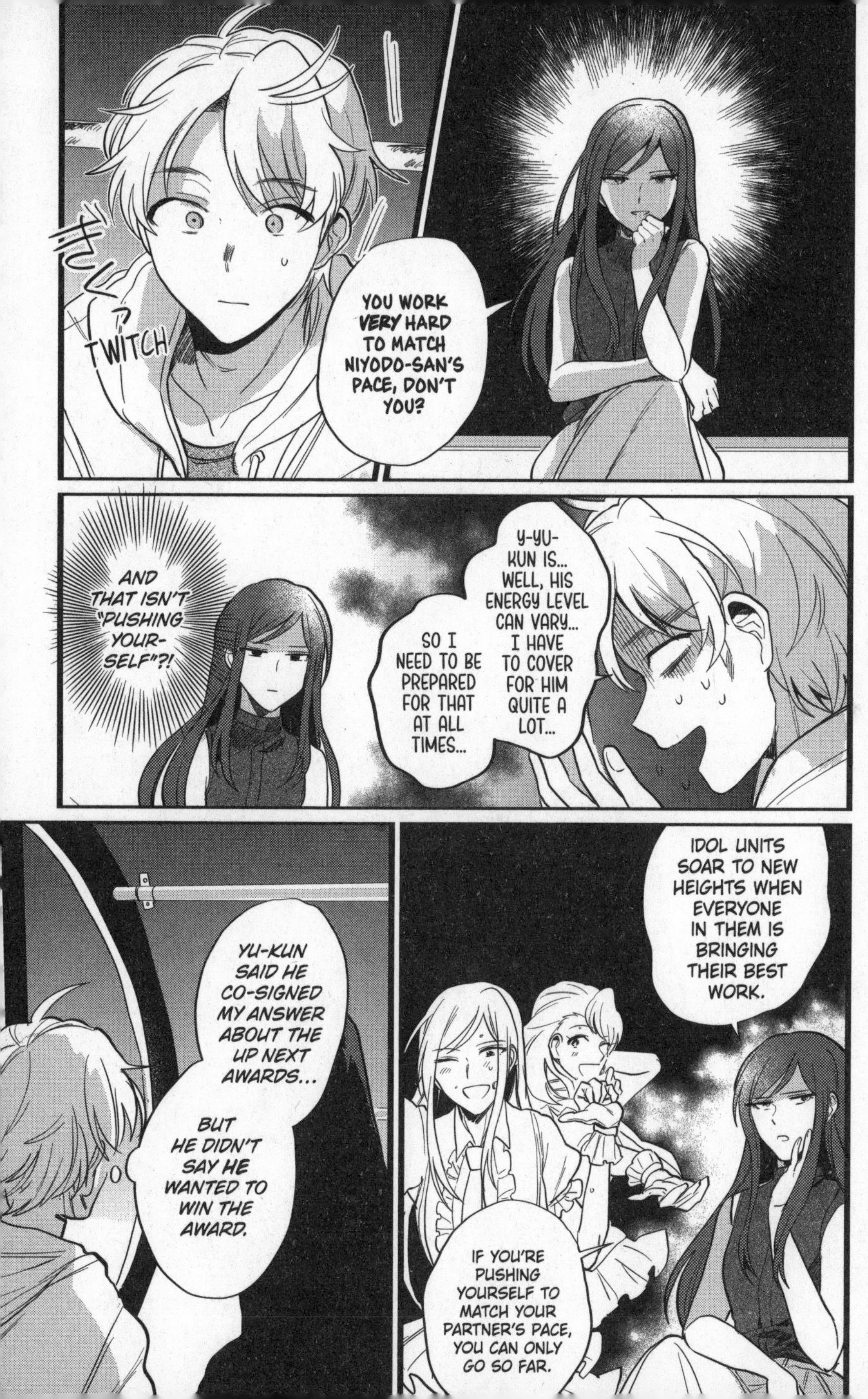
YOU WORK VERY HARD TO MATCH NIYODO-SAN'S PACE, DON'T YOU?
きくっ
TWITCH
Y-YU-KUN IS... WELL, HIS ENERGY LEVEL CAN VARY... I HAVE TO COVER FOR HIM QUITE A LOT...
SO I NEED TO BE PREPARED FOR THAT AT ALL TIMES...
AND THAT ISN'T "PUSHING YOURSELF"?!
IDOL UNITS SOAR TO NEW HEIGHTS WHEN EVERYONE IN THEM IS BRINGING THEIR BEST WORK.
IF YOU'RE PUSHING YOURSELF TO MATCH YOUR PARTNER'S PACE, YOU CAN ONLY GO SO FAR.
YU-KUN SAID HE CO-SIGNED MY ANSWER ABOUT THE UP NEXT AWARDS...
BUT HE DIDN'T SAY HE WANTED TO WIN THE AWARD.

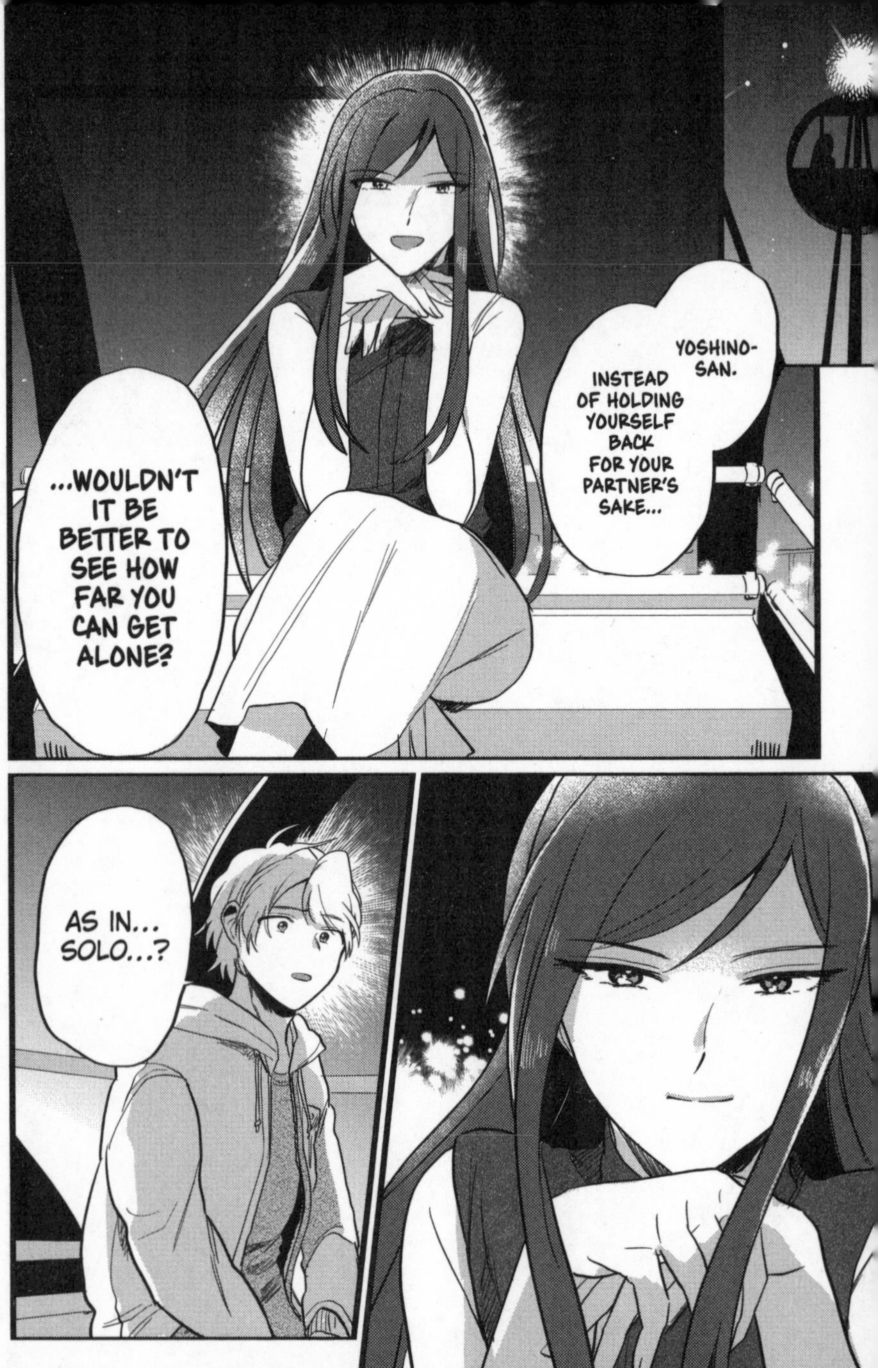
YOSHINO-SAN.
INSTEAD OF HOLDING YOURSELF BACK FOR YOUR PARTNER'S SAKE...
...WOULDN'T IT BE BETTER TO SEE HOW FAR YOU CAN GET ALONE?
AS IN... SOLO...?

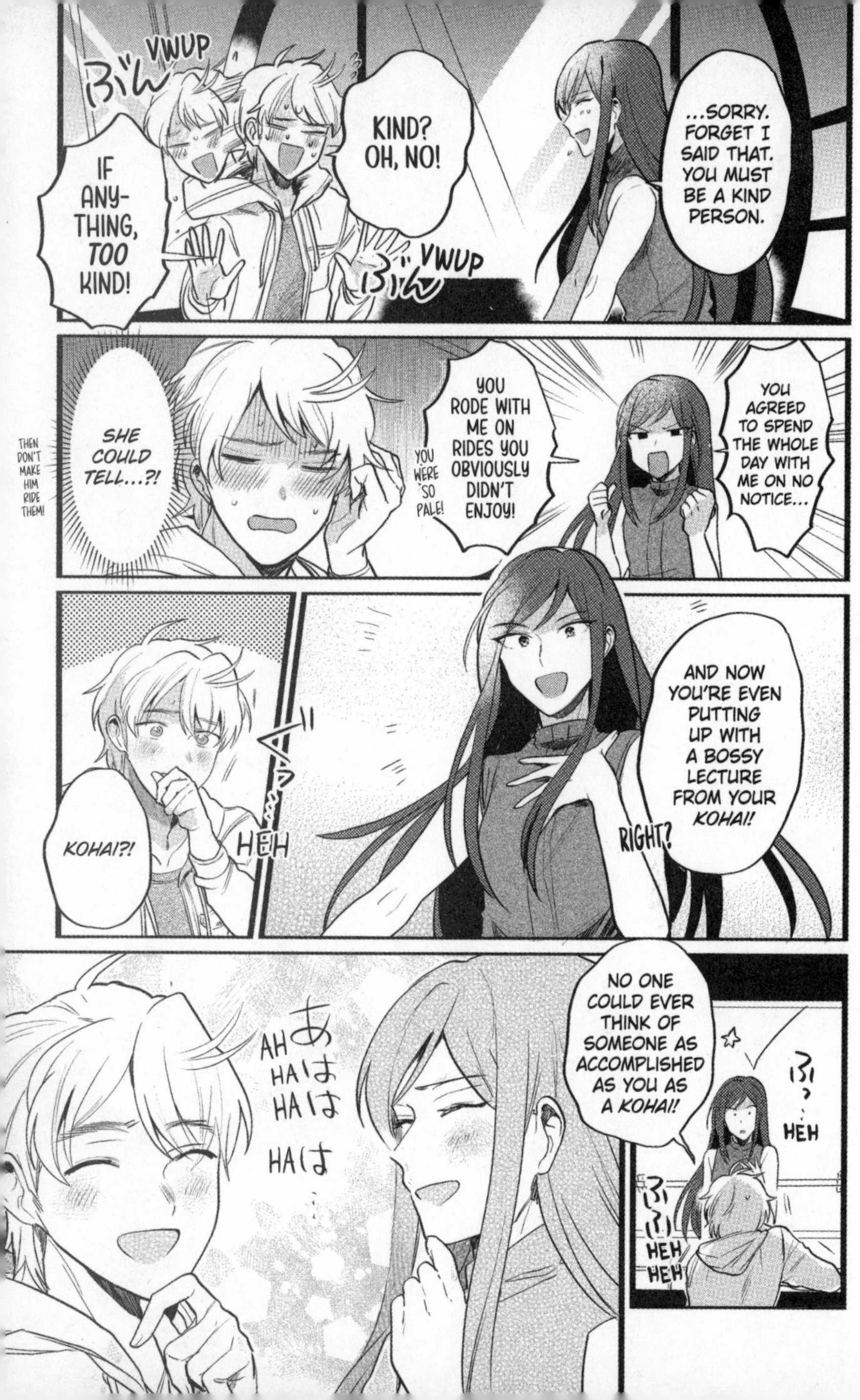
...SORRY. FORGET I SAID THAT. YOU MUST BE A KIND PERSON.
KIND? OH, NO!
VWUP
ぶん
VWUP
ぶん
IF ANY-THING, TOO KIND!
YOU AGREED TO SPEND THE WHOLE DAY WITH ME ON NO NOTICE...
YOU RODE WITH ME ON RIDES YOU OBVIOUSLY DIDN'T ENJOY!
YOU WERE SO PALE!
SHE COULD TELL...?!
THEN DON'T MAKE HIM RIDE THEM!
AND NOW YOU'RE EVEN PUTTING UP WITH A BOSSY LECTURE FROM YOUR KOHAI!
RIGHT?
HEH
KOHAI?!
NO ONE COULD EVER THINK OF SOMEONE AS ACCOMPLISHED AS YOU AS A KOHAI!
ふっ HEH
ふふ HEH HEH
AH あ HA は HA は HA は

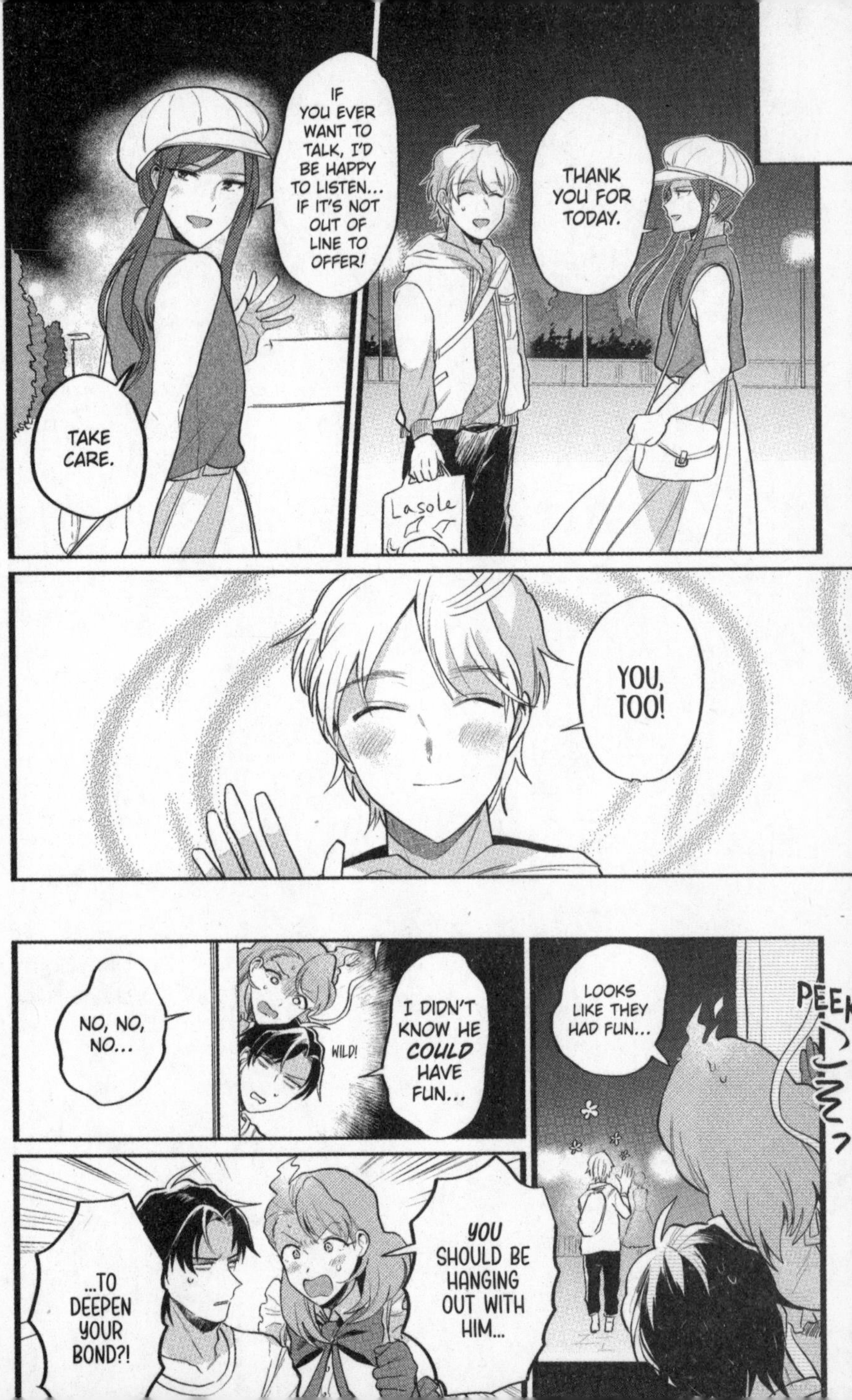
THANK YOU FOR TODAY.
IF YOU EVER WANT TO TALK, I'D BE HAPPY TO LISTEN... IF IT'S NOT OUT OF LINE TO OFFER!
TAKE CARE.
Lasole
YOU, TOO!
LOOKS LIKE THEY HAD FUN...
PEEK
I DIDN'T KNOW HE *COULD* HAVE FUN...
WILD!
NO, NO, NO...
*YOU* SHOULD BE HANGING OUT WITH HIM...
...TO DEEPEN YOUR BOND?!

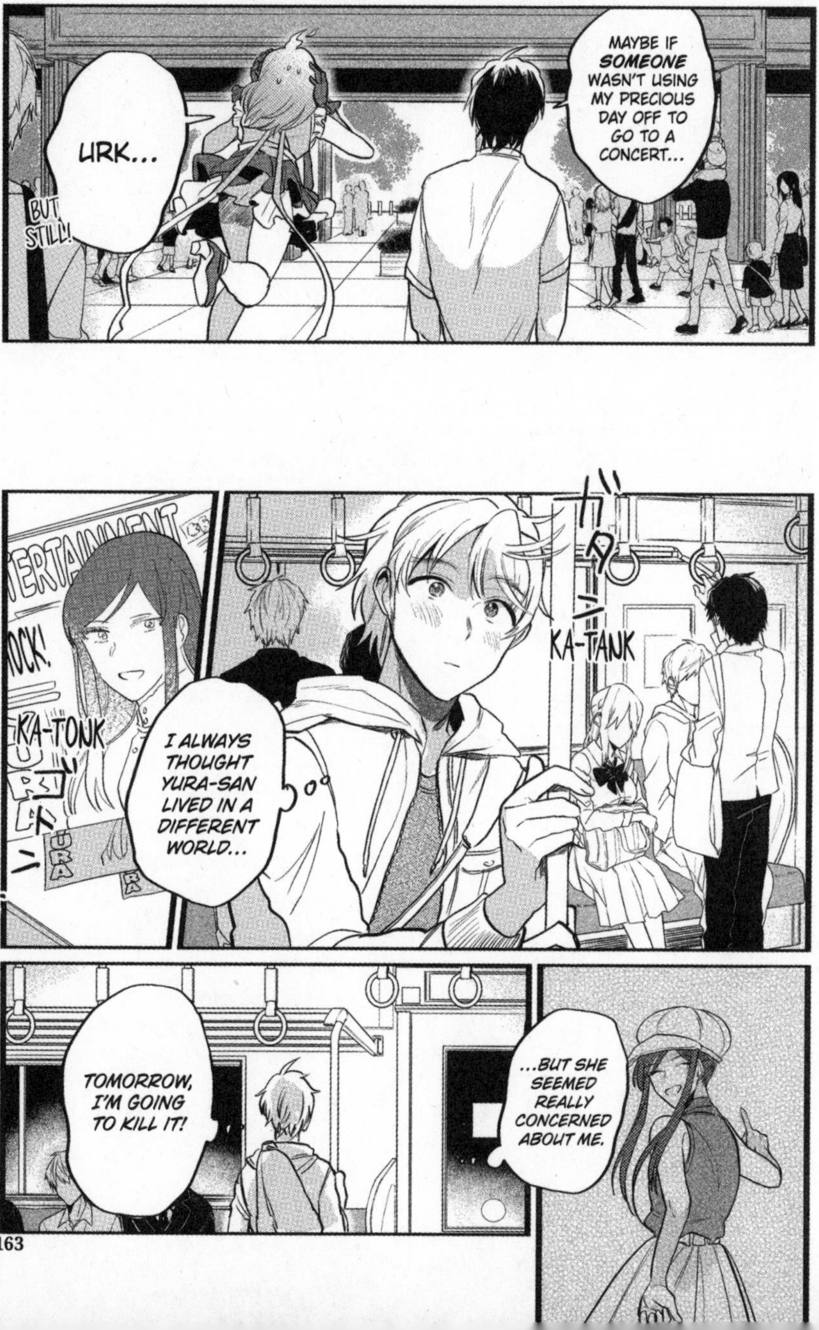
MAYBE IF *SOMEONE* WASN'T USING MY PRECIOUS DAY OFF TO GO TO A CONCERT...
URK...
BUT STILL!
KA-TANK
I ALWAYS THOUGHT YURA-SAN LIVED IN A DIFFERENT WORLD...
ENTERTAINMENT
ROCK!
KA-TONK
URA
...BUT SHE SEEMED REALLY CONCERNED ABOUT ME.
TOMORROW, I'M GOING TO KILL IT!

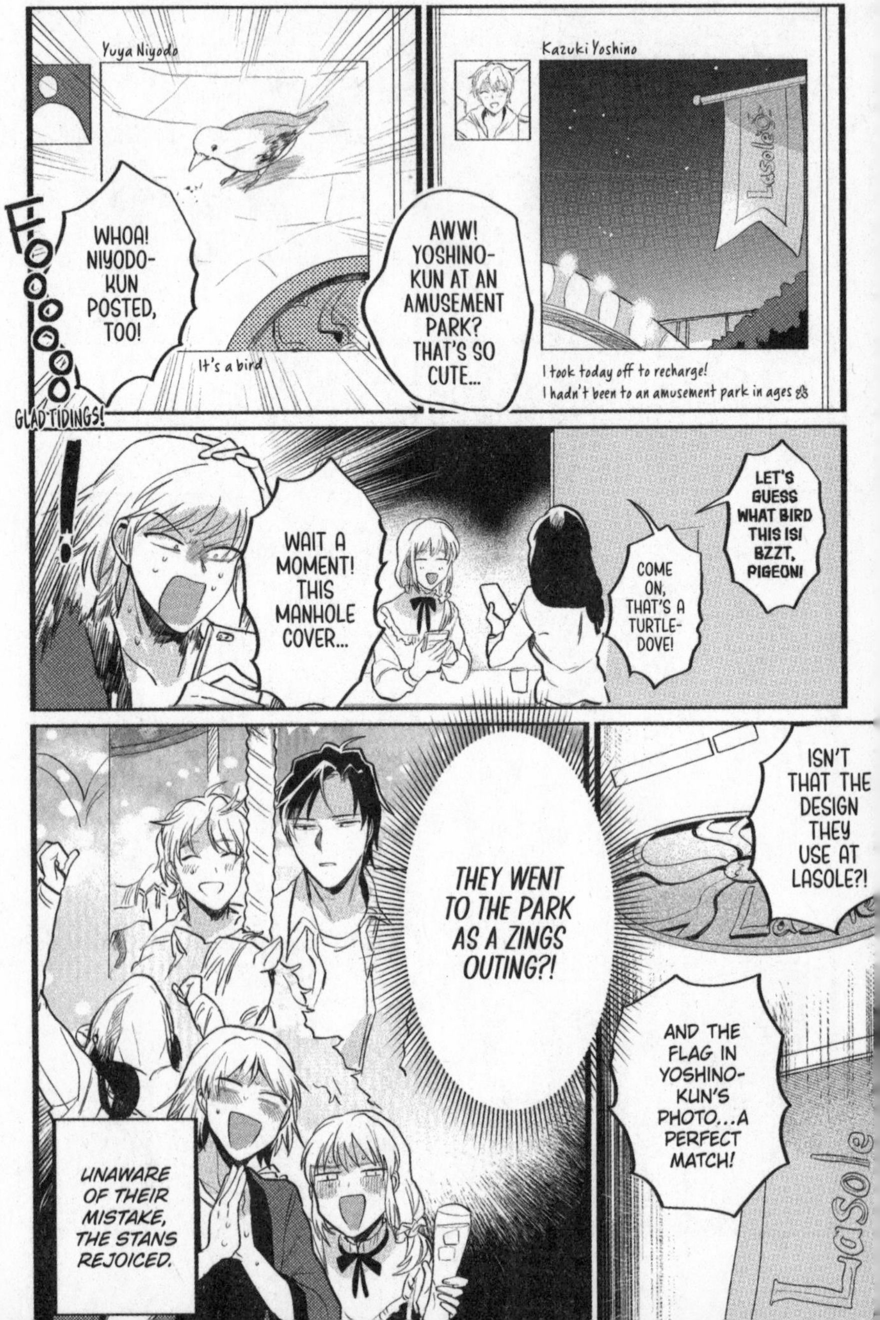
Kazuki Yoshino
I took today off to recharge!
I hadn't been to an amusement park in ages
AWW! YOSHINO-KUN AT AN AMUSEMENT PARK? THAT'S SO CUTE...
Yuya Niyodo
It's a bird
WHOA! NIYODO-KUN POSTED, TOO!
FOOOOOOO
GLAD TIDINGS!
LET'S GUESS WHAT BIRD THIS IS! BZZT, PIGEON!
COME ON, THAT'S A TURTLE-DOVE!
WAIT A MOMENT! THIS MANHOLE COVER...
!
ISN'T THAT THE DESIGN THEY USE AT LASOLE?!
AND THE FLAG IN YOSHINO-KUN'S PHOTO...A PERFECT MATCH!
Lasole
THEY WENT TO THE PARK AS A ZINGS OUTING?!
UNAWARE OF THEIR MISTAKE, THE STANS REJOICED.

# Set 22

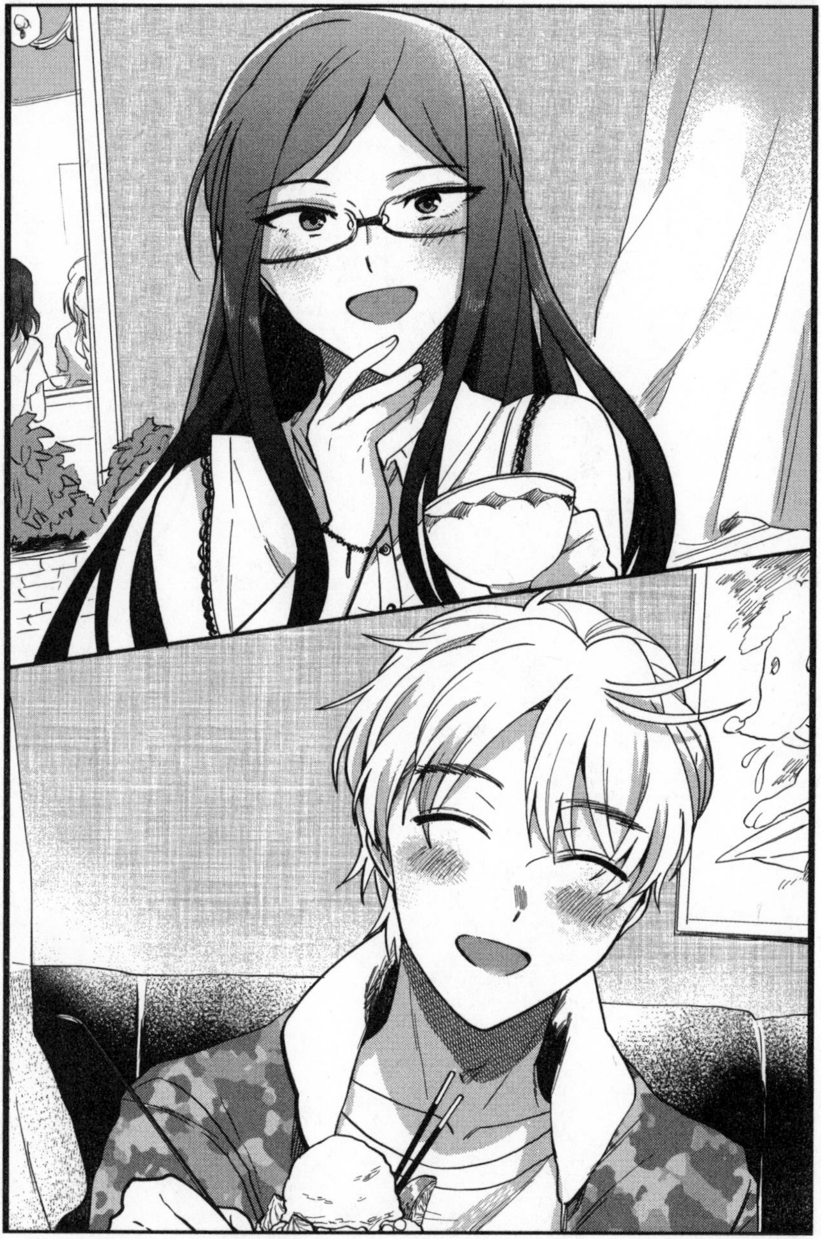

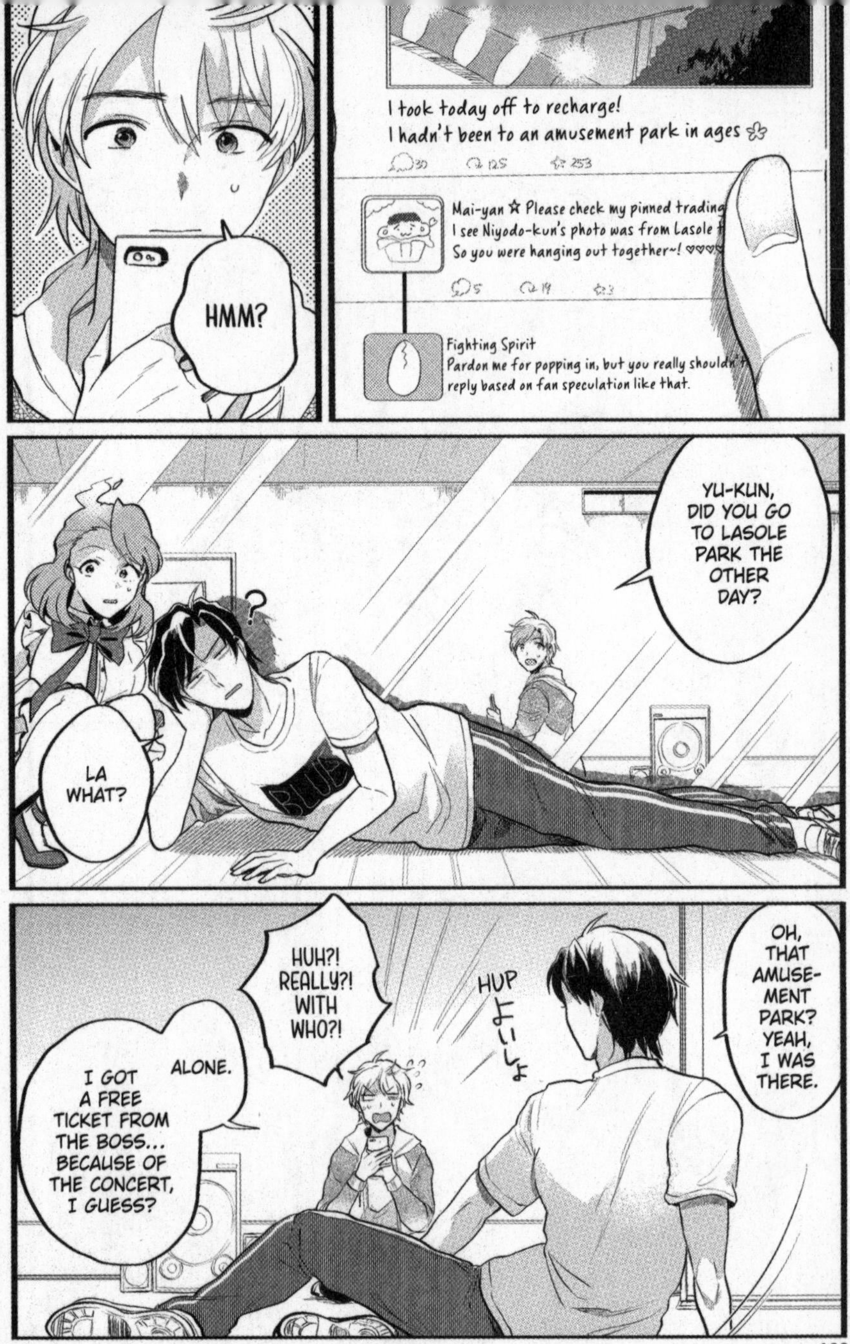
I took today off to recharge!
I hadn't been to an amusement park in ages
30 125 253
Mai-yan☆ Please check my pinned trading
I see Niyodo-kun's photo was from Lasole
So you were hanging out together~! ♡♡♡
Fighting Spirit
Pardon me for popping in, but you really shouldn't
reply based on fan speculation like that.
HMM?
YU-KUN, DID YOU GO TO LASOLE PARK THE OTHER DAY?
LA WHAT?
OH, THAT AMUSEMENT PARK? YEAH, I WAS THERE.
HUP
よいしょ
HUH?! REALLY?! WITH WHO?!
ALONE.
I GOT A FREE TICKET FROM THE BOSS... BECAUSE OF THE CONCERT, I GUESS?

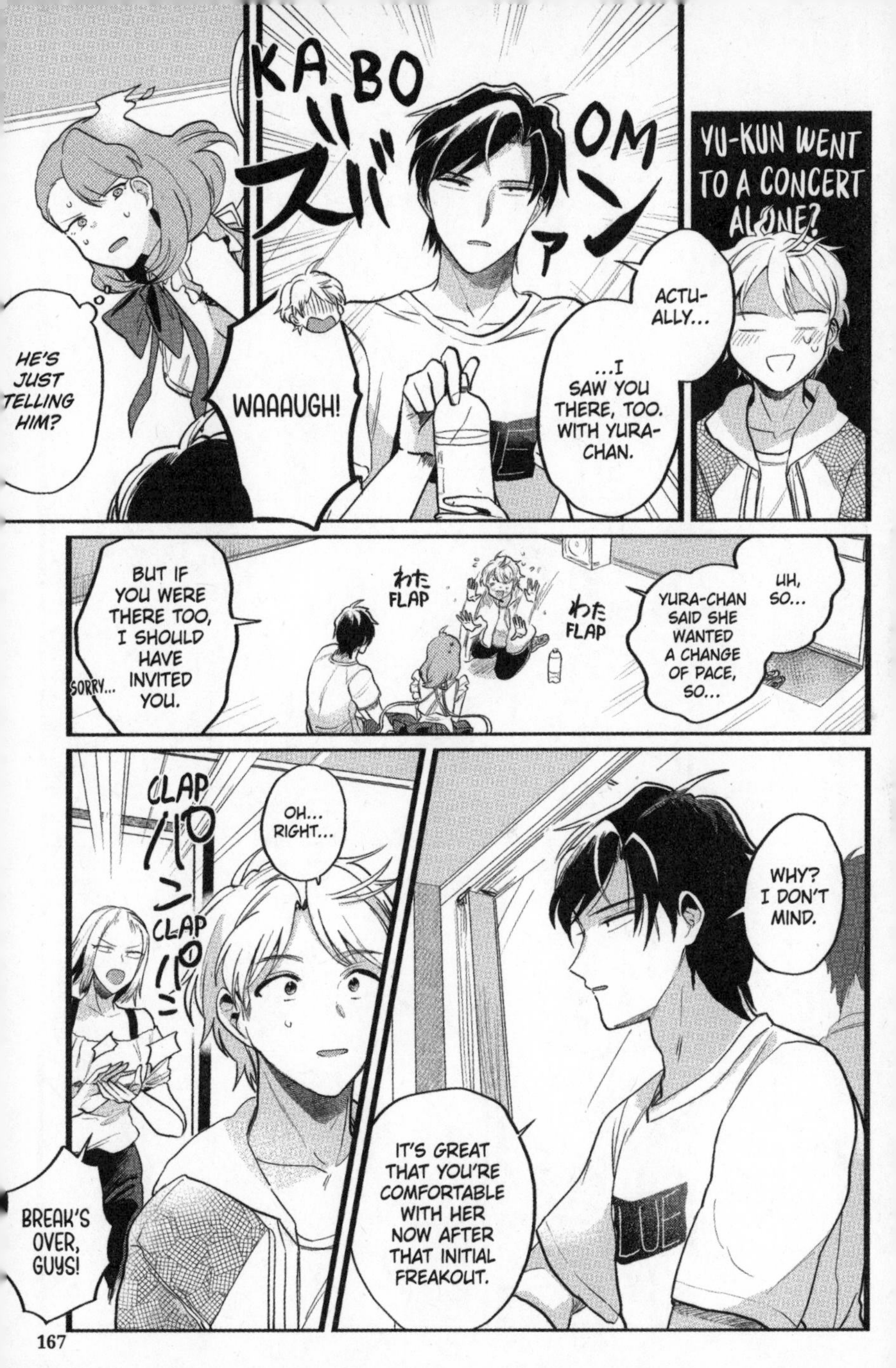
YU-KUN WENT TO A CONCERT ALONE?
ズバーン KABOOM
ACTU-ALLY...
...I SAW YOU THERE, TOO. WITH YURA-CHAN.
WAAAUGH!
HE'S JUST TELLING HIM?
UH, SO...
YURA-CHAN SAID SHE WANTED A CHANGE OF PACE, SO...
わた FLAP
わた FLAP
BUT IF YOU WERE THERE TOO, I SHOULD HAVE INVITED YOU.
SORRY...
WHY? I DON'T MIND.
IT'S GREAT THAT YOU'RE COMFORTABLE WITH HER NOW AFTER THAT INITIAL FREAKOUT.
OH... RIGHT...
CLAP パン
CLAP パン
BREAK'S OVER, GUYS!

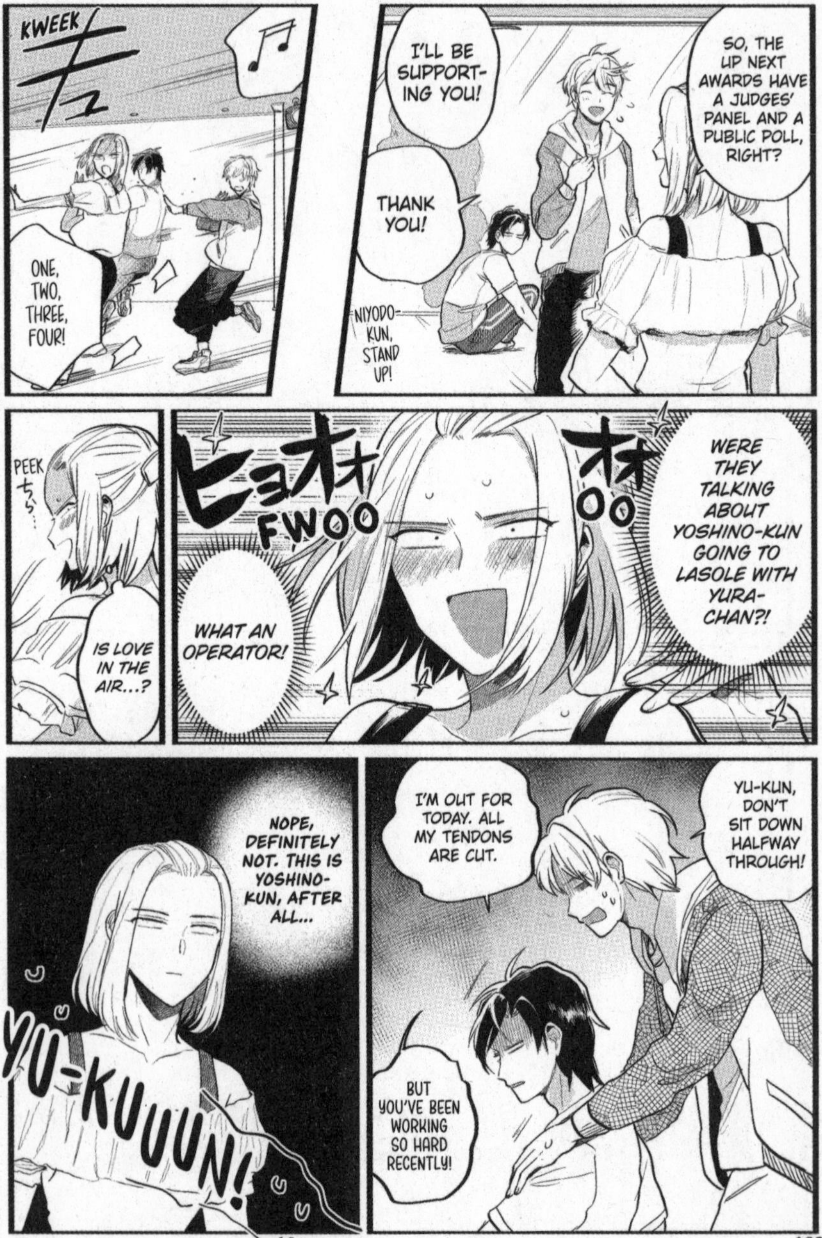
SO, THE UP NEXT AWARDS HAVE A JUDGES' PANEL AND A PUBLIC POLL, RIGHT?
I'LL BE SUPPORTING YOU!
THANK YOU!
NIYODO-KUN, STAND UP!
KWEEK
キュ
ONE, TWO, THREE, FOUR!
WERE THEY TALKING ABOUT YOSHINO-KUN GOING TO LASOLE WITH YURA-CHAN?!
ヒョオオ FWOO
オオ OO
WHAT AN OPERATOR!
PEEK ちら…
IS LOVE IN THE AIR...?
YU-KUN, DON'T SIT DOWN HALFWAY THROUGH!
I'M OUT FOR TODAY. ALL MY TENDONS ARE CUT.
BUT YOU'VE BEEN WORKING SO HARD RECENTLY!
NOPE, DEFINITELY NOT. THIS IS YOSHINO-KUN, AFTER ALL...
YU-KUUUUN!

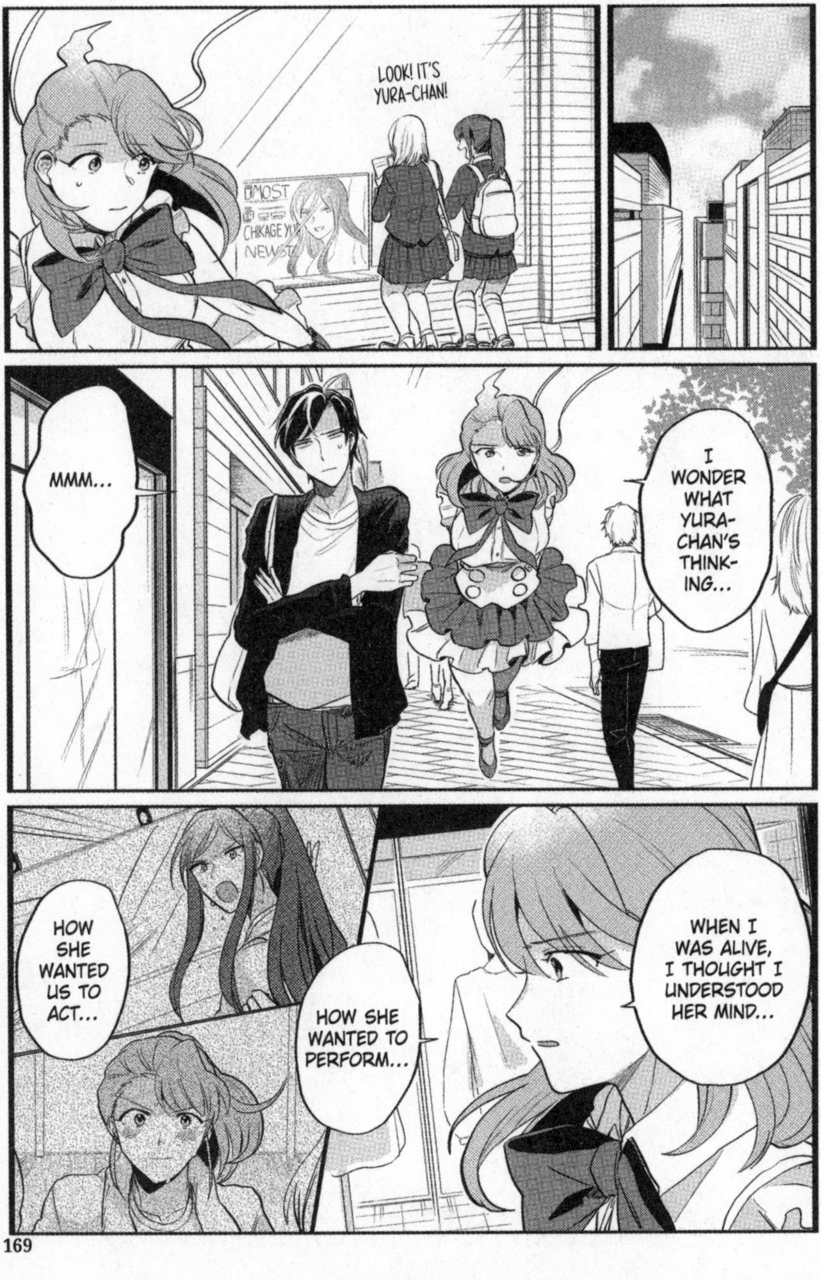
LOOK! IT'S YURA-CHAN!
MOST
I WONDER WHAT YURA-CHAN'S THINKING...
MMM...
WHEN I WAS ALIVE, I THOUGHT I UNDERSTOOD HER MIND...
HOW SHE WANTED TO PERFORM...
HOW SHE WANTED US TO ACT...

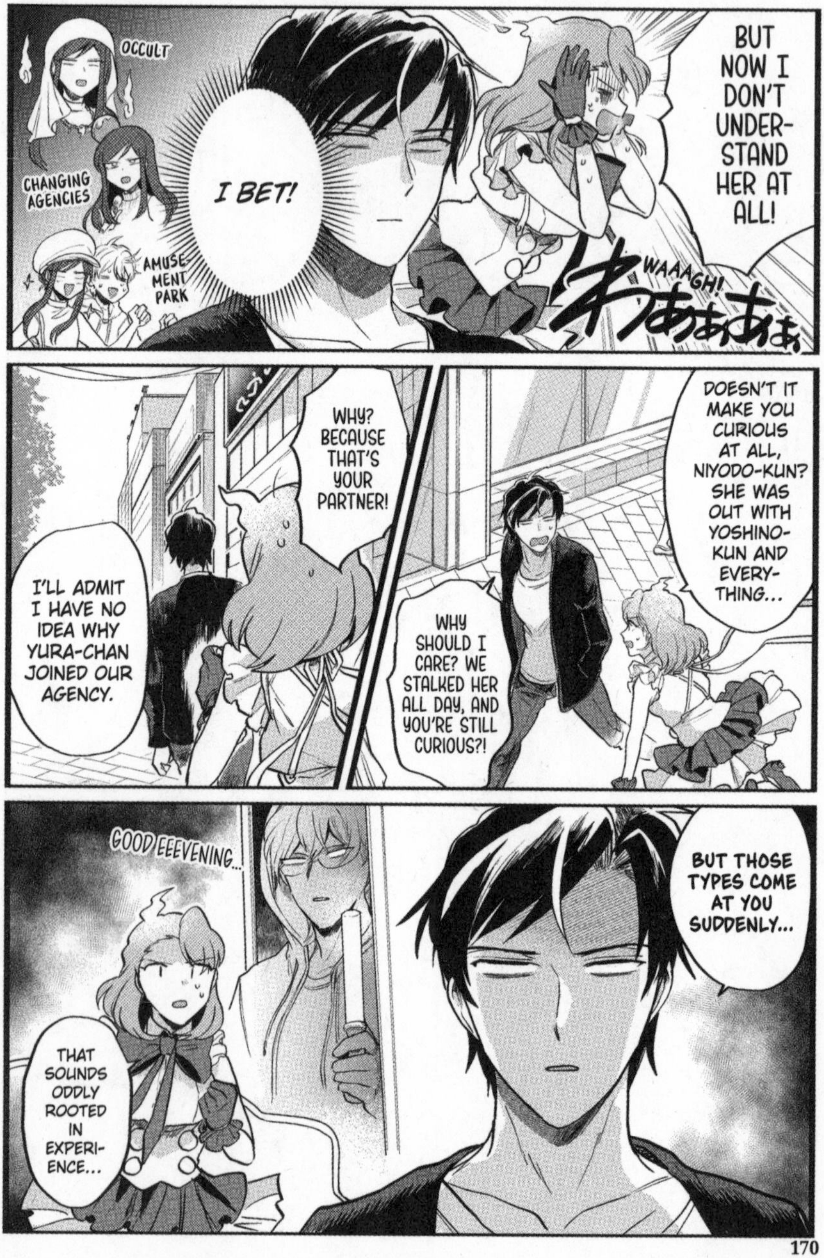
BUT NOW I DON'T UNDERSTAND HER AT ALL!
WAAAGH!
I BET!
OCCULT
CHANGING AGENCIES
AMUSEMENT PARK
DOESN'T IT MAKE YOU CURIOUS AT ALL, NIYODO-KUN? SHE WAS OUT WITH YOSHINO-KUN AND EVERYTHING...
WHY SHOULD I CARE? WE STALKED HER ALL DAY, AND YOU'RE STILL CURIOUS?!
WHY? BECAUSE THAT'S YOUR PARTNER!
I'LL ADMIT I HAVE NO IDEA WHY YURA-CHAN JOINED OUR AGENCY.
BUT THOSE TYPES COME AT YOU SUDDENLY...
GOOD EEEVENING...
THAT SOUNDS ODDLY ROOTED IN EXPERIENCE...

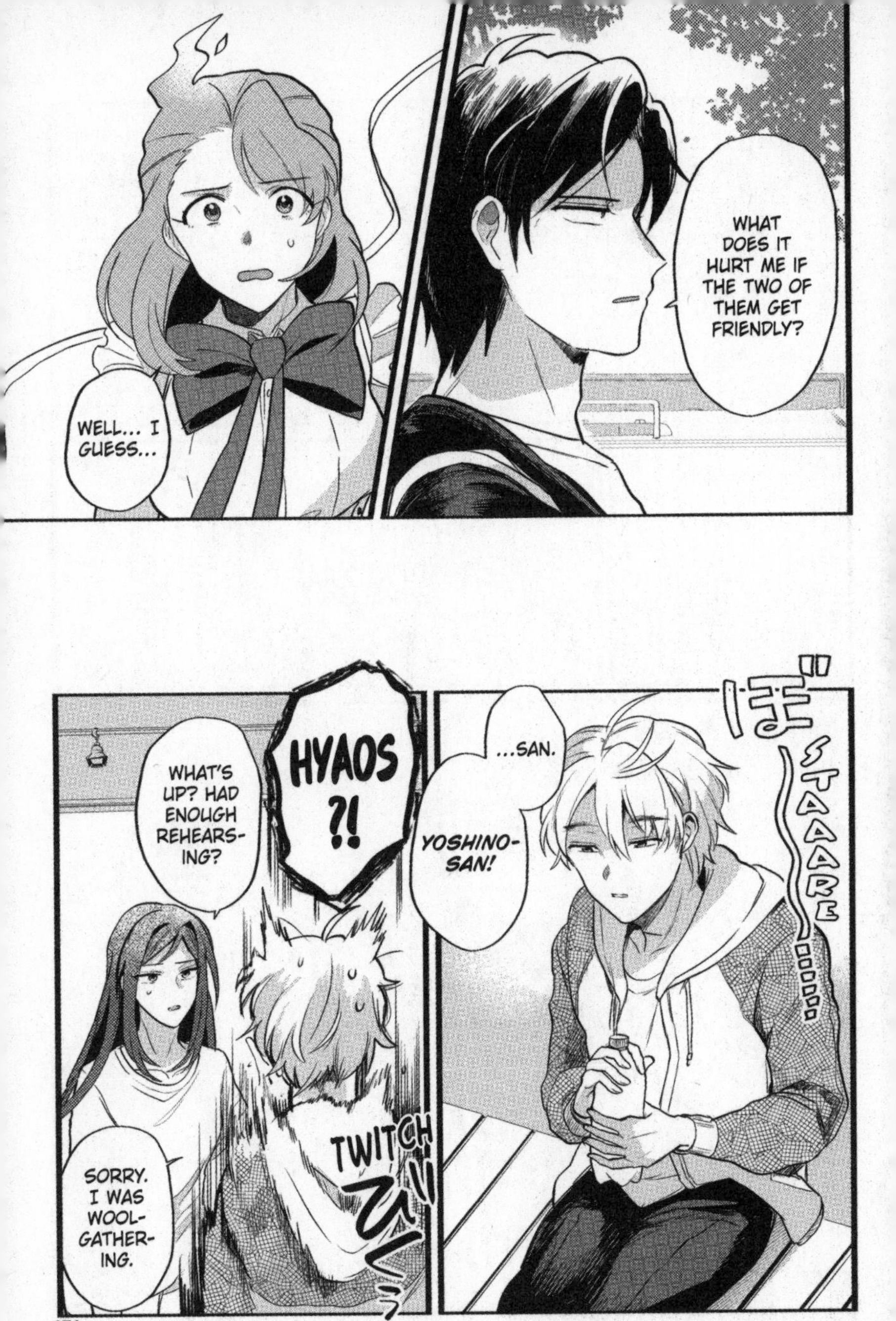
WHAT DOES IT HURT ME IF THE TWO OF THEM GET FRIENDLY?
WELL... I GUESS...
ぼー
STAAAARE......
...SAN.
YOSHINO-SAN!
HYAOS ?!
WHAT'S UP? HAD ENOUGH REHEARS-ING?
TWITCH
びくっ
SORRY. I WAS WOOL-GATHER-ING.

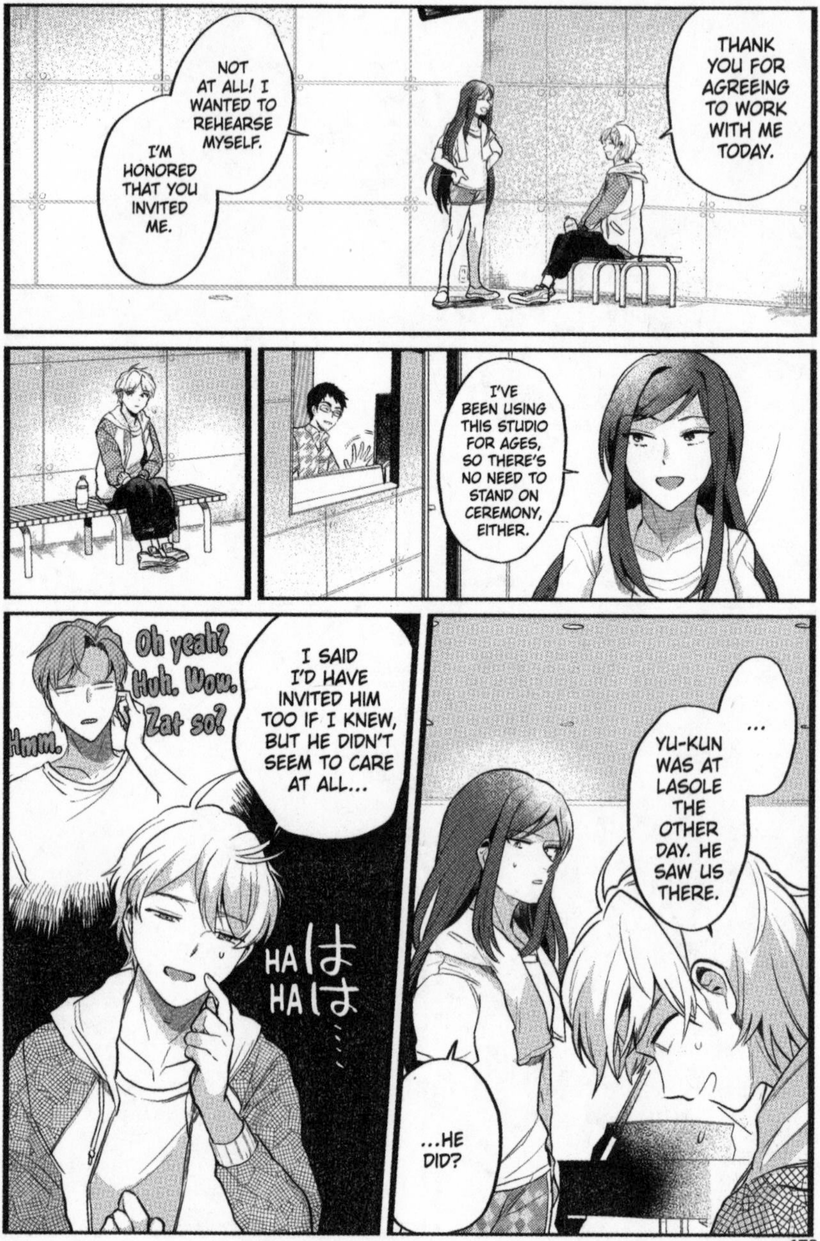
THANK YOU FOR AGREEING TO WORK WITH ME TODAY.
NOT AT ALL! I WANTED TO REHEARSE MYSELF.
I'M HONORED THAT YOU INVITED ME.
I'VE BEEN USING THIS STUDIO FOR AGES, SO THERE'S NO NEED TO STAND ON CEREMONY, EITHER.
...
YU-KUN WAS AT LASOLE THE OTHER DAY. HE SAW US THERE.
...HE DID?
I SAID I'D HAVE INVITED HIM TOO IF I KNEW, BUT HE DIDN'T SEEM TO CARE AT ALL...
Oh yeah? Huh. Wow. Zat so?
Hmm.
HA HA
はは

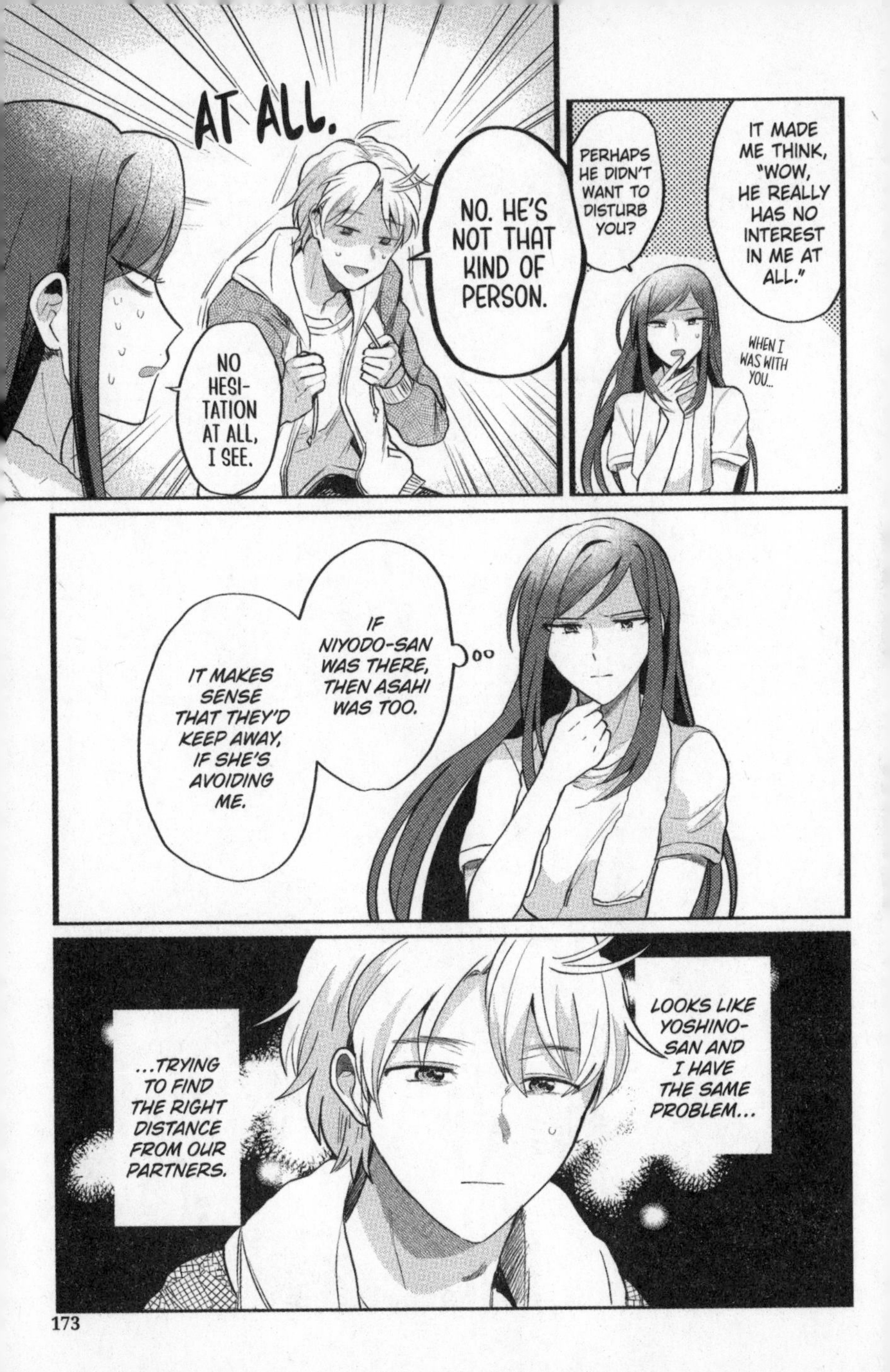
IT MADE ME THINK, "WOW, HE REALLY HAS NO INTEREST IN ME AT ALL."
PERHAPS HE DIDN'T WANT TO DISTURB YOU?
WHEN I WAS WITH YOU...
NO. HE'S NOT THAT KIND OF PERSON.
AT ALL.
NO HESITATION AT ALL, I SEE.
IF NIYODO-SAN WAS THERE, THEN ASAHI WAS TOO.
IT MAKES SENSE THAT THEY'D KEEP AWAY, IF SHE'S AVOIDING ME.
LOOKS LIKE YOSHINO-SAN AND I HAVE THE SAME PROBLEM...
...TRYING TO FIND THE RIGHT DISTANCE FROM OUR PARTNERS.

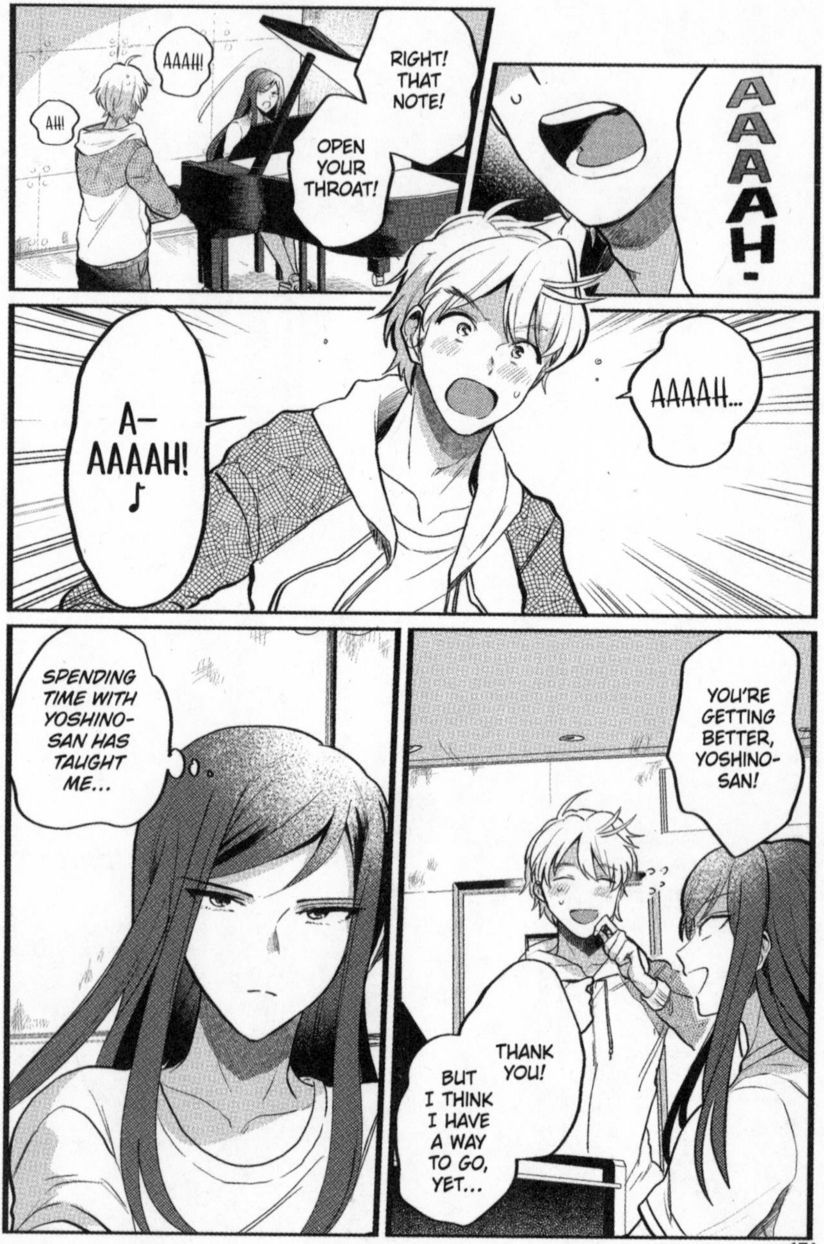
AAAAH!
RIGHT! THAT NOTE!
AAAH!
OPEN YOUR THROAT!
AH!
AAAAH...
A- AAAAH! ♪
YOU'RE GETTING BETTER, YOSHINO-SAN!
THANK YOU!
BUT I THINK I HAVE A WAY TO GO, YET...
SPENDING TIME WITH YOSHINO-SAN HAS TAUGHT ME...

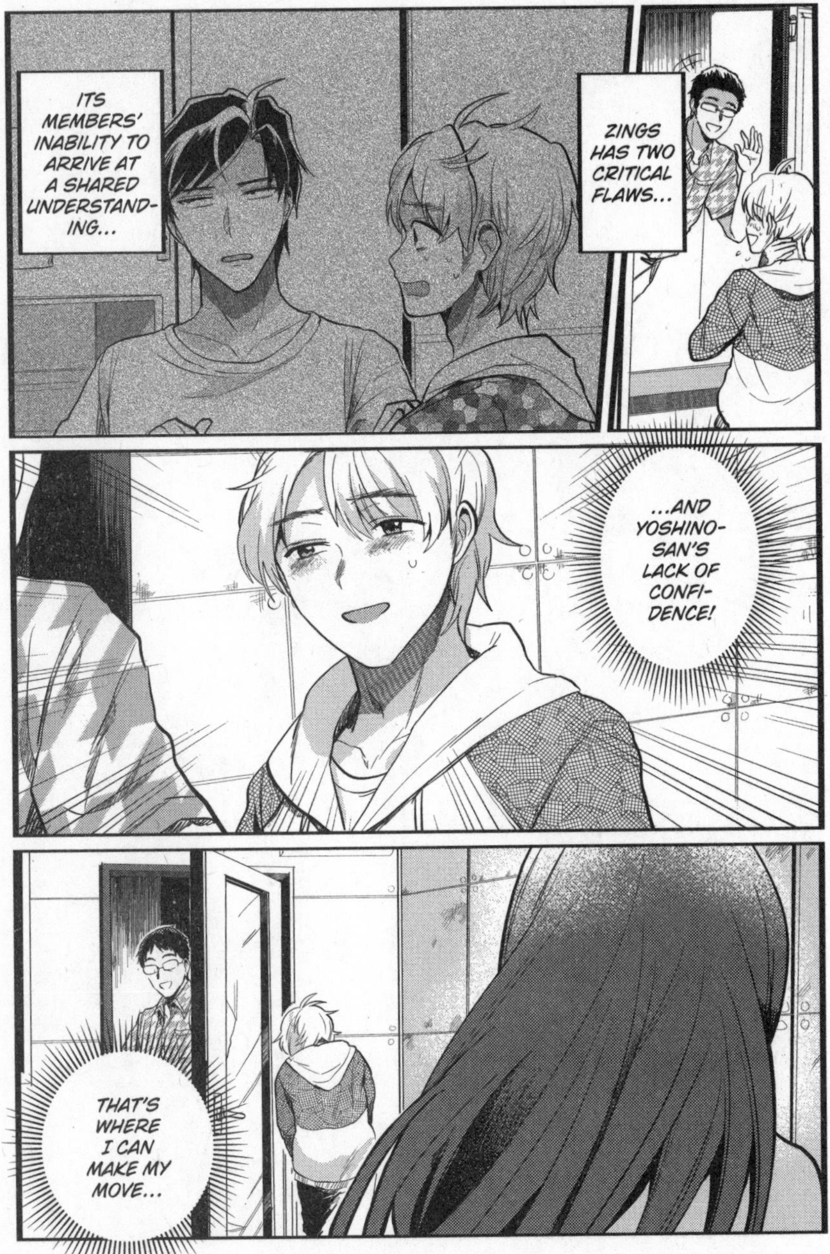
ZINGS HAS TWO CRITICAL FLAWS…
ITS MEMBERS' INABILITY TO ARRIVE AT A SHARED UNDERSTANDING…
…AND YOSHINO-SAN'S LACK OF CONFIDENCE!
THAT'S WHERE I CAN MAKE MY MOVE…

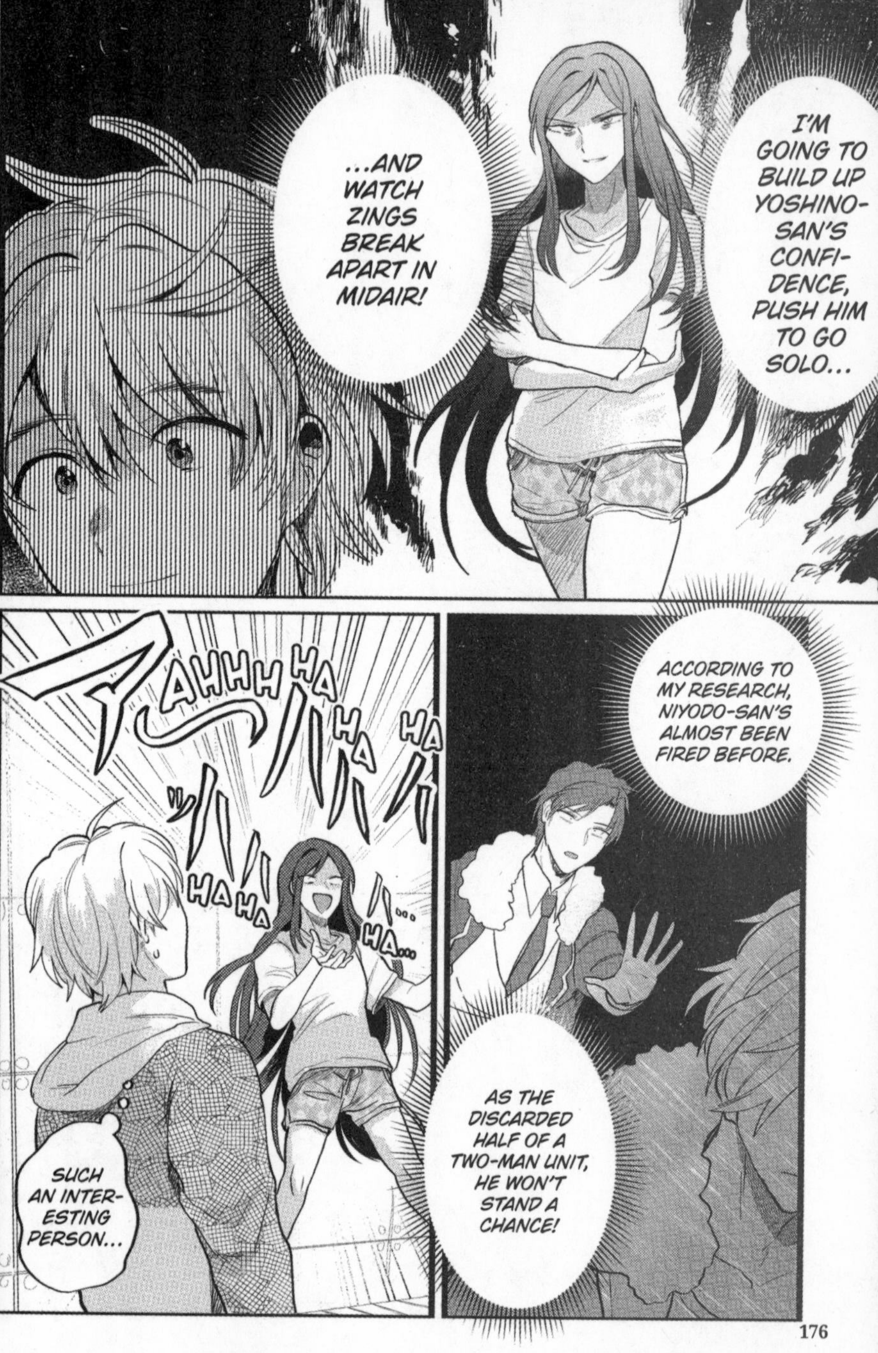
I'M GOING TO BUILD UP YOSHINO-SAN'S CONFI-DENCE, PUSH HIM TO GO SOLO...
...AND WATCH ZINGS BREAK APART IN MIDAIR!
ACCORDING TO MY RESEARCH, NIYODO-SAN'S ALMOST BEEN FIRED BEFORE.
AS THE DISCARDED HALF OF A TWO-MAN UNIT, HE WON'T STAND A CHANCE!
AHHH HA HA HA HA HA HA HA...
SUCH AN INTER-ESTING PERSON...

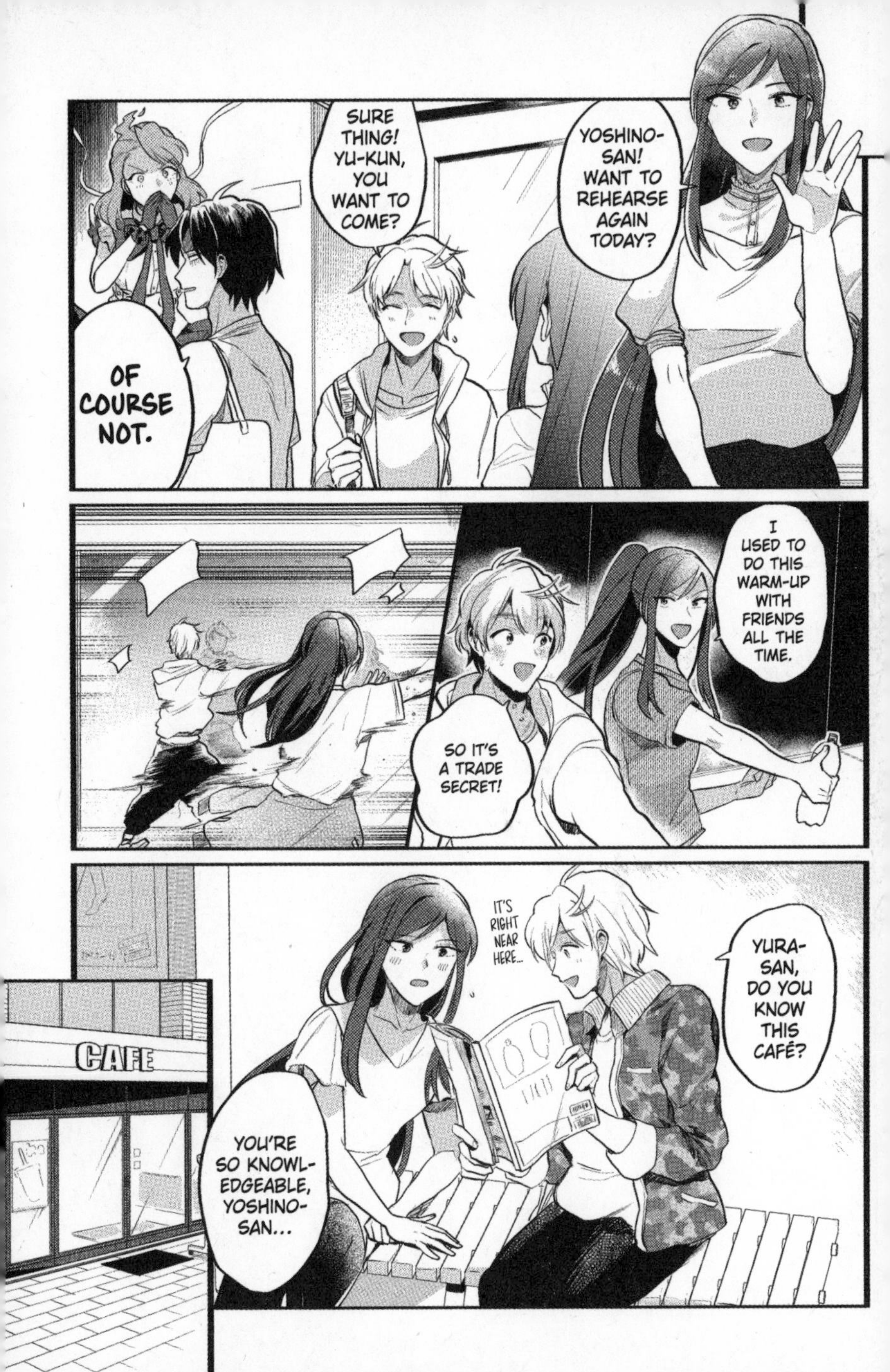
YOSHINO-SAN! WANT TO REHEARSE AGAIN TODAY?
SURE THING! YU-KUN, YOU WANT TO COME?
OF COURSE NOT.
I USED TO DO THIS WARM-UP WITH FRIENDS ALL THE TIME.
SO IT'S A TRADE SECRET!
YURA-SAN, DO YOU KNOW THIS CAFÉ?
IT'S RIGHT NEAR HERE...
YOU'RE SO KNOWLEDGEABLE, YOSHINO-SAN...
CAFE

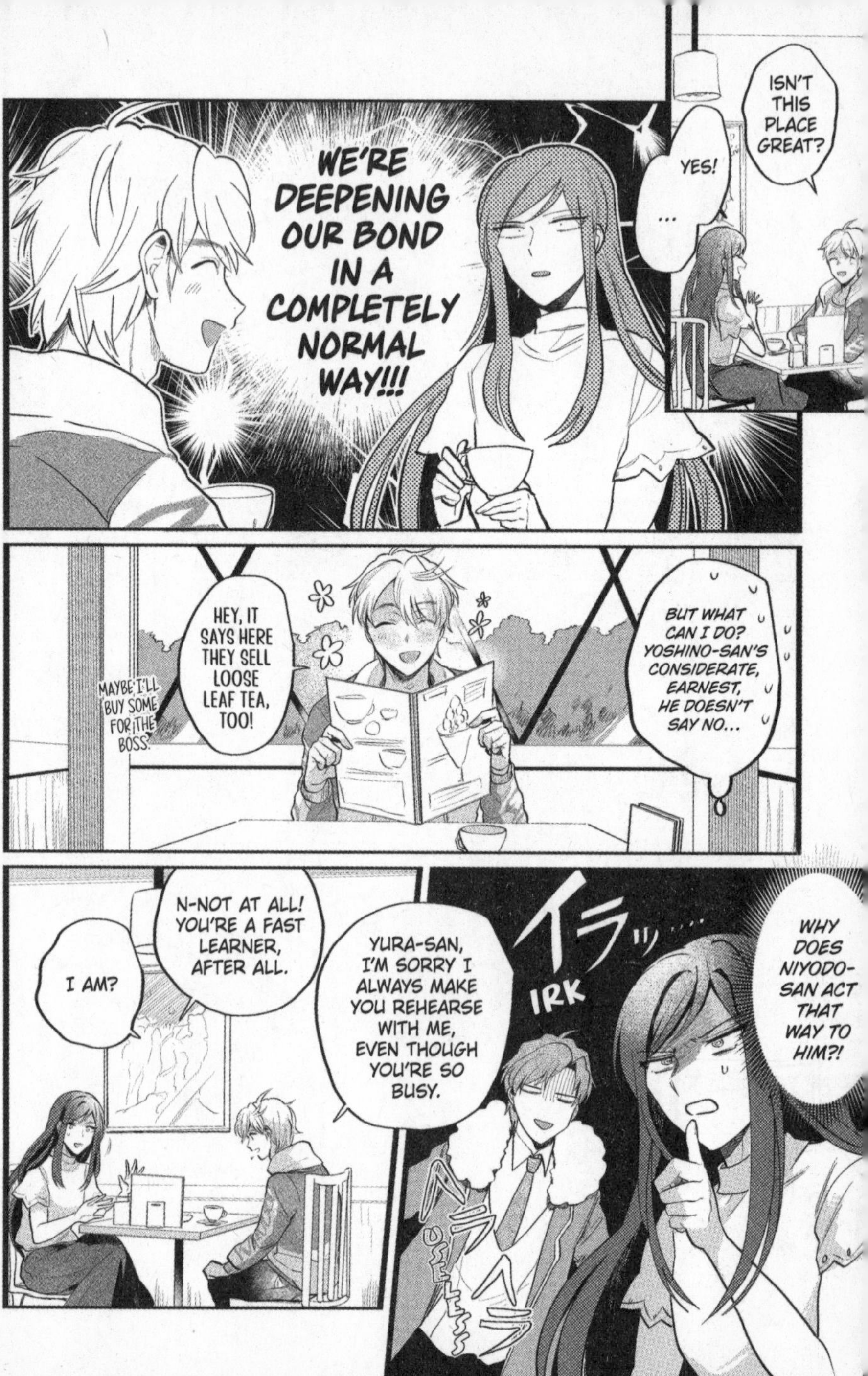
ISN'T THIS PLACE GREAT?
YES!
...
WE'RE DEEPENING OUR BOND IN A COMPLETELY NORMAL WAY!!!
BUT WHAT CAN I DO? YOSHINO-SAN'S CONSIDERATE, EARNEST, HE DOESN'T SAY NO...
HEY, IT SAYS HERE THEY SELL LOOSE LEAF TEA, TOO!
MAYBE I'LL BUY SOME FOR THE BOSS.
WHY DOES NIYODO-SAN ACT THAT WAY TO HIM?!
IRK
YURA-SAN, I'M SORRY I ALWAYS MAKE YOU REHEARSE WITH ME, EVEN THOUGH YOU'RE SO BUSY.
N-NOT AT ALL! YOU'RE A FAST LEARNER, AFTER ALL.
I AM?

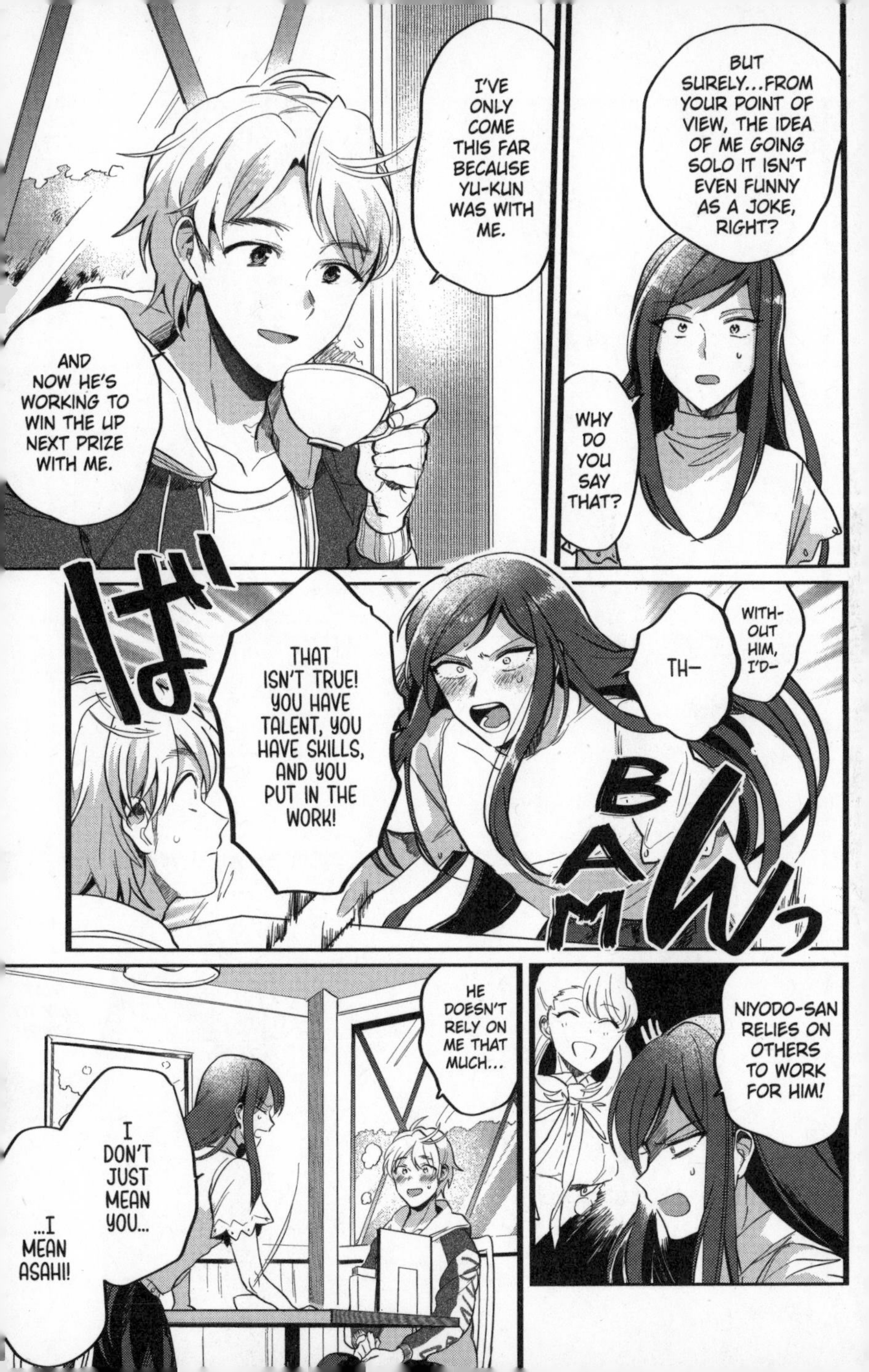
BUT SURELY...FROM YOUR POINT OF VIEW, THE IDEA OF ME GOING SOLO IT ISN'T EVEN FUNNY AS A JOKE, RIGHT?
WHY DO YOU SAY THAT?
I'VE ONLY COME THIS FAR BECAUSE YU-KUN WAS WITH ME.
AND NOW HE'S WORKING TO WIN THE UP NEXT PRIZE WITH ME.
WITH-OUT HIM, I'D—
TH—
BAM
THAT ISN'T TRUE! YOU HAVE TALENT, YOU HAVE SKILLS, AND YOU PUT IN THE WORK!
ば
NIYODO-SAN RELIES ON OTHERS TO WORK FOR HIM!
HE DOESN'T RELY ON ME THAT MUCH...
I DON'T JUST MEAN YOU...
...I MEAN ASAHI!

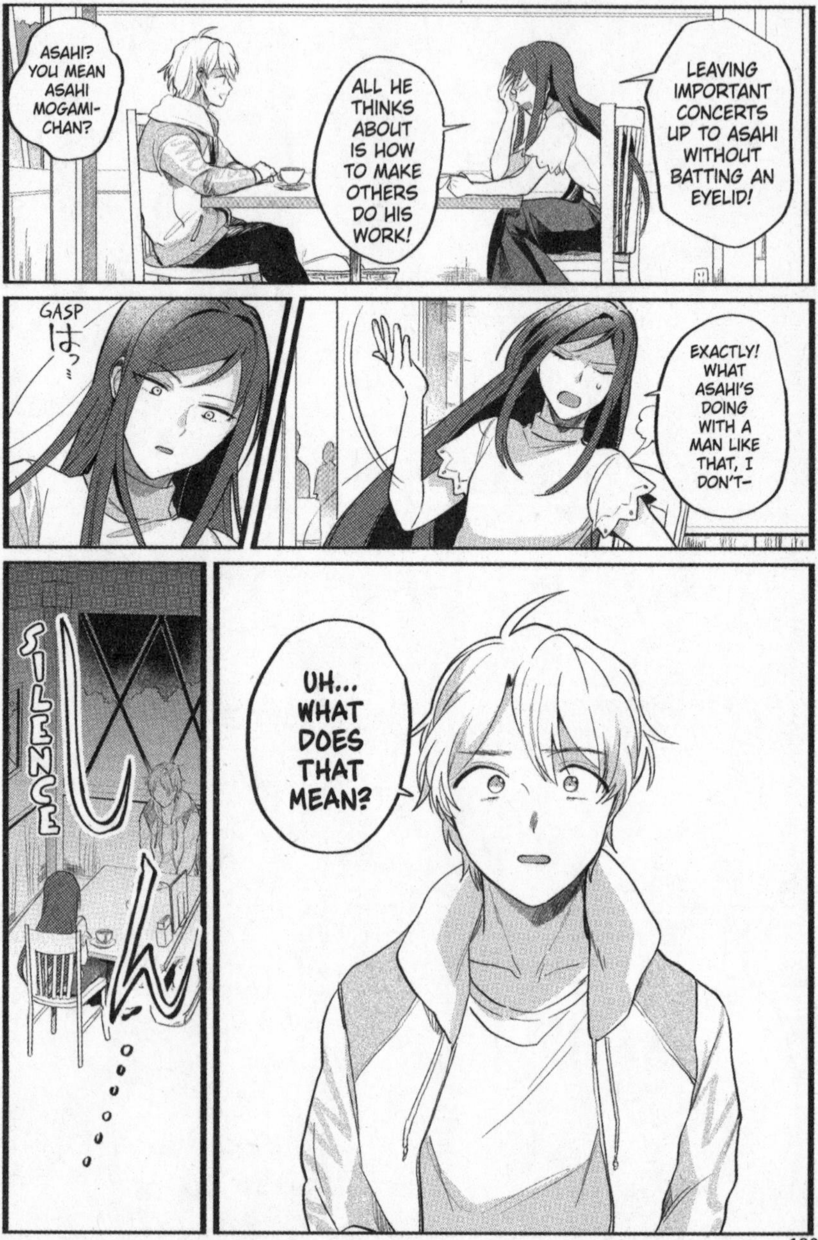
LEAVING IMPORTANT CONCERTS UP TO ASAHI WITHOUT BATTING AN EYELID!
ALL HE THINKS ABOUT IS HOW TO MAKE OTHERS DO HIS WORK!
ASAHI? YOU MEAN ASAHI MOGAMI-CHAN?
EXACTLY! WHAT ASAHI'S DOING WITH A MAN LIKE THAT, I DON'T-
GASP
はっ
UH... WHAT DOES THAT MEAN?
SILENCE
しん……

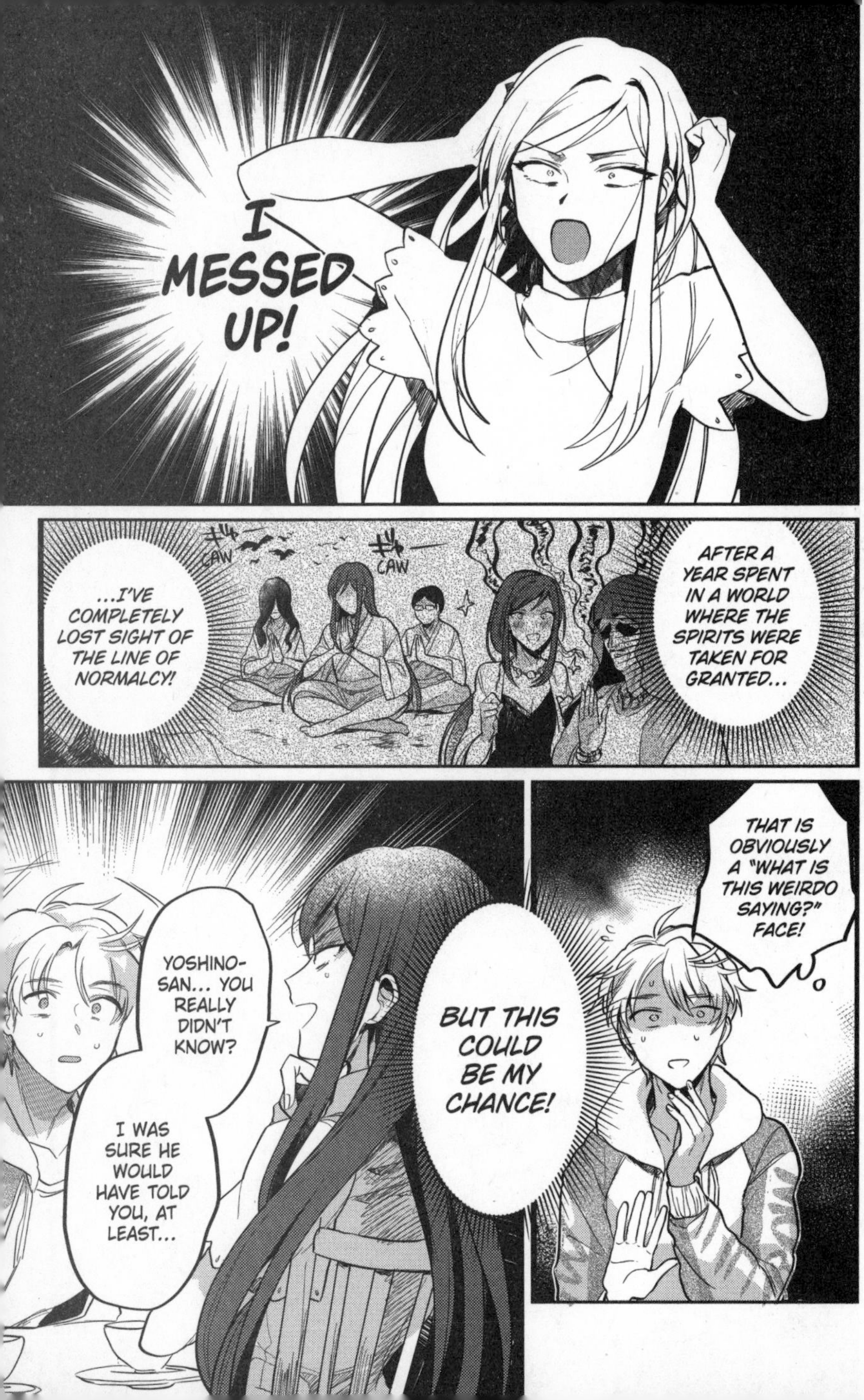
I MESSED UP!
AFTER A YEAR SPENT IN A WORLD WHERE THE SPIRITS WERE TAKEN FOR GRANTED...
CAW
CAW
...I'VE COMPLETELY LOST SIGHT OF THE LINE OF NORMALCY!
THAT IS OBVIOUSLY A "WHAT IS THIS WEIRDO SAYING?" FACE!
BUT THIS COULD BE MY CHANCE!
YOSHINO-SAN... YOU REALLY DIDN'T KNOW?
I WAS SURE HE WOULD HAVE TOLD YOU, AT LEAST...

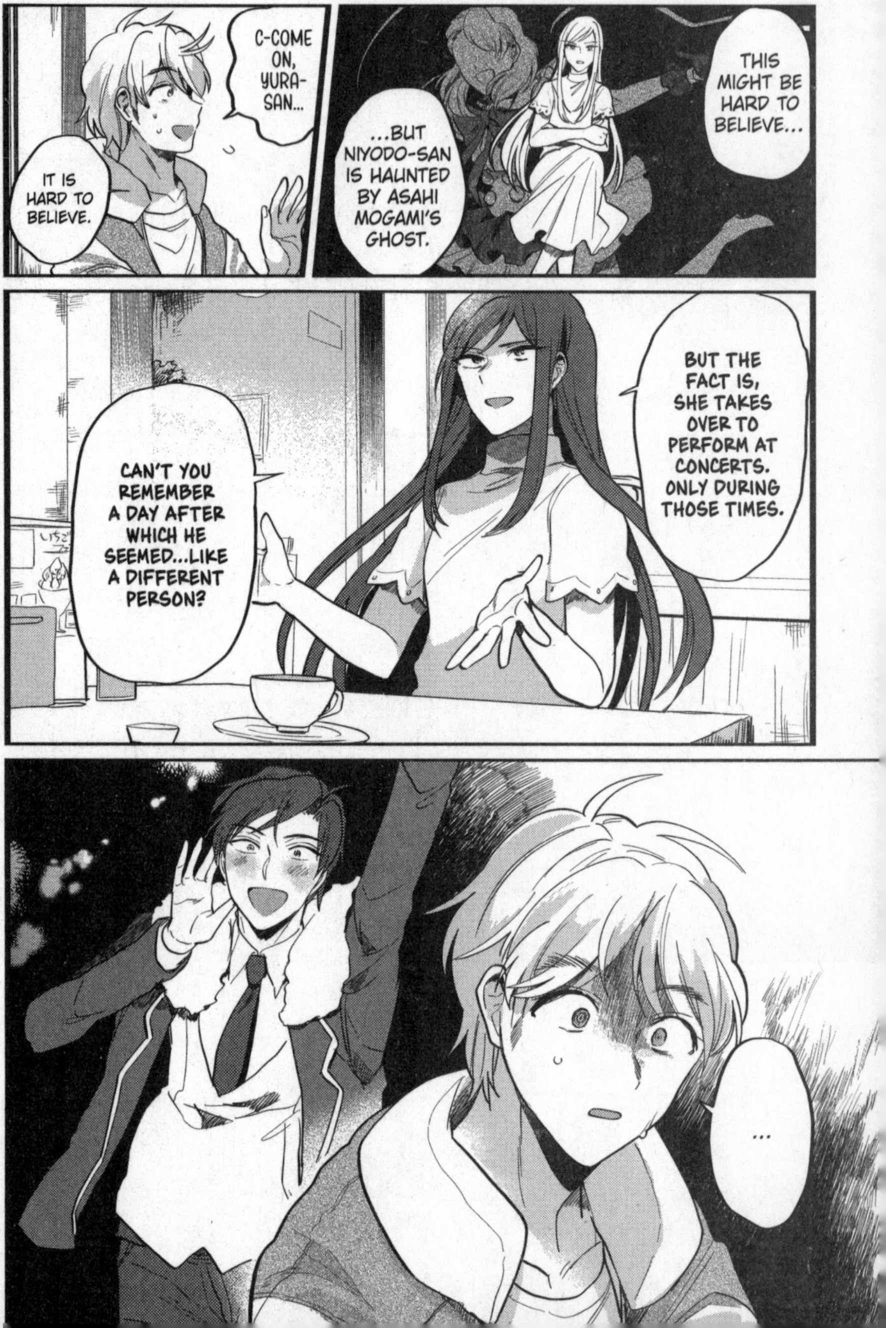
THIS MIGHT BE HARD TO BELIEVE...
...BUT NIYODO-SAN IS HAUNTED BY ASAHI MOGAMI'S GHOST.
C-COME ON, YURA-SAN...
IT IS HARD TO BELIEVE.
BUT THE FACT IS, SHE TAKES OVER TO PERFORM AT CONCERTS. ONLY DURING THOSE TIMES.
CAN'T YOU REMEMBER A DAY AFTER WHICH HE SEEMED...LIKE A DIFFERENT PERSON?
...

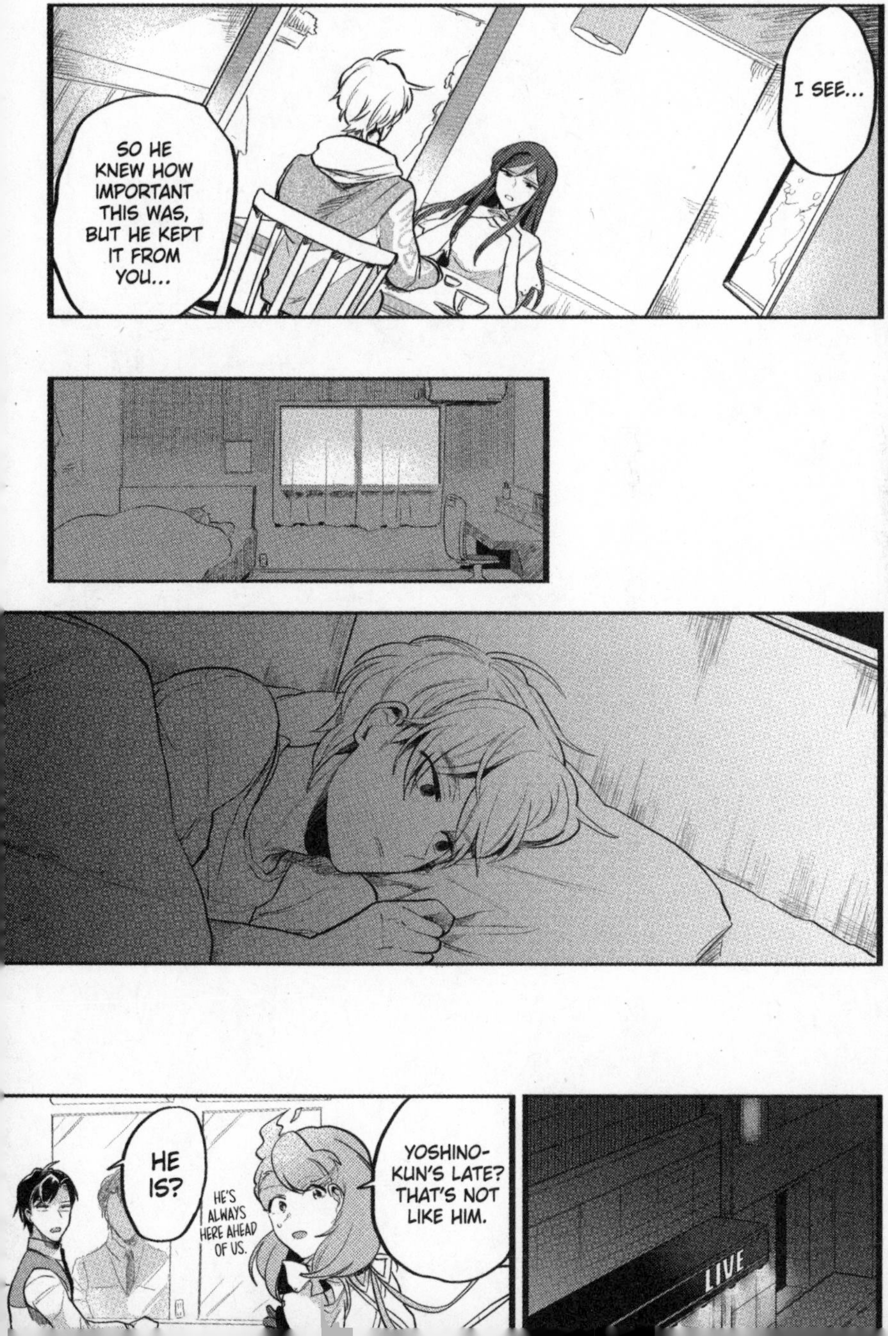
I SEE...
SO HE KNEW HOW IMPORTANT THIS WAS, BUT HE KEPT IT FROM YOU...
LIVE
YOSHINO-KUN'S LATE? THAT'S NOT LIKE HIM.
HE'S ALWAYS HERE AHEAD OF US.
HE IS?

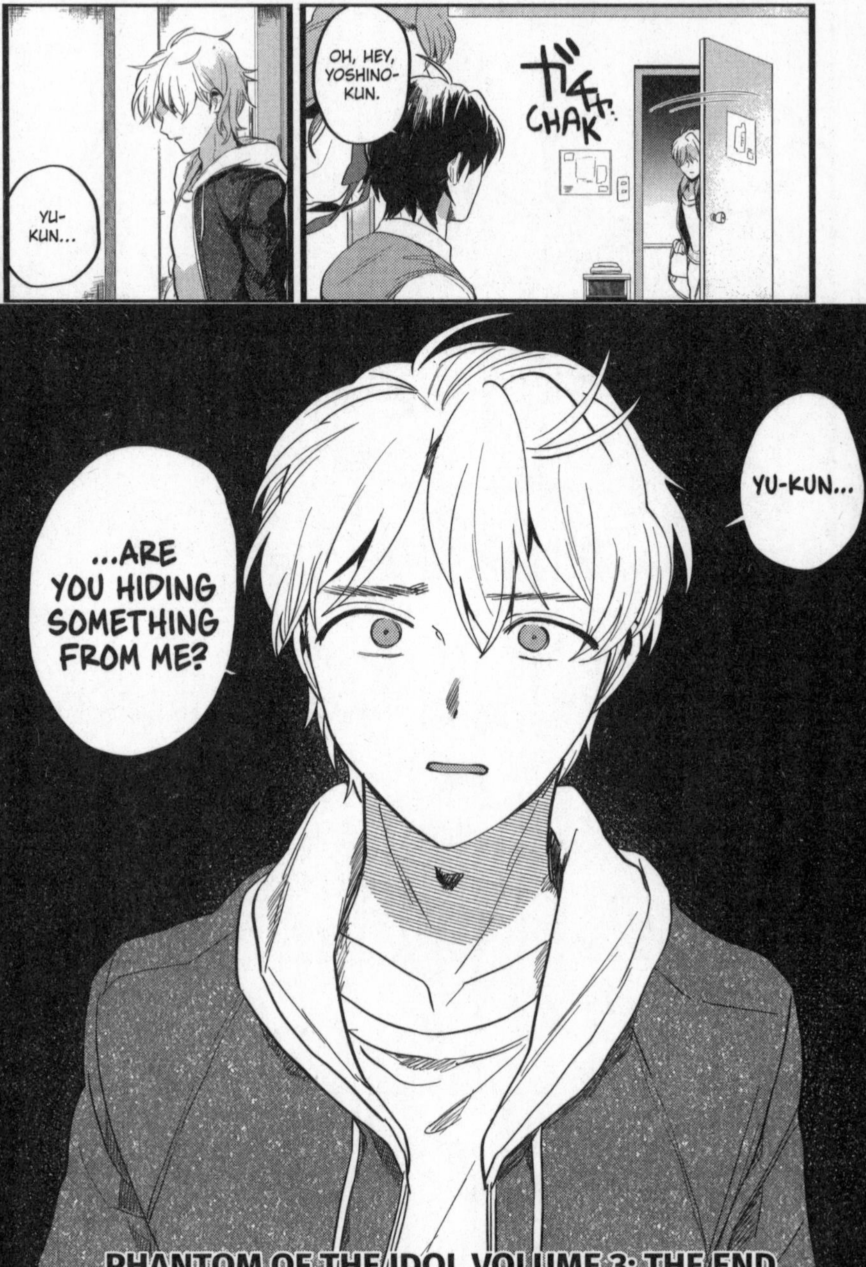
ガチャ
CHAK
OH, HEY, YOSHINO-KUN.
YU-KUN...
YU-KUN...
...ARE YOU HIDING SOMETHING FROM ME?
PHANTOM OF THE IDOL VOLUME 3: THE END

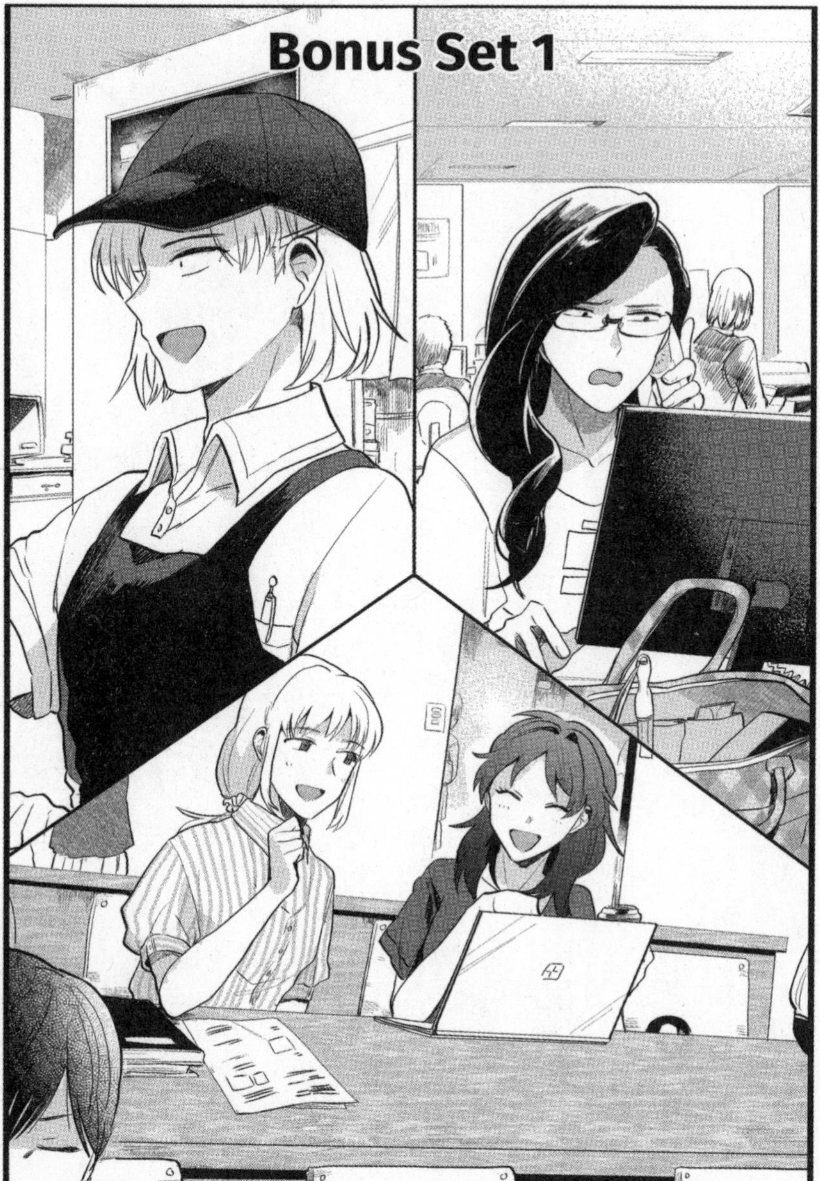
Bonus Set 1

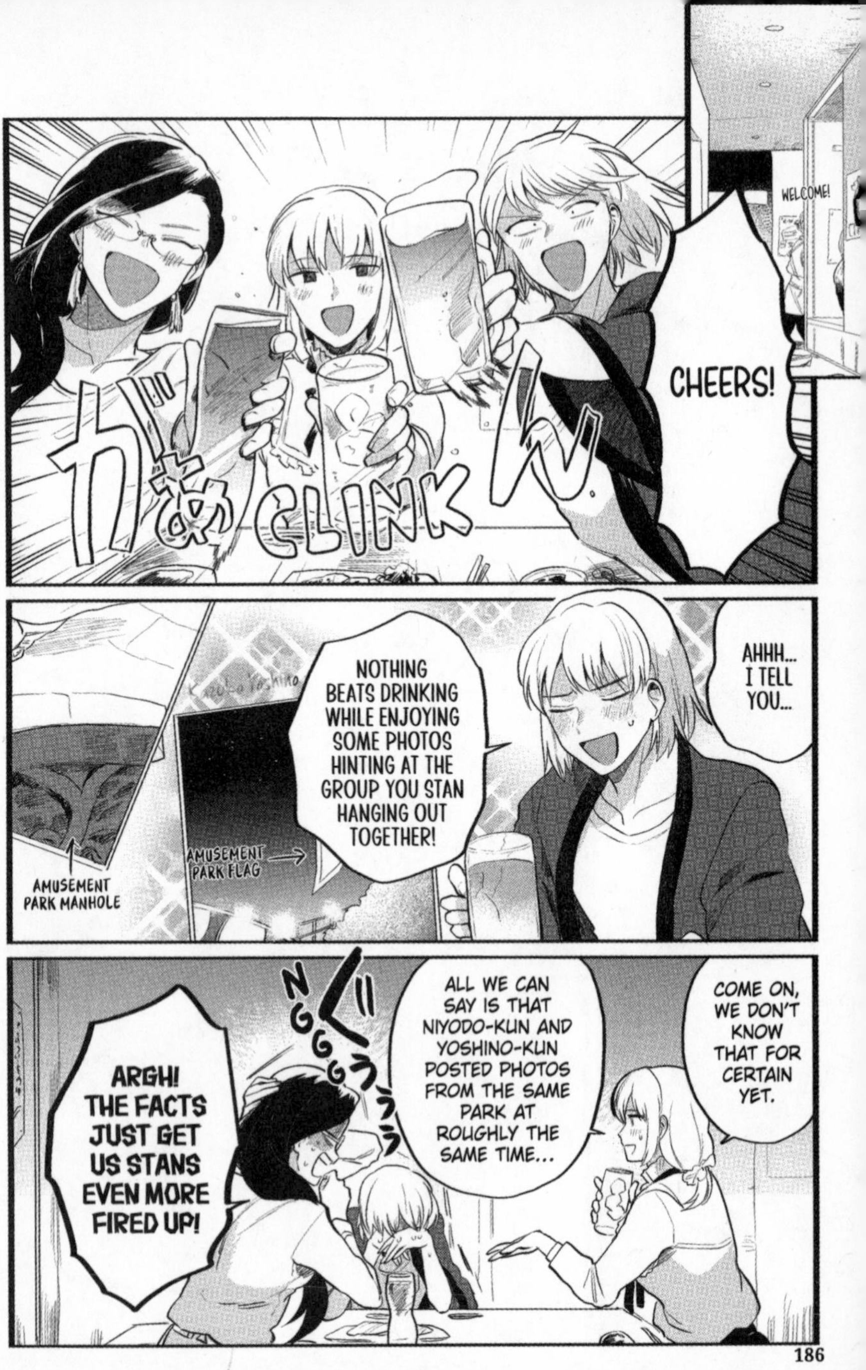
WELCOME!
CHEERS!
CLINK
AHHH... I TELL YOU...
NOTHING BEATS DRINKING WHILE ENJOYING SOME PHOTOS HINTING AT THE GROUP YOU STAN HANGING OUT TOGETHER!
AMUSEMENT PARK FLAG
AMUSEMENT PARK MANHOLE
COME ON, WE DON'T KNOW THAT FOR CERTAIN YET.
ALL WE CAN SAY IS THAT NIYODO-KUN AND YOSHINO-KUN POSTED PHOTOS FROM THE SAME PARK AT ROUGHLY THE SAME TIME...
NGGGG
ARGH! THE FACTS JUST GET US STANS EVEN MORE FIRED UP!

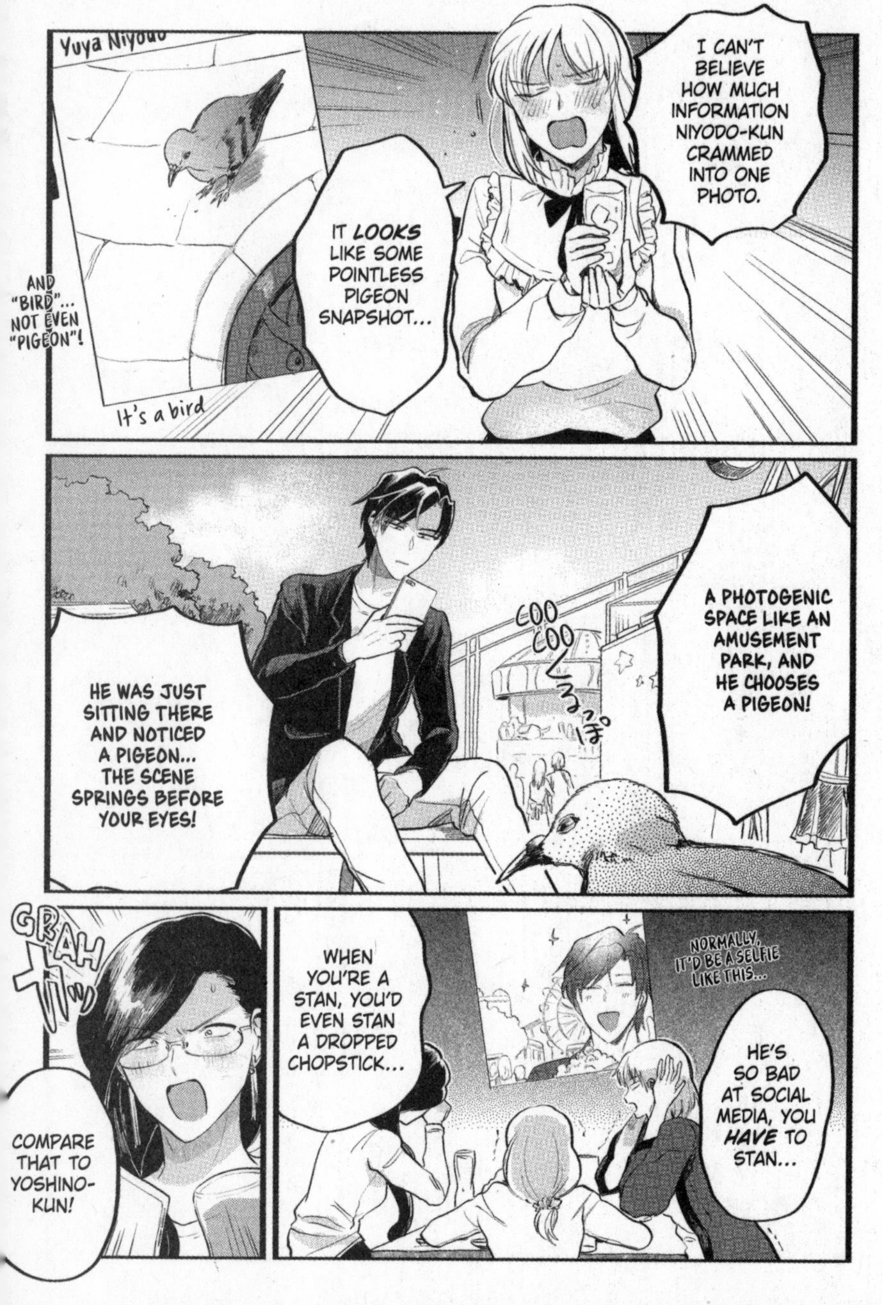
I CAN'T BELIEVE HOW MUCH INFORMATION NIYODO-KUN CRAMMED INTO ONE PHOTO.
Yuya Niyodo
IT *LOOKS* LIKE SOME POINTLESS PIGEON SNAPSHOT...
AND "BIRD"... NOT EVEN "PIGEON"!
It's a bird
A PHOTOGENIC SPACE LIKE AN AMUSEMENT PARK, AND HE CHOOSES A PIGEON!
COO COO
くるっぽ
HE WAS JUST SITTING THERE AND NOTICED A PIGEON... THE SCENE SPRINGS BEFORE YOUR EYES!
NORMALLY, IT'D BE A SELFIE LIKE THIS...
HE'S SO BAD AT SOCIAL MEDIA, YOU *HAVE* TO STAN...
WHEN YOU'RE A STAN, YOU'D EVEN STAN A DROPPED CHOPSTICK...
GRAH
COMPARE THAT TO YOSHINO-KUN!

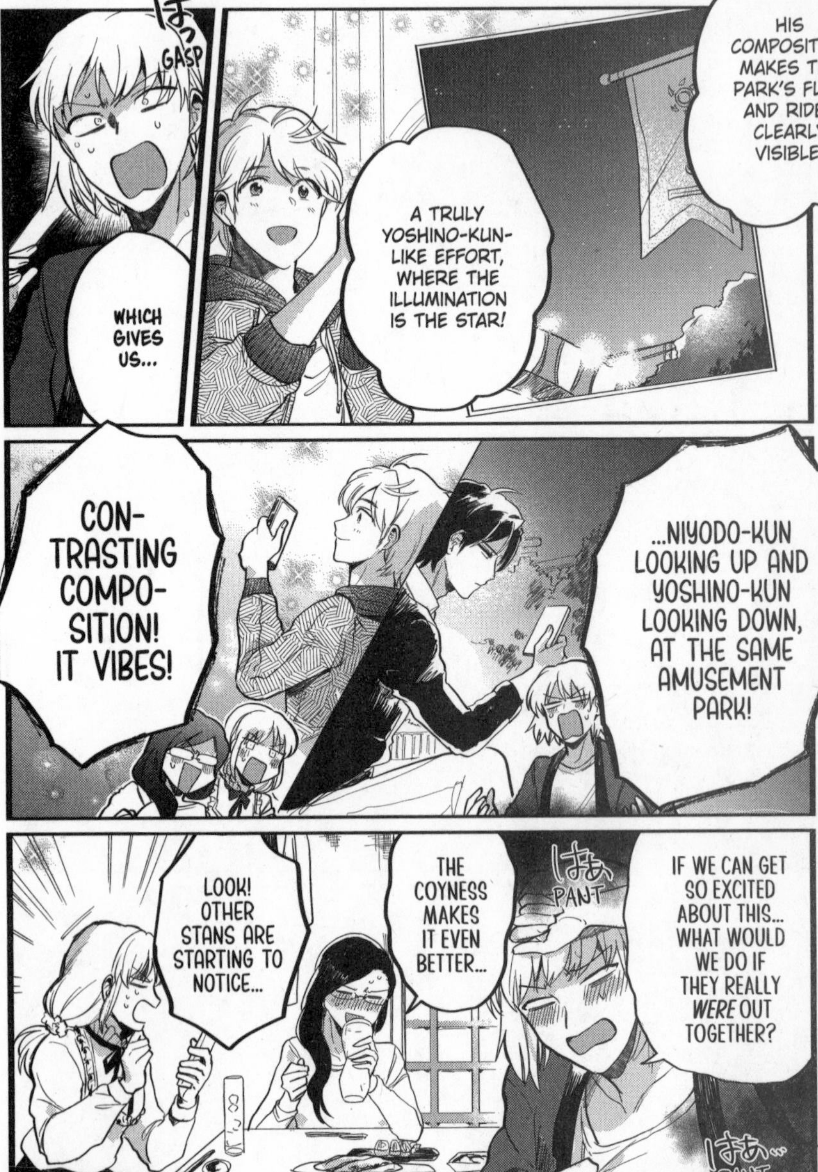
HIS COMPOSITION MAKES THE PARK'S FLAG AND RIDES CLEARLY VISIBLE!
A TRULY YOSHINO-KUN-LIKE EFFORT, WHERE THE ILLUMINATION IS THE STAR!
はっ
GASP
WHICH GIVES US...
...NIYODO-KUN LOOKING UP AND YOSHINO-KUN LOOKING DOWN, AT THE SAME AMUSEMENT PARK!
CON-TRASTING COMPO-SITION! IT VIBES!
はあ
PANT
IF WE CAN GET SO EXCITED ABOUT THIS... WHAT WOULD WE DO IF THEY REALLY *WERE* OUT TOGETHER?
THE COYNESS MAKES IT EVEN BETTER...
LOOK! OTHER STANS ARE STARTING TO NOTICE...
はあ…
PANT

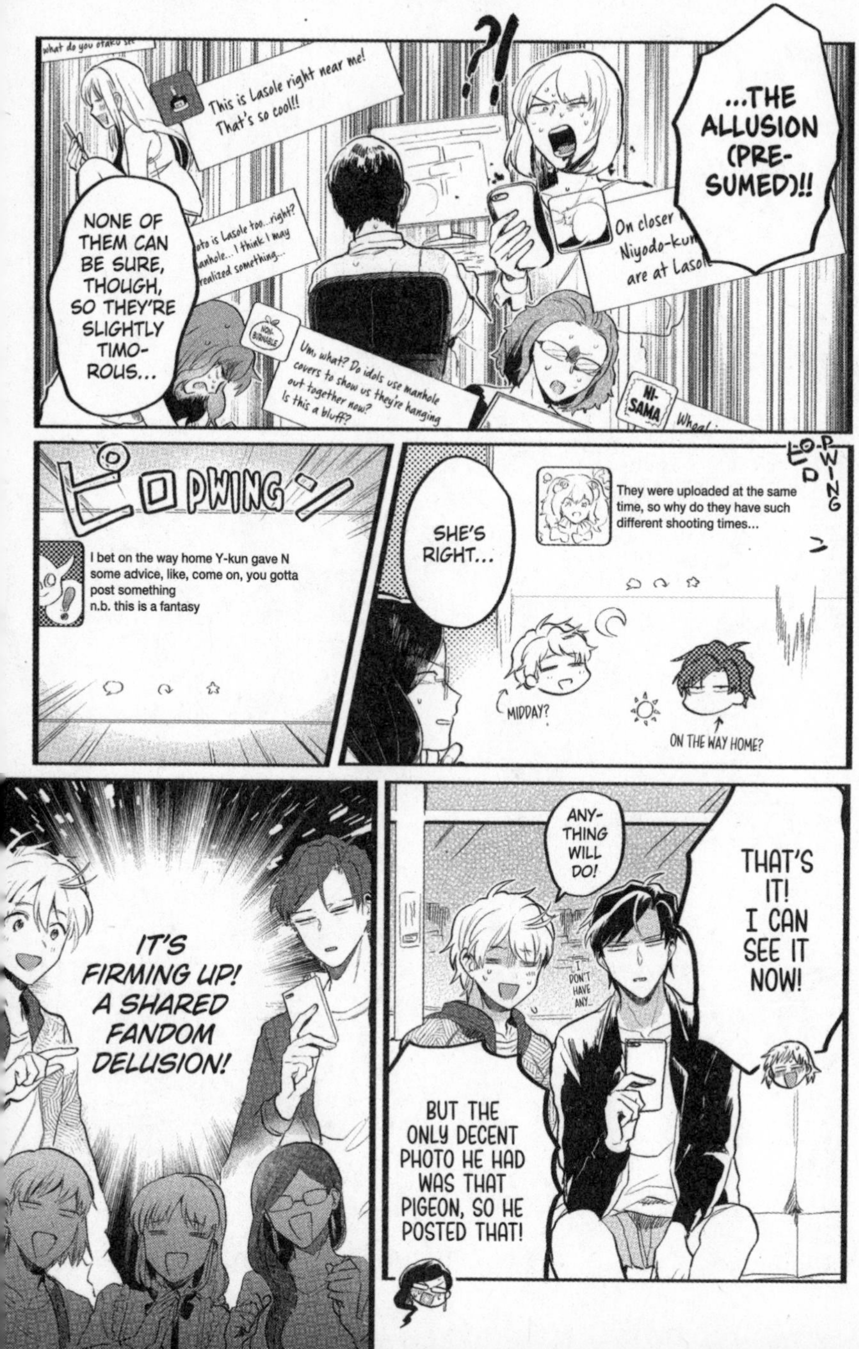
?!
...THE ALLUSION (PRE-SUMED)!!
On closer
Niyodo-kun
are at Lasol
This is Lasole right near me! That's so cool!!
what do you otaku
NONE OF THEM CAN BE SURE, THOUGH, SO THEY'RE SLIGHTLY TIMO-ROUS...
is Lasole too...right?
I think I may
realized something...
NON-BURNABLE
Um, what? Do idols use manhole covers to show us they're hanging out together now? Is this a bluff?
NI-SAMA
PWING
They were uploaded at the same time, so why do they have such different shooting times...
SHE'S RIGHT...
ON THE WAY HOME?
MIDDAY?
PWING
I bet on the way home Y-kun gave N some advice, like, come on, you gotta post something
n.b. this is a fantasy
THAT'S IT! I CAN SEE IT NOW!
ANY-THING WILL DO!
I DON'T HAVE ANY...
BUT THE ONLY DECENT PHOTO HE HAD WAS THAT PIGEON, SO HE POSTED THAT!
IT'S FIRMING UP! A SHARED FANDOM DELUSION!

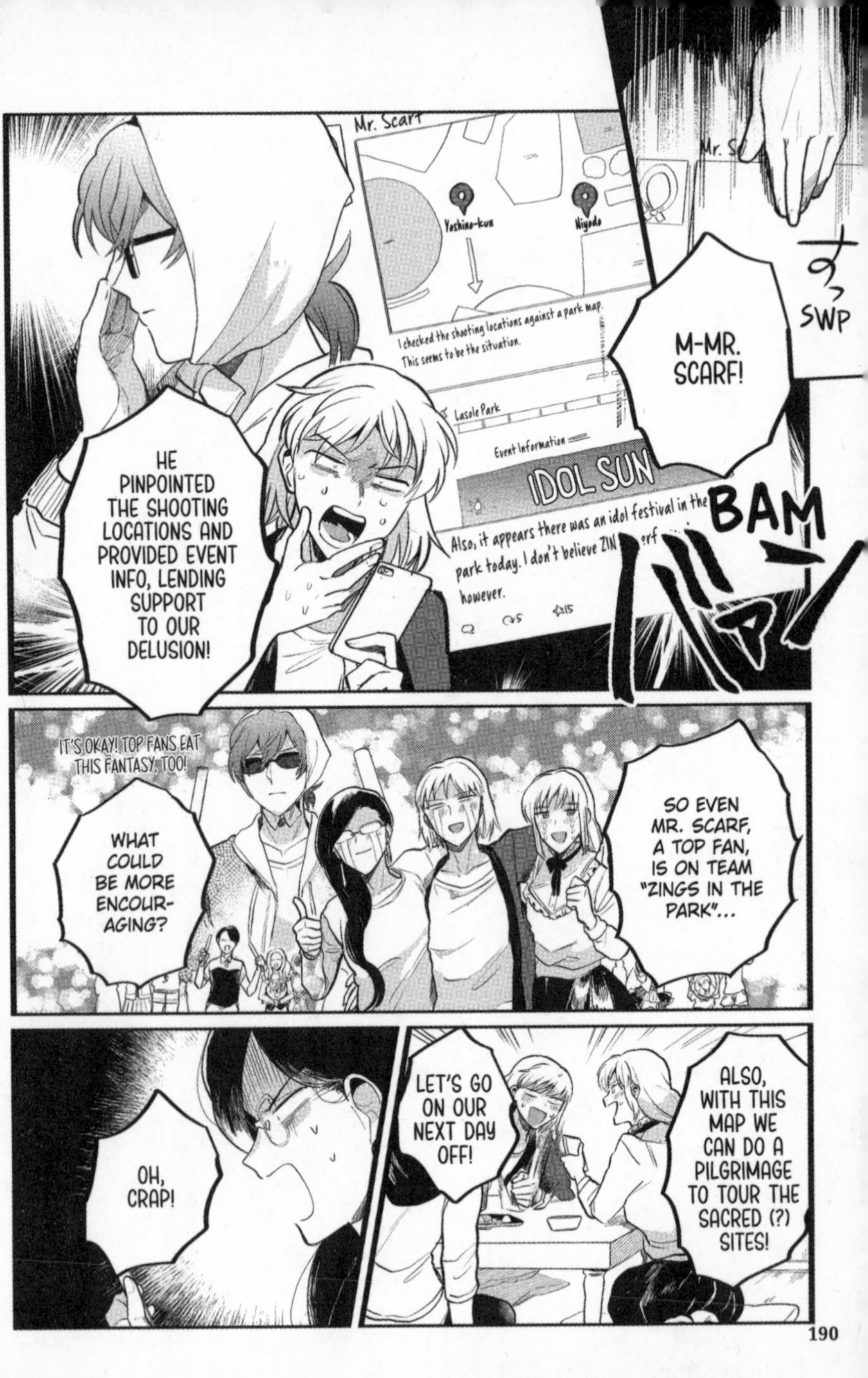

Mr. S
すっ
SWP
M-MR. SCARF!
Mr. Scarf
Yoshino-kun
Niyodo
I checked the shooting locations against a park map.
This seems to be the situation.
Lasole Park
Event Information
IDOL SUN
Also, it appears there was an idol festival in the
park today. I don't believe ZIN
however.
HE PINPOINTED THE SHOOTING LOCATIONS AND PROVIDED EVENT INFO, LENDING SUPPORT TO OUR DELUSION!
BAM
バァン
SO EVEN MR. SCARF, A TOP FAN, IS ON TEAM "ZINGS IN THE PARK"...
IT'S OKAY! TOP FANS EAT THIS FANTASY, TOO!
WHAT COULD BE MORE ENCOUR-AGING?
ALSO, WITH THIS MAP WE CAN DO A PILGRIMAGE TO TOUR THE SACRED (?) SITES!
LET'S GO ON OUR NEXT DAY OFF!
OH, CRAP!

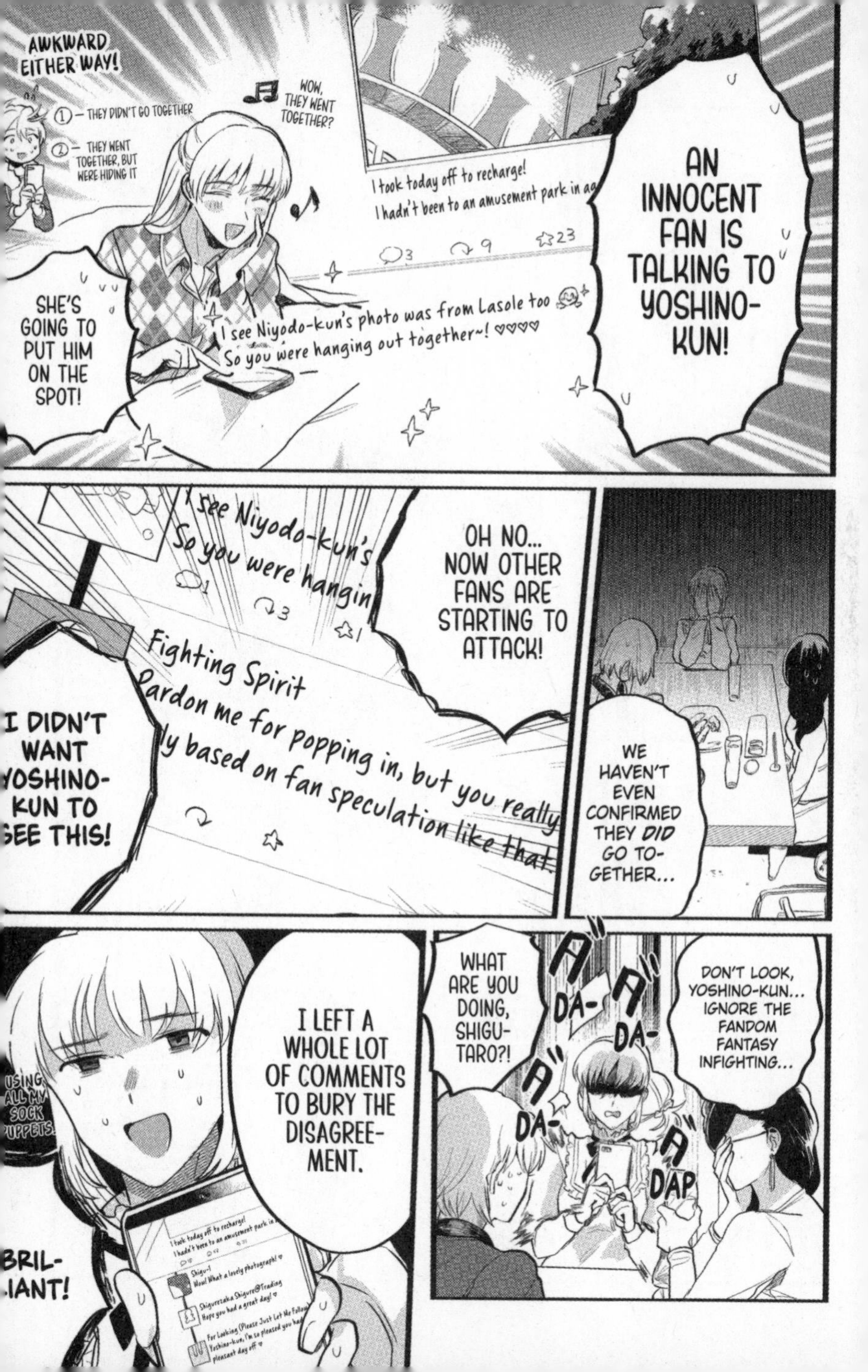
AN INNOCENT FAN IS TALKING TO YOSHINO-KUN!
I took today off to recharge!
I hadn't been to an amusement park in ag
3
9
23
WOW, THEY WENT TOGETHER?
AWKWARD EITHER WAY!
① — THEY DIDN'T GO TOGETHER
② — THEY WENT TOGETHER, BUT WERE HIDING IT
I see Niyodo-kun's photo was from Lasole too
So you were hanging out together~! ♡♡♡♡
SHE'S GOING TO PUT HIM ON THE SPOT!
WE HAVEN'T EVEN CONFIRMED THEY *DID* GO TOGETHER...
OH NO... NOW OTHER FANS ARE STARTING TO ATTACK!
I see Niyodo-kun's
So you were hangin
1
3
1
Fighting Spirit
Pardon me for popping in, but you really
ly based on fan speculation like that.
I DIDN'T WANT YOSHINO-KUN TO SEE THIS!
DON'T LOOK, YOSHINO-KUN... IGNORE THE FANDOM FANTASY INFIGHTING...
DA-
DA-
DA-
DAP
WHAT ARE YOU DOING, SHIGUTARO?!
I LEFT A WHOLE LOT OF COMMENTS TO BURY THE DISAGREEMENT.
USING ALL MY SOCK PUPPETS!
I took today off to recharge!
I hadn't been to an amusement park in
Shigu-1
Wow! What a lovely photograph!
Shigurezaka Shigure@Trading
Hope you had a great day!
For Looking (Please Just Let Me Follow)
Yoshino-kun, I'm so pleased you had a pleasant day off
BRILLIANT!

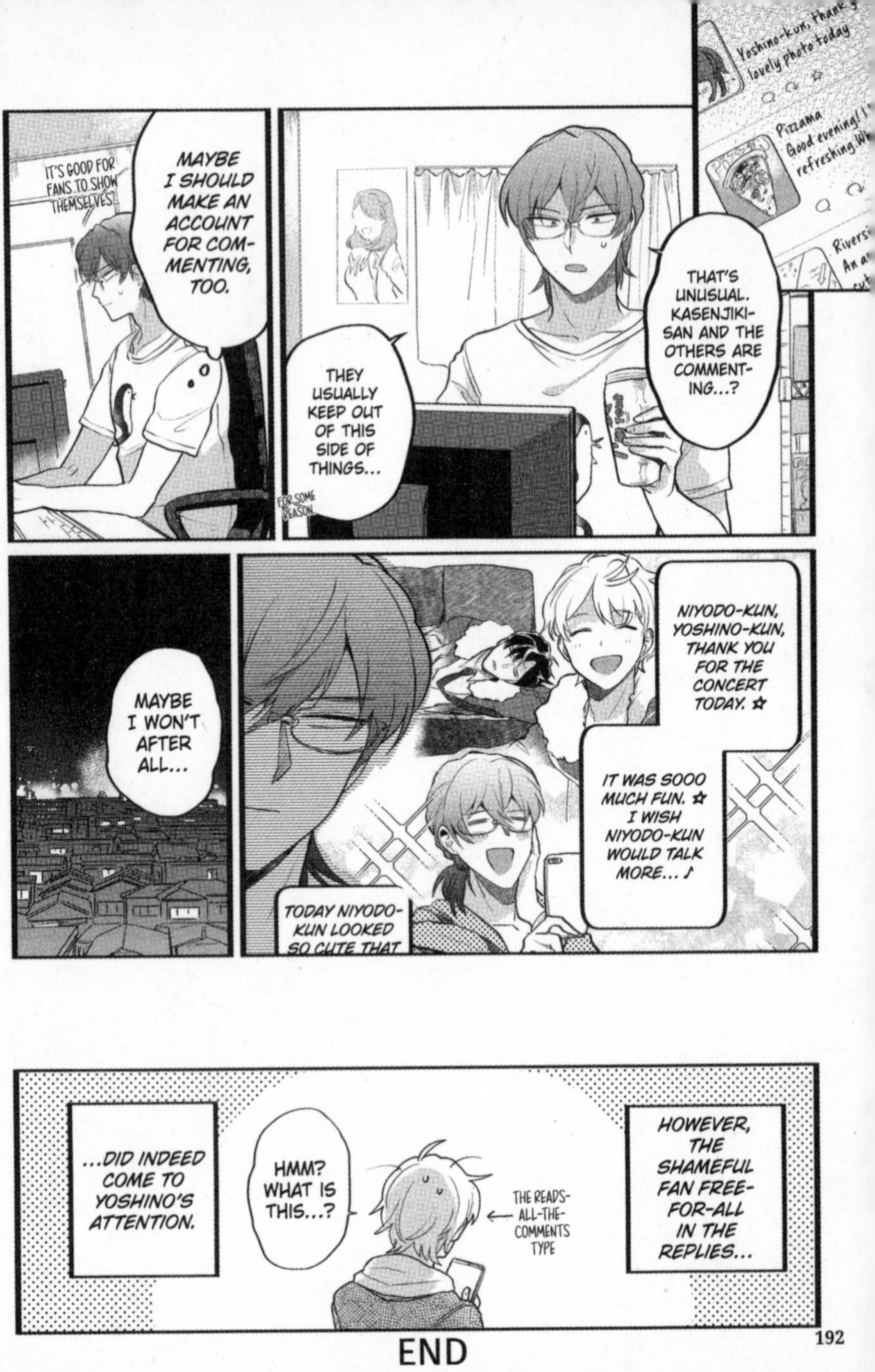
Yoshino-kun, thank
lovely photo today ☆
Pizzama
Good evening!
refreshing.
THAT'S UNUSUAL. KASENJIKI-SAN AND THE OTHERS ARE COMMENTING...?
THEY USUALLY KEEP OUT OF THIS SIDE OF THINGS...
FOR SOME REASON
MAYBE I SHOULD MAKE AN ACCOUNT FOR COMMENTING, TOO.
IT'S GOOD FOR FANS TO SHOW THEMSELVES!!
NIYODO-KUN, YOSHINO-KUN, THANK YOU FOR THE CONCERT TODAY. ☆
IT WAS SOOO MUCH FUN. ☆ I WISH NIYODO-KUN WOULD TALK MORE... ♪
TODAY NIYODO-KUN LOOKED SO CUTE THAT
MAYBE I WON'T AFTER ALL...
HOWEVER, THE SHAMEFUL FAN FREE-FOR-ALL IN THE REPLIES...
THE READS-ALL-THE-COMMENTS TYPE
HMM? WHAT IS THIS...?
...DID INDEED COME TO YOSHINO'S ATTENTION.

END

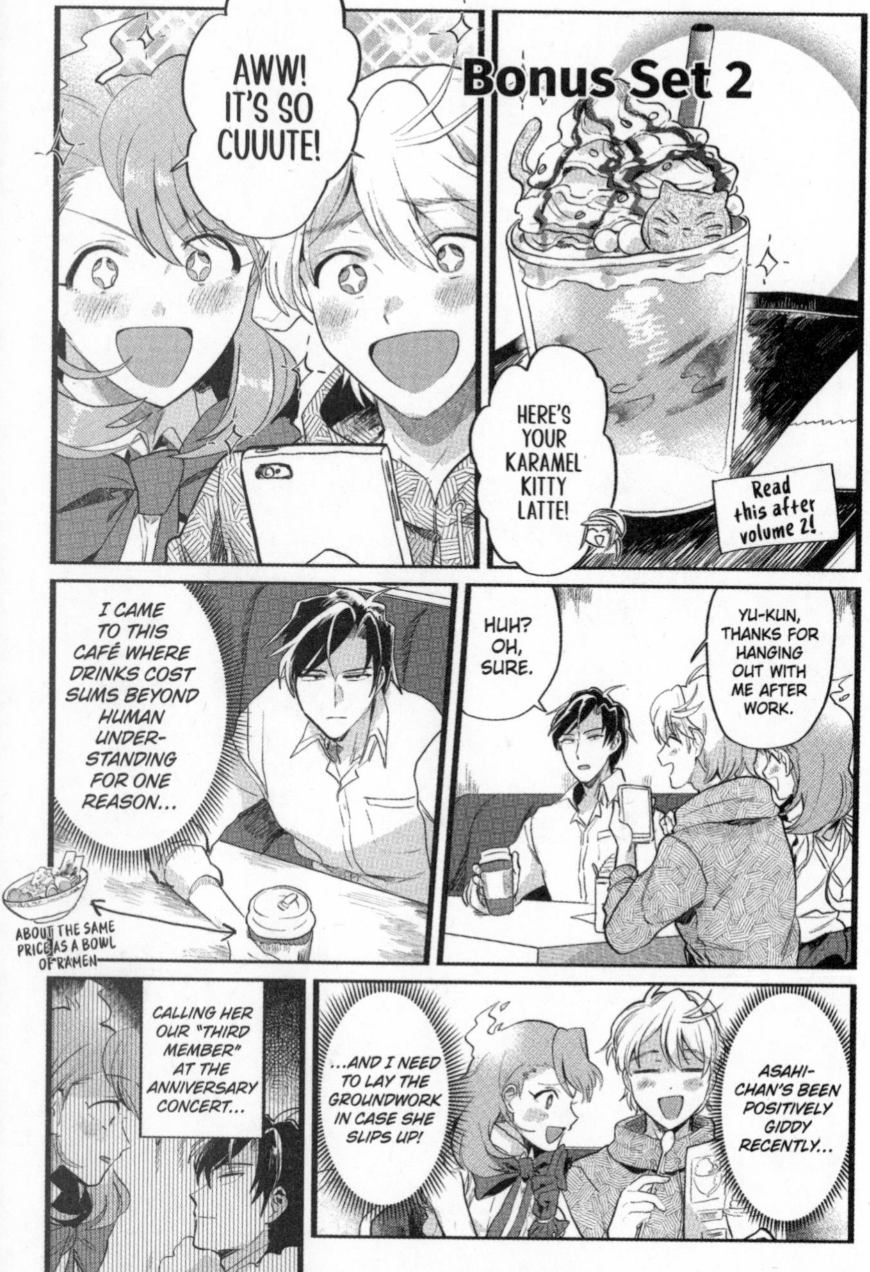
Bonus Set 2
HERE'S YOUR KARAMEL KITTY LATTE!
Read this after volume 2!
AWW! IT'S SO CUUUTE!
YU-KUN, THANKS FOR HANGING OUT WITH ME AFTER WORK.
HUH? OH, SURE.
I CAME TO THIS CAFÉ WHERE DRINKS COST SUMS BEYOND HUMAN UNDER-STANDING FOR ONE REASON...
ABOUT THE SAME PRICE AS A BOWL OF RAMEN
ASAHI-CHAN'S BEEN POSITIVELY GIDDY RECENTLY...
...AND I NEED TO LAY THE GROUNDWORK IN CASE SHE SLIPS UP!
CALLING HER OUR "THIRD MEMBER" AT THE ANNIVERSARY CONCERT...

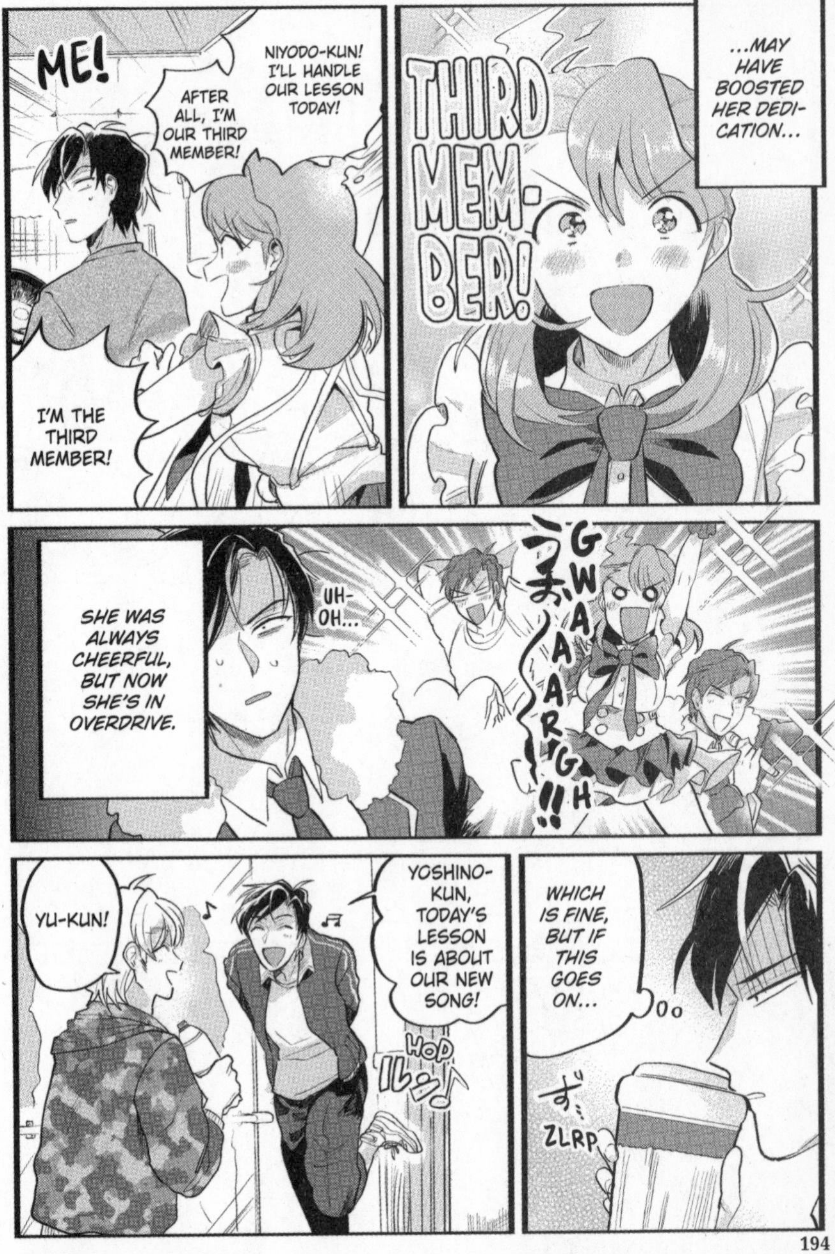
...MAY HAVE BOOSTED HER DEDICATION...
THIRD MEMBER!
ME!
NIYODO-KUN! I'LL HANDLE OUR LESSON TODAY!
AFTER ALL, I'M OUR THIRD MEMBER!
I'M THE THIRD MEMBER!
GWAAAARGH!!
UH-OH...
SHE WAS ALWAYS CHEERFUL, BUT NOW SHE'S IN OVERDRIVE.
WHICH IS FINE, BUT IF THIS GOES ON...
ZLRP
YOSHINO-KUN, TODAY'S LESSON IS ABOUT OUR NEW SONG!
HOP
YU-KUN!

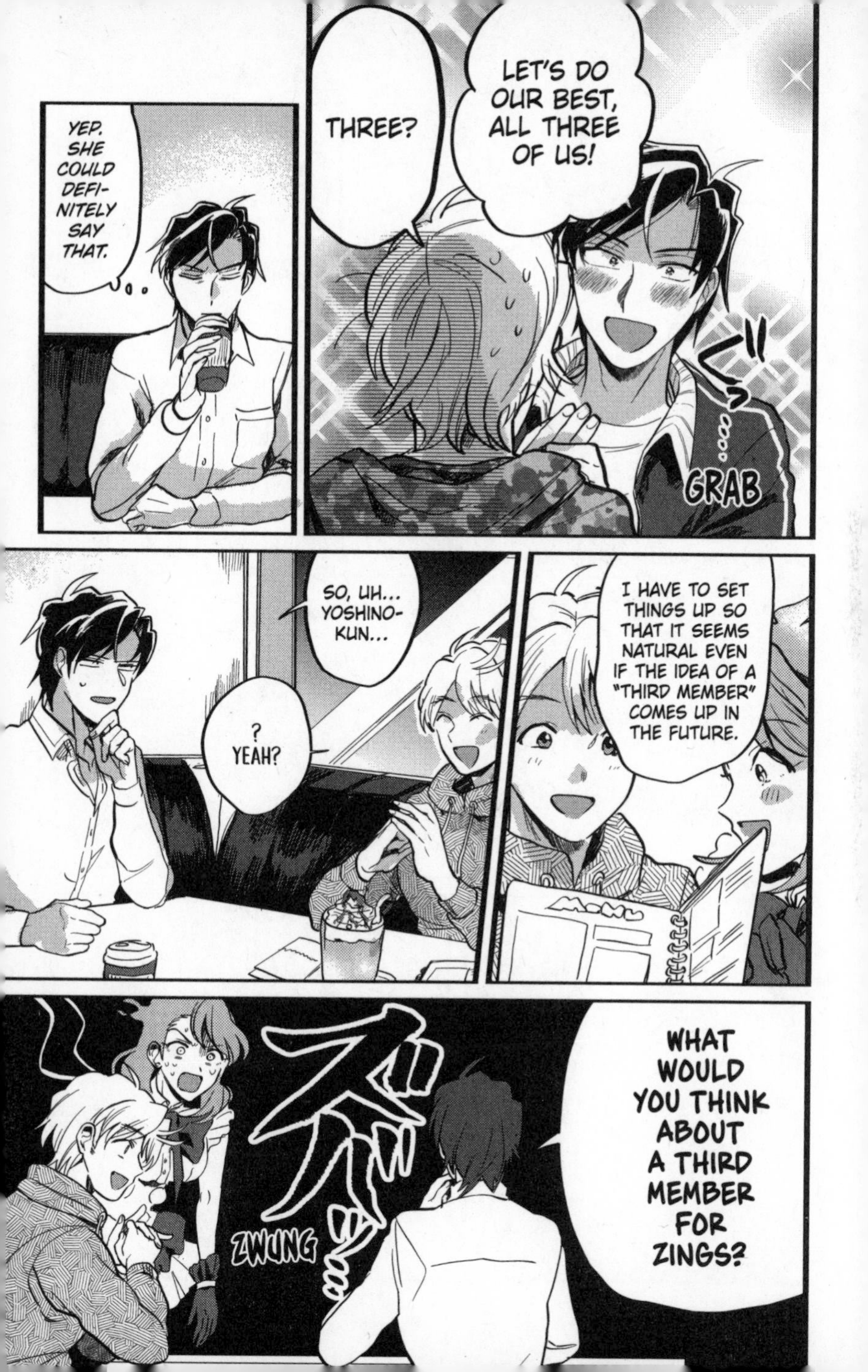
LET'S DO OUR BEST, ALL THREE OF US!
THREE?
GRAB
YEP. SHE COULD DEFINITELY SAY THAT.
I HAVE TO SET THINGS UP SO THAT IT SEEMS NATURAL EVEN IF THE IDEA OF A "THIRD MEMBER" COMES UP IN THE FUTURE.
SO, UH... YOSHINO-KUN...
? YEAH?
WHAT WOULD YOU THINK ABOUT A THIRD MEMBER FOR ZINGS?
ZWUNG

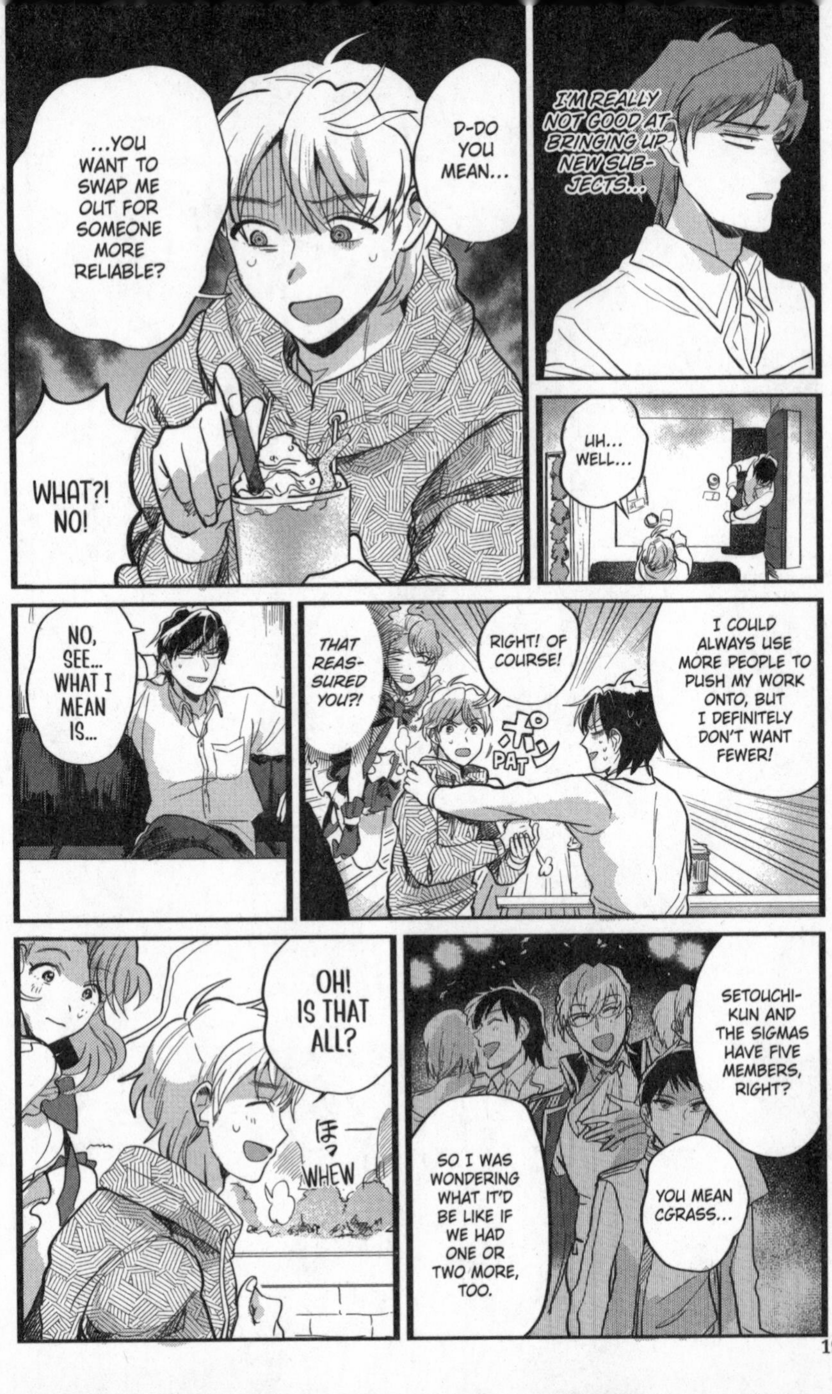
I'M REALLY NOT GOOD AT BRINGING UP NEW SUB-JECTS...
UH... WELL...
D-DO YOU MEAN...
...YOU WANT TO SWAP ME OUT FOR SOMEONE MORE RELIABLE?
WHAT?! NO!
I COULD ALWAYS USE MORE PEOPLE TO PUSH MY WORK ONTO, BUT I DEFINITELY DON'T WANT FEWER!
RIGHT! OF COURSE!
ポン
PAT
THAT REAS-SURED YOU?!
NO, SEE... WHAT I MEAN IS...
SETOUCHI-KUN AND THE SIGMAS HAVE FIVE MEMBERS, RIGHT?
YOU MEAN CGRASS...
SO I WAS WONDERING WHAT IT'D BE LIKE IF WE HAD ONE OR TWO MORE, TOO.
OH! IS THAT ALL?
ほっ
WHEW

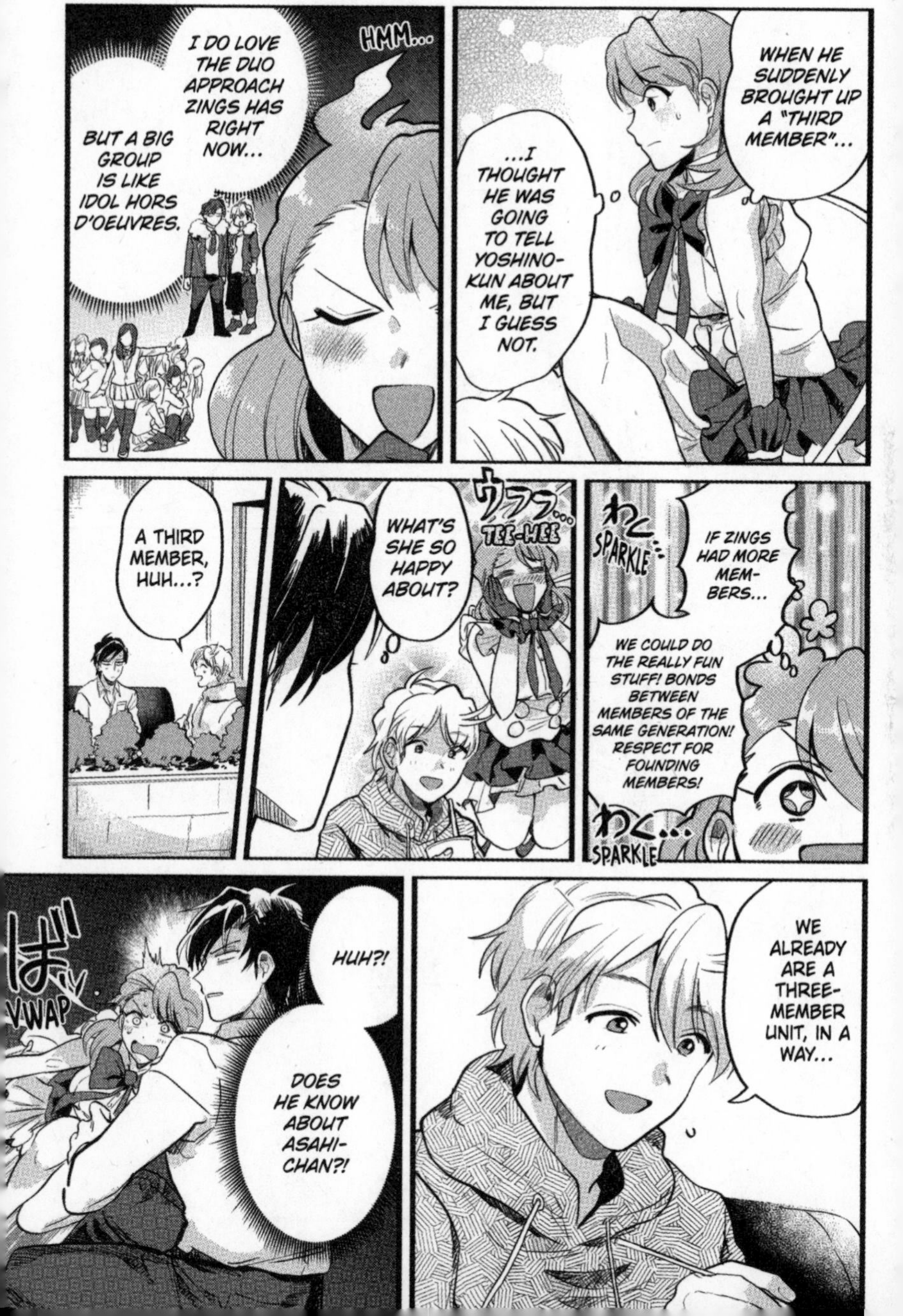
WHEN HE SUDDENLY BROUGHT UP A "THIRD MEMBER"...
...I THOUGHT HE WAS GOING TO TELL YOSHINO-KUN ABOUT ME, BUT I GUESS NOT.
HMM...
I DO LOVE THE DUO APPROACH ZINGS HAS RIGHT NOW...
BUT A BIG GROUP IS LIKE IDOL HORS D'OEUVRES.
わく
SPARKLE
IF ZINGS HAD MORE MEM-BERS...
WE COULD DO THE REALLY FUN STUFF! BONDS BETWEEN MEMBERS OF THE SAME GENERATION! RESPECT FOR FOUNDING MEMBERS!
わく...
SPARKLE
ウフフ...
TEE-HEE
WHAT'S SHE SO HAPPY ABOUT?
A THIRD MEMBER, HUH...?
WE ALREADY ARE A THREE-MEMBER UNIT, IN A WAY...
ば
VWAP
HUH?!
DOES HE KNOW ABOUT ASAHI-CHAN?!

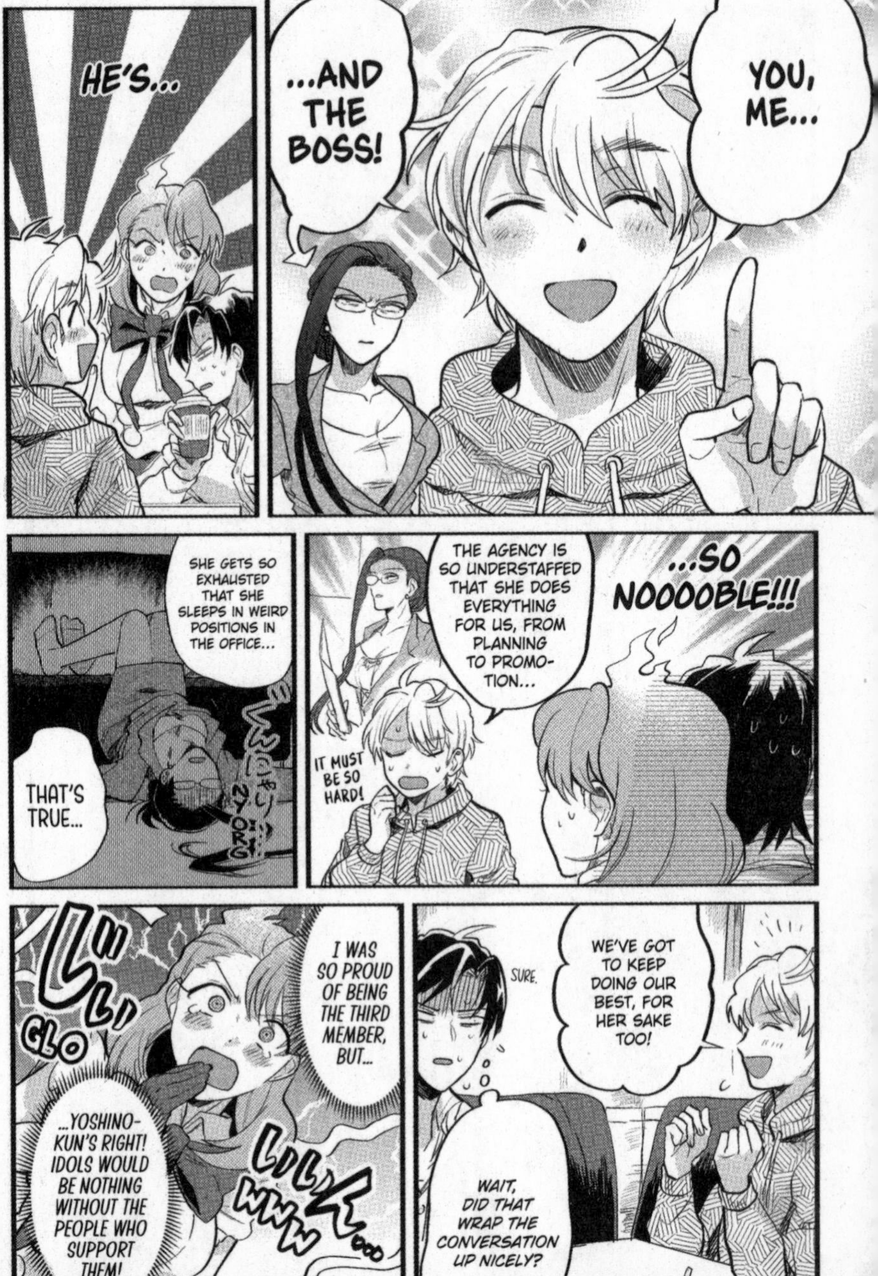
YOU, ME...
...AND THE BOSS!
HE'S...
...SO NOOOOBLE!!!
THE AGENCY IS SO UNDERSTAFFED THAT SHE DOES EVERYTHING FOR US, FROM PLANNING TO PROMO-TION...
IT MUST BE SO HARD!
SHE GETS SO EXHAUSTED THAT SHE SLEEPS IN WEIRD POSITIONS IN THE OFFICE...
THAT'S TRUE...
WE'VE GOT TO KEEP DOING OUR BEST, FOR HER SAKE TOO!
SURE.
WAIT, DID THAT WRAP THE CONVERSATION UP NICELY?
I WAS SO PROUD OF BEING THE THIRD MEMBER, BUT...
GLO
...YOSHINO-KUN'S RIGHT! IDOLS WOULD BE NOTHING WITHOUT THE PEOPLE WHO SUPPORT THEM!

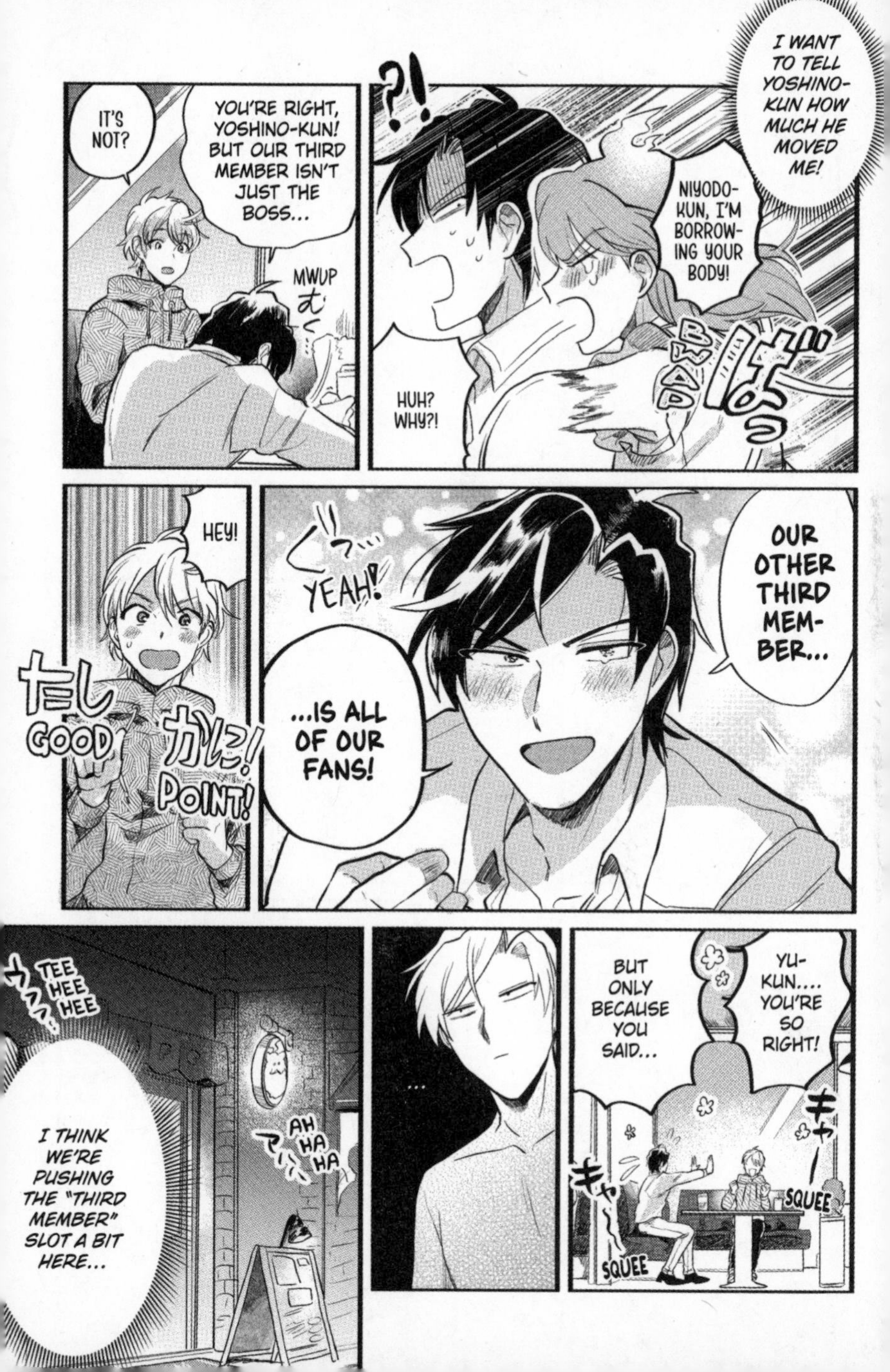
I WANT TO TELL YOSHINO-KUN HOW MUCH HE MOVED ME!
?!
NIYODO-KUN, I'M BORROWING YOUR BODY!
BWAP ぱっ
HUH? WHY?!
YOU'RE RIGHT, YOSHINO-KUN! BUT OUR THIRD MEMBER ISN'T JUST THE BOSS...
IT'S NOT?
MWUP むく...
OUR OTHER THIRD MEMBER...
ぐっ YEAH!
...IS ALL OF OUR FANS!
HEY!
たしかに! GOOD POINT!
YU-KUN.... YOU'RE SO RIGHT!
BUT ONLY BECAUSE YOU SAID...
キャー SQUEE
キャ SQUEE
...
うふふ TEE HEE HEE
あはは AH HA HA
I THINK WE'RE PUSHING THE "THIRD MEMBER" SLOT A BIT HERE...

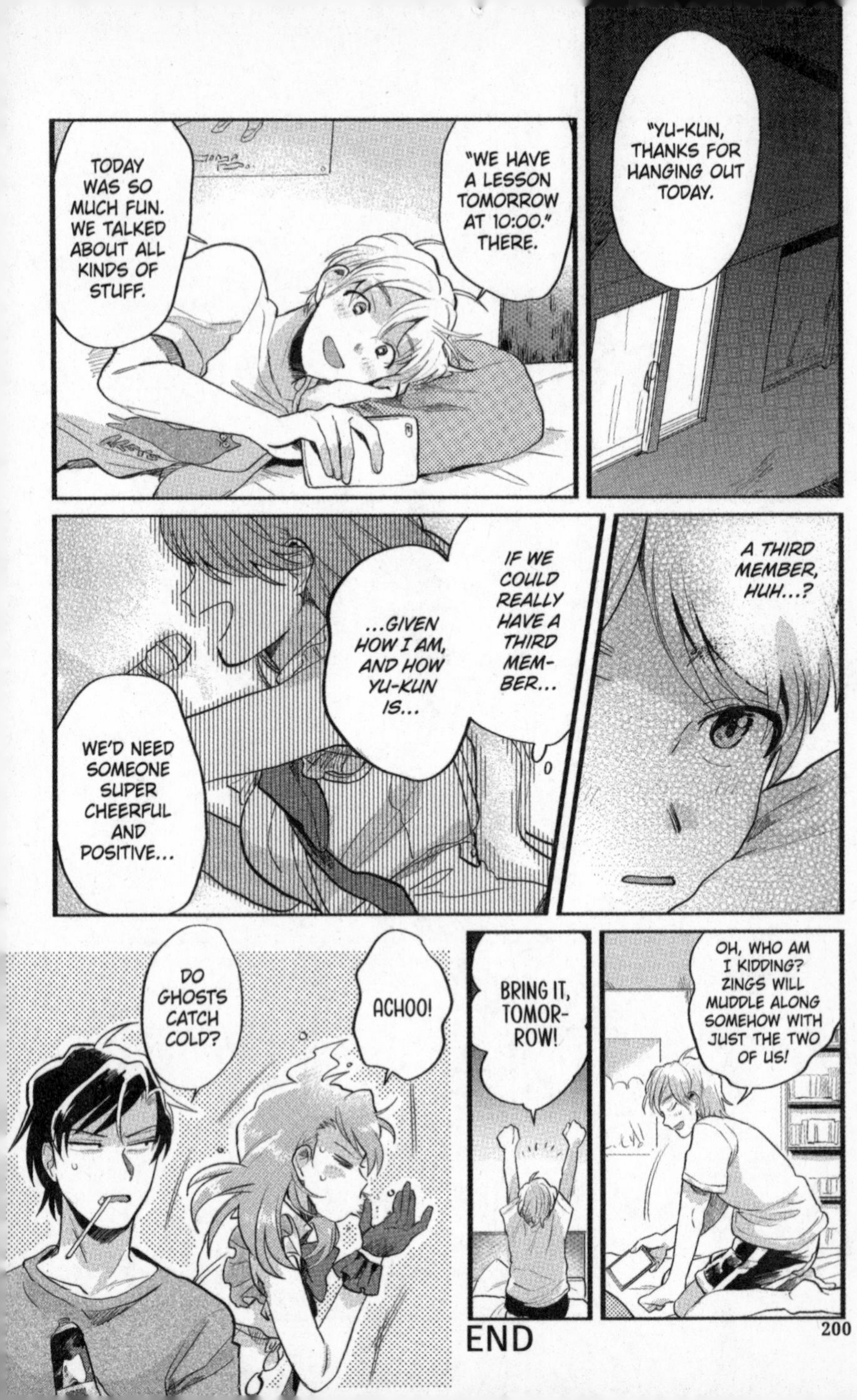
"YU-KUN, THANKS FOR HANGING OUT TODAY.
"WE HAVE A LESSON TOMORROW AT 10:00." THERE.
TODAY WAS SO MUCH FUN. WE TALKED ABOUT ALL KINDS OF STUFF.
A THIRD MEMBER, HUH...?
IF WE COULD REALLY HAVE A THIRD MEM-BER...
...GIVEN HOW I AM, AND HOW YU-KUN IS...
WE'D NEED SOMEONE SUPER CHEERFUL AND POSITIVE...
OH, WHO AM I KIDDING? ZINGS WILL MUDDLE ALONG SOMEHOW WITH JUST THE TWO OF US!
BRING IT, TOMOR-ROW!
ACHOO!
DO GHOSTS CATCH COLD?

END

# AFTERFLAVONE

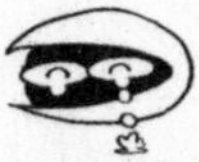

Hello! I'm *Phantom of the Idol* artist Isoflavone Hijiki. Strange name, right...? (Third time)
This is our second arc. Second! Aaah!!! I never dreamed I'd be able to do this.
The ending of Volume 2 was supposed to be the finale for *Phantom of the Idol*,
but then it threw a tantrum and said, "I don't want to end!"
And, with your help, it was revived! Volume 3! It's like a dream...
How can I ever express my gratitude enough?
Coming third in the Next Manga Grand Prize 2019, holding a ZINGS event...
I was blessed by surprises I never even imagined.
*Phantom of the Idol* truly is supported by everyone reading this—so many people!
Thank you for everything!
Even if I didn't make a manga of it, I thought that Niyodo and Asahi-chan and the
others would be living somewhere, but...when you do make a manga of it,
you realize some things for the first time.
"Oh, yeah, Niyodo is the type to say this kind of thing,"
"Yoshino-kun can be like that," that sort of thing.
There are lots of things I could only have realized by drawing *Phantom of the Idol*!
I'm so happy! Conveying this understanding through manga is my job...right?
Probably? (Weak-spirited)

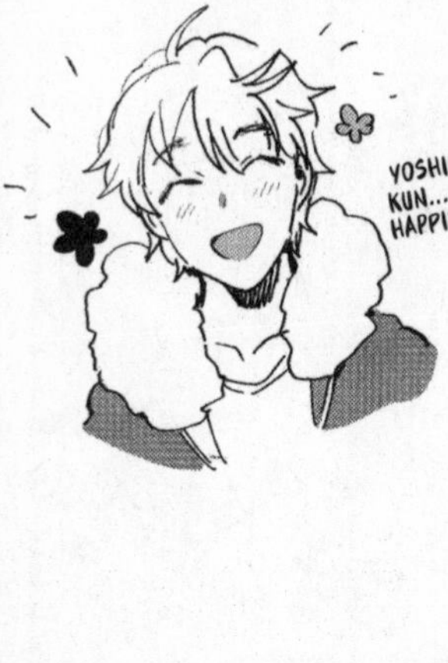
YOSHINO-KUN... FIND HAPPINESS!

## SPECIAL THANKS

Arata Natsuki-sensei
Arata-san is helping with backgrounds from arc 2!
The beautiful backgrounds are Arata-san's,
the others are mine...

Thank you so much!

&

Everyone who supports me

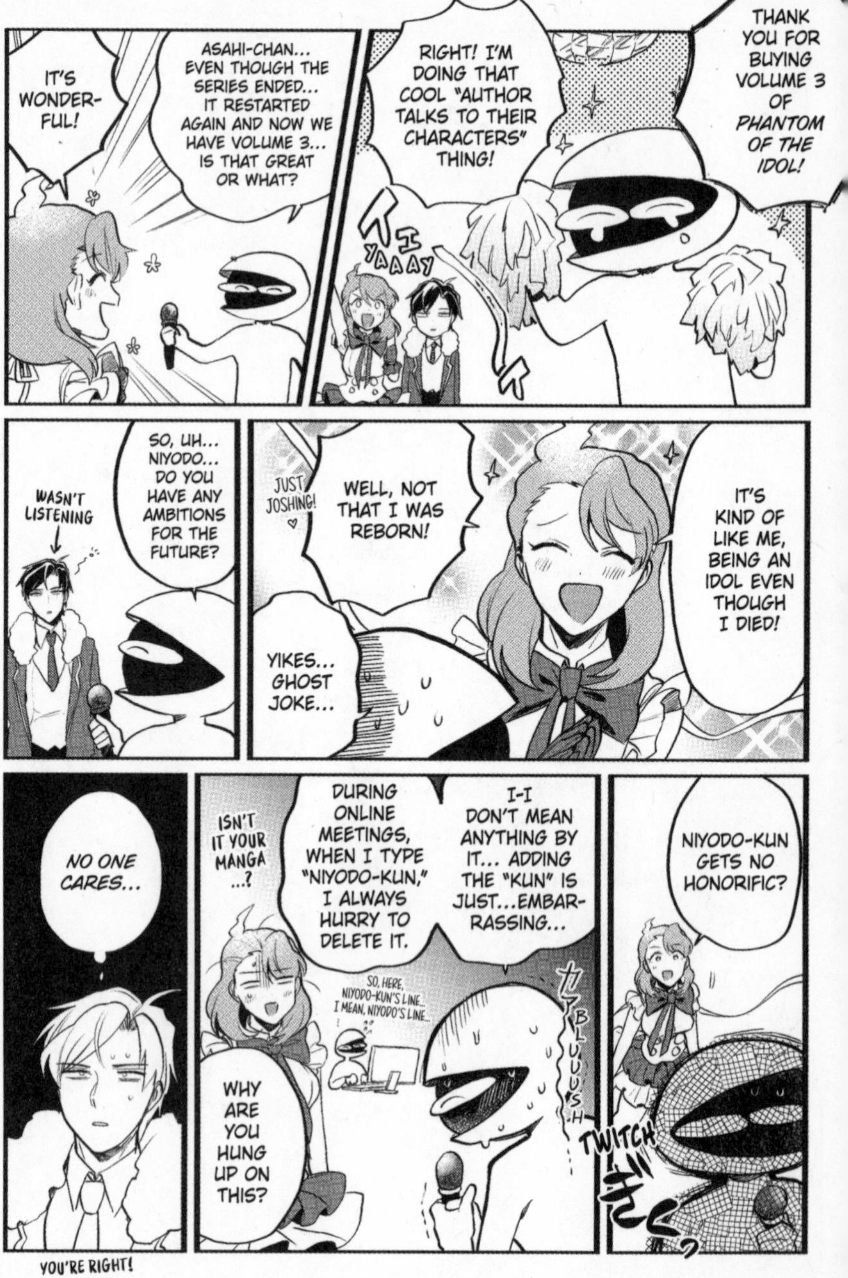
THANK YOU FOR BUYING VOLUME 3 OF *PHANTOM OF THE IDOL!*
RIGHT! I'M DOING THAT COOL "AUTHOR TALKS TO THEIR CHARACTERS" THING!
YAAAY
ASAHI-CHAN... EVEN THOUGH THE SERIES ENDED... IT RESTARTED AGAIN AND NOW WE HAVE VOLUME 3... IS THAT GREAT OR WHAT?
IT'S WONDERFUL!
IT'S KIND OF LIKE ME, BEING AN IDOL EVEN THOUGH I DIED!
WELL, NOT THAT I WAS REBORN!
JUST JOSHING!
YIKES... GHOST JOKE...
SO, UH... NIYODO... DO YOU HAVE ANY AMBITIONS FOR THE FUTURE?
WASN'T LISTENING
NIYODO-KUN GETS NO HONORIFIC?
TWITCH
I-I DON'T MEAN ANYTHING BY IT... ADDING THE "KUN" IS JUST...EMBARRASSING...
BLUUUUSH
DURING ONLINE MEETINGS, WHEN I TYPE "NIYODO-KUN," I ALWAYS HURRY TO DELETE IT.
ISN'T IT YOUR MANGA ...?
SO, HERE, NIYODO-KUN'S LINE... I MEAN, NIYODO'S LINE...
WHY ARE YOU HUNG UP ON THIS?
NO ONE CARES...
YOU'RE RIGHT!

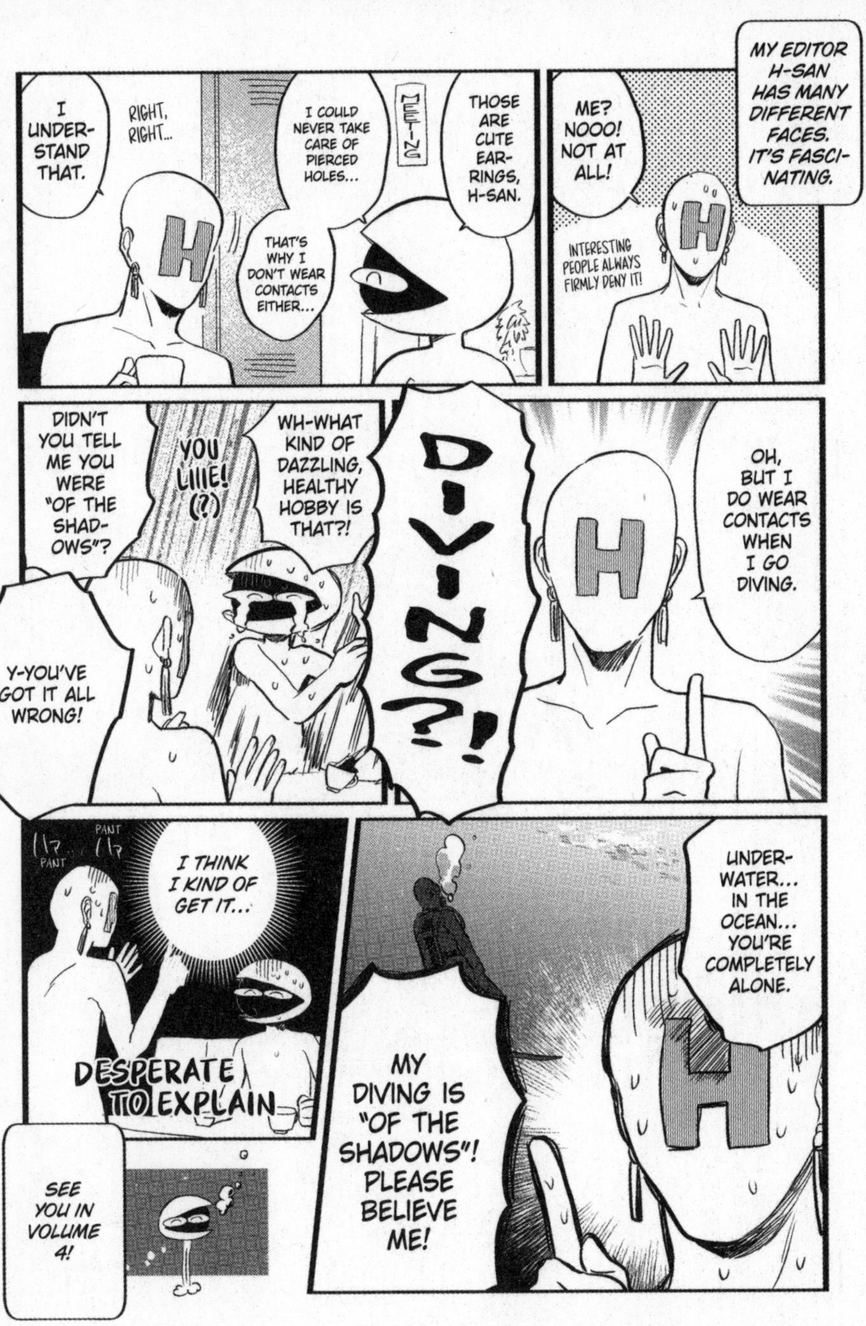
MY EDITOR H-SAN HAS MANY DIFFERENT FACES. IT'S FASCINATING.
ME? NOOO! NOT AT ALL!
INTERESTING PEOPLE ALWAYS FIRMLY DENY IT!
THOSE ARE CUTE EARRINGS, H-SAN.
MEETING
I COULD NEVER TAKE CARE OF PIERCED HOLES...
THAT'S WHY I DON'T WEAR CONTACTS EITHER...
RIGHT, RIGHT...
I UNDERSTAND THAT.
OH, BUT I DO WEAR CONTACTS WHEN I GO DIVING.
DIVING?!
WH-WHAT KIND OF DAZZLING, HEALTHY HOBBY IS THAT?!
YOU LIIIE! (?)
DIDN'T YOU TELL ME YOU WERE "OF THE SHADOWS"?
Y-YOU'VE GOT IT ALL WRONG!
UNDERWATER... IN THE OCEAN... YOU'RE COMPLETELY ALONE.
MY DIVING IS "OF THE SHADOWS"! PLEASE BELIEVE ME!
PANT PANT
I THINK I KIND OF GET IT...
DESPERATE TO EXPLAIN
SEE YOU IN VOLUME 4!

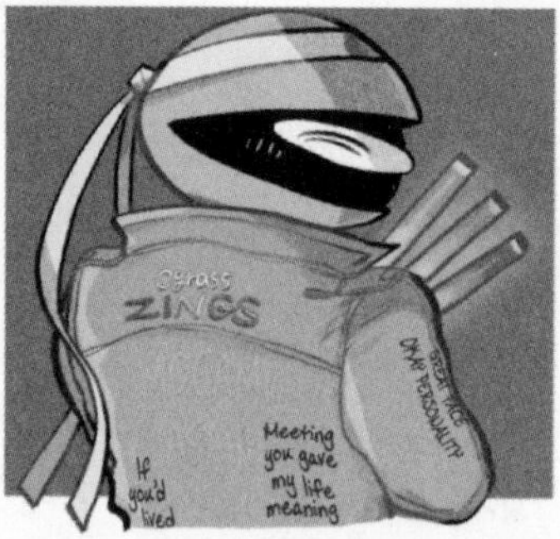
ZINGS
Meeting you gave my life meaning
If you'd lived

ISOFLAVONE HIJIKI

THANKS TO EVERYONE'S SUPPORT,
WE'VE REACHED VOLUME 3!
I WANT THIS TO BE A MANGA
FOR PEOPLE WHO READ LIKE
THE WIND FOR HONOR'S SAKE.
SEE YOU ON THE STREETS!

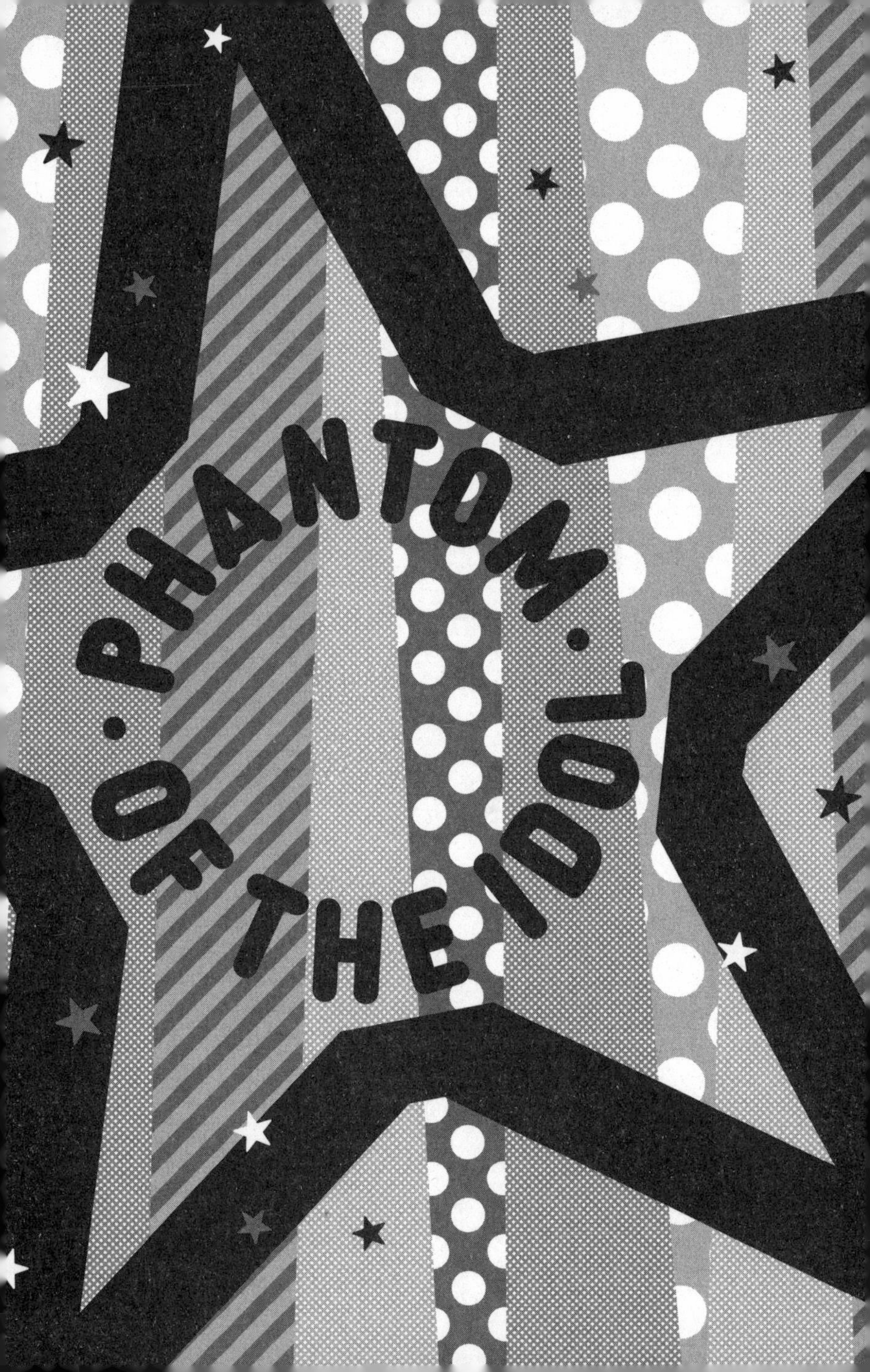
PHANTOM OF THE IDOL

# Translation Notes

**Grave-visiting outfit, page 8**
During the Bon festival in summer, many people in Japan visit their family homes and visit the graves of relatives buried in local cemeteries. During this grave visit, they will clean, which may involve weeding. This is distinct from attending memorial services, so clothing is chosen for comfort!

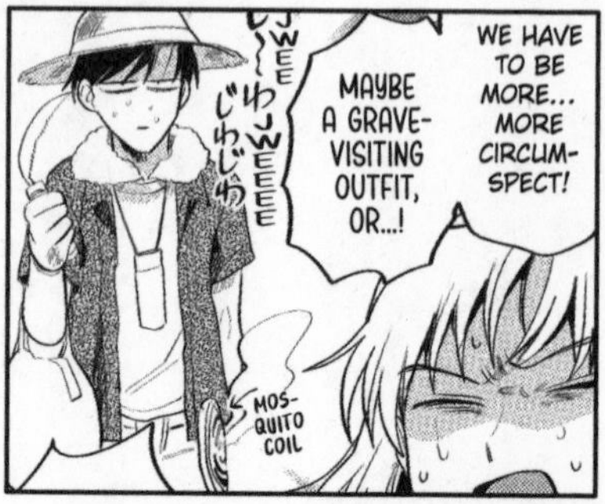
WE HAVE TO BE MORE... MORE CIRCUMSPECT!
MAYBE A GRAVE-VISITING OUTFIT, OR...!
JWEE
JWEEEE
MOS-QUITO COIL

**Season of Reading, page 17**
Autumn is known as the "Season of Reading" (*dokusho no aki*) in Japan, because the weather is perfect for curling up with a book. It is also called the "Season of Sports" (*supotsu no aki*), the "Season of Healthy Appetites" (*shokuyoku no aki*), and the "Season of Art" (*geijutsu no aki*), of course...

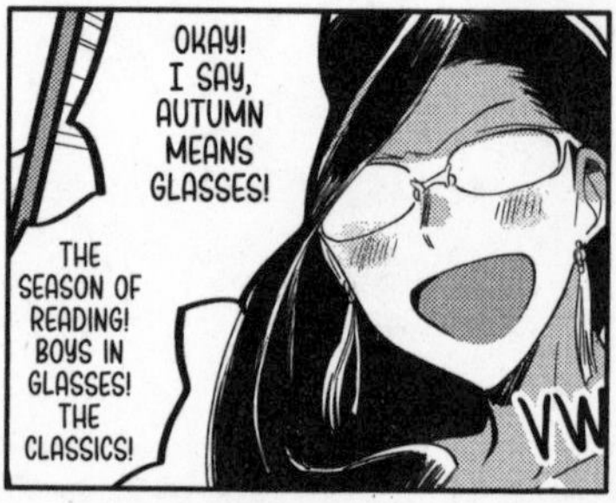
OKAY! I SAY, AUTUMN MEANS GLASSES!
THE SEASON OF READING! BOYS IN GLASSES! THE CLASSICS!

**"My Country Home," page 73**
"Furusato," a beloved Japanese song about a rural hometown with lyrics about chasing rabbits and fishing.

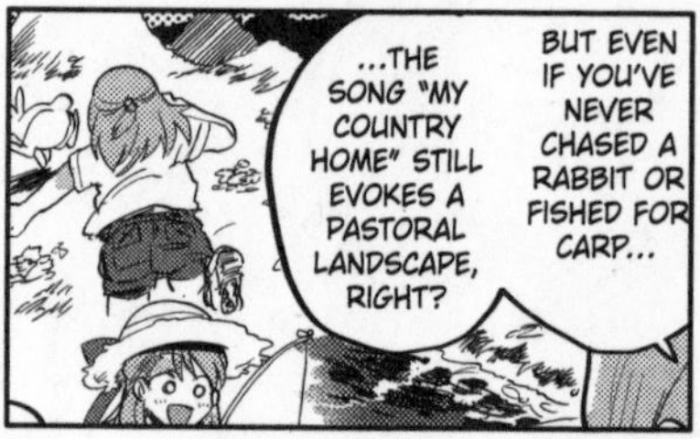
BUT EVEN IF YOU'VE NEVER CHASED A RABBIT OR FISHED FOR CARP...
...THE SONG "MY COUNTRY HOME" STILL EVOKES A PASTORAL LANDSCAPE, RIGHT?

**Same round of auditions, page 93**
Large idol groups often hold regular auditions to recruit new members, replacing the ones who graduate after several years with the group.

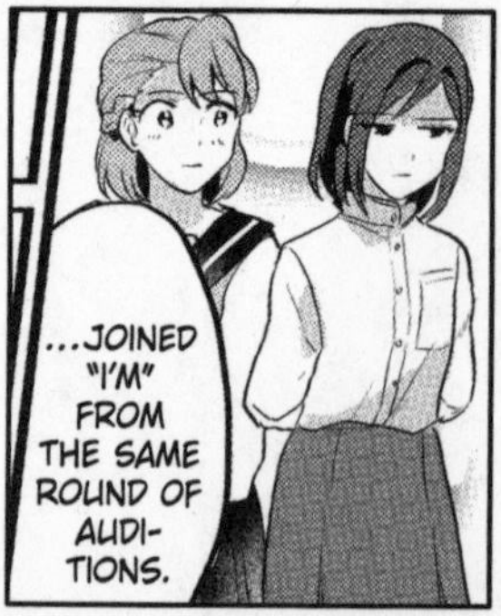
...JOINED "I'M" FROM THE SAME ROUND OF AUDI-TIONS.

*Itako*, **page 115**
A kind of female medium from northern Japan, known for communicating with the dead.

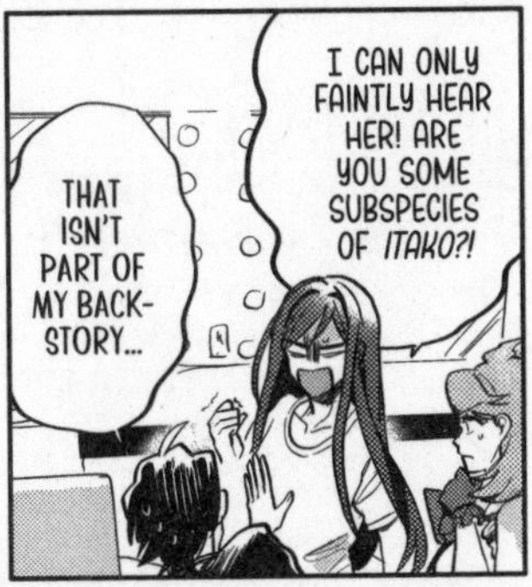
I CAN ONLY FAINTLY HEAR HER! ARE YOU SOME SUBSPECIES OF *ITAKO*?!
THAT ISN'T PART OF MY BACK-STORY...

*Kohai*, **page 127**
The opposite of a *senpai*, a *kohai* is someone who entered your workplace or school after you, placing them lower in the seniority hierarchy.

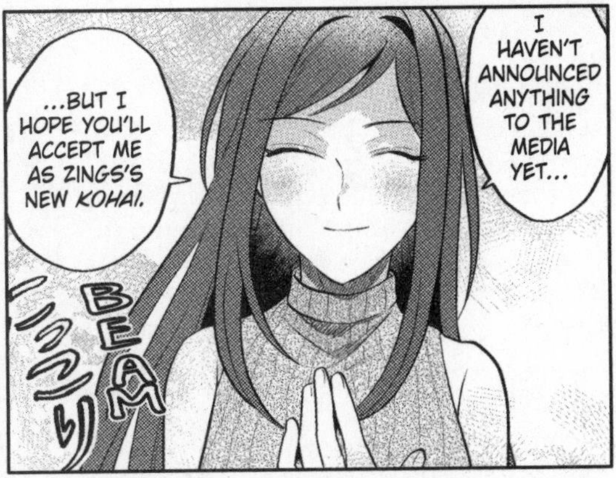
I HAVEN'T ANNOUNCED ANYTHING TO THE MEDIA YET...
...BUT I HOPE YOU'LL ACCEPT ME AS ZINGS'S NEW *KOHAI*.
BEAM

**Achoo!, page 200**
In Japan, there is a saying that when you sneeze, it means somebody is thinking or talking about you.

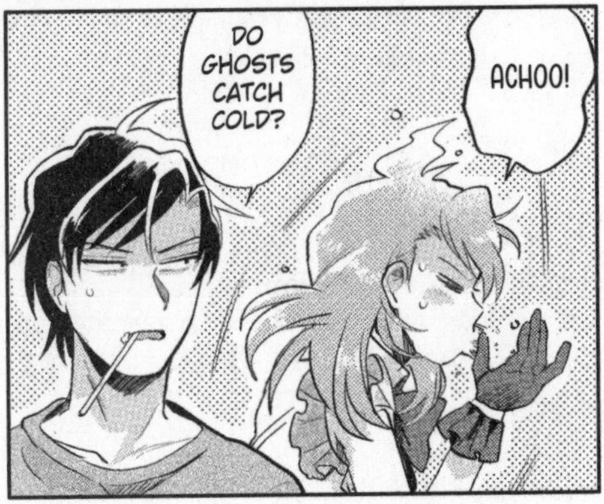
ACHOO!
DO GHOSTS CATCH COLD?

*Phantom of the Idol* 3 is a work of fiction. Names, characters, places, and incidents are the products of the author's imagination or are used fictitiously. Any resemblance to actual events, locales, or persons, living or dead, is entirely coincidental.

A Kodansha Trade Paperback Original



Published in the United States by
Kodansha USA Publishing, LLC, New York.

Publication rights for this English edition arranged through
Kodansha Ltd., Tokyo.

First published in Japan in 2020 by Ichijinsha Inc., Tokyo
as *Kami Kuzu Aidoru*, volume 3.

ISBN: 978-1-64651-586-8

Printed in the United States of America.

9 8 7 6 5 4 3 2 1

Translation: Max Greenway
Lettering: Michael Martin
Editing: Maggie Le
Kodansha USA Publishing edition cover design by Matthew Akuginow

Publisher: Kiichiro Sugawara

Director of Publishing Services: Ben Applegate
Director of Publishing Operations: Dave Barrett
Associate Director of Publishing Operations: Stephen Pakula
Publishing Services Managing Editors: Alanna Ruse, Madison Salters, with Grace Chen
Senior Production Manager: Angela Zurlo

KODANSHA.US

KODANSHA